SpringerWienNewYork

Tort and Insurance Law
Vol. 18

Edited by the
European Centre of Tort
and Insurance Law

together with the

Research Unit for European Tort Law
of the Austrian Academy of Sciences

Miquel Martín-Casals (ed.)

Children in Tort Law
Part II: Children as Victims

With Contributions by

Bertil Bengtsson	Olivier Moréteau
Willem H. van Boom	Luca Nocco
Melissa Moncada Castillo	Ken Oliphant
Giovanni Comandé	Caroline Pellerin-Rugliano
Laurence Francoz-Terminal	Jordi Ribot
Susanna Hirsch	Josep Solé Feliu
Jiří Hrádek	Pieter De Tavernier
Igor V. Kornev	Maria Manuel Veloso
Fabien Lafay	Gerhard Wagner
Miquel Martín-Casals	Felix Wieser

SpringerWienNewYork

European Centre of Tort and Insurance Law
Landesgerichtsstraße 11
1080 Vienna, Austria
Tel.: +43 1 40127 1688
Fax: +43 1 40127 1685
E-Mail: ectil@ectil.org

Austrian Academy of Sciences
Research Unit for European Tort Law
Landesgerichtsstraße 11
1080 Vienna, Austria
Tel.: +43 1 40127 1687
Fax: +43 1 40127 1685
E-Mail: etl@oeaw.ac.at

This work is published with the financial support of
the Austrian Science Fund (FWF)

Gedruckt mit Förderung des
Fonds zur Förderung der wissenschaftlichen Forschung (FWF)

Printed in Germany

Springer-Verlag Wien New York is part of
Springer Science + Business Media
springeronline.com

Typesetting: Composition & Design Services, Minsk, Belarus
Printing and binding: Strauss GmbH, 69509 Mörlenbach, Germany

Printed on acid-free and chlorine-free bleached paper
SPIN: 11605034

With 2 Figures

CIP data applied for

ISSN 1616-8623
ISBN-10 3-211-31130-0 SpringerWienNewYork
ISBN-13 978-3-211-31130-1 SpringerWienNewYork

Preface

This book is the second and final part of the research project "Children in Tort Law" funded by the European Science Foundation in 2001. Whereas the first book "Children in Tort Law Part I: Children as Tortfeasors", published in February 2006, focused on the legal problems posed by children causing harm to others, this volume deals with the other side of the coin. Here children are considered from the point of view of victims who have suffered damage caused by adults or by other children and which must be redressed according to tort law rules. In this area one of the main issues arises when the conduct of the child has also contributed to the damaging result, i.e. when there is contributory negligence of the victim. The traditional approach considers that the child must accept a reduction of his or her damages claim if the tortfeasor can establish that the victim failed to comply with the general duty of self-protection, a sort of "mirror image" of the duty of care placed upon the tortfeasor. By contrast, a more modern approach holds that, at least in some areas where third-party liability is compulsory, such as road-traffic accidents, children should be accorded a privilege or a broader exemption from the defence of contributory negligence.

The book includes country reports from Austria, Belgium, the Czech Republic, England and Wales, France, Germany, Italy, the Netherlands, Portugal and Spain, two brief notes on Russia and Sweden and a Comparative Report. It concludes with a paper entitled "*Final Conclusions: Policy Issues and Tentative Answers*" where Gerhard Wagner organises and comments on the lively two-day discussion on the whole project held by most members of the working team in Tossa de Mar (Spain) at the end of September 2005.

I would like to thank all contributors to this book for their reports and for their contributions in the debates as well as Katrin Karner, Denis Kelliher, Markus Kellner, Fiona Salter-Townshend and Thomas Thiede at the European Centre of Tort and Insurance Law (Vienna) and to Sonja Breßer and Jan Schletz at the University of Bonn for their valuable assistance in the preparation of the publication of this book. I would also like to thank Gerhard Wagner for the organisation of a very pleasant and productive meeting in Bonn. Finally, I would like to express my gratitude to Jordi Ribot, Josep Solé and Albert Ruda, my colleagues at the Observatory of European and Comparative Law at the University of Girona (OECPL), who organised the two meetings held in Spain and who, over a time span of five years, assisted me in the coordination of this project.

Girona, September 2006 — Miquel Martín-Casals

Table of Contents

QUESTIONNAIRE

I. Factual Introduction

1. What are the most common causes of injury to children in your jurisdiction? In what proportion of cases are actions brought for damages in tort? How many of these are successful? (Plus any other relevant factual data.)

II. Damage Caused by Parents and Other Specific Third Parties

2. In what circumstances may a parent be held liable for an injury sustained by his or her child?

(a) In what circumstances may a parent be held liable for injury resulting from his or her intentional conduct? (Liability for intent.) In particular, in what circumstances may the parent be held liable for injury resulting from his or her physical chastisement of the child?

(b) In what circumstances may a parent be held liable for injury resulting from his or her unintentional conduct? (Liability for fault.) Are there special rules for liability of the parents? E.g. are parents liable only in case of gross negligence? Are parents held to a lower or higher standard of care? In what circumstances may a parent be held liable for injury resulting from his or her failure to protect the child from harm? (Liability for omissions.)

3. In what circumstances may a third party (e.g. a school or local authority social services department) be held liable for failing to render a child positive assistance (e.g. by preventing parental abuse)?

4. What limitations periods are applied to a child's claim?

III. Contributory Negligence

5. Are there any special provisions concerning contributory negligence if the tortfeasor is a child?

6. What are the rules governing contributory negligence of the child? Do such principles follow the same lines as those governing the negligence issue itself (mirror-image)?

7. Does the fixed minimum age for children to be liable, if any exists, also apply to the contributory negligence of the child?

8. What is the standard of care governing the behaviour of children in the context of contributory negligence? Is such standard determined by the same principles and criteria which are relevant to the duty of care incumbent upon the child in the context of him or her being held liable?

IV. Contribution in Equity

9. Is there a parallel (mirror-image) to liability in equity in the field of contributory negligence? If so, do the criteria determining liability in equity of the child also apply to the issue of holding him or her accountable for his or her contributory negligence?

10. If answered affirmatively: Is the fact that the child is privately or socially insured against the accident a factor to be considered? Is the existence of liability insurance of the tortfeasor to be taken into account? What factors have a bearing on the assessment of equitable contribution?

V. Miscellaneous

11. What are the rules for a situation in which the child is guilty of contributory negligence but the parents have also breached their duty to supervise? Is the child held accountable in any way for his or her parents' breach of the duty to supervise so that his or her claim for damages is reduced?

12. Do the rules of contributory negligence also apply in the area of strict liability?

13. Do the rules of contributory negligence apply in the area of strict liability for traffic-accidents or other areas of tort liability?

14. Are adults held to a higher standard of care in their interactions with children, or when children are or may be around?

VI. Insurance Matters

15. Are pupils covered by private or public accident (first-party) insurance?

16. Does this insurance cover any damage incurred on the way to school and back?

17. Are there restrictions on damages recoverable by the child, e.g. with respect to loss of future earnings?

VII. Damage Issues

18. If damages for loss of earnings are available, what are the principles governing their assessment?

19. Which of the child's non-material interests are protected in your jurisdiction? May the child, for example, sue for impairment of intellectual or social development, the onset of behavioural problems or reduced employment prospects?

20. Are there special rules for the assessment of damages sustained by a child, e.g. with respect to pain and suffering?

21. Does a small child have a claim for damages for pain and suffering if he or she is deprived of his or her parents by a tortious act? If so, may the claim be denied on the ground that the child does not feel the loss?

22. With respect to a damage claim for the costs of medical treatment: May the tortfeasor defend himself by pointing to the fact that the parents have a duty to maintain the child?

23. In case of wrongful life: Does the child have a damage claim against the physician or a health care institution?

24. Concerning liability for pre-natal injuries: Are third parties liable to the child? May the mother be liable to the child, for example, for excessive consumption of alcohol or even for an omission to procure treatment?

Country Reports

CHILDREN AS VICTIMS UNDER AUSTRIAN LAW

Susanna Hirsch

I. Factual Introduction

1. What are the most common causes of injury to children in your jurisdiction? In what proportion of cases are actions brought for damages in tort? How many of these are successful? (Plus any other relevant factual data.)

Information available regarding accidents of young people in Austria is provided for persons under the age of fifteen. Unfortunately the statistics do not distinguish between externally caused accidents and accidents that have not been caused by a third person. 1

The data shows that, in 2004, forty children under the age of fifteen died in accidents. The fatal accidents most often result from road traffic and drowning. 2

Table 1. Accidents involving children under the age of fifteen in 2004[1]

Fatal accidents	40
Accidents causing invalidity	700
Accidents necessitating a hospital stay	23,200
Accidents	173,500

Children's accidents in general, however, are most likely to happen in flats (floor, furniture, electronic devices), in playgrounds, at school whilst practising sports, and while playing soccer, skiing or riding a bicycle. Thus, the most common sources of accidents differ quite considerably between fatal accidents and the totality of accidents. 3

[1] Source: Institut "Sicher Leben", Unfalldatenbank 2004, © Institut "Sicher Leben", Wien.

Table 2. Areas of accidents involving children under the age of fifteen in 2004[2]

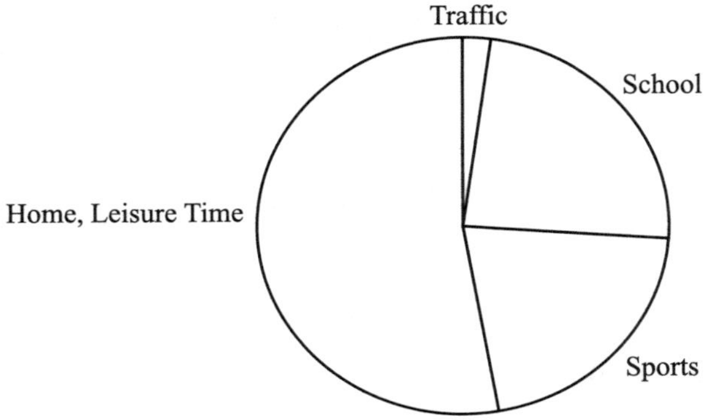

II. Damage Caused by Parents and Other Specific Third Parties

2. In what circumstances may a parent be held liable for an injury sustained by his or her child?

(a) In what circumstances may a parent be held liable for injury resulting from his or her intentional conduct? (Liability for intent.) In particular, in what circumstances may the parent be held liable for injury resulting from his or her physical chastisement of the child?

4 If parents harm their child intentionally, the general rules on tort law are applicable.

5 Regarding the physical chastisement of children, according to § 146a *Allgemeines Bürgerliches Gesetzbuch* (Austrian Civil Code, ABGB), the use of violence and the infliction of physical or mental pain to the child are considered unlawful. There exists no parental right of chastisement.[3] Other forms of violence such as detention or the infliction of mental pain are, however, considered admissible as far as they are reasonable and serve a pedagogical purpose.[4] A further limit is seen in the proportionality of violence and pain, on the one hand, and the purpose pursued, on the other hand. The age, the development and the personality of the child also have to be taken into account.[5]

(b) In what circumstances may a parent be held liable for injury resulting from his or her unintentional conduct? (liability for fault) Are there special rules for liability of the parents? E.g. are parents liable only in case of gross negli-

[2] Source: Institut "Sicher Leben", Unfalldatenbank 2004, © Institut "Sicher Leben", Wien.

[3] J. Stabentheiner in: P. Rummel, *Kommentar zum ABGB I* (3rd edn. 2000), § 146a no. 2.

[4] J. Stabentheiner in: P. Rummel (supra fn. 3), § 146a no. 2; B. Verschraegen in: M. Schwimann, *Praxiskommentar zum ABGB I* (3rd edn. 2005), § 146a no. 3.

[5] B. Verschraegen in: M. Schwimann (supra fn. 4), § 146 a no. 4.

gence? Are parents held to a lower or higher standard of care? In what circumstances may a parent be held liable for injury resulting from his or her failure to protect the child from harm? (Liability for omissions.)

In the Austrian legal system there exist no special provisions regarding the parents' liability for negligent behaviour vis à vis their children. In doctrine however, Selb holds that the parents should only be held liable if they neglected the care they use in exercising their own affairs, as is provided for explicitly in Germany by § 1664 *Bürgerliches Gesetzbuch* (German Civil Code, BGB).[6] This would mean a modification of the generally applicable yardstick, since §§ 1294, 1297 ABGB provide that an objective standard is to be applied regarding the degree of attention and diligence. 6

Also Koziol supports mitigation of liability within the family. With reference to § 88 StGB[7] he suggests to limit the liability of the parents to cases of gross negligence or intent.[8] 7

Regarding liability for omissions, the Austrian legislator has not established a general duty to prevent the damaging behaviour of others by acting in a certain way.[9] Omissions are however considered wrongful if the law imposes special *Fürsorgepflichten* (duties to provide welfare maintenance); moreover if a *Schutzgesetz* (protective law) or contractual duties demand a certain behaviour. More generally, the endangerement of somebody else's goods by omission is considered wrongful whenever the weighing of interests justifies the establishment of a duty to act in a certain way.[10] Thus, a duty to act is to be assumed whenever somebody could easily have avoided a considerable infringement of a third person's goods without endangering himself.[11] 8

Regarding parents, liability for omissions may arise from the neglect of their *Fürsorgepflichten* for the child. According to § 144 in connection with § 146 ABGB, the parents have the duty to take care of the minor, which comprises in particular safeguarding his physical welfare and health as well as providing direct supervision. Thus, liability of the parents can be established if they culpably neglected this duty and did not protect the child from harm. 9

If the parents did not prevent the child from damage caused by third parties, they can be held liable alongside the direct tortfeasor according to §§ 1301, 1302 ABGB. 10

6 W. Selb, Schädigung des Menschen vor der Geburt – ein Problem der Rechtsfähigkeit, [1966] *Archiv für die civilistische Praxis* (AcP), 76 et seq.

7 § 88 sec. 2 subpara. 1 StGB provides that if children are personally injured by their parents, the latter are not to be punished in the case of slight negligence.

8 For further information see H. Koziol, *Haftpflichtrecht II* (2nd edn. 1984), 126.

9 H. Koziol, *Haftpflichtrecht I* (3rd edn. 1997), no. 4/60; regarding German Law, c.f. E. Deutsch, *Allgemeines Haftungsrecht* (2nd edn. 1995), no. 103.

10 H. Koziol (supra fn. 9), no. 4/60.

11 H. Koziol (supra fn. 9), no. 4/61.

3. In what circumstances may a third party (e.g. a school or local authority social services department) be held liable for failing to render a child positive assistance (e.g. by preventing parental abuse)?

11 As mentioned above, there is no general duty to act in order to prevent others from being injured.[12] In criminal law, § 286 StGB penalises omitting the prevention of a criminal act if it could have been prevented easily and without exposing oneself or relatives to the danger of a considerable harm or loss.[13] In private law, however, the duty to help or to prevent somebody else from being injured must not be reduced to this or other criminal law provisions.[14] The duty to act is to be assumed whenever a person could easily have avoided a considerable infringement of someone else's goods without endangering herself.[15] Thus, third parties may be held liable if they fail to render a child positive assistance under such circumstances.

a) Liability for omission of schools:

12 Regarding schools, there exist special provisions that establish duties of information designed to help preventing the child from harm. According to § 48 *Schulunterrichtsgesetz* (Statute on School Instruction, SchUG), the school principal has to inform the competent *Jugendwohlfahrtsträger* (youth welfare institution)[16] in accordance with § 37 *Jugendwohlfahrtsgesetz* (Statute on Youth Welfare, JWG), whenever the legal guardians obviously neglect their duties. It is to be considered such a neglect if the parents do not prevent the child from being sexually abused (see supra no. 9). § 37 JWG itself provides that the public authorities, in particular as far as they are competent for institutions that provide the care and instruction of minors,[17] have to inform the youth welfare institution about all facts they have come to know, if these facts are necessary for the fulfilment of youth welfare.

13 It has to be asked whether the neglect of these duties of information entails official liability. According to § 1 sec. 1 the *Amtshaftungsgesetz* (Official Liability Act, AHG), the federation, the member states, the "districts", the local communities, other public corporations and the social insurance institutions (short: legal entities) are to be held liable for damage, which their organs caused wrongfully and with fault in implementation of legislation. The formulation "in implementation of legislation" signifies that the AHG regards only damage in the field of public administration and not in the field of private economic administration.[18] As the school and educational system is part of the

[12] H. Koziol (supra fn. 9), no. 4/60.
[13] H. Koziol (supra fn. 9), no. 4/61.
[14] Such as §§ 94 or 95 StGB; see H. Koziol (supra fn. 9), no. 4/61.
[15] H. Koziol (supra fn. 9), no. 4/61.
[16] According to § 4 JWG, the youth welfare institution is the *Land* (member state of the federation of Austria).
[17] And the organs of public supervision.
[18] I.e. if the state does not act with imperium but uses the legal forms also available to its legal subjects (R.Walter/H. Mayer (eds.), *Bundesverfassungsrecht* (9th edn. 2000), no. 560).

public administration,[19] it is to be assumed that also these duties of information fall in the field of public administration. Thus, the Official Liability Act is applicable. Which legal entity is to be held liable depends on whose functions the organ inflicting the damage is exercising (theory of function).[20] According to art. 14 sec. 1 *Bundes-Verfassungsgesetz* (Federal Constitution of Austria, B-VG),[21] the legislation and implementation of school and education matters lies within the competence of the federation. Therefore, the legal entity to be held liable is the federation. Still, the question arises whether liability according to the AHG also comprises liability for omission. § 1 sec. 1 AHG, employs the term "behaviour" which according to the general rules of private law comprises actions as well as omissions if there was a duty to act. In this case, the duty to act arises from public *Fürsorgepflichten*.

b) Liability for omission of the youth welfare institution:

Regarding the youth welfare institution, § 2 sec. 2 JWG provides the duty to grant public youth welfare if and as far as the legal guardian does not ensure the child's welfare.[22] Moreover, the youth welfare institution has to intervene in the family sphere and relations if this is necessary in order to insure the child's welfare. This is in particular true if violence is resorted to or physical or mental pain is inflicted (§ 2 sec. 3 JWG). 14

If possible, the youth welfare institution has to bring about an adequate solution to the problem without special proceedings only in consultation with the legal guardians. Where required, it has to arrange for the necessary steps (§ 30 JWG) and, as the case may be, invoke the aid of the court (§ 215 ABGB). If delays are dangerous, however, the youth welfare organisation provisionally can take the necessary steps itself (§ 215 sec. 1 second sentence ABGB).[23] 15

If the youth welfare institution culpably neglects these public *Fürsorgepflichten*, the question arises, whether official liability can be established, as the youth welfare organisation is the *Land* (member state of the Federation of Austria) (see fn. 16). As mentioned above, according to § 1 sec. 1 AHG the federation, the member states, the "districts", the local communities, other public corporations and the social insurance institutions (short: legal entities) are to be held liable for damage, which their organs caused wrongfully and with fault in implementation of legislation. Whether youth welfare falls in the 16

[19] H. Koziol/St. Frotz, [1979] *Recht der Schule* (RdS), 98; W. Schragel, *Amtshaftungsgesetzkommentar* (3rd edn. 2003), no. 78.

[20] See e.g. R.Walter/H. Mayer, (supra fn. 18), no. 1285; H. Koziol (supra fn. 8), 380; W. Schragel (supra fn. 19), no. 51 et seq.; H. Koziol/St. Frotz, [1979] RdS, 98.

[21] Austria is a federal state composed of nine autonomous member states. The Constitution in its artt. 10 to 15 contains the so-called *Kompetenzverteilung* (distribution of competence), which regulates the separation of legislative and executive powers between the *Bund* (federation) and the *Länder* (member states).

[22] As far as the child's welfare necessitates it, the public youth welfare may also interfere with family relations and spheres (§ 2 sec. 3 JWG).

[23] W. Schragel (supra fn. 19), no. 108.

field of public administration cannot be generally said. It depends on the substance and the signification of the single provisions of the JWG.[24] In general, youth welfare is to be qualified private economic administration of the youth welfare institutions, i.e. the *Länder*.[25] However, as mentioned above, if delays are dangerous, the youth welfare institution is authorised to provisionally take the necessary steps itself, i.e. to give sovereign orders and take public executive measures. If in such a case damage is caused, the *Land* may be held liable according to the Official Liability Act (see § 4 sec. 1 JWG).[26] This is also true in the case of the culpable omission of such necessary sovereign acts.[27]

4. What limitations periods are applied to a child's claim?

17 Regarding time limitation of the child's claim against his parents, § 1495 ABGB provides a special regulation: The beginning and the running of the limitation period are suspended as long as the child is in the parents' custody. This is also true with respect to adoptive parents and adoptive children.[28] Regarding foster parents, an analogous application of § 1495 ABGB is held possible if the foster parents were entrusted with custody.[29]

III. Contributory Negligence

5. Are there any special provisions concerning contributory negligence if the tortfeasor is a child?

18 In the Austrian legal system, § 1304 ABGB contains the general rule on contributory negligence: If not only the tortfeasor but also the victim acted with fault, damages have to be divided proportionally.

19 An exception to this general rule is provided by § 1308 ABGB which regulates contributory negligence if the tortfeasor is a minor: The injured party cannot claim any compensation if he induced the damaging behaviour of the minor with fault. § 1308 ABGB thus excludes the application of §§ 1309 and 1310 ABGB.[30]

[24] W. Schragel (supra fn. 19), no. 108.
[25] W. Schragel (supra fn. 19), no. 108.
[26] W. Schragel (supra fn. 19), no. 108.
[27] According to § 215 sec. 1 second sentence ABGB, the youth welfare organisation provisionally can take the necessary steps itself if delays are dangerous. This discretionary power, however, has to be made use of in the intendment of the law. In this case, it therefore has to conform to the child's welfare. The misuse of discretionary power is wrongful. (See e.g. W. Schragel (supra fn. 19), nos. 149 and 151.)
[28] M. Bydlinski in: P. Rummel, *Kommentar zum ABGB II/3* (3rd edn. 2002), § 1495 no. 3.
[29] P. Mader/S. Janisch in: M. Schwimann, *Praxiskommentar zum ABGB VI* (3rd edn. 2006), § 1495 no. 4.
[30] R. Reischauer in: P. Rummel, *Kommentar zum ABGB II* (2nd edn. 1992), § 1308 no. 1.

It has to be stressed that § 1308 ABGB is applicable only if the injured has induced the damaging behaviour of the tortfeasor.[31] "Inducing" is understood as a behaviour of the victim which typically causes the tortfeasor's illicit reaction.[32] If the victim, on the other hand, only fulfilled another, independent condition for the damage to occur, the general provision of § 1304 ABGB has to be applied.[33] 20

As to the degree of fault, intentional as well as negligent inducement lead to the minor's relief from liability. 21

However, the *Oberste Gerichtshof* (Austrian Supreme Court, OGH) held that a slightly negligent act of the victim could be left out of account if the wrongdoer acted with intent.[34] This corresponds to the courts' practice regarding the division of the loss according to the general rule of § 1304 ABGB.[35] The application of these considerations to § 1308 ABGB has been heavily criticised in doctrine.[36] A minor who feels challenged (and this is the prime case of § 1308 ABGB) would often react intentionally.[37] Not to apply § 1308 ABGB to such cases is considered a contradiction of the purpose of this provision, i.e. to protect the minor because of his immaturity and to remove the victim's right to damages completely if he induced the damaging act.[38] As the purposes of §§ 1308 and 1304 ABGB would not correspond in this respect, Wolff's considerations were not applicable to the prior provision. 22

Special attention has to be drawn to cases in which one minor induces the damaging behaviour of another minor.[39] In the judicial practice, such cases are quite frequent. To apply § 1308 ABGB without distinction would lead to the unsatisfactory result that the injured minor does not receive any compensation.[40] This would contradict the *telos* of § 1308 ABGB that considers minors worthier of protection than majors and therefore provides an exception to the 23

[31] H. Koziol (supra fn. 9), no. 12/18; K. Wolff in: H. Klang, *Kommentar zum ABGB* (2nd edn. 1964), 75; [1974] *Evidenzblatt der Rechtsmittelentscheidungen in: Österreichische Juristen-Zeitung* (EvBl), 234. This is also held by the courts when stressing that the victim must have outrightly induced the damaging behaviour of the minor. See for example [1981] *Zeitschrift für Verkehrsrecht* (ZVR), no. 168.

[32] R. Reischauer in: P. Rummel (supra fn. 30), § 1308 no. 2. Since minors are likely to react in an immature way, the range of reactions that have to be reckoned with is rather broad (Cf. also R. Reischauer in: P. Rummel (supra fn. 30), § 1308 no. 2).

[33] H. Koziol (supra fn. 9), no. 12/18; R. Reischauer in: P. Rummel (supra fn. 30), § 1308 no. 5; [1981] ZVR, no. 168.

[34] [1933] *Zentralblatt für die juristische Praxis* (ZBl), 289.

[35] Cf. OGH 28 April 1981, 4 Ob 35/81; OGH 27 October 1981, 5 Ob 560/81; OGH 3 April 1986, 8 Ob 538/85; OGH 30 October 1996, 9 ObA 2233/96i; K. Wolff in: H. Klang, (supra fn. 31), 64.

[36] H. Koziol (supra fn. 9), no. 12/18; R. Reischauer in: P. Rummel (supra fn. 30), § 1308 no. 3.

[37] R. Reischauer in: P. Rummel (supra fn. 30), § 1308 no. 3.

[38] H. Koziol (supra fn. 9), no. 12/18.

[39] Generally, if the victim is a person under fourteen years of age, § 1304 ABGB is applied in conjunction with § 1310 ABGB which is employed analogously.

[40] H. Koziol (supra fn. 9), no. 12/19.

general rule. If, however, both, tortfeasor and victim are minors, they are equally worthy of protection and the application of different yardsticks is not justified.[41] Among persons equally worthy of protection, the loss has to be divided according to § 1304 ABGB.[42] Thus, if the victim is a minor, the rules on establishing a minor's liability have to be applied analogously.

24 If, on the other hand, only the injured is a minor whereas the tortfeasor is of majority age, § 1308 ABGB is to be applied analogously, when establishing contributory negligence of the minor: If the tortfeasor has induced the minor victim's misbehaviour, the tortfeasor cannot plead contributory negligence.[43]

6. What are the rules governing contributory negligence of the child? Do such principles follow the same lines as those governing the negligence issue itself (mirror-image)?

25 As to contributory negligence, the general rule of § 1304 ABGB provides that damages have to be reduced where not only the wrongdoer, but also the victim acted culpably. Regarding contributory negligence, the principles decisive in establishing liability in general have to be applied correspondingly, since contributory negligence, too, is a question of imputing damage ("mirror-image").[44] Thus, if the victim is a person under fourteen years of age, in the absence of specific provisions the §§ 1308 et seq. and 153 ABGB on establishing liability of a minor have to be applied analogously.[45]

26 Accordingly, if the injured party is a minor, the tortfeasor cannot plead contributory negligence, unless the minor did not apply the objectively necessary care with respect to his own goods and is in a better position to bear the loss because of his pecuniary circumstances (§ 1310 ABGB analogously).[46] Thus contributory negligence of mentally deranged persons and minors can only be established in exceptional cases.[47] In this respect the Supreme Court also stresses that the behaviour of minors has to be considered with more leniency than the behaviour of persons of majority.[48]

[41] *Entscheidungen des österreichischen Obersten Gerichtshofes in Zivilsachen* (SZ) 33/54.

[42] H. Koziol (supra fn. 9), no. 12/19; R. Reischauer in: P. Rummel (supra fn. 30), § 1308 no. 5; *Ehe- und familienrechtliche Entscheidungen* (EFSlg) 38.565; EFSlg 41.089; EFSlg 48.626. The former court practice strived to obtain an adequate solution by stressing that the tortfeasor had not outright induced the damaging behaviour. See for example [1958] *Juristische Blätter* (JBl), 401 et seq.; SZ 33/54; [1961] JBl, 282.

[43] R. Reischauer in: P. Rummel, (supra fn. 30), § 1310 no. 20.

[44] H. Koziol (supra fn. 9), no. 12/1.

[45] H. Koziol (supra fn. 9), no. 12/13.

[46] See M. Hinteregger, Contributory Negligence in Austria in: U. Magnus/M. Martín-Casals (eds.), *Unification of Tort Law: Contributory Negligence* (2004), no. 27.

[47] However, sometimes even contributory negligence of children under seven is established.

[48] See e.g. [1986] ZVR, no. 77; [1987] ZVR, no. 80; R. Reischauer in: P. Rummel (supra fn. 30), § 1310 no. 14.

7. Does the fixed minimum age for children to be liable, if any exists, also apply to the contributory negligence of the child?

In the Austrian legal system, there is no such fixed minimum age for children to be liable. Since "minors", i.e. persons under fourteen, regularly lack discernment, also regarding contributory negligence they are rebuttably presumed not to be capable of acting reasonably. Thus, contributory negligence has to be established according to their individual capacity from case to case. 27

Persons over fourteen years of age, on the other hand, are presumed to have sufficient powers of discernment to be fully responsible for their tortious behaviour (§ 153 ABGB). This is true also regarding contributory negligence, as § 153 ABGB has to be applied analogously according to the "mirror-image principle". 28

8. What is the standard of care governing the behaviour of children in the context of contributory negligence? Is such standard determined by the same principles and criteria which are relevant to the duty of care incumbent upon the child in the context of him or her being held liable?

Contributory negligence is not negligence in the technical sense. In particular it does not presuppose wrongful behaviour, but only the absence of the necessary care with respect to the injured's own goods.[49] If the injured has carelessly treated his own goods, this behaviour is not wrongful, since there is no legal duty to protect one's own goods from being damaged.[50] Thus, the application of § 1304 ABGB does not necessarily presuppose wrongful behaviour.[51] The absence of care brings about a situation by which the injured is less worthy of protection and in which the tortfeasor cannot be burdened with the obligation to compensate the whole damage.[52] The standard of care required with respect to one's own goods corresponds to the standard of care necessary with regard to somebody else's goods.[53] 29

Regarding fault, it has to be repeated that contributory negligence is not negligence in the technical sense. Still, according to the "principle of equal treatment", the same rules used in establishing liability are applicable. The damage is (partly) imputed to the injured if he behaved in a way that – with respect to somebody else's goods – would justify a subjective reproach of lack of willpower. The individual abilities have to be considered. Regarding the degree of attention and diligence, however, as in establishing liability, an objective stan- 30

[49] H. Koziol (supra fn. 9), no. 12/7.
[50] H. Koziol (supra fn. 9), no. 12/3.
[51] However, it is imaginable that the injured acts careless in his own matters and at the same time wrongful because he infringes an imperative rule. For further information see H. Koziol (supra fn. 9), no. 12/6.
[52] H. Koziol (supra fn. 9), no. 12/7.
[53] R. Reischauer in: P. Rummel (supra fn. 30), § 1304 no. 1.

dard is to be applied (§§ 1294, 1297 ABGB). The ordinary degree of attention and diligence of children of the particular age is required.

IV. Contribution in Equity

9. Is there a parallel (mirror-image) to liability in equity in the field of contributory negligence? If so, do the criteria determining liability in equity of the child also apply to the issue of holding him or her accountable for his or her contributory negligence?

31 According to the "mirror-image principle" (see supra fn. 31), the rules concerning liability in equity have to be applied analogously in the field of contributory negligence.[54] Thus, contributory negligence can be based on the absence of the objectively necessary care with respect to one's own goods in connection with the consideration of the financial circumstances of the injured and the tortfeasor.

32 However, it appears that no decisions exist in this respect.

10. If answered affirmatively: Is the fact that the child is privately or socially insured against the accident a factor to be considered? Is the existence of liability insurance of the tortfeasor to be taken into account? What factors have a bearing on the assessment of equitable contribution?

33 It appears that there are no decisions in which the courts take into account the fact of the child being covered by insurance. This seems quite inconsequential as insurance coverage is considered as a part of the minor's assets when establishing liability in equity.

34 Another factor that has a bearing on the assessment of equitable contribution is the degree of "wrongfulness". As the degree of wrongfulness can vary, according to the principle of mirror-image, also the degree of the absence of the necessary care with respect to one's own goods can be varying. In most cases, the varying weight is considered when judging the weight of fault and shall thus not be taken into account twice. The degree of the absence of the necessary care can however gain separate importance for apportioning the damage, when the imputation of the damage is not based on a subjective reproach, but when the absence of the objectively necessary care is decisive. This can be the case in § 1310 ABGB and its analogous application in the field of contribution of the injured.[55]

[54] Cf. H. Koziol (supra fn. 9), no. 12/13.
[55] H. Koziol (supra fn. 9), no. 12/16.

V. Miscellaneous

11. What are the rules for a situation in which the child is guilty of contributory negligence but the parents have also breached their duty to supervise? Is the child held accountable in any way for his or her parents' breach of the duty to supervise so that his or her claim for damages is reduced?

Only in contractual relationships can fault on behalf of the legal representative be attributed to the minor when establishing contributory negligence (§ 1313a ABGB analogously).[56] In tort law, according to the prevailing opinion, the fault of the person charged with the duty to supervise is not imputable to the child.[57] Damages of the injured are not to be reduced because of the neglect of duty on the part of the supervisor. 35

At first sight, this may appear inconsequential, as the prevailing opinion holds that the misconduct of a helper, who contributed to the principal's damage while acting in his interest, is imputable to the injured principal also in tort law (§ 1313a ABGB analogously).[58] This differing treatment is however justified, as there are some fundamental differences between the relationship of the minor and the guardian and the relationship between principal and helper. Unlike the principal, the minor cannot choose his guardian and the minor is usually not in a better position to bear the damage. Furthermore, the guardian is meant to serve the minor's protection. This protection would be reversed if the minor was imputed with the tortious misconduct of the supervisor. Finally, from § 1309 ABGB it emerges that only the guardian but not the minor himself shall be held liable if the guardian neglects his duty to supervise.[59] Therefore, compensation of the injured minor must not be reduced if the guardian neglected his duty to supervise.[60] 36

On the other hand, the guardian's culpable neglect of the duty to supervise is considered a tort with respect to the injured minor.[61] Thus, the person charged with the duty to supervise can be held liable alongside the "external" tortfeasor – proportionately if proportions can be determined, or otherwise joint and severally.[62] In the case of joint and several liability a recourse of the person who entirely indemnified the injured is possible.[63] 37

[56] The imputation of the legal representative's behaviour in contractual relationships is provided by § 1313a ABGB for establishing liability which is applied analogously when establishing contributory negligence.

[57] H. Koziol (supra fn. 9), no. 12/73; SZ 20/246; SZ 25/318; contrary: K. Wolff in: H. Klang (supra fn. 31), 66.

[58] H. Koziol (supra fn. 9), no. 12/74. For further information see also H. Koziol (supra fn. 9), no. 12/64 et seq.; R. Reischauer in: P. Rummel (supra fn. 30), § 1304 no. 7.

[59] H. Koziol (supra fn. 9), no. 12/74; R. Reischauer in: P. Rummel (supra fn. 30), § 1310 no. 19.

[60] M. Hinteregger in: U. Magnus/M. Martín-Casals (supra fn. 46), no. 28.

[61] R. Reischauer in: P. Rummel (supra fn. 30), § 1310 no. 19; SZ 20/246.

[62] R. Reischauer in: P. Rummel (supra fn. 30), § 1310 no. 19; SZ 20/246.

[63] SZ 20/246; R. Reischauer in: P. Rummel (supra fn. 30), § 1310 no. 19.

38 If the persons charged with the duty to supervise can be held liable alongside the third person, the damages of the minor must not be reduced at all because of contributory negligence. As liability of minors is subsidiary to the liability of the supervisor, according to the "mirror-image principle" contributory negligence of the minor can only be established if the supervisor himself cannot be liable, if he is unable to indemnify the recoverer or if he is of unknown abode (§ 1310 and § 1309 analogously).

12. Do the rules of contributory negligence also apply in the area of strict liability?

39 According to the prevailing opinion, the rules on contributory negligence apply as well in the area of strict liability.[64] This is explicitly provided for by all specific strict liability statutes.[65] Also if provisions on strict liability should not contain a corresponding rule, it is common opinion that § 1304 ABGB has to be applied analogously.[66] Imputability of the damage to the injured depends on the same criteria that are to be considered when establishing liability of the tortfeasor.

40 The proportioning of shares is however quite difficult. The prevailing opinion[67] holds that in most cases the operational risk can be equated with slight negligence.[68]

13. Do the rules of contributory negligence apply in the area of strict liability for traffic-accidents or other areas of tort liability?

41 The Statute on liability for keeping railways and motor vehicles contains an explicit provision concerning contributory negligence. § 7 of the *Eisenbahn- und Kraftfahrzeughaftpflichtgesetz* (Statute on Liability for Keeping Railways and Motor Vehicles, EKHG) provides that § 1304 ABGB on contributory negligence has to be applied, the fault of the injured thus leading to a reduction of compensation. However, it is held that if the operational risk far outweighs the negligence of the injured, the tortfeasor has to compensate the whole damage.[69] On the other hand, gross contributory negligence with respect to small operational risk can lead to the total release from liability.

64 See H. Koziol (supra fn. 9), nos. 12/26 et seq.
65 M. Hinteregger (supra fn. 46), no. 22.
66 H. Koziol (supra fn. 9), no. 12/26.
67 H. Koziol (supra fn. 9), no. 12/27; R. Welser in: R. Sprung/B. König (eds.), *Das österreichische Schirecht* (1977), 418.
68 For further information see H. Koziol (supra fn. 9), no. 12/27.
69 H. Koziol (supra fn. 9), no. 12/26.

14. Are adults held to a higher standard of care in their interactions with children, or when children are or may be around?

In establishing wrongfulness, on the one hand, "*Schutzgesetze*" (protective statutes) are decisive. They require a certain behaviour and thereby forbid abstractly dangerous behaviour by formulating imperative rules (§ 1311 sent. 2 case 2 ABGB). A descriptive example for the requirement of a higher standard of care with respect to children is provided by § 3 StVO[70]: Every user of the road may rely on other persons observing the provisions regarding the use of the road, unless he has to presume that the person is a child. 42

However, the legal system does not always provide imperative rules, but it recognises protected positions by assigning rights or assets and thereby prohibits creating concrete dangers to those rights. Wrongfulness is then based on the interference with a protected position by violating an objective duty of care. For determining the required duty of care, among other criteria, the probability of the behaviour creating a damage, i.e. the dangerousness, is decisive. If children are or may be around, the probability of creating a damage is increased, since children are often not able to judge neither the situation nor the consequences of their behaviour and therefore often act in an "uncontrolled" way and are less able to protect themselves. Therefore the required duty of care is higher. 43

VI. Insurance Matters by Dr. Felix Wieser

15. Are pupils covered by private or public accident (first-party) insurance?

16. Does this insurance cover any damage incurred on the way to school and back?

a) Public accident (first-party) insurance:

Pupils are covered by public accident insurance against the consequences of accidents which happen during classes, during school events or on the way to school (§ 8 sec. 1 subpara. 3 lit. h *Allgemeines Sozialversicherungsgesetz* – General Social Insurance Act, ASVG). According to court practice, the protected sphere goes even further: Every activity, which is to be considered the exercise of the role of a pupil or a student, is covered.[71] Pupils are therefore entitled to claims which sometimes go far beyond what they could gain from legal health insurance. (Pupils are usually covered by legal health insurance by non-contributory co-insurance with their parents.) Because of accident insurance, they can obtain, in particular, an injury benefit (§ 212 ASVG), a disablement annuity (§ 204 ASVG) and indemnification of integrity (§ 213a ASVG). 44

[70] § 3 *Straßenverkehrsordnung* (Road Traffic Act, StVO) regulates the so-called *"Vertrauensgrundsatz"* (principle of reliance).

[71] OGH 23 November 1993, [1994] *Österreichische Juristen-Zeitung* (ÖJZ), 168 et seq.

The latter serves to make up for non-pecuniary loss[72] and is akin to damages for pain and suffering and to compensation for defacing (§§ 1325 et seq. ABGB). However, it is granted only on very restrictive conditions. Regarding the assignment of the claim to the social insurance institution (legal cession according to §§ 332 et seq. ASVG)[73], the indemnification of integrity is seen in congruency to damages for pain and suffering and to compensation for defacing. Therefore, the claim for damages for pain and suffering is devolved upon the social insurance institution insofar as the latter has to pay an indemnification of integrity. Thus, if the injured pupil is entitled to an indemnification of integrity, his claim for damages for pain and suffering and for compensation for defacing persist only as far as these claims exceed the amount of the indemnification of integrity.

45 Unfavourable for the pupil is the applicability of the so-called "employer's privilege concerning liability".[74] According to this, the pupil is not entitled to a damages' claim against those persons who are equated with the employer or the supervisor in business, i.e. the operator of an institution where pupils are trained and the teacher. This is true also regarding damages for pain and suffering – even in those cases in which the injured is not entitled to an indemnification of integrity. However, if the tortfeasor is a fellow pupil, the "employer's privilege concerning liability" is not applicable and the injured is entitled to a claim for damages for pain and suffering against his fellow pupil. In Austria, no "fellow worker's privilege concerning liability" in this respect exists.

b) Private accident (first-party) insurance

46 Children can also be covered by private accident insurance. However, no special legal provisions in this respect exist. The designing of the accident insurance policies is in general left to contracting parties. Statistics, which could provide information on the percentage of children covered by accident insurance in Austria, are lacking. Such accident insurance policies are often sold via schools. School principals, teachers or parents' associations take out group accident insurance for the pupils. The contracting party and payer of the premiums is then the parent's association or sometimes the teacher. Often teachers hand out payment forms, which have been prepared by a private insurance company, to the pupils and request them to hand the forms on to their parents. If the parents then pay the premium, the child is covered by accident insurance. The contractual partner in such a case is the child who is represented by one or both of his parents. Of significant importance is also the so-called "family insurance", an insurance, which, too, is taken out by one or both parents, and which provides coverage for the parents as well as for the children of the family. In this case the parents are the policy holders and the children are co-insured. Accident insurance in Austria is generally offered in the form of a

72 See W. Holzer, The Impact of Social Security Law on Tort Law in Austria in: U. Magnus (ed.), *The Impact of Social Security Law on Tort Law* (2003), nos. 15, 39 et seq.

73 As to *cessio legis* and congruency see W. Holzer (supra fn. 72), no. 13 respectively no. 23.

74 As to the employer's privilege see W. Holzer (supra fn. 72), nos. 14 et seq.

capital-sum insurance. This means that the amount of the indemnification depends on capital-sums stipulated in the contract. Thus, the damage which occurs in the concrete case, assessed according to the principles of tort law, or according to the principles of legal accident insurance is not decisive. The following types of claims are typical: (i) Benefits in case of permanent invalidity. The degree of invalidity is calculated according to a so-called "valuation of limbs list" contained in the General Insurance Conditions. This means that a certain degree of invalidity is assigned to the loss of a limb or of an organ. (ii) Benefits in the case of hospitalisation. The amount depends upon the sum stipulated in the contract for a day of hospitalisation. (iii) Benefits on the occurrence of death. An interesting detail is the fact that the insurance benefits on the occurrence of the death of a child do not consist of a certain sum agreed upon, as is the case when adults die, but that the benefits correspond to the actual costs of the funeral. Some benefits, that are however of minor importance, are rendered in the manner of indemnity insurance, which means that the actual expenditure is reimbursed. Among these benefits number: the costs of a rescue operation, of transport and, as already mentioned, the costs of the funeral of a child.

Regarding private accident insurance, the following particular rules apply. 47
(These particularities mainly result from the fact of the private accident insurance being a capital-sum insurance and not an indemnity insurance – apart from the exceptions mentioned supra): (i) The benefits from private insurance do not affect those from social insurance and vice versa. The benefits are not congruent and are thus due in parallel. (ii) The legal cession of § 67 VVG[75] does not take place. Despite the contributions of the insurer, the injured keeps possible damages' claims against a third person. (iii) Several private insurance policies can be taken out in parallel; in the event of damage, every insurer is obliged to provide indemnification. The existence of double or multiple insurance coverage does not lead to a reduction of the claims. The so-called principle of interdicted enrichment is not applicable. Nonetheless, prior to entering into a contract, accident insurers in general request information on whether further accident insurance policies have been taken out or not. The decision on whether a contract is concluded is then based on this information. Moreover, in general the policy holder obliges himself to notify the insurance company when taking out further accident insurance policies. The insurer usually reserves the right to denounce the contract in this case. (iv) Negligence of the insured does not influence the merits or the extent of the amount of indemnification by the private accident insurer. Only damage intentionally caused by the insured is generally excluded from being covered. However, the parties are free to stipulate further exclusions. Typically excluded are e.g. accidents which re-

[75] § 67 sec. 1 phrase 1 *Verwaltungsvollstreckungsgesetz* (Act on the Enforcement of Administrative Decisions, VVG) reads as follows: "If the insured is entitled to a damages' claim against a third person, the claim devolves upon the insurer, as far as the latter compensates the insured for his damage."

sult from the exercise of certain dangerous kinds of sport or from a loss of consciousness due to the consumption of alcohol, drugs or medicine.

17. Are there restrictions on damages recoverable by the child, e.g. with respect to loss of future earnings?

48 There are no special restrictions on damages for children. They are entitled to obtain compensation for every kind of damage, without any contractual or financial limitation. However, special problems might occur in the inquiry of the damage or with the calculation of the extent of damages in the case of an injured child. These can be important for the assessment of damages, which depend on the hypothetical development of the child had the damage not occurred; like, for example, damages for loss of earnings. In calculating the amount of loss in case of a child being injured and suffering physical or psychological harms which affected its earning ability, several factors will be taken into account, namely, which school the child would attend and graduate from, which studies the child would finish, which occupation the child would have and how much money the child would earn had the injuring event not occurred. Although statements and assumtions on these topics are judged to be highly uncertain, this, however, does not alter the fact that Austrian jurisprudence provides compensation of such losses and awards damages on an individual basis, depending on the concrete circumstances of each case.

VII. Damage Issues

18. If damages for loss of earnings are available, what are the principles governing their assessment?

49 The earnings that are lost and that will be lost in the future are to be compensated for in every case of personal injury.[76] The loss has to be assessed on probability according to the usual course of events.[77] However, the calculation of earnings that will be lost is rather problematic if the tortfeasor is a child who has been prevented from receiving professional training because of the injury. It remains unclear which education he would have completed and which position he would have reached.

50 The damage can be calculated in a subjective-concrete or in an objective-abstract way. When calculating the damage in a subjective way, according to the "*Differenzmethode*", the actual loss because of the personal injury is to be ascertained.[78]

51 However, damage can also be assessed in an objective-abstract way, which means that the subjective circumstances of the injured are not taken into ac-

[76] H. Koziol (supra fn. 8), 131.
[77] H. Koziol, Damages under Austrian Law in: U. Magnus (ed.), *Unification of Tort Law: Damages* (2001), no. 83; H. Koziol (supra fn. 8), 132.
[78] H. Koziol (supra fn. 8), 132.

count. Only the objective reduction or loss of earning capacity is to be considered. Thus, the injured person can claim compensation even if she suffers no actual loss of earnings.[79] Austrian scholars justify the objective-abstract calculation by referring to the "*Rechtsfortwirkungsfunktion*". This expresses the idea that the infringed right of the injured party or its object of legal protection continues to exist in the injured party's claim for compensation.[80]

Regarding the question of how the compensation for loss of earnings has to be awarded, the ABGB does not lay down exact rules. According to the prevailing opinion, in general the damages have to be awarded as a rent, because a rent can be adjusted to the real developments and needs not be based on presumptions as much.[81] A lump sum may only be rewarded if there are weighty arguments.[82] More recent statutes, such as the EKHG[83] regulate the question corresponding to the prevailing opinion.[84] 52

19. Which of the child's non-material interests are protected in your jurisdiction? May the child, for example, sue for impairment of intellectual or social development, the onset of behavioural problems, or reduced employment prospects?

Non-material damage is damage which does not entail a measurable reduction of the injured's patrimony.[85] It can be the consequence of a pecuniary damage or occur independently of it as so-called mere pain or the consequences of the injury of personal rights.[86] Every person is entitled to personal rights – independent of her age (see § 16 ABGB). Such personal rights are for example the right to physical soundness, the right to freedom, to honour, the right to one's name and the right to one's image. Beyond that, several other personal rights exist, which cannot be outlined that clearly. 53

Whether the immaterial damage is compensable depends on different factors that have to be weighed: In particular, the value that is given to the injured interest by the legal system and the relevancy of the impairment is to be considered. In this regard, it is decisive whether the injury can be objectified,[87] which depends very much on whether the infringed interest has clear outlines. Moreover, the extent of fault is to be taken into account when establishing liability for immaterial damage. In general, immaterial damage has to be compensated only in cases of gross negligence according to the §§ 1323, 1324 ABGB un- 54

[79] H. Koziol in: U. Magnus (supra fn. 77), no. 16; H. Koziol (supra fn. 8), 134 et seq.
[80] H. Koziol in: U. Magnus (supra fn. 77), no. 4.
[81] H. Koziol (supra fn. 8), 133.
[82] [1975] ZVR, no. 198; [1990] ZVR, no. 121; H. Koziol in: U. Magnus (supra fn. 77), no. 63; R. Reischauer in: P. Rummel (supra fn. 30), § 1325 no. 27.
[83] § 14 EKHG.
[84] H. Koziol in: U. Magnus (supra fn. 77), no. 64.
[85] H. Koziol (supra fn. 9), no. 2/102.
[86] E. Karner/H. Koziol, Der Ersatz ideellen Schadens im österreichischen Recht und seine Reform, *15. Österreichischer Juristentag* (ÖJT) II/1 (2003), 11 and 24.
[87] E. Karner/H. Koziol (supra fn. 86), 23 and 34.

less special provisions[88] are applicable.[89] Some scholars hold that in a flexible combination with the factors mentioned above, a high degree of fault can outweigh a lesser degree of the injury's relevancy.[90]

55 With respect to the encroachment of intellectual or social development and to the onset of behavioural problems there exist no decisions of the courts. Compensation follows the rules outlined above.

56 Regarding reduced employment prospects, § 1326 ABGB and § 13 subpara. 5 EKHG are applicable and contain special provisions: If a person has been defaced as the result of personal injury, the tortfeasor has to compensate for the impairment of the injured's better advancement. The impairment of better advancement mainly comprises the reduction of marriage chances or of employment prospects.[91] § 1326 ABGB thus clarifies that a loss resulting from personal injury also has to be compensated even if it does not consist of lost earnings and even if it does not reduce the ability to work. Compensation takes place at every degree of fault.[92]

57 A particularity of § 1326 ABGB lies in the fact that the actual occurrence of a damage need not be very probable. A rather low degree of probability suffices.[93] This is true especially if the future course of life of the defaced is completely unclear and the impairment of a better advancement can only be inferred from general life experience. That is in particular the case if the injured is a child.[94]

58 Whether § 1326 ABGB regards only pecuniary loss or also immaterial damage is controversial. This question is, however, of minor importance as both opinions support the adjudgment of immaterial damage. If they are not granted under § 1326 ABGB, they are taken into account when assessing damages for pain and suffering.[95]

[88] Such as § 1325 ABGB regarding damages for pain and suffering.

[89] E. Karner/H. Koziol (supra fn. 86), 38 and 105. The OGH, however, is more restrictive and rejects compensation if the right to freedom is negligently impaired ([1990] EvBl 135; H. Koziol, (supra fn. 9), no. 11/18).

[90] E. Karner/H. Koziol (supra fn. 86), 144.

[91] B.A. Koch/H. Koziol, Schadenersatz für Körperverletzung in Österreich in: B.A. Koch/H. Koziol (eds.), *Compensation for Personal Injury in a Comparative Perspective* (2003), no. 59; H. Koziol (supra fn. 8), 144.

[92] B.A. Koch/H. Koziol in: B.A. Koch/H. Koziol (supra fn. 91), no. 59; H. Koziol (supra fn. 8), 144.

[93] B.A. Koch/H. Koziol in: B.A. Koch/H. Koziol (supra fn. 91), no. 59; H. Koziol (supra fn. 8), 144; [1963] ZVR, 69; [1974] ZVR, 42; [1981] ZVR, 231; [1982] ZVR, 332.

[94] OGH 30 March 1978, 2 Ob 15/78.

[95] H. Koziol (supra fn. 8), 143; B.A. Koch/H. Koziol in: B.A. Koch/H. Koziol (supra fn. 91), no. 59.

20. Are there special rules for the assessment of damages sustained by a child, e.g. with respect to pain and suffering?

The ABGB does not provide detailed guidelines for the assessment of damages for pain and suffering. According to § 1325 ABGB, compensation for pain and suffering has to be "appropriate to the ascertained circumstances". 59

Firstly it has to be mentioned that the age per se is not decisive. Thus, also an infant is entitled to damages for pain and suffering. However, the age is of indirect importance, as permanent injury can prejudice a young victim in many fields and experiences of life that are already lived through in elder age. This regards for example marriage, family planning or professional career. In this regard, also a recent decision[96] stated that the paraplegia of a very young man justified higher damages with respect to his emotional pain. Thus, not simply the duration of the personal injury and its consequences is considered, but the fact that the young victim is much more prevented from developing his personality than an elder person and thereby sustains higher immaterial damage.[97] 60

Furthermore, the duration of the injury is decisive when assessing damages for pain and suffering. In this respect it is therefore held that the permanent injury of a child justifies higher damages than the personal injury of an older person.[98] 61

21. Does a small child have a claim for damages for pain and suffering, if he or she is deprived of his or her parents by a tortious act? If so, may the claim be denied on the ground that the child does not feel the loss?

Close relatives are entitled to damages for pain and suffering if they suffered a shock from watching the injury or the death of the immediate victim or from the message thereof if the shock amounts to a bodily injury (e.g. a reactive depression).[99] 62

However, according to a very recent decision, in cases of gross negligence or intent near relatives can also obtain compensation for "pain of grief" that cannot be qualified as a bodily injury.[100] Corresponding solutions are supported for exceptional "mere emotional damage" owing to very serious injuries of near relatives.[101] In this respect the question arises whether the claim of the child can be denied because it cannot feel the loss as it is too young. This has not yet been decided by the Supreme Court. However, it has to be considered 63

96 [2001] ZVR, no. 54.
97 E. Karner/H. Koziol, (supra fn. 86), 126.
98 E. Karner/H. Koziol (supra fn. 86), 126 et seq.
99 [1995] ZVR, no. 46; [1997] ZVR, no. 75; B.A. Koch/H. Koziol in: B.A. Koch/H. Koziol (supra fn. 91), no. 70.
100 [2001] ZVR, no. 73; B.C. Steininger, Austrian Report in: H. Koziol/B.C. Steininger, *European Tort Law 2001* (2002), nos. 69 et seq.
101 B.A. Koch/H. Koziol in: B.A. Koch/H. Koziol (supra fn. 91), no. 70.

that also very young children have a very intense relationship to their parents, especially to the mother. On the other hand, it is held that the child would not be entitled to a damages claim for pain of grief if at no time a close relationship between the parent and the child existed or if they have become totally estranged from one another.[102]

22. With respect to a damage claim for the costs of medical treatment: May the tortfeasor defend himself by pointing to the fact that the parents have a duty to maintain the child?

64 The tortfeasor cannot defend himself by pointing to the fact that the parents have to pay the costs of medical treatment because of their legal duty to maintain the child. According to the prevailing opinion, in such a case of "mere shift of damage", the tortfeasor is not released from liability. Furthermore the purpose of the contribution is decisive. Since the payment of the costs of medical treatment is not meant to release the tortfeasor, but only to serve the injured child, these payments are not to be deducted from the damages.[103]

65 Moreover, the question has to be raised, who can claim damages for the costs of medical treatment paid by the parent, since the parent is not "directly injured".[104] However, the Austrian Supreme Court admits also a damages claim of the parents regarding the costs of medical treatment they had to bear because of their legal obligation to provide maintenance.[105] Thus, either the parent or the directly injured child can claim damages.[106]

23. In case of wrongful life: Does the child have a damage claim against the physician or a health care institution?

66 The term "wrongful life" refers to the claim of a child, who was born handicapped, against the physician, because he did not prevent the child's birth. The "wrongful life" claim is thus problematic insofar as the physician did not cause the handicap of the child but was only causal for the child being born.[107] Therefore, the claim can only regard the fact that the child was born at all and now has to live a toilsome, often painful life that necessitates a lot of expenses.[108] The child would have been spared this if the physician had duly informed the mother and if the mother had therefore aborted the child or the parents had refrained from procreation.[109]

[102] E. Karner/H. Koziol (supra fn. 86), 84.
[103] H. Koziol (supra fn. 9), no. 13/11.
[104] SZ 35/32; for further information see H. Koziol (supra fn. 9), nos. 13/9 et seq.
[105] SZ 35/32; H. Koziol (supra fn. 9), no. 13/18; F. Harrer in: M. Schwimann (supra fn. 29), § 1325 no. 18.
[106] F. Harrer in: M. Schwimann (supra fn. 29), § 1325 no. 18.
[107] Ch. Hirsch, *Arzthaftung bei fehlgeschlagener Familienplanung* (2002), 219 et seq.
[108] H. Koziol (supra fn. 9), no. 2/30; Ch. Hirsch (supra fn. 107), 225.
[109] H. Koziol (supra fn. 9), no. 2/30.

The Austrian Supreme Court, with reference to the *Bundesgerichtshof* (German Supreme Court, BGH), did not consider such a claim justified.[110] The OGH emphasised that the lack of information by the physician had not caused the handicap. In such a case, the court stressed, the utmost limits of possible legal regulation of claims were reached. One had to accept one's life as it was created by nature and therefore had no right to it being prevented or exterminated by others. Even if abortion is lawful under certain circumstances, according to the prevailing opinion neither the *nasciturus* nor a person already born has a right to be killed.[111] 67

Also in doctrine a damages claim of the child is rejected by the prevailing opinion. Regarding omitted abortion, the physician's behaviour is not considered wrongful with respect to the child, since the *naciturus* has no right to be killed.[112] On the other hand, also if the parents would have refrained from procreation if they had been duly informed by the physician, the child's claim is denied because of the absence of an ascertainable damage.[113] F. Bydlinski stresses in this respect that there are no valid criteria for judging whether non-existence or life as a handicapped is better, and the opposite condition therefore to be qualified as a damage.[114] 68

24. Concerning liability for pre-natal injuries: Are third parties liable to the child? May the mother be liable to the child, for example, for excessive consumption of alcohol or even for an omission to procure treatment?

According to § 22 ABGB, also unborn children have the right of protection by the law from the time of their conception on. An injury of the *nasciturus* is a personal injury in the sense of § 1325 ABGB which has to be compensated according to the general rules.[115] On the other hand, the injury can also be caused by tortious actions committed when the child was not yet conceived. The damages claim of the child in this respect was controversial, since an uninjured existence had never existed, whose condition had then been impaired by the damaging act. However, the prevailing opinion approves a damages claim, as it is considered an injury of the born person if in the context of her coming into existence actions took place that later caused her being born sick. Thus, it is held irrelevant when the injuring action took place.[116] 69

Regarding liability of the mother who injured the *nasciturus*, the mother could be held liable according to the general rules for personal injury. As to a mitigation of the liability of parents see infra no. 6 et seq. 70

[110] [1999] JBl, 593.
[111] [1999] JBl, 593; H. Koziol (supra fn. 9), no. 2/31.
[112] H. Koziol (supra fn. 9), no. 2/31; E. Karner/H. Koziol (supra fn. 86), 73.
[113] E. Karner/H. Koziol (supra fn. 86), 73; Ch. Hirsch (supra fn. 107), 253.
[114] F. Bydlinski, Das Kind als Schadensursache im Österreichischen Recht in: U. Magnus/J. Spier, *European Tort Law – Liber amicorum for Helmut Koziol* (2000), 64.
[115] H. Koziol (supra fn. 8), 124; E. Karner/H. Koziol (supra fn. 86), 73.
[116] W. Selb, [1966] AcP, 76 et seq; H. Koziol (supra fn. 8), 124 et seq.

Children as Victims under Belgian Law

Pieter De Tavernier

I. Damage Caused by Parents and Other Specific Third Parties

1. In what circumstances may a parent be held liable for an injury sustained by his or her child?

In Belgium, there are no particular rules which govern the tortious conduct of a parent vis-à-vis his child. The general rules of tort liability (artt. 1382–1386 *bis* Belgian Civil Code) are applicable. Nothing prevents children from bringing an action for compensation for damage caused intentionally or unintentionally by his or her parents.[1] In fact, however, only in a limited number of cases are civil actions brought by children against their parents. 1

The problem has hardly been examined in literature. There is very little case law. One important decision, however, has to be mentioned, namely the decision of the *Court de cassation* of 10 October 1972. A father's daughter in law is accidentally killed in a car accident. The father's son starts an action against his father to obtain moral compensation for the loss of his wife. The court of first instance found that the defendant was liable. Consequently, the father had to pay compensation for the moral and material damage that his son had suffered by the death of his wife. Before the Court of Appeal, the father argued that the fact he was held to pay damages to his son constituted a violation of another interest, namely the interest of affection and respect that a son is due to his father. The Court of Appeal did not agree with the argument of the father. To held a parent liable for an injury sustained by one of his children is neither immoral nor unlawful and cannot be considered as an abuse of law. The court stated that families, today, are characterised by a growing individualism and that there are many specific statutory rules concerning conflicts within families. The Court of Appeal concluded that the existence of family doesn't create immunity for 2

[1] B. Weyts, Familiebanden, aansprakelijkheid en verzekeringen, [2004–05] *Rechtskundig Weekblad* (R.W.), 82–83, nos. 7–9.

actions based on liability law. The *Court de cassation* upheld this decision of the Court of Appeal.[2]

(a) In what circumstances may a parent be held liable for injury resulting from his or her intentional conduct? (Liability for intent.) In particular, in what circumstances may the parent be held liable for injury resulting from his or her physical chastisement or the child?

3 Intentional acts committed by a parent have not been the subject of specific legislation. But such acts are, undoubtedly, covered by art. 1382 Civil Code: "*Elke daad [act] van de mens, waardoor aan een ander schade wordt veroorzaakt, verplicht degene door wiens schuld de schade is ontstaan, deze te vergoeden.*" In other words, when parents harm their child intentionally, the general rules of Belgian tort law are applicable.

4 Belgian penal law contains specific provisions regarding criminal acts between parents and children. In cases of abuse of parental authority, i.e when a parent exceeds the scope of authority granted to him or her, different sanctions exist. The Act of 28 November 2000[3] introduced a new system of augmented sanctions in cases of criminal behaviour against children, e.g. in case of intentional injuries caused to minors.[4] Furthermore, there exist specific criminal sanctions, e.g. in cases of neglect of children ("*kinderverwaarlozing*")[5] or incest.[6]

5 Concerning the parental *ius corrigendi*, I believe that there is a fundamental difference between an occasional parental slap on the one hand and the frequent and intense harassment or beating on the other. A specialist in youth protection law has written: "*Het bestuur over de persoon van de minderjarige houdt in dat de ouders hun kinderen mogen straffen wanneer deze ongehoorzaam zijn. Men spreekt dan in de rechtsleer van het "recht op tuchtiging", een middel om de ouders de mogelijkheid te geven hun opvoedend toezicht en hoede te realiseren en dus hun kinderen op te voeden*" [The control on the person of the minor implies that parents may punish their disobedient children. Parents have a "right of chastisement". This is an instrument for parents to re-

[2] *Hof van Cassatie* (Court of Cassation, Cass.) 10 October 1972, [1973] *Arresten van het Hof van Cassatie* (Arr. Cass.), 146, [1972–73] R.W., 718 and [1973] *Journal des Tribunaux* (J.T.), 164, commented by A. Tunc; about this decision, see: A. Van Oevelen, Enige aspecten van aansprakelijkheid jegens kinderen in: M. Coene (ed.), *Het statuut van het kind* (1980), 170 et seq.

[3] Act of 28 November 2000 concerning the criminal protection of minors; see about this Act: B. Weyts (supra fn. 1), 86, no. 17; C. De Roy, De Wet op de strafrechtelijke bescherming van minderjarigen: nieuwe strafbaarstellingen en grotere territoriale gelding in: *Reeks Advocatenpraktijk* (2002), 50; G. Vermeulen, Strenger en ook beter? Over de fragmentarische aanscherping van de strafrechtelijke berscherming van minderjarigen in de wet van 28 november 2000 in: *Gandaius Actueel* VII (2002), 1–27.

[4] See art. 405*bis Strafwetboek* (Belgian Criminal Code, Sw.)

[5] Artt. 423–424 Sw.

[6] Art. 372 subs. 2 Sw.

alise their educational supervision and custody and, by this way, to educate their children].[7] However, some authors argue that even a pedagogical slap is not admitted. In the so-called "*Memorandum Vlaams Beleid 2004–2009 met oog voor kinderrechten* [children's rights]", for instance, it is stated: "*Bovendien vragen we dat, binnen deze context, de zogenaamde 'pedagogische' tik – een contradictio in terminis – blijvend ter discussie gesteld wordt. Nog teveel volwassenen vinden dit een vanzelfsprekend onderdeel van het ouderlijk gezag. Binnen het ruimer kader van opvoedingsondersteuning, dient via sensibilisering duidelijk gemaakt te worden dat lijfstraffen niet langer getolereerd kunnen worden in een respectvolle ouder-kindrelatie*" [We ask that the discussion on the the so-called pedagogical slap – which has to be considered as a *contraditio in terminis* – never stops. Too many adults think that the parental slap is an evident part of exercising parental authority. Within the wide framework of educational support, all involved parties must be made aware that chastisement is no longer tolerable in a respectful parent-child relationship].

(b) In what circumstances may a parent be held liable for injury resulting form his or her unintentional conduct? (Liability for fault.) Are there special rules for liability of the parents? E.g. are parents liable only in case of gross negligence? Are parents held to a lower or higher standard of care? In what circumstances may a parent be held liable for injury resulting from his or her failure to protect the child from harm? (Liability for omissions.)

As already emphasised, Belgian law relating to civil liability does not impose 6
specific duties or standards of behaviour in respect of parent's treatment of their children. Liability for negligence and for omission are the subject of identical treatment under the terms of art. 1383 Civil Code: "*Ieder is aansprakelijk niet alleen voor schade welke hij door zijn daad* [intent], *maar ook voor die welke hij door zijn nalatigheid* [omission] *of door zijn onvoorzichtigheid* [negligence] *heeft veroorzaakt*".

Regarding parents, liability for omissions may arise from the neglect of their 7
so-called parental duties ("*oudelijke plichten*"). Parents are subject to specific duties with respect to their children, being responsible for their development ("*opleiding*"), their cost of living ("*levensonderhoud*") and education ("*opvoeding*").[8] Where a parent fails in one of these duties, Belgian law has at its disposal a variety of measures.

Apart from youth protection measures on the basis of the *Youth Protection* 8
Act, the judge may, for instance, verify if the parental authority might be exercised in violation of the interest of the child or not.[9] In some cases, Belgian law expressly allows the judge to intervene in the exercise of parental authori-

[7] E. Verhellen, *Jeugdbeschermingsrecht* (1996), 185.
[8] See A. Heyvaert, *Het personen- en gezinsrecht ont(k)leed* (2000), 223 et seq.; P. Senaeve, *Compendium van het personen- en familierecht*, 2, *Familierecht* (2003), 159 et seq.
[9] See Cass. 9 February 1978, [1978–79] R.W., 605; see also B. Weyts (supra fn. 1), 85, no. 15.

ty. For instance, art. 148 Civil Code determines that a minor child cannot contract a marriage without permission of his parents. When parents refuse their child permission to contract in marriage, the tribunal may consider that refusal as being abusive. In that circumstance, the child can sue his parent(s) on the basis of art. 1382 Civil Code. Since the Act of 19 January 1990, art. 179 Civil Code allows holding a parent liable when the refusal of permission to the child to contract in marriage is rejected by the tribunal.[10]

9 On the basis of the *Youth Protection Act* itself, several measures may be taken, such as the withdrawal of parental authority by the Youth tribunal ("*Jeugdrechtbank*").[11]

10 The existence of measures within or outside of the scope of the Youth Protection Act does not diminish the possibility to hold parents liable on the grounds of artt. 1382–1383 Civil Code. The behaviour of the parents is compared with that of a *bonus pater familias*, i.e. a normal prudent adult in similar circumstances.[12] Although his behaviour is principally judged *in abstracto*, the judgement is rendered more concrete by the circumstances in which the damage was caused. The family tie may play a role on examining the existence of a fault by one or both parents on the basis of artt. 1382–1383 Civil Code. For example, the parental duty to raise their child must be assessed in a reasonable way.[13]

2. In what circumstances may a third party (e.g. a school or local authority social services department) be held liable for failing to render a child positive assistance (e.g. by preventing parental abuse)?

i) Civil liability[14]

11 There are no specific statutory rules governing the liability of schools or local authorities with a statutory supervisory task. The general rules of tort law of the Belgian Civil Code (artt. 1382–1386*bis*) apply. Damage inflicted by a pupil can be caused *grosso modo* by (1) an unlawful act of (an organ of an agent of) the school's governing body, (2) defective premises or the collapse of a building (art. 1386 Belgian Civil Code) or (3) may be inflicted by another pupil subjected to the education authority. The behaviour of the supervisor or the school's governing body etc. is compared with that of a supervisor or school's governing body etc. which exhibits normal prudence and care in similar circumstances. Supervisors, educators, the school's governing body, etc. should take reasonable care that the pupil will not cause unlawful harm to others or

[10] B. Weyts (supra fn. 1), 85–86, no. 15.
[11] B. Weyts (supra fn. 1), 86, no. 16.
[12] B. Weyts (supra fn. 1), 86, no. 18.
[13] B. Weyts (supra fn. 1), 86, no. 18.
[14] See about this topic D. Deli, Civil liability within the education system: the Belgian framework, [2002] *European Journal for Education Law and Policy*, vol. 6, 15–23.

that damage will not be inflicted on a pupil. This reasonable care does not only concern supervision, but also the organisation of that supervision.

Who can be held liable for failing to render for a child positive assistance? 12
First, the supervisor, the teacher, the educator, etc. can be held liable for a supervisory fault (act or omission), or a fault concerning the organisation of the supervision, on grounds of artt. 1382–1383 Civil Code, or, when the defendant can be considered as a "teacher", on grounds of art. 1384, para. 4, Civil Code. *Secondly*, the school or the institution charged with the supervision of the child (youth welfare institutions, etc.) can be held liable for a fault concerning the organisation of the supervision, on grounds of artt. 1382–1383 Civil Code. *Thirdly*, the school can be held liable for the fault committed by one of the staff members of the school, on grounds of artt. 1382–1383 Civil Code (legal persons of public law) or on grounds of artt. 1384, para. 3, Civil Code (legal persons of private law).

Although the "fault" is principally judged *in abstracto*, the judgement is ren- 13
dered more concrete by the circumstances in which the damage was caused. One of these circumstances is the professional activity of the person whose acts are judged, i.e. "being a specialist" in a certain field. Principally, the acts of a supervisor, educator, institution, etc. presuppose specific skills and will therefore be compared with the behaviour of a regular supervisor, educator, institution, etc, acting carefully and reasonably. The judgement *in abstracto* of the act will be rendered *in concreto* afterwards by considering the time and place in which it took place. The judge has several criteria at his disposal to assess whether or not the supervisor has taken reasonable care: (1) the nature of the activity, e.g. a dangerous game played by children; (2) the number of children who have to be supervised; (3) the character of the child or (4) the means of coercion the school or institution can use.

Concerning the liability of the supervisor of a school, it must be emphasised 14
that *predictability* of the damage is an essential component of the "fault" concept alongside the wrongful conduct and the tortious capacity of the tortfeasor. The foreseeable nature of the damage, referring not to the size but to the existence itself of the damage, is regarded as one of the most essential elements to determine the (non-)respect of the general carefulness standard.

ii) Cases of criminal liability[15]

Because of the growing social awareness concerning the – unfortunately often 15
occurring – violation of the physical and psychological integrity of children, the responsibility of persons having much contact with children has been substantially increased. This phenomenon particularly affects the participants in education.

[15] D. Deli, [2002] *European Journal for Education Law and Policy*, 23–24.

16 The offence of careless negligence is described and considered as a criminal act in art. 422*bis* of the Belgian Criminal Code and punishes anyone who neglects to help someone in great danger. The careless negligence is one of the so-called *omission offenses*. This means that someone has neglected to act in a situation where action is imposed by the law. The duty to provide help exists also with regard to minors who are in any kind of serious danger. Pursuant to art. 422*bis* Criminal Code, it is indisputable that anyone who knows about any kind of abuse, either sexually, physically or psychologically, has the obligation to intervene and act in the most appropriate way. Since teachers, school heads and others carrying responsibility towards pupils due to their professional activities will be confronted more often with such reprehensible acts than others, they above all are subject to criminal liability when they do not meet this obligation.

17 Within the same scope lies the problem of *professional secrecy* of the staff members in education. Due to their special position, education people will learn more often about unlawful acts committed (by and) on pupils. This can result in a strange paradox: on the one hand they are legally obliged to give help pursuant to art. 422*bis* Criminal Code, whereas it is forbidden to communicate secret affairs confided to them on the grounds of their duty to confidentiality and professional secrecy.[16] As a result, professional secrecy may cause delicate problems. Damage can sometimes be avoided by communicating certain confidential data to certain persons. The secrecy duty is only lifted when a confidant is called on to testify in court or where the law obliges him/her to release those secrets. Nevertheless, the keeper of the secret has the right to remain silent before a judge so that he/she him/herself decides whether it is advisable to speak or to keep silent. Except for these cases, the confidant will always have to judge whether it is advisable to communicate certain data to certain persons by weighing his/her interests. In fact, professional secrecy has no absolute value in se and serves both public and private interests. There are of course cases where the right to hear the truth is more important than the right to secrecy. Since professional secrecy is intended above all to protect the one who communicates the data there can be no secrecy duty if this would be disadvantageous for the person involved. The major criterion must therefore be the possible advantage the person involved will have if he/she (the confidant) talks or remains silent.

3. What limitations periods are applied to a child's claim?

18 Since the Act of 10 June 1998, the limitation periods concerning tort claims of children are as follows. Firstly, there is a five year period running from the day following the day on which the victim has knowledge of his damage (or of the aggravation of his damage) <u>and</u> the identity of the person who is liable for this damage.[17] Secondly, the claim is barred in any case after twenty years, running

[16] See e.g. art. 458 Sw.

[17] Art. 2262*bis* § 1, subs. 2 *Burgerlijk Wetboek* (Belgian Civil Code, B.W.).

from the moment of the tortious act.[18] This system is the same as in the Netherlands.[19] The limitation period, however, is suspended during the minority of the child.[20]

II. Contributory Negligence

4. Are there any special provisions concerning contributory negligence if the tortfeasor is a child?

As a rule, general rules of tort law apply. Damage caused by the fault of a third party and the victim's own fault, will not be compensated entirely. Neither does the Belgian law of torts allow a complete denial of compensation to a contributorily negligent victim. Compensation awarded to contributorily negligent victims will be diminished in proportion to the contribution of the victim's fault in the occurrence of the damage. Contributory negligence will thus generally lead to a reduction of damages. The threefold requirement to establish fault liability is also used to assess contributory negligence. The tortfeasor has to prove a fault in a causal relationship with the damage which has occurred. 19

However, there is one special provision concerning contributory negligence if the child is a tortfeasor. In the first paragraph of art. 29*bis* of the Act of 21 November 1989 on the compulsory automobile liability insurance (the so-called *W.A.M.* Act), we read the conditions which apply in order to get compensation for personal injury suffered by vulnerable victims of traffic accidents. The sixth phrase of that first paragraph of art. 29*bis* W.A.M. Act excludes victims from compensation when they have wanted both the accident and its consequences to happen ("*die het ongeval en zijn gevolgen hebben gewild*"). Regarding minor children, the same phrase states that this exclusion can only be applied to minors *older than 14 years of age*. Minors *younger than 14 years of age* can get compensation, even when they wanted both the accident and its consequences to happen.[21] 20

5. What are the rules governing contributory negligence of the child? Do such principles follow the same lines as those governing the negligence issue itself? (mirror-image?)

Regarding children, the tortious capacity has to be examined. With regard to this capacity, the conditions applying to contributory negligence are identical to the ones under general fault liability law. In contrast with, for example, Dutch law, contributory negligence of the child in Belgian law is clearly the mirror-image of tortious liability of the child. Contributory negligence will 21

[18] Art. 2262*bis* § 1, subs. 3 B.W.

[19] See W.H. Van Boom, Children as Victims under Dutch Law in: M. Martín-Casals (ed.), *Children in Tort Law Part II: Children as Victims* (2006), no. 12.

[20] Art. 2252 B.W.; see on this topic: A. Van Oevelen, Recente ontwikkelingen inzake de bevrijdende verjaring in het burgerlijk recht, [2000–01] R.W., 1437–1438.

[21] Cf. also the answer to question 6.

only be recognised if the subjective element of the necessary fault (i.e. the tortious capacity of the child) can be established.[22]

22 There is one special provision concerning contributory negligence if the tortfeasor is a child, namely in the case of compensation of traffic victims. In that case, contributory negligence had been subject to severe criticism until the promulgation of special legislation introducing a regime of "automatic" compensation for *personal* injury suffered by vulnerable victims of traffic accidents. This new regime has reduced the possibility to invoke contributory negligence of non-motorised victims. The legal basis of this new regime is art. 29*bis* of the Act of 21 November 1989 on the compulsory automobile liability insurance.[23] In the first paragraph of art. 29*bis* of this so-called *W.A.M.* Act, we read the conditions in order to get compensation for personal injury suffered by vulnerable victims of traffic accidents. The sixth phrase of that first paragraph of art. 29*bis* W.A.M.-Act excludes victims from compensation when they have wanted both the accident and its consequences to happen ("*die het ongeval en zijn gevolgen hebben gewild*"). Regarding minor children, the same phrase states that this exclusion can only be applied to minors *older than 14 years old*. Minors *younger than 14 years old* can get compensation, even when they wanted both the accident and its consequences to happen.[24]

6. Does the fixed minimum age for children to be liable, if any exists, also apply to the contributory negligence of the child?

23 In the Belgian legal system, there is no such minimum age for children to be liable. Children can only be addressed personally if they have reached the so-called age of discretion ("*jaren des onderscheids*"). As already explained in of my contribution to *Part I: Children as Tortfeasors*, this criterion is not bound to a specific age. It has to be assessed by the judges as a matter of fact, depending on, for example, the child's intellectual development.[25] Mentally ill minors or minors suffering from sudden illnesses, such as epilepsy, also lack the necessary tortious capacity.

For instance, the *Court de cassation* did not accept a defence based on contributory negligence against a child whose conduct met all necessary elements of the objective element of fault, but who had not reached the "age of discretion". It concerned a decision of the *Court de cassation* of 13 October 1999.[26] On 22 February 1989, the Brussels Court of Appeal decided that a 9

[22] H. Cousy/D. Droshout, Contributory negligence under Belgian Law in: U. Magnus/M. Martín-Casals (eds.), *Unification of Tort Law: Contributory Negligence* (2003), 30, no. 14; B. Weyts, *De fout van het slachtoffer in het buitencontractueel aansprakelijkheidsrecht* (2003), 85 et seq., nos. 95 et seq.

[23] Text after the modifying Act of 19 January 2001, in force since 3 March 2001.

[24] See on this matter H. Cousy/D. Droshout in: U. Magnus/M. Martín-Casals (supra fn. 22), 35, no. 30; B. Weyts (supra fn. 22), 143–144, no. 165.

[25] B. Weyts (supra fn. 22), 85 et seq., nos. 95 et seq.

[26] [1999] Arr. Cass., 1255 and [1999] *Pasicrisie* (Pas.), I, 528; see about this decision: B. Weyts (supra fn. 22), 88–89, no. 98; H. Cousy/D. Droshout in: U. Magnus/M. Martín-Casals (supra fn. 22), 37, no. 37.

year-old child, entering a bus through an open window and putting it in motion, had not yet reach the "age of discretion".[27] The Court of Appeal of Mons stated, in a decision of 29 February 1988, that an eleven-year-old child, knowing the risk of fire, commits a fault by setting a match to paper, especially when the child does so in a cellar.[28]

7. What is the standard of care governing the behaviour of children in the field of contributory negligence? Is such standard determined by the same principles and criteria which are relevant to the duty of care incumbent upon the child in the context of him or her being held liable?

In a decision of 24 October 1974, the Belgian *Court de cassation* has decided 24
that the age of a child is irrelevant to the assessment of whether he or she has committed an unlawful act or not.[29] For the reasons stated in *Part I: Children as Tortfeasors*, I do not agree with this point of view. Indeed, the comparison of the behaviour of the minor with that of the *bonus pater familias* entails that no account should be taken of the intellectual or psychological factors of the child, but that is not to say that the internal circumstances of the minor child, insofar as they are *objectifiable*, cannot be taken into account. I believe that comparison of the behaviour of the child with that of the *bonus pater familias* is, after all, only possible if the person who exhibits normal care and caution is placed in the same circumstances as the minor child who has committed the unlawful act that has caused the damage. Consequently, the standard of care employed in assessing whether a child is guilty of contributory negligence is that of an ordinarily prudent and reasonable child of the claimant's age. There are several decisions in which the courts have taken into account the age of the child.[30]

III. Contribution in Equity

8. Is there a parallel (mirror-image) to liability in equity in the field of contributory negligence? If so, do the criteria determining liability in equity of the child also apply to the issue of holding him or her accountable for his or her contributory negligence?

Yes. The rules concerning liability in equity have to be applied analogously in 25
the field of contributory negligence. In *Part I: Children as Tortfeasors*, I have already explained that the legislator has deemed it necessary to allow an unaccountable person to be held (partially or fully) liable for damages he has caused. According to art. 1386*bis* Civil Code, in cases where damages to an-

[27] [1990] *Tijdschrift voor Verzekeringen* (De Verz.), 168.

[28] Court of Appeal of Mons 29 February 1988, [1990] *Revue générale des assurances et des responsabilités* (R.G.A.R.), no. 11636.

[29] Cass. 24 October 1974, [1974–75] R.W., 1185, cmt.

[30] E.g. *Rechtbank van Eerste Aanleg* (Civil Tribunal, Rb.) of Leuven 21 September 1994, [1996] R.G.A.R., no. 12696. See also Court of Appeal of Bergen 29 February 1988, [1990] R.G.A.R., no. 11636.

other person caused by a person who is in a state of insanity, serious mental disturbance or mental impairment, to such that he is unfit to control his acts, the judge can sentence him to partial or full repayment of the amount that would have applied had he had full control over his actions. In such cases, the judge rules in equity, taking into account the circumstances and the situation of the parties involved. Art. 1386*bis* Civil Code was provided for persons who are unaccountable on grounds of their mental state, and not for *infantes*. It is said that a tortfeasor can also invoke this article *vis-à-vis* a victim that would have been contributorily negligent had he not been mentally ill.[31]

26 Yes. It seems that the same criteria determining liability in equity of the mentally ill child apply to the issue of holding the child accountable for his or her contributory negligence.

9. If answered affirmatively: Is the fact that the child is privately or socially insured against the accident a factor to be considered? Is the existence of liability insurance of the tortfeasor to be taken into account? What factors have a bearing on the assessment of equitable contribution?

27 Yes. The fact that the mentally ill child is privately or socially insured against the accident is considered expressly as a financial component that justifies that the child, despite the fact that it lacks tortious capacity, can be held accountable for its contributory negligence.

28 Yes. The existence of liability insurance of the tortfeasor is taken into account. When assessing the equitable contribution, the financial circumstances of the two parties involved have to be taken into consideration.

29 The judge may take into account the nature and the gravity of the unlawful act committed by the tortfeasor. He can also allow his equity assessment to depend on the gravity of the damage the mentally ill child has suffered. Likewise, the gravity of the fault of the mentally ill minor victim may be taken into account in order to refuse full compensation for damage to the mentally ill child or to order only partial compensation to the child. Indeed, as the degree of wrongfulness in the behaviour of the mentally ill minor can vary, also the degree of absence of the necessary care with respect to his or her own goods can vary.

[31] L. Cornelis, Beginselen van het Belgische buitencontractuele aansprakelijkheidsrecht. De onrechtmatige daad in: *Reeks Aansprakelijkheidsrecht, no. 7* (1989), 176.

IV. Miscellaneous

10. What are the rules for a situation in which the child is guilty of contributory negligence but the parents have also breached their duty to supervise? Is the child held accountable in any way for his or her parents' breach of the duty to supervise so that his or her claim for damages is reduced?

Children are not identified with the negligence of persons that are taking care of them. A reduction of liability because of contributory negligence is only possible if the child commits both the objective and subjective element of a fault itself. Negligence of a person who has to take care of a child will never give rise to personal liability of the child or to contributory negligence of the child. In other words, damages of the injured are not to be reduced because of a neglect of duty on the part of the supervisor.[32] 30

However, a tortfeasor can also base his defence upon the presumption *iuris tantum* provided by art. 1384, para. 2, Civil Code, making parents (or a parent) vicariously liable for the faulty behaviour of their child(ren). As already examined in *Part I: Children as Tortfeasors*, such is possible as soon as the behaviour of the child complies with the objective element of fault (thus also if a child cannot be considered contributorily negligent because the childlacks the necessary tortious capacity because he or she has not yet reached the 'age of discretion'). Parents can rebut the presumption of art. 1384, para. 2, Civil Code by proving both sufficient supervision and good education. From a technical point of view, it should be stressed that a defence based upon art. 1384 Civil Code will not lead to a reduction of the child's claim because of contributory negligence. The third tortfeasor's obligation to compensate will be reduced because of the strict liability of parents for their children. 31

In practice, both the defence based on art. 1382 Civil Code and the one based on art. 1384, para. 2, Civil Code, will be combined as soon as all necessary requirements are met. 32

11. Do the rules of contributory negligence also apply in the area of strict liability?

Unless specific strict liability regimes contain exceptions, contributory negligence of a (minor) victim will be taken into account in cases of strict liability. A strictly liable party can claim a reduction of damage it has to compensate on the basis of the own fault of the (minor) victim. With regard to product liability, this principle is, for instance, confirmed explicitly by existing legislation.[33] 33

[32] H. Cousy/D. Droshout in: U. Magnus/M. Martín-Casals (supra fn. 22), 37, no. 38.

[33] See art. 8.2. Council Directive 85/374/EEC of 25 July 1985 on the approximation of the laws, regulations and administrative provisions of the Member States, implemented under Belgian law by art. 10 (2) Act of 25 February 1991 concerning the liability of defective products.

12. Do the rules of contributory negligence apply in the area of strict liability for traffic-accidents or other areas of tort liability?

34 Under specific legislation protecting vulnerable persons who are victims of traffic accidents, compensation can only be refused if the victim wanted both the accident and its consequences to happen. Contributory negligence is always excluded if the victim is under fourteen years of age (cf. supra question no. 6).

13. Are adults held to a higher standard of care in their interactions with children, or when children are or may be around?

35 Yes. The case law on traffic accidents involving children confirms this approach.[34] An example for the requirement of a higher standard of care with respect to children is provided by art. 40.2 Road Traffic Code: "*De bestuurder moet dubbel voorzichtig zijn ten aanzien van kinderen* [The driver must be twice as careful with regard to children]".

36 Testing the behaviour of adults (parents, teachers, etc.) against the general duty of care happens *in abstracto*. Thus, the adults must prove that they have behaved as a *bonus pater familias*, i.e. that they have acted as a normal prudent adult in similar circumstances. Although the "fault" is principally judged *in abstracto*, the judgement is rendered more concrete by the circumstances in which the damage was caused. The interaction with children or children in the next neighbourhood are to be considered as one of these circumstances the judge can take into account in assessing if an adult has or has not behaved as a *bonus pater familias*.

V. Insurance Matters

14. Are pupils covered by private or public accident (first-party) insurance?

37 Schools have *no legal duty* to provide accident insurance to cover the accidents their pupils suffer. However, most schools take out *voluntary* accident insurance. Moreover, the existence of such an insurance is explicitly mentioned as a condition to be *subsidized* by the competent public authorities.

15. Does this insurance cover any damage incurred on the way to school and back?

38 Although no legal duty to insure exists, all school policies covering the accidents their pupils (and other members of the school community) suffer *also* cover the risk of accidents (not the risk of liability!) on the way to school and back.

[34] See on this matter A. Van Oevelen in: M. Coene (supra fn. 2), 174 et seq.

16. Are there restrictions on damages recoverable by the child, e.g. with respect to loss of future earnings?

There are no restrictions on damages when the victims are children. Future earnings are compensated according to the *loss of chance* doctrine.[35] 39

VI. Damage Issues

17. If damages for loss of earnings are available, what are the principles governing their assessment?

In Belgium, the question of loss of earnings is treated according to the doctrine of loss of a chance. The opportunity lost, however, cannot be too hypothetical. Courts require *in the first place* that the chance must be *real* ("*reëel*"). This means that only the loss of a serious chance ("*ernstige kans*") can be considered as damage. The victim could reasonably expect the chance at the current time. No compensation is provided for a purely hypothetical loss of opportunity.[36] *In the second place*, the loss of the chance to achieve the earnings in the future must be certain ("*vaststaan*").[37] In case law, there are many examples of this rule, including that of students being unable to progress to the next class at school as a result of an accident.[38] 40

18. Which of the child's non-material interests are protected in your jurisdiction? May the child, for example, sue for impairment of intellectual or social development, the onset of behavioural problems, or reduced employment prospects?

Non-material interests of victims are protected, regardless of whether they are adults or children. The impairment of intellectual or social development may result in a claim for so-called "*genoegensschade*" (equivalent to "loss of amenity").[39] This term refers to a decline in the victim's quality of life caused by the injury, a decline that might, for example, prevent the victim from practising certain leisure activities (sports, etc.) or participating in social events. 41

As far as I know, no cases exist of claimants having alleged that their school negligently failed to address their special educational needs, with the consequent impairment of their intellectual and social development. However, the 42

[35] See on this matter: D. Simoens, Recente ontwikkelingen inzake schade en schadeloosstelling in: B. Tilleman/I. Claeys (eds.), *Buitencontractuele aansprakelijkheid* (2004), 319–321, nos. 91–93.

[36] See D. Simoens in: B. Tilleman/I. Claeys (supra fn. 35), 319–320, nos. 91–92.

[37] D. Simoens in: B. Tilleman/I. Claeys (supra fn. 35), 319–320, nos. 91–92.

[38] D. Simoens in: B. Tilleman/I. Claeys (supra fn. 35), 321, no. 93 and D. Simoens, *Buitencontractuele aansprakelijkheid*, II, *Schade en schadeloosstelling* (1999), 134–137, no. 70; see for example Court of Appeal of Brussels 20 February and 17 April 1996, resp. [1997] R.G.A.R., no. 12822 and [1997] R.G.A.R., no. 12838.

[39] See W. Peeters/J.L. Desmecht, Indicatieve tabel 1 mei 2004, [2003–04] *Nieuw Juridisch Weekblad* (N.J.W.), issue 72, 9.

possibility of such actions for educational negligence has not been excluded by Belgian doctrine.

19. Are there special rules for the assessment of damages sustained by a child, e.g. with respect to pain and suffering?

43 There are no special rules for the assessment of damages when the victims are children and the same rules applicable to adults apply to children.

20. Does a small child have a claim for damages for pain and suffering if he or she is deprived of his or her parents by a tortious act? If so, may the claim be denied on the ground that the child does not feel the loss?

44 Yes. Close relatives of a victim are entitled to damages for pain and suffering arising from his or her death. However, in cases of fatal injury caused to the parent of the child, the award is fixed – according to the so-called "*Indicatieve tabellen*" – at the amount of € 7,500 when the child was living together with his of her parent and € 3,750 when the child was no longer living together with his or her parent. This kind of damages is not always awarded. Furthermore, the amounts of resp. € 7,500 and € 3,750 can be increased or decreased on the basis of concrete circumstances.[40]

45 As compensation is admitted for pain and suffering of a child which is deprived of a parent by a tortious act, the question arises if this possibility is denied when the child is too young to feel the loss? The answer to this question is negative. For example, the Court of Appeal of Brussels has awarded a moral compensation of 200,000 BEF (€ 4,958) to a child of one year old whose mother died in a car accident. According to the "*Indicatieve tabellen*", the amount of damages for pain and suffering of a child which is deprived of a parent by a tortious act cannot be differentiated on the basis of the age of the child.[41]

21. With respect to a damage claim for the costs of medical treatment: May the tortfeasor defend himself by pointing to the fact that the parents have a duty to maintain the child?

46 No.

22. In case of wrongful life: Does the child have a damage claim against the physician or a health care institution?

47 Legal scholarship has already devoted much attention to the topic.[42] In two recent cases, a wrongful life claim of a child was declared admissible. In the

[40] W. Peeters/J.L. Desmecht, [2003–04] N.J.W., 9, nos. 52–53.

[41] Court of Appeal of Brussels 18 October 1989, [1990] De Verz., 177, cmt. Brasseur.

[42] T. Balthasar, Frans Hof van Cassatie aanvaardt vordering van kind bij prenatale fout, [2001] *De Juristenkrant*, issue no. 22, 12; R.O. Dalcq/J. Dalcq, Commentaires, [2000] *Le Journal des*

first case, a child was born with hypoplasia (*syndrome des mains et pieds fendus*). With regard to the claim of the child (represented by his parents), the Civil Tribunal of Brussels decided: "The child is born with the serious handicap, the source of an undeniable prejudice, because of bad information given to the parents. Before the birth and the right of the child to live depend on his parents. These parents, who were badly informed, have accepted the birth of the child. The child undoubtedly suffers a damage of having been born with a serious handicap which the child did not choose". The Tribunal refers to the French *Perruche*-case, in which the French Court de cassation decided: "[...] *un enfant né handicapé peut demander la réparation du préjudice résultant de son handicap si ce dernier est en relation de causalité directe avec les fautes commises par le médecin dans l'exécution du contrat formé avec sa mère et qui ont empêché celle-ci d'exercer son choix d'interrompre sa grossesse*" [a child born with a disability can be granted compensation with regard to its own losses that resulted from its disability, if this disability was in causative relationship with the faults committed by the doctor [...] who prevented the mother from exercising her right to terminate the pregnancy]. The Civil Tribunal of Brussels continued its reasoning as follows: "According to 350, 4 of the Criminal Code, an abortion was possible. The fact that the parents, and consequently the child, could not take the advantage of that abortion constitutes a prejudice for both the parents and the child. Consequently, the action of the child has to be declared admissible".[43] In another case, the Civil Tribunal of Brussels has ruled in a similar way. The Tribunal stated: "The claim introduced by the legal representative of a child with a serious impairment caused by an incurable genetic anomaly (trisomy 21) against the doctors who are reproached for not having detected that anomaly before the birth of the child and consequently having deprived the mother of carrying out a therapeutical interruption of pregnancy tends to the reparation of a wrongful life". However, the Tribunal emphasised "that the postulated damages were limited to the *consequences* of the impairment", and "the question was *not* the compensation for the damage of *being born or not*".[44]

procès (Journ. Proc.), issue no. 404, 11–16; E. De Kesel, Wrongful birth en wrongful life. Een stand van zaken, [2004] N.J.W., 546–551; J.-L. Fagnart, To be or not to be, [2000] Journ. Proc., issue no. 404, (19) 24; S. De Meuter, Wrongful life – Wrongful Birth – Wrongful conception or pregnancy claim: inventarisatie van de begrippen – theoretisch raamwerk – proeve van probleemoplossing in: *Liber Amicorum Prof. Em. E. Krings* (1991), 61 et seq.; J.L. Fagnart, To be or not to be, [2000] Journ. Proc., issue no. 404, 19–24; R. Kruithof, Schadevergoeding wegens de geboorte van een ongewenst kind?, [1986–87] R.W., 2737–2778; Y.-H. Leleu, Le droit à la libre disposition du corps à l'épreuve de la jurisprudence Perruche, [2002] R.G.A.R., no. 13466; J. Ter Heerdt, "Wrongful life" en "Wrongful birth": een "never ending story": twee arresten die de controverse rond vorderingen tot schadevergoeding voor de geboorte van een ongewenst of gehandicapt kind weer volop in de schijnwerper plaatsen, [2001–02] *Tijdschrift voor Gezondheidsrecht* (T. Gez.), 250–255; C. Trouet, Wrongful birth and wrongful life: nieuwe risico's bij preconceptioneel en prenataal onderzoek, [1998–99] T. Gez., 284–288;.W. Van Gerven et al., Tort Law (2000), 91–98, 114–118 and 133–136.

43 Civil Tribunal of Brussels 7 June 2002, [2002] *Tijdschrift voor Belgisch Burgerlijk Recht* (T.B.B.R.), (483) 484.

44 Civil Tribunal of Brussels 21 April 2004, [2004] J.T., 716.

23. Concerning liability for pre-natal injuries: Are third parties liable to the child? May the mother be liable to the child, for example for excessive consumption of alcohol or even for an omission to procure treatment?

48 The child has the right to be compensated for pre-natal injuries caused by a third party, even when at the time of being injured the child was not yet born if the following conditions are fulfilled: (1) There must be a possibility of a viable child at the moment of the birth and (2) the pre-natal injury must still exist at the moment of the birth. The injury can also be caused by tortious actions committed when the child was not yet conceived.[45]

49 There are no cases known with regard to the liability of mothers for damage caused to their children due to excessive consumption of alcohol or an omission to procure treatment during pregnancy, but legal doctrine in Belgium does not exclude the possibility of compensation. However, the requirements for establishing liability (fault, damage and causal relationship between the fault and the damage) may be very difficult to prove in practice.[46]

[45] E. De Kesel [2004] N.J.W., 547, no. 5; R. Kruithof [1986–87] R.W., 2746, no. 8.

[46] See on this matter: E. De Kesel [2004] N.J.W., 549, no. 14; J.-L. Fagnart [2000] Journ. Proc., issue no. 404, (19) 24.

Children as Victims under Czech Law

Jiří Hrádek

I. Factual Introduction

1. What are the most common causes of injury to children in your jurisdiction? In what proportion of cases are actions brought for damages in tort? How many of these are successful? (Plus any other relevant factual data.)

The statistics published by the Czech Ministry of Justice on its website[1] do not provide a sufficient answer to the question of what the most common cases are and the proportion of actions are brought for damage as they do not include all necessary particulars. However, the following information answering the question in part may be found within the statistics. 1

There were 196,897 proceedings held by district and regional courts in the Czech Republic concerning civil law matters in 2002, 188,000 in 2001 and about 207,000 in 2000. According to the statistics, about 5,260 cases were based on provisions of the Civil Code concerning tort law. Besides this group, there were approximately another 5,000 cases based on the provisions of commercial and labour laws relating to tort law, which provide a rather autonomous legislation in relation to the Civil Code within the Czech legal system. 2

According to this data, proceedings under the provisions of the Civil Code's tort law represent only about 2.5 per cent of all cases held in 2002; however, the number of lawsuits that were successful is another question. Claims for damage compensation by minors were the subject of proceedings in 52 cases in 2002 (2000 – 76, 2001 – 72). 3

[1] <http://www.justice.cz/cgi-bin/sqw1250.cgi/zresortu/stati/st_vyber.sqw?s=C>.

II. Damage Caused by Parents and Other Specific Third Parties

2. In what circumstances may a parent be held liable for an injury sustained by his or her child?

(a) In what circumstances may a parent be held liable for injury resulting from his or her intentional conduct? (Liability for intent.) In particular, in what circumstances may the parent be held liable for injury resulting from his or her physical chastisement of the child?

4 A parent can be held liable for damage sustained by his or her child when the parent has breached the legal duty of parental care in such a way that the damage incurred is the direct or indirect result thereof. It is irrelevant which laws were breached, whether provisions of civil, administrative or criminal law.

5 The liability of a parent consists namely in the general duty to take care of the child based on a provision of sec. 31 of the Family Act – parental responsibility (*rodičovská zodpovědnost*).[2] This provision lays down the principle that parents may use all appropriate measures in bringing the child up, to the extent that the child's dignity is not harmed and its health and physical, emotional, intellectual and moral development is not threatened. Therefore, the use of physical or emotional violence on children is basically not prohibited.[3]

6 The parents shall especially take into account all the circumstances regarding the purpose and results of the upbringing. However, equal attention should be drawn to the second part of the rule mentioned in the provision: all measures used by the parents should be appropriate to the purpose. Additionally, in assessing the proportionality of the measure used, not only objective criteria shall be taken into account, but also subjective criteria, e.g. the particular development of the individual, his or her age, personality, etc.[4]

7 On the basis of the above-mentioned principle, the general rules of tort law set forth within the Civil Code are applicable also in the event of intentionally inflicted harm. It is important to emphasise that fault is presumed in Czech law (sec. 420 subs. 3 of the Civil Code), even if only unwilful negligence is presumed. Therefore, in the case of intent or gross negligence, the injured party shall also prove this volitional component of the wrongdoer's conduct.

[2] Act no. 94/1993 Coll., *zákon o rodině* (Family Act).

[3] This provision of the Czech Family Act was inspired by artt. 16 and 19 of the Convention on the Rights of the Child.

[4] M. Hrušáková, *Zákon o rodině – Komentář (Family Act – Commentary)* (2nd edn. 2001), 100.

(b) In what circumstances may a parent be held liable for injury resulting from his or her unintentional conduct? (Liability for fault.) Are there special rules for liability of the parents? E.g. are parents liable only in case of gross negligence? Are parents held to a lower or higher standard of care? In what circumstances may a parent be held liable for injury resulting from his or her failure to protect the child from harm? (Liability for omissions.)

The Family Act (sec. 31 et seq.) constitutes only the main principles, stating what parental care (parental responsibility) is, what the purposes of the upbringing are, and which disciplinary measures the parent may use, but no special provisions regarding the liability of parents for negligent conduct towards their child are set forth. 8

Therefore, the particular extent of care required depends on the objective standards which are common to all similar cases, regardless of whether the relationships are between children and parents or between parents and third parties. There is no Czech legislation equivalent to § 1664 *Bürgerliches Gesetzbuch* (German Civil Code, BGB). This undifferentiated legislation means, in effect, that parents are subject to the duty to protect the child, his or her interests, property or other values covered by parental responsibility, from damage to the extent which is equal to *diligens pater familias* (standard duty of care).[5] 9

Because there are no special conditions regarding liability for the unintentional conduct of parents, the liability of parents towards the child should be governed by the same principles as other cases of liability based on negligence, i.e. liability shall be subject to sec. 420 of the Civil Code. In other words, the parent shall be held liable if he or she has caused damage breaching his or her legal duty to properly carry out parental responsibility – *inter alia* the duty to supervise the child. 10

The breach of parental duty may also consist of an omission of proper performance. However, a basic condition is that the parent must be subject to the imposed duty to take action before causation between damage and behaviour can be established. Because the parental responsibility, as set forth in the Family Act, includes all elements of care of the child – including the upbringing, supervisory or protective duty of the parent – parental care shall be understood as the duty to take action. As Czech law does not expressly distinguish between harm caused by gross negligence and omission, the breach of the duty to supervise the child can therefore cause the same results as any other breach of legal duty as determined under sec. 420 of the Civil Code. 11

[5] M. Pokorný/J. Salač in: O. Jehlička/J. Švestka/M. Škárová et al., *Občanský zákoník – Komentář (Civil Code – Commentary)* (8th edn. 2003), 486.

3. In what circumstances may a third party (e.g. a school or local authority social services department) be held liable for failing to render a child positive assistance (e.g. by preventing parental abuse)?

12 Pursuant to sec. 420 of the Civil Code a condition for liability based on omission is that the legal duty to take action must be imposed on a subject, and the subject breaches this duty. Neither the Civil Code nor the Family Act set forth such a duty of third parties (save for the duty of a parent). Therefore, there is no general duty to act in order to prevent children from harm, even if it is disputable whether an individual should not prevent another from threatened harm when this act to prevent the damage requires neither great effort from the individual nor is there any danger of damage to the individual's property. Although this kind of obligation is not imposed by the Civil Code, it would be possible to consider such a duty pursuant to sec. 415 – prevention of harm – *per analogiam*. However, this issue has not been discussed in the legal writing and the courts have not decided on it yet.

13 Act no. 359/1999 Coll. on the Social and Legal Protection of Children sets forth that anybody may inform a body competent for the protection of children of a breach or abuse of duties resulting from the parental duty to care. However, this right to inform presents no obligation, and consequently a person who does not inform shall not therefore be held liable. An individual or legal person is not subject to the duty to take action and they shall not be held liable by virtue of the omission to act.

14 Otherwise, this duty can be found in School Act,[6] which sets out in sec. 29 *inter alia* the duty to ensure the security and protection of children, for boarding schools or other institutions liability shall be established for the period of the minor's stay. In addition, the statutory legislation of the Ministry of Education, in particular in Decree no. 1/2001 on work rules for teacher and school staff, requires that the teacher maintain sufficient control over the behaviour of children in order to prevent damage. In accordance with these laws, the pedagogical employees must prevent damage if the act to prevent harm does not threaten to cause damage to the employee or to a third party, or he or she informs the director of the institution.

15 However, this point of consideration, based on the lack of provisions in civil law, does not change the criminal law provisions under the Criminal Code.[7] Pursuant to sec. 168 of the Criminal Code, the non-reporting of a criminal offence shall be considered a criminal offence, as well as pursuant to sec. 167 of the Criminal Code, the non-prevention of an offence, when the person had qualified knowledge about the offence.

[6] Act no. 561/2004 Coll., *zákon o předškolním, základním, středním, vyšším odborném a jiném vzdělávání – školský zákon* (School Act).

[7] Act no. 141/1961 Coll., *trestní zákoník* (Criminal Code).

The possible liability of public bodies presents another point of view. Some state bodies are regarded as having responsibility for the protection of children under Act no. 359/1999 Coll., and by virtue of this competence, failing to render active assistance may be considered to be a breach of their duties and incur liability. 16

In a case in which the competent bodies, either public or self-governmental, have breached their duty, liability is determined according to the provisions of Act no. 82/1998 Coll. on state liability (State Liability Act). Such liability can be specified as strict liability, and it is of no importance whether the particular employee/wrongdoer was at fault in their actions or not. In such a case, only the result counts, i.e. whether the damage was caused by the breach of the duty to protect children by measures specified in the particular legal act. In accordance with the State Liability Act, the employee shall not be personally liable (provided he or she did not act intentionally) but only the competent body, which is, however, entitled to obtain damages from the employee. 17

4. What limitations periods are applied to a child's claim?

There is no special provision regarding the child's claim for compensation, however, pursuant to sec. 114 of the Civil Code the commencement of the limitation period in case of damage caused by parents (legal representatives) to their minor children is suspended, the only exception herefrom is the limitation period for recurrent payments (alimony)[8] and interests. Pursuant to sec. 113 of the Civil Code, in the case of rights of persons who must have a legal representative, or rights against such persons, the limitation period shall not commence to run until such representative is appointed. Once commenced, the limitation period shall continue to run but it shall not terminate any earlier than one year after the appointment of the legal representative or after the inhibition otherwise ceased to exist. Therefore, save for the exceptions mentioned, a claim for compensation for material harm becomes statute-barred two years from the date when the injured party realised for the first time that it had suffered damage and determined who was liable for the damage. Such a claim generally runs out three years after the wrongful event regardless of when the above knowledge was gained, however case law also considers the occurrence of the damage for the commencement of such a period[9] as decisive. Furthermore, should such damage have been caused intentionally, the right only becomes statute-barred ten years after the objective occurrence.[10] 18

This differentiation means that two kinds of limitation periods are laid down by law in the Czech Republic; firstly, a subjective two-year limitation period, and secondly, a three-year or ten-year objective period. The subjective period 19

[8] Sec. 98 of the Family Act.
[9] Supreme Court 1 Cz 29/1990.
[10] Sec. 106 of the Civil Code.

commences with knowledge of the damage, the objective with the wrongful event (occurrence of the damage).

20 There is an exception regarding damage to the health of the injured person, only a subjective limitation period is allowed for this damage and all components of the damage to health, for instance, the loss of earnings or payments for compensation of physical injury,[11] which are understood as independent claims to compensation.

21 A claim for compensation of non-material harm pursuant to sec. 11 et seq. is not subject to any limitation period. However, monetary compensation for the interference with personality rights is, in accordance with the opinion expressed in the case law and legal writing, subject to the general 3-year limitation period pursuant to sec. 101 of the Civil Code.

III. Contributory Negligence

5. Are there any special provisions concerning contributory negligence if the tortfeasor is a child?

22 In accordance with sec. 441 of the Civil Code, if the damage caused was also the fault of the injured party, this party bears corresponding liability for the damage. If the damage was exclusively the injured party's fault, then it shall bear the liability alone.[12]

23 However there are no special provisions regarding contributory negligence and minors as tortfeasors. In each case the general provisions concerning liability (sec. 420 of the Civil Code) shall be applied, together with provisions concerning the general conditions for liability of minors pursuant to sec. 422 of the Civil Code and provisions concerning contributory negligence pursuant to sec. 441 of the Civil Code.

24 This means that the capacity of the minor to commit a delict, i.e. the proof of ability to act reasonably and the ability to consider the consequences of his own conduct, must be established. A child without such capacity cannot be held liable.[13] But it is possible that the minor's supervisor, being jointly and severally liable along with the child, may be unable to prove that he or she acted properly in supervising the child and remain liable.

25 Czech law does not know a similar provision to § 1308[14] of the *Allgemeines Bürgerliches Gesetzbuch* (Austrian Civil Code, ABGB) (even though the

[11] M. Pokorný/J. Salač in: O. Jehlička/J. Švestka/M. Škárová et al. (supra fn. 5), 106.

[12] Supreme Court, 25 Cdo 1427/2001.

[13] Supreme Court, 4 Cz 53/84.

[14] *„Wenn Personen, die den Gebrauch der Vernunft nicht haben, oder Unmündige jemanden beschädigen, der durch irgendein Verschulden selbst Veranlassung gegeben hat, so kann dieser keinen Ersatz beanspruchen."*

ABGB was in effect in former Czechoslovakia until 1950 and many cases were decided thereunder by the Supreme Court),[15] nor has a similar interpretation of sec. 441 in connection with sec. 422 of the Civil Code been sought by the legal writing.

6. What are the rules governing contributory negligence of the child? Do such principles follow the same lines as those governing the negligence issue itself (mirror-image)?

The Czech Civil Code includes under the heading "*spoluzavinění poškozeného*" (contributory negligence of the injured) in Part III. on the common provisions regarding compensation for damage, a particular provision concerning the situation when the injured party was also at fault and caused damage together with the wrongdoer. 26

The legislator sets forth this general provision on contributory negligence; however, it does not take into account any special conditions for the liability of minors, or consider any special provision to cover it (save for the application of sec. 422 of the Civil Code). Thus the same principles shall be applied hereto as govern the establishment of liability pursuant to the general clause concerning damages (mirror-image). 27

This means that causality between the breach of legal duty or legal event and fault must be established, as well as the causality between the fault and the damage caused.[16] In this respect, however, a significant difference can be found between liability based on fault pursuant to sec. 420 and contributory negligence. The difference lies in the presumption of fault,[17] which shall not be applied to cases of contributory negligence. 28

Whilst the provision sec. 420 regulates cases of harm caused to a third party protected in the opinion of Czech legal writing by the presumption of fault, damage caused to one's own property is not a typical case of wrongful activity which causes damage to a third party, but a breach of duty imposed on its owner to prevent property from being damaged.[18] However, this breach of duty is latent until it is activated when another person negligently causes damage to the owner. In such a situation, the general rule presuming fault based on sec. 420 subs. 3 cannot be applied. 29

[15] Rv I 378/31, Rc 11608.
[16] M. Pokorný/J. Salač in: O. Jehlička/J. Švestka/M. Škárová et al. (supra fn. 5), 541.
[17] Sec. 420 subs. 3 of the Civil Code.
[18] Supreme Court, 25 Cdo 1427/2001.

7. Does the fixed minimum age for children to be liable, if any exists, also apply to the contributory negligence of the child?

30 There is no fixed minimum age for the liability of minors in the Civil Code. However, a certain limitation can be found in that the minor shall be subject to limited liability pursuant to sec. 422 of the Civil Code only if he or she was able to control his or her conduct and consider the consequences thereof. These conditions shall therefore be crucial when considering the wrongful activity of the minor, and this provision shall be applied to all situations that arise under liability based on fault.

8. What is the standard of care governing the behaviour of children in the context of contributory negligence? Is such standard determined by the same principles and criteria which are relevant to the duty of care incumbent upon the child in the context of him or her being held liable?

31 Firstly, the general norm of conduct required by sec. 415 of the Czech Civil Code should be cited. It sets forth that everybody is obliged to behave in such a way that no damage to health, property, nature or the environment occurs. This provision expresses the principle of "prevention of impending damage" that presents a general standard conduct-clause to all provisions of Czech tort law.[19]

32 However, additionally to that, sec. 422 of the Civil Code relating to minor's liability must be applied. Under this provision, a minor is liable for damage he caused if he is capable of controlling his own conduct and judging its consequences, i.e. this provision attaches no importance to the age of the minor *per se* (objective standards) but focuses mainly on the character of the individual and his abilities (subjective standards).

33 In conclusion, even though the standard of care clause generally expresses the standard governing the behaviour of children in the context of contributory negligence, in the case of a minor the minor's own abilities, both mental (judging consequences) and volitional (controlling his/her own conduct) must be taken into account when determining the standard of care. Therefore, the standard is determined by the same principles and criteria that are relevant to the duty of care incumbent upon the child in the context of it being held liable.

[19] M. Pokorný/J. Salač in: O. Jehlička/J. Švestka/M. Škárová et al. (supra fn. 5), 415.

IV. Contribution in Equity

9. Is there a parallel (mirror-image) to liability in equity in the field of contributory negligence? If so, do the criteria determining liability in equity of the child also apply to the issue of holding him or her accountable for his or her contributory negligence?

Czech tort law does not acknowledge liability in equity. 34

10. If answered affirmatively: Is the fact that the child is privately or socially insured against the accident a factor to be considered? Is the existence of liability insurance of the tortfeasor to be taken into account? What factors have a bearing on the assessment of equitable contribution?

This question cannot be answered. 35

V. Miscellaneous

11. What are the rules for a situation in which the child is guilty of contributory negligence but the parents have also breached their duty to supervise? Is the child held accountable in any way for his or her parents' breach of the duty to supervise so that his or her claim for damages is reduced?

When the minor is a wrongdoer and the parents have breached their duty to 36
supervise the minor, the Civil Code states that the principle of joint liability shall be applied. Another situation arises when the minor is guilty of contributory negligence. In this case, harm is caused to his or her own property and therefore relates to the specific relationship existing between the minor and the supervisors, who are to prevent him or her and his or her property from being damaged.

The City Court in Prague ruled[20] that if the parents of a minor breached their 37
duty to supervise the minor, this circumstance shall not be considered as joint fault with the injured party. On the contrary, the parents shall be jointly liable with the person who is the third party wrongdoer, and their liability shall be divided in accordance with their shares in the damage caused.[21] In that case, the Court decided on a matter when the minor did not possess the capacity to commit a delict, and a similar situation must also arise when the injured party has a limited capacity for committing delicts. It is to be understood that the parent, through his or her conduct, caused in contribution a part of the damage

[20] R 44/1974.

[21] In the particular case, two ten-year-old children together did experiments with chemical substances along with their older friend. The older boy had experience with such experiments and therefore was aware of the possible results, while the younger ones were not able to consider the danger and consequences of their activity. The parents of both younger boys also had knowledge of the activities. By virtue of these circumstances, the court firstly rejected hereby the contributory fault of the minors and secondly rejected the attribution of the parents' fault based on their breach of duty to supervise the child.

and therefore shall not be subject to joint liability with the minor but with the other wrongdoer pursuant to sec. 438 of the Civil Code. In conclusion, in a case of contributory negligence the parents shall be subject to joint liability with the wrongdoer.

12. Do the rules of contributory negligence also apply in the area of strict liability?

38 The provisions of sec. 441 do not expressly apply to cases of strict liability; however, the judicature has acknowledged many times that this regulation shall be applied *per analogiam* to strict liability cases.[22] Also, the legislator acknowledges in the official reasoning to sec. 441 that it is applicable both to cases of liability based on fault and on strict liability, and the provision for dividing liability according to shares of the wrongdoer shall be applied *per analogiam.*

39 This means that in the case of strict liability the sources of the risk must be taken into account, especially their contribution to the cause of damage and the influence on the extent of damage caused.[23]

40 The judicature has already acknowledged, in cases of liability based on fault, that damage negligently caused by the injured party can also be taken into account when the tortfeasors acted intentionally.[24] In a case of strict liability the Supreme Court has ruled that the provision concerning contributory negligence shall be applied also if the victim is a child with no capacity to commit delicts in contributory negligence, because this missing capacity does not mean that, e.g. the operator of a means of transport, shall bear the whole damage caused alone. The principle must be that where there is no exclusive causation by a certain person, there is no reason for exclusive liability.[25]

13. Do the rules of contributory negligence apply in the area of strict liability for traffic-accidents or other areas of tort liability?

41 In cases R 3/1984 and R 28/1973, the Supreme Court has used the provision of sec. 441 of the Civil Code *per analogiam*, wherein both cases had the same object of proceedings, the liability of the provider of a means of transport based on provision of sec. 427 et seq. (strict liability).

42 In the case R 28/1973 the court dealt with the issue of compensation for farmers who incurred damage after a locomotive started a fire in a grain field, and it consequently completely burned down. The court ruled that although the

[22] R 3/1984, R 28/1973.

[23] M. Pokorný/J. Salač in: O. Jehlièka/J. Švestka/M. Škárová et al. (supra fn. 5), 542.

[24] However, in such cases the contribution of the injured party is mostly very small so that the negligence in relation to the intent is of no real importance and it shall not be taken into account – R 27/1977.

[25] R 3/1984; Supreme Court, 25 Cdo 2233/99.

farmers had not caused the damage, the fact that they had not collected the straw was a contributing factor, and therefore they were held liable together with the railway company, pursuant to sec. 441.

Case R 3/1984 presents a collection of decisions regarding the issue of transport. In one case the former Supreme Court of the Slovak Republic decided whether sec. 441 was also applicable in the case of strict liability. It found that even if contributory negligence is not determined as an explicit reason for avoiding strict liability, it must be understood from its general character that the particular share of the damage caused by the injured party in the framework of contributory negligence shall be borne by this party. 43

In conclusion, it can be alleged that the provision on contributory negligence shall be applied also to cases of strict liability, in particular cases concerning issues of transport. 44

14. Are adults held to a higher standard of care in their interactions with children, or when children are or may be around?

The Czech Civil Code uses a general clause regulating in general the standard of care. Pursuant to this general clause, everybody is obliged to behave in such a way that no damage to health, property, nature and the environment occurs (sec. 415). This rule is understood as the principle of the prevention of impending damage and a breach of this clause represents a breach of legal duty which is a substantial criterion for assessing liability pursuant to sec. 420 of the Civil Code. Therefore, this rule has to be applied also to the conduct of adults during their interaction with children. 45

The Civil Code does not make any exact specification in that particular direction; however, from the general provision it can be derived that the parent has to conduct him or herself in a way that corresponds to the particular situation (*diligens pater familias*), for instance in interaction with any children, including children in the immediate neighbourhood or when the activity could involve children. An adult has to consider these circumstances, including the abilities of the children as provided by sec. 422, i.e. the decision-making and the volitional ability. 46

VI. Insurance Matters

15. Are pupils covered by private or public accident (first-party) insurance?

If a person can be considered subject to the Labour Code's provisions,[26] then he or she shall also be subject to public accident insurance caused during or in connection with the performance of work. Every employer who has at least one employee is obliged to conclude this insurance agreement with one of two 47

[26] Act no. 65/1965 Coll., *zákoník práce* (Labour Code).

licensed insurance companies.[27] In the case of an accident, the employee then obtains a claim against his employer and he subsequently against his insurer. However, in certain cases specified by law, the employee has a direct claim against the insurer.[28]

48 The application of the Labour Code's provision to this question consists of sec. 206 of the Code. This provision states that students in primary schools, secondary schools, university-level students, etc. and other categories of employee shall be equal to other categories mentioned in sec. 205, and by virtue of this provision, they shall be subject to the system of compensation based on the Labour Code. Therefore, when a minor-student suffers harm to his or her health during class, he or she may file a claim against the school for compensation.

49 Of course, a pupil may also be subject to private accident insurance concluded on an optional basis. However, in the case of such insurance the relationship between the insurer and the insured is exclusively subject to the provisions of the Act no. 37/2004 Coll., on Insurance Contracts.[29] The insured person would, in the case of an insurance event, raise a claim directly, based on the provisions of the insurance contract, against the insurer and other particulars would also be governed by the mutual contract.

50 Czech insurance companies offer many kinds of insurance and it is up to the discretion of the legal representatives of the child whether the minor shall be covered by which kind of insurance. There are two kinds of insurance: The child can be an independent subject of an insurance contract, or the insurance may be included in the family insurance policy.

16. Does this insurance cover any damage incurred on the way to school and back?

51 Sec. 190 subs. 1 of the Labour Code regulates that if an employee suffers harm to his or her health while performing work duties or in direct connection therewith (work-related injury – *pracovní úraz*), the employer with which the employee had an employment relationship at the time of the injury shall be liable for damage caused by that injury. However, the following paragraph already excludes from the definition of work accident such damage as occurs to the employee on the way to or from work.

52 There is no legal definition in the Code, but the academic writing and case law define this term as a journey from the employee's place of residence to the usual entrance of the employer's building or any different entrance to the

[27] Sec. 205d of the Labour Code.
[28] Sec. 205d subs. 8 of the Labour Code.
[29] Act no. 37/2004 Coll., *o pojistné smlouvě* (Act on Insurance Contracts).

building designated by the employer (place of work).[30] The second part of the definition determines situations when the place of work is changeable in time, as, for example, in the construction or forest industry.

Pursuant to sec. 206 of the Labour Code, since the pupil shall be a subject of public accident insurance, this provision must also be applicable *per definitionem* to school accidents. 53

In optional insurance, the parties to the insurance contract determine the exact conditions of their relationship, so that the answer to this question depends on the particular insurance conditions of the insurer. 54

17. Are there restrictions on damages recoverable by the child, e.g. with respect to loss of future earnings?

No, there is no special provision within Czech law that would restrict the damages recoverable by the child. The only possible limitation is presented by sec. 450 of the Civil Code, which allows the judge to restrict, in favour of the wrongdoer, compensation in a particular case as long as the requirements set forth by the Civil Code are met. 55

There are two categories of damages which can be obtained in the case of damage to health: firstly, compensation for pain suffered and aggravation of social position, and secondly compensation for a loss of earnings and other losses suffered as result of the damage to health pursuant to sec. 445–449a of the Civil Code (loss of earnings, loss of pension, loss of maintenance, costs of medical treatment and funeral costs). Whereas the first category is compensated by a lump sum, and the amount is determined by the court pursuant to a point scale laid down by a Decree of the Ministry of Social Affairs,[31] the other one mainly depends on the difference of income before and after the damage occurred. 56

Compensation for the aggravation of social position does not provide for any special determination in a case in which the harm is suffered by a child – the Decree allows only a small, reasonable variation from the set amount. 57

Compensation for a loss of earnings depends on the previous earnings of the child; however, a minor typically has no earnings before an accident, so the "average earnings" presumed in calculating the loss cannot correspond to real conditions.[32] The Civil Code and its statutory legislation deal explicitly with 58

[30] J. Bičovský/M. Holub et al., *Odpovědnost za škodu v právu občanském, pracovním, obchodním a správním (Liability for damage in civil, labour, commercial and administrative law)* (2003), 141 et seq.

[31] Decree no. 440/2001 Coll.

[32] Academic writing maintains the opinion that e.g. in the case of a woman being at home and obtaining no salary, the earnings must be set as the costs of equal work done by a third party if hired.

the situation of students when they have no real earnings, in particular Decree no. 258/1995 Coll. In accordance with such law, the minimal earnings for the purpose of the Civil Code shall be determined pursuant to sec. 17 subs. 6 of the Act no. 1/1992 on Wages,[33] which states that if the average wage of the employee is lower than the minimum wage [...] the average wage shall be equal to such minimum wage.[34]

59 As the minimum earnings of a minor shall be determined in accordance with labour law provisions, the court has no discretionary power to consider particular circumstances of the case or the financial situation of the injured party, for instance whether the child attended a school, his or her particular abilities and the results of his or her former studies, etc. These circumstances must be taken into account when considering the aggravation of the social position of the minor and enumerating the compensation in a lump sum.

VII. Damage Issues

18. If damages for loss of earnings are available, what are the principles governing their assessment?

60 The provisions sec. 445 et seq. of the Civil Code set forth that a loss of earnings shall be compensated by periodical payments amounting to the difference between the average income before and after the damage occurred. The wrongdoer shall compensate the injured party in money for the harm caused. However, it is a condition hereof that not only the damage exist but also that the difference mentioned above is not covered by the benefits of the social security system, in particular sick pay or partial or full invalidity annuity.

61 A loss of earnings can be divided into two periods: during the inability to work and thereafter. The first category presents the difference between the average income before the damage and the sick pay paid by the social security system,[35] the second category separates those cases in which the injured party is able to work after the sick pay period has finished from those in which he or she is no longer able to work. If the injured party can work, but his or her ability has diminished, he or she shall be compensated for the established difference of income. Should he or she not be able to work, the injured party becomes entitled to an invalid's annuity and the compensation payable will be calculated as the difference between the particular annuity and the former average income. The judicature has specified what should be understood under the term "income". It considers all forms of income which are subject to income tax and further similar income and honorariums as income. This defini-

[33] Act no. 1/1992 Coll., *o mzdě, odměně za pracovní pohotovost a o průměrném výdělku* (Act on Wages, Standby Remuneration and Average Earnings).

[34] With Decree no. 464/2003 Coll., the Czech government recently set the minimum wage at 6,700 Czech Crowns (CZK) per month.

[35] Act no. 54/1956 Coll., *o zdravotním pojištění zaměstnanců* (Act on Health Insurance of Employees).

tion shall also be applied to payments for services provided before an accident when it is used after the accident (R 31/1979).[36]

In all variations, the wrongdoer has to compensate the injured party only for the specific loss of income received after the harm to health occurred. 62

Besides this kind of damages, the injured party might also claim compensation for aggravation of social position, pursuant to sec. 444 of the Civil Code. However, the amount of compensation is calculated pursuant to a point scale (with possible analogy)[37] and is awarded as a lump sum. In this kind of compensation, certain subjective considerations are allowed. 63

19. Which of the child's non-material interests are protected in your jurisdiction? May the child, for example, sue for impairment of intellectual or social development, the onset of behavioural problems, or reduced employment prospects?

There are no special rules within Czech legislation regulating the protection of the non-material interests of children. Due to this fact, the protection of these interests is divided into the two following groups: the protection of bodily integrity and health and the protection of personality rights in general. 64

If harm to the health of a minor is caused, the minor consequently has a claim against the wrongdoer, pursuant to sec. 444 of the Civil Code, for compensation, in particular for pain suffered and aggravation of social position. The sum of compensation shall be determined according to the Decree of the Ministry of Social Affairs no. 440/2001 Coll., which lays down exact rules for the assessment of payments for particular kinds of damage to health. The newest amendment to the Civil Code, which established the new sec. 444 subs. 3 of the Civil Code,[38] has also introduced lump sum compensation for moral distress suffered in the case of the killing of a relative or other close person. The amounts of the compensation payable are determined directly in the Civil Code. 65

All other non-material interests must be protected as personality rights pursuant to sec. 11 et seq. of the Civil Code, i.e. especially life or health, human dignity, civic honour, privacy or other non-material values of each person. It is not possible to enumerate all the values that are protected, and therefore it is possible that in a particular case the court would allow a claim, for example for the protection of the social or intellectual development of a minor. 66

[36] M. Pokorný/J. Salač in: O. Jehlička/J. Švestka/M. Škárová et al. (supra fn. 5), 445.
[37] J. Bičovský/M. Holub (supra fn. 30), 103.
[38] Act no. 47/2004 Coll.

67 The wrongdoer that caused such harm would be obliged, consequently, to compensate the minor for the aggravation of the situation, either by appropriate satisfaction or by monetary compensation.[39]

68 In respect to the compensation, for example for aggravation of social development or for reduced employment prospects, material and non-material damage shall be distinguished. Whereas the non-material damage shall be subject to sec. 11 et seq. or sec. 444 of the Civil Code, material damage must be considered pursuant to sec. 420 of the Civil Code.

69 The victim must prove that the behaviour of a possibly liable person caused interference with his or her personal rights. This can be very complicated in most cases, especially as far as situations like the degree of education that could have been reached or a future social life are concerned, all of which cannot be presumed with great probability. Therefore, such claims for damages concerning non-material harm do not generally have great success.

20. Are there special rules for the assessment of damages sustained by a child, e.g. with respect to pain and suffering?

70 There are no special rules for the assessment of damages sustained by a child for pain and suffering; the whole system of compensation for physical injury and diminished social position is based on a system of classifying each injury on a point scale basis. The judge shall simply apply this schedule to the particular case (the value is determined by a physician), in exceptional cases special circumstances of the particular case can be taken into account, and hereafter the judge may use his discretionary power to reduce or increase the amount of compensation payable.[40] Within this system, injuries are considered on an objective basis and are measured with reference to a point scale system, whereby every point is equivalent to CZK 120 (€ 4).[41]

71 The latest amendment to the Civil Code attached a new paragraph to sec. 444 providing for compensation for moral distress suffered in the event of a relative or other close person being killed. Therefore, two systems of assessment of damages can be found in the Civil Code: a point scale system for pain suffered and aggravation of social position and fixed amounts for distress caused by homicide of a relative or other close person.

[39] Sec. 13 of the Civil Code.
[40] Sec. 7 subs. 3 of the Decree no. 440/2001 Coll.
[41] Sec. 7 subs. 2 of the Decree no. 440/2001 Coll.

21. Does a small child have a claim for damages for pain and suffering, if he or she is deprived of his or her parents by a tortious act? If so, may the claim be denied on the ground that the child does not feel the loss?

Compensation for non-material damage suffered by the child can either be claimed pursuant to sec. 444 subs. 3 or sec. 11 et seq. of the Civil Code. 72

If the child suffered stress and shock due to a tortious act and this harm can be qualified as coming under sec. 444 subs. 2 of the Civil Code (damage to his or her health – under application of analogy), damages might be awarded. Regarding damages for harm suffered, it shall be mentioned that according to the constant case law of Czech courts no adequate causality between damage to the health of a third party and the conduct of the wrongdoer can be found, because the damage to health is already the fact which alone is the result of the act of the wrongdoer.[42] Consequently, most likely no damages will be awarded in similar cases.[43] 73

Otherwise, in accordance with the new legislation laid down by the amendment to the Civil Code, the child has a claim for compensation pursuant to sec. 444 subs. 3 of the Civil Code, i.e. compensation for moral distress suffered in the event that a relative or other close person is a victim of homicide (see above). This compensation is determined as a fixed sum and amounts to CZK 240,000 (€ 8,000) when the injured party is a child and the fatal injury was caused to his parent. 74

Besides the compensation based on provisions of sec. 444 of the Civil Code, compensation pursuant to sec. 11 is also possible. Shock, stress or similar psychological harm correspond mostly to interference with interests protected by the appropriate provisions of the Civil Code, namely under the protection of life, health, the privacy and personality. 75

There are two rulings in the Czech Republic on this issue. They are decision 23 C 52/96 of the Regional Court Ostrava and 2 Co 96/99 of the Higher Court in Prague.[44] Both cases use such an interpretation of sec. 11 of the Civil Code, which states that a breach of one person's right to life could interfere with the privacy of another person. Such a consideration assumes, however, that there are various social, moral and cultural relations based on their private and family life, and the breach of one person's right to life damages private relations and the private sphere. 76

The Czech Constitutional Court also considered this issue in decision II US 517/99 concerning art. 8 ECHR when it alleged that part of a person's private 77

[42] Supreme Court, 25 Cdo 1455/2003.
[43] Supreme Court, 2 Cz 36/76.
[44] J. Švestka in: O. Jehlička/J. Švestka/M. Škárová et al., *Občanský zákoník – Komentář (Civil Code – Commentary)* (8th edn. 2003), § 11.

life is created by the family relationship and this relation consists not only of moral or social relations, but also in the material interests of a person.[45]

22. With respect to a damage claim for the costs of medical treatment: May the tortfeasor defend himself by pointing to the fact that the parents have a duty to maintain the child?

78 Pursuant to sec. 449 of the Civil Code in the event of damage to health, the injured party shall also be compensated for useful expedients connected to medical treatment. This presumes, even if it is not explicitly mentioned, the fulfillment of two basic conditions: Several costs incurred by the injured person in connection with damage to his or her health and no compensation of such expenditures by the payment of social security benefits from the health insurance company. That means, however, that this provision does not cover the common costs of living that arise in the course of a normal life, for instance the costs of the maintenance of a child, but only special costs that were usefully spent on medical treatment, etc.

79 Case law acknowledges that all expenses that help to improve the physical or mental condition of the injured party shall be ranged under this term, e.g. not only the cost of prostheses, therapy, or dietary food, but also the expenses of the visitors of the injured party or the costs of personal assistance or other similar costs incurred in connection with the damage to the health of the injured party.[46]

80 Therefore, any objection on the part of the wrongdoer claiming that the parents should cover all costs at their own expense on the basis of their duty to maintain the child would not be allowed, as all expenses that shall be compensated by the wrongdoer must be considered as special costs connected with the damage caused.

23. In case of wrongful life: Does the child have a damage claim against the physician or a health care institution?

81 There is no relevant decision of the Czech courts concerning the issue of wrongful life. Neither the Supreme Court nor the lower courts have dealt with a similar issue, or at least their decision has not been published. Also, academic opinion has not considered this issue, so that there is nothing which could be introduced as a representative opinion in the theory of the Czech Republic.[47]

[45] These decisions contributed to the support for the aforementioned amendment to the Civil Code, so that it would no longer be necessary to consider a similar construction in all cases of death of a close person and in the event of a fatal injury or the death of a relative, also a claim for compensation based on sec. 444 of the Civil Code could be used.

[46] Supreme Court, R III/1967.

[47] Some opinions are presented by O. Dostál who has dealt with medical law, e.g. O. Dostál, Náhrada škody způsobené lékařským zákrokem – základní pravidla a problémy, [2002] *Právo a medicína* (MP) (<http://www.medico.juristic.cz>).

24. Concerning the liability for pre-natal injuries: Are third parties liable to the child? May the mother be liable to the child, for example for excessive consumption of alcohol or even for an omission to procure treatment?

This issue too has not been discussed in the Czech Republic; however, Czech 82
law includes a provision based on sec. 7 subs. 1 of the Civil Code that construes a fiction that a *nasciturus* (unborn human), though not a living human, shall be considered as having full legal capacity before birth if later born alive. In our opinion, this provision allows us to understand general personal rights as falling under the protection of sec. 11 et seq. or sec. 420 et seq. and, consequently, once the person is born alive he or she acquires full legal capacity and becomes the subject of a right to claim compensation based on damage to health or to bodily integrity.[48]

Therefore, it should be possible to hold a mother, who in an excessive manner, 83
consumed alcohol or other similarly harmful substances, liable for damage caused to the *nasciturus*. However, it must be proved that the mother's conduct during the pregnancy was the exclusive cause of the damage sustained, for instance for the abnormal development of the child's mind or for harm to bodily integrity.

This can be very complicated to prove in a particular case, because should the 84
mother consume an excessive amount of alcohol before she conceived then nobody can know whether it was just the consumption after this event that was the adequate cause. Apart from the issue of adequate cause, the causality itself is also a question. It is extremely complicated to prove that merely the consumption of an addictive substance, or some other substance, was the cause of the harm sustained. However, this issue can now more easily be resolved using modern scientific methods.

[48] Supreme Court ČSSR, *Nejvyšší soud o občanském soudním řízení v některých věcech pracovněprávních, občanskoprávních a rodinněprávních (Sborník stanovisek, závěrů, rozborů a zhodnocení soudní praxe, zprávo rozhodování soudů a soudních rozhodnutí Nejvyššího soudu) (The Supreme Court on the civil proceedings in some civil, family and labour law matters)* (1980), 179.

Children as Victims under the Law of England and Wales

Ken Oliphant

I. Factual Introduction

1. What are the most common causes of injury to children in your jurisdiction? In what proportion of cases are actions brought for damages in tort? How many of these are successful? (Plus any other relevant factual data.)

The Royal Society for the Prevention of Accidents has reported that, in 2000, 491 children under the age of 15 died in accidents or as a result of violence in the United Kingdom, and that, in 1999, there were 2,281,963 injuries requiring hospital treatment sustained by children in the same age range whilst at home or engaging in leisure activities.[1] Of the latter, 393,778 injuries were suffered at places of education (some 150,334 in school playgrounds and 114,064 in school/college sports areas).[2] Road casualty figures for 2001 record the deaths of 219 children under the age of 16, plus 4,769 serious injuries and 33,362 slight injuries. 107 of the deaths were of child pedestrians.[3] The Society has also reported that accidents are the commonest cause of death in children over one year of age, and that the cost to the National Health Service of treating children involved in accidents as outpatients and inpatients is over £ 200 million a year.[4] 1

In 1978, the Pearson Commission, a Royal Commission on Civil Liability and Compensation for Personal Injury, reported that, "[i]n practice, few children seek tort compensation"[5] and that injured children were much less likely to 2

[1] Royal Society for the Prevention of Accidents, *Child Accident Statistics* (2002), tables 1 and 5. <http://www.rospa.com/factsheets/pdfs/child_accidents.pdf> (accessed 17 May 2004). See tables 1 and 2, below. These figures may be compared with the total population figure of approximately 11.8 million for the 0–15 age group: <www.statistics.gov.uk>.

[2] Royal Society for the Prevention of Accidents (supra fn. 1), table 6.

[3] Royal Society for the Prevention of Accidents (supra fn. 1), table 2.

[4] *RoSPA Factsheet – Child Safety in the Home,* <http://www.rospa.co.uk/CMS/> (accessed 17 May 2004).

[5] Royal Commission on Civil Liability and Compensation for Personal Injury (Chairman: Lord Pearson), *Report* (1978) [hereafter: *Pearson Report*], vol. 1, § 1494. Nevertheless, personal injury claims are the biggest single category of children's civil litigation (approximately 17,000 claims in 1997–98): see J. Masson/A. Orchard, *Children and Civil Litigation*, Lord Chancellor's Department Research Series no. 10/99 (1999), § 2.6.

Table 1. Accidental and other violent deaths in childhood, all places, by age group, United Kingdom 2000.[6]

EXTERNAL CAUSE	<1	1–4	5–9	10–14	Under 15
Road transport	31	7	48	88	174
Water/Rail/Air transport	0	0	0	1	1
Poisonings	3	0	1	6	10
Falls	6	2	3	6	17
Fire/flames	15	2	12	9	38
Drowning/Choking/Suffocation	41	25	10	18	94
Other accidents	6	4	12	15	37
SUB TOTAL ACCIDENTS	102	40	86	143	371
Suicide	0	0	0	12	12
Homicide	12	14	13	11	50
Open verdict	7	27	7	17	58
ALL ACCIDENTS/VIOLENCE	121	81	106	183	491
POPULATION	2,889,573	685,601	3,862,777	3,884,564	11,322,515

Table 2. Home and leisure injuries to children under 15, involving hospital treatment, estimates for the United Kingdom 1999 (2000).[7]

TYPE OF ACCIDENT	0–4		5–14		Under 15		TOTAL
	Home	Leisure	Home	Leisure	Home	Leisure	(H+L)
Falls	260	83	176	490	436	573	1008
Struck by object/person	112	37	134	360	246	398	643
Crushing/cutting/piercing	51	14	68	68	119	82	202
Bites/stings	9	3	13	13	22	16	37
Foreign bodies	42	6	22	14	64	20	84
Poisonings	28	2	3	2	31	3	35
Hot liquid/object	34	2	14	3	48	5	53
Other	43	14	35	127	78	141	219
TOTAL	579	161	464	1077	1044	1238	2282

receive tort compensation than injured adults. The evidence of the Commission's own empirical survey was that only about one percent of children injured after birth obtained any compensation at all through tort, as compared with about seven percent of adults suffering personal injuries.[8] It attributed the very small percentage of children receiving damages in part to the large proportion of cases where the injury was no one else's fault, and in part to the

[6] Royal Society for the Prevention of Accidents (supra fn. 1), table 1.

[7] Royal Society for the Prevention of Accidents (supra fn. 1), table 5.

[8] *Pearson Report* (supra fn. 5), vol. 1, § 1494. But cf. *Latham v Johnson* [1913] 1 *Law Reports, King's Bench* (KB) 388, 413 per Hamilton LJ: "Children's cases are always troublesome. English law has been very ready to find remedies for their injuries."

difficulty a child could have in giving a coherent account of the accident.[9] In the evidence advanced before the Commission, this factor was picked out as one reason why children often failed to recover damages following road accidents where the cause could not be established, an additional factor being that there was frequently no unbiased adult witness.[10] Other reasons may also be advanced for why children so rarely sue, for example, that a high proportion of their injuries occur in contexts where claims-consciousness, or insurance-consciousness, is low (e.g. at home or in the school playground), that broken limbs and bruises have in the past been accepted as an inevitable risk of childhood, and that children's injuries rarely result in out-of-pocket financial losses.

In recent times, some of these attitudes have begun to change. There has been 3
a spectacular growth of particular types of claim involving children, generally against institutional defendants. First, growing numbers of claims are now being brought against local authorities on the basis of alleged negligence in the performance of their child welfare responsibilities. The allegation may be that the local authority failed to take vulnerable children into protective care despite evidence of parental abuse,[11] or wrongly took a particular child into care,[12] or that the authority's treatment of a child in its care fell below the standards of responsible parenthood.[13] The claim may also be brought by members of a foster family into which the local authority places an unsuitable child who has been in its protective care.[14] A second category of claim relates to the responsibility of local authorities to provide appropriate schooling for children with special educational needs (e.g. where they have dyslexia).[15] Lastly, there is increasing litigation arising out of allegations of child abuse, very often in the care homes in which vulnerable children have been placed by local authorities. One issue that has recently been addressed in this context is whether the owners of the home are vicariously liable for deliberate sexual abuse perpetrated by their employees.[16]

II. Damage Caused by Parents and Other Specific Third Parties

2. In what circumstances may a parent be held liable for an injury sustained by his or her child?

The basis on which parents may be held liable for injuries sustained by their 4
children has been considered in several parts of the common law world,

[9] *Pearson Report* (supra fn. 5), vol. 2, § 254.
[10] *Pearson Report* (supra fn. 5), vol. 1, § 1495.
[11] See, e.g., *X v Bedfordshire County Council* [1995] *Law Reports, Appeal Cases (Third Series)* (AC) 655.
[12] *M v Newham Borough Council, sub. nom. X v Bedfordshire County Council* [1995] 2 AC 633.
[13] *Barrett v London Borough of Enfield* [2001] 2 AC 550.
[14] *W v Essex County Council* [2001] 2 AC 592.
[15] *Phelps v London Borough of Hillingdon* [2001] 2 AC 619.
[16] Answer: Yes, if the employee had a responsibility for the child's welfare (*Lister v Hesley Hall Ltd* [2002] 1 AC 215).

though there has been little express consideration of the issue in English law. In the United States, a leading case of 1891[17] ruled that parents should have immunity from liability to their children for personal torts (in that case, false imprisonment). The immunity, which applied to torts of both intention and negligence, achieved widespread acceptance in other states. It was justified on the basis of a perceived need to guard against fraudulent collusion between (insured) parent and child, the depletion of family funds at the expense of the claimant's siblings, and possible domestic disharmony. Not all have found these concerns sufficient justification, and in very many states the immunity was first limited in scope, then abrogated.[18]

5 No court in the British Commonwealth has recognised a comparable immunity. In the Australian High Court's decision in *Hahn v Conley*,[19] Barwick CJ expressly affirmed that, "if there be a cause of action available to the child, the blood relationship of the defendant to the child will not constitute a bar to the maintenance by the child of the appropriate proceeding to enforce the cause of action." In England and Wales, unlike Scotland,[20] the matter appears not to have arisen for express decision, but the same has been assumed to be the case on numerous occasions.[21] By exception to this general approach, however, the High Court has ruled that a person who negligently injures himself, and thereby causes psychiatric harm to a close relative who witnesses the injury or comes upon its immediate aftermath, owes the latter no duty of care, having regard to (*inter alia*) the undesirability of litigation between family members.[22] There has, in addition, been a notable reluctance on the part of Commonwealth courts to find parents liable for nonfeasance in preventing injury to their child. An openly-admitted policy consideration here is the risk that families might be threatened with financial ruin if a third party sued by a child in the family were to seek contribution from the parents as joint tortfeasors and the parents were uninsured.[23] Different jurisdictions have, however, developed different doctrinal mechanisms to reflect this concern.

[17] *Hewellette v George* (1891) 68 *Mississippi Reports* 703, 9 *Southern Reporter* 885 (Supreme Court of Mississippi). For a general account, see W.P. Keeton et al., *Prosser and Keeton on Torts* (5th edn. 1984), 904–907.

[18] See, e.g., *Rousey v Rousey* (1987) 528 *Atlantic Reporter, Second Series* (A 2d) 416 (District of Columbia Court of Appeals); G.C. Christie/J.E. Meeks, *Cases and Materials on the Law of Torts* (2nd edn. 1990), 1234–1243.

[19] (1971) 126 *Commonwealth Law Reports* (CLR) 276, 283. See also *Fidelity & Casualty Co of New York v Marchand* [1924] *Supreme Court Reports* (SCR) 86 (Supreme Court of Canada) and *McCallion v Dodd* [1966] *New Zealand Law Reports* (NZLR) 710 (New Zealand Court of Appeal).

[20] *Young v Rankin* [1934] *Session Cases* (SC) 499 (Court of Session (Inner House)).

[21] See, e.g., *Ash v Lady Ash* (1696) *Comberbach's King's Bench Reports* (Comb) 357, 90 *English Reports* (ER) 526.

[22] *Greatorex v Greatorex* [2000] 1 *Weekly Law Reports* (WLR) 1970. The rule applies not only where the child suffers psychiatric injury as a result of the parent's injury but also where their positions are reversed (as was the case on the facts).

[23] *Rogers v Rawlings* [1969] *Queensland Reporter* (Qd R) 262, 273 per Hart J; *McCallion v Dodd* [1966] NZLR 710, 727 per Turner J.

(a) In what circumstances may a parent be held liable for injury resulting from his or her intentional conduct? (Liability for intent.) In particular, in what circumstances may the parent be held liable for injury resulting from his or her physical chastisement of the child?

A parent may be liable for a trespass to the person of his or her child, that is, for assault, battery or false imprisonment.[24] The scope of these torts is limited in various respects – they do not, for example, extend to nonfeasance[25] – but deliberate wrongdoing falling outside their scope may be actionable under the rule in *Wilkinson v Downton*,[26] which admits a general (though infrequently invoked) liability for the intentional infliction of harm. There are no cases precisely in point,[27] but it appears that the liability would arise if parents were deliberately to starve their child or refrain from taking necessary steps to render or obtain medical assistance.[28] Under statute, neglect of parental responsibilities (e.g. the provision of adequate food, clothing, medical aid and lodging) in respect of a child under the age of 16 may lead to a criminal conviction for cruelty,[29] but it seems unlikely that breach of the statute would be actionable in damages in a civil court. The claim would have to be brought in negligence at common law. 6

It is a defence at common law that the injury resulted from the child's reasonable punishment ("lawful chastisement"),[30] but statute now prevents the defence being raised in respect of any battery causing the child actual bodily harm.[31] In other cases, the reasonableness of the force used is tested by the nature and context of the defendant's behaviour, its duration, the physical and mental consequences for the child (provided, of course, that they fall short of actual bodily harm), the child's age and personal characteristics, and the de- 7

[24] *Ash v Lady Ash* (1696) Comb 357, 90 ER 526.

[25] *Innes v Wylie* (1844) 1 *Carrington & Kirwan's Nisi Prius Reports* 257, 174 ER 800.

[26] [1897] 2 *Law Reports, Queen's Bench (3rd Series)* (QB) 57.

[27] Cf. *Godwin v Uzoigwe* [1993] *Family Law* (Fam Law) 65 (couple's liability for "intimidation" of a 16-year-old girl they took into their household and treated as a drudge and a skivvy).

[28] Cf. *R v Gibbons and Procter* (1918) 13 *Criminal Appeal Reports* (Cr App R) 134 (criminal conviction for murder).

[29] Children and Young Persons Act 1933, sec. 1.

[30] *R v H* [2001] *England and Wales Court of Appeal (Criminal Division)* (EWCA Crim) 1024, [2002] 1 Cr App R 7 (use of leather belt). This was a criminal case, but the same undoubtedly holds true in tort law too. Note also the deemed consent of those participating in lawfully conducted games or sports (*Attorney General's Reference (no. 6 of 1980)* [1981] QB 715), or engaging in "horseplay" (*R v Jones* [1987] *Criminal Law Review* (Crim LR) 123). Parents also have the right to discipline and control their children in other respects, though their ability to make the child act against its wishes diminishes as the child gets older: see, e.g., *R v Rahman* (1985) 81 Cr App R 349 (father guilty of false imprisonment in pushing 14-year-old daughter into car against her wishes with a view to making her visit sick grandmother in Bangladesh).

[31] Children Act 2004, sec. 5(3). "Actual bodily harm" bears the meaning it has in English criminal law (sec. 5(4)), where it "includes any hurt or injury calculated to interfere with the health or comfort of the prosecutor. Such hurt or injury need not be permanent, but must, no doubt, be more than merely transient and trifling" (*R v Donovan* [1934] 2 KB 498, 509 per Swift J). Psychiatric injury may be "actual bodily harm" if it amounts to an identifiable clinical condition (*R v Chan-Fook* [1994] 1 WLR 689).

fendant's reasons for administering the punishment. Corporal punishment does not necessarily involve a breach of art. 3 of the European Convention on Human Rights: it is only "degrading" if it attains a particular level of severity, which is to be assessed relative to the facts of each case, including in particular the punishment's nature and extent.[32] Although the common law extended the defence of lawful chastisement to schools and others acting *in loco parentis*,[33] statute now prevents school teachers from relying upon it to justify the corporal punishment of a pupil.[34] Such conduct may therefore be actionable as a battery, whether it results in actual bodily harm or not. The same prohibition now also applies to child minders.[35]

(b) In what circumstances may a parent be held liable for injury resulting from his or her unintentional conduct? (Liability for fault.) Are there special rules for liability of the parents? E.g. are parents liable only in case of gross negligence? Are parents held to a lower or higher standard of care? In what circumstances may a parent be held liable for injury resulting from his or her failure to protect the child from harm? (Liability for omissions.)

8 Where the child is injured by the parent's positive act (e.g. careless driving), it is clear that a liability may arise in negligence. It is also clear that a parent may, in principle, be held liable in certain circumstances for nonfeasance (e.g. failing to keep the child from straying into danger) but the basis of the liability is uncertain. Some authorities suggest that the parent's duty to supervise the child and prevent it from suffering injury arises by virtue of the blood relationship;[36] others that it arises only on those occasions when the parent has accepted a responsibility for the child's care. In *Hahn v Conley*,[37] for example, where

[32] *R v H* [2001] EWCA Crim 1024, [2002] 1 Cr App R 7, interpreting *A v United Kingdom* [1998] 2 *Family Law Reports* (FLR) 959.

[33] But this could violate the parents' right to respect for their philosophical convictions under art. 2 of Protocol no. 1 ECHR if they had advised the school of their objections to corporal punishment: *Campbell and Cosans v United Kingdom* (1982) 4 *European Human Rights Reports* (EHRR) 293.

[34] Education Act 1996, sec. 548 (as amended). The statutory bar does not violate the rights of parents under the Human Rights Act 1998, and applies even to a case where the parent purports to "delegate" the right to administer corporal punishment to the teacher: *R (Williamson) v Secretary of State for Education and Employment* [2005] *United Kingdom House of Lords* (UKHL) 15, [2005] 2 AC 246.

[35] Day Care and Child Minding (National Standards) (England) Regulations 2003, *Statutory Instruments* (SI) 2003/1996, reg. 5.

[36] See, e.g., Hart J's dictum in his minority concurring judgment in the Full Court of Queensland's decision in *Rogers v Rawlings* [1969] Qd R 262, 272–3: a parent "is always automatically a neighbour in Lord Atkin's sense, whilst the child needs care." See also the observations of North P in *McCallion v Dodd* [1966] NZLR 710, 721: "I am not prepared to equate the position of a parent with that of a stranger. A stranger would render himself liable in negligence only if he had on a particular occasion assumed or accepted the care and custody of the child. It seems to me, however, that parents are in a somewhat different position, and at all times while present are under a legal duty to exercise reasonable care to protect their child from foreseeable danger."

[37] (1971) 126 CLR 276.

the High Court of Australia took a restrictive view of the circumstances in which a parent's positive duty of care will arise, Barwick CJ stated:[38]

> "Whilst perhaps there is no clear decision of an appellate court in the United Kingdom, New Zealand or Australia to that effect, I think that the view for which there is the most judicial support and the view which commends itself to me is that the moral duties of conscientious parenthood do not as such provide the child with any cause of action when they are not, or badly, performed or neglected. Further, I think that the predominant judicial view to be extracted from those cases, and again a view which commends itself to me as correct is that, whilst in particular situations and because of their nature or elements, there will be a duty on the person into whose care the child has been placed and accepted to take reasonable care to protect the child against foreseeable danger, there is no general duty of care in that respect imposed by the law upon a parent simply because of the blood relationship. Also parents like strangers may become liable to the child if the child is led into danger by their actions."

It is apparent that this amounts to a rejection of the idea that parents have a general duty to their children, persisting for the duration of their childhood, in favour of the idea that even the parental duty of care is only assumed on particular occasions. This approach also appealed to the majority of the New Zealand Court of Appeal in *McCallion v Dodd*.[39] But the issue has never been authoritatively decided in England, the courts having invariably been prepared to assume the existence of a parental duty of supervision on the facts of those cases that have arisen.[40] There are admittedly dicta which suggest that there is an area of parental discretion into which the courts should not intrude,[41] but this seems not to limit the parent's duty to protect the child from specific physical danger, only to guard the parent against claims of arrested development relating to the child's general upbringing.[42]

Of course, even where a duty of care is recognised, the courts are likely to ac- 9
cord significant weight to the wide discretion that parents have in raising their children in determining whether there has been a breach of the duty. They are wary of imposing too onerous an obligation. There are almost infinite circum-

[38] (1971) 126 CLR 276, 283–4. In similar vein, Barwick CJ also observed: "parenthood is not itself the source of the duty" ((1971) 126 CLR 276, 284). See also (1971) 126 CLR 276, 294 per Windeyer J, Menzies J (with whom Walsh J agreed) can also be regarded as implicitly taking the same view (see especially (1971) 126 CLR 276, 289).

[39] [1966] NZLR 710, especially at 725 per Turner J, and 729 per McCarthy J, North P, however, took a different approach (as noted at fn. 36, above). See also *Rogers v Rawlings* [1969] Qd R 262, 273 per Lucas J and 278–9 per Douglas J.

[40] See *Julie Eastham v B. Eastham and I. Eastham* [1982] *Current Law Yearbook* (CLY) 2141 and *Surtees v Kingston-upon-Thames Borough Council* [1991] 2 FLR 559.

[41] *Barrett v Enfield London Borough Council* [2001] 2 AC 550, 587 per Lord Hutton. (See also the *dicta* of Lord Woolf MR, when the same case was in the Court of Appeal, at [1998] QB 367, 377).

[42] On which, see no. 31 below.

stances in which a child can injure itself if left alone, and a duty of constant supervision would represent an impossible burden, especially given the additional responsibilities (e.g. to other children) that parents have to juggle.[43] A busy housewife, for example, cannot be expected to tie her child to her apron strings and keep it out of reach of all danger at all times.[44] But the standard of care is not regarded as "lower" or "higher" than that applying in other circumstances: the standard is always that of the reasonable person, though no doubt the duty's practical content is often more onerous where the defendant is a parent rather than a stranger.

3. In what circumstances may a third party (e.g. a school or local authority social services department) be held liable for failing to render a child positive assistance (e.g. by preventing parental abuse)?

10 Duties analogous to those on parents may of course be placed on others who assume responsibility for a child's welfare, for example, the child's school. So, in one case, the local education authority was held liable where an infant was let out of school early, before her mother arrived to pick her up, and she walked onto the road and was hit by a lorry.[45] Another aspect of the school's duty is to protect its pupils from bullying, even – in exceptional cases – if the bullying takes place off the school premises.[46] It may be noted that the duty goes not only to the child's physical safety but also to its personal development, and may extend to the identification of the child's special educational needs, if any, and the implementation of an appropriate response.[47]

11 A much-litigated issue in recent times has been the liability of local authorities for the work of their social services departments. Every local authority has a general duty to safeguard and promote the welfare of "children in need" within its area.[48] The authority must make inquiries about any child in its area who it has reason to believe is suffering, or is likely to suffer, significant harm, and it must take such action as it considers necessary to safeguard or promote the child's welfare.[49] In an appropriate case, it may apply for a court order placing the child in its care or under its supervision.[50] These duties do not give rise directly to enforceable private rights, so their breach is not actionable in damag-

[43] *Surtees v Kingston-upon-Thames Borough Council* [1991] 2 FLR 559 (two-year old scalded by hot water after being left unattended next to the wash basin by her foster mother; no breach of duty). See also the Canadian case of *Arnold v Teno* [1978] 2 SCR 287 (mother not negligent in allowing her young daughter to leave the house to go to the ice-cream truck parked on the other side of a quiet residential street; it was enough that she had warned her to watch out for traffic).

[44] *Posthuma v Campbell* (1984) 37 *South Australian State Reports* (SASR) 321, 331 per Jacobs J.

[45] *Barnes v Hampshire County Council* [1969] 1 WLR 1563.

[46] *Bradford-Smart v West Sussex County Council* [2002] 1 *Family Court Reporter* (FCR) 425 (no breach of duty on the facts).

[47] *Phelps v Hillingdon London Borough Council* [2001] 2 AC 619.

[48] Children Act 1989, sec. 17.

[49] Children Act 1989, sec. 47.

[50] Children Act 1989, sec. 31.

es,[51] but their negligent exercise may give rise to a liability in common law negligence – provided a duty of care arises in the circumstances of the individual case. This is an area in which the law is in a considerable state of flux.

In *X v Bedfordshire County Council*,[52] five children in the same family claimed that they had suffered ill-treatment by their parents and ill-health as a result of insanitary conditions in the home. They alleged that their local authority had been negligent in failing to take them into care with due expedition. In a preliminary hearing, the House of Lords ruled that the claims should be struck out as revealing no arguable cause of action, the children having failed to demonstrate at the third stage of the *Caparo* test[53] that it would be fair, just and reasonable to impose a duty of care. Amongst the considerations that drove their Lordships to this conclusion was the prospect that money and human resources would be diverted away from the performance of the social services for which they were provided, and the risk that the threat of liability might cause local authorities to adopt a detrimentally defensive approach to their duties. The children subsequently brought a case in the European Court of Human Rights, which upheld their claim of a violation of art. 3 of the Convention: the local authority had breached its positive obligation of protecting the children from inhuman or degrading treatment.[54] The Court found that the United Kingdom was also in breach of its obligation under art. 13 to provide an effective remedy for the authority's breach of art. 3, and awarded the children compensation. The House of Lords' decision preceded the implementation of the Human Rights Act in October 2000, but now that the Convention rights have been incorporated into English law, and public authorities have a duty to act compatibly with them, it appears that the balance of policy considerations has changed. As, following *Z v United Kingdom*, local authorities have a positive obligation to protect children from inhuman or degrading treatment by their parents, and can be sued for compensation under the Act's own remedial mechanism, the imposition on them of a common law duty of care "should not have a significantly adverse effect on the manner in which they perform their duties."[55] This consideration emboldened the Court of Appeal in a recent case to conclude that it was no longer bound by the authority of the *Bedfordshire* case, and to rule that local authority social workers did owe a duty of care to a child whom they were considering taking into care.[56] 12

[51] *X v Bedfordshire County Council* [1995] 2 AC 633.
[52] [1995] 2 AC 633.
[53] Known after *Caparo Industries plc v Dickman* [1990] 2 AC 605.
[54] *Z v United Kingdom* [2001] 2 FLR 612. See K. Oliphant, England and Wales in: H. Koziol/B. Steininger (eds.), *European Tort Law 2001* (2002), 133–9.
[55] *D v East Berkshire Community NHS Trust* [2003] *England and Wales Court of Appeal (Civil Division)* (EWCA Civ) 1151, [2004] QB 558, § 83.
[56] *D v East Berkshire Community NHS Trust* [2003] EWCA Civ 1151, [2004] QB 558. In fact, the claim was for taking the child into care unnecessarily, so the facts were closer to *M v Newham London Borough Council* (which the House of Lords heard with the *Bedfordshire* case), than to the *Bedfordshire* case itself. In *TP and KM v United Kingdom* [2001] 2 FLR 549, the Strasbourg court found that the circumstances of the child's detention in Newham Council's

13 Even before these developments, the House of Lords had itself backtracked substantially on its *Bedfordshire* decision. In *Barrett v Enfield London Borough Council*,[57] their Lordships declined to strike out a claim relating to the claimant's allegedly-negligent treatment in the 16-year period in which he was in the care of social services following his being taken away from his violent and abusive mother at the age of 10 months. In *W v Essex County Council*,[58] the House found that the local authority owed an arguable duty of care not only to children in the household in which it placed a child for fostering, but also to the parents, who alleged that they had suffered psychiatric injury as a result of learning that the foster child had committed sexual assaults on the other children. In both cases, the House of Lords found that the balance of policy considerations arguably made it fair, just and reasonable to recognise a duty of care. Their Lordships attached much less weight to the considerations that had tipped the balance in the *Bedfordshire* case, one Law Lord being moved to describe the risk of detrimentally defensive conduct as "normally [...] a factor of little, if any, weight."[59]

4. What limitations periods are applied to a child's claim?

14 Time ordinarily runs from the date on which the cause of action accrues, but, in the case of injury to a child, it runs from the date on which the claimant attains the age of majority (18).[60] From that point, the normal limitation period is applicable. For personal injury caused by negligence, this is three years[61] – subject to an extension in the case of latent injury.[62] The court also has a discretion to allow a claim out of time if it would be equitable to allow it to proceed, having regard to the prejudice the claimant would suffer if the claim were barred and that which the defendant would suffer if it went ahead.[63] For personal injury caused intentionally, the limitation period is six years,[64] but there is no provision allowing extension in the case of latent injury, and no discretion to allow claims out of time. Before the decision of the House of Lords in *Stubbings v Webb*,[65] it was thought

care were in violation of her art. 8 rights. See K. Oliphant, England and Wales in: H. Koziol/B. Steininger (supra fn. 54), 139–43. The local authority's duty to the child was not at issue when the case was appealed to the House of Lords (*D v East Berkshire Community Health NHS Trust* [2005] UKHL 23, [2005] 2 AC 373) but the Law Lords accepted that "the law has moved on" since the *Bedfordshire* case (§ 82 per Lord Nicholls).

57 [2001] 2 AC 550.

58 [2001] 2 AC 592. Cf. *D v East Berkshire Community Health NHS Trust* [2005] UKHL 23, [2005] 2 AC 373 (healthcare and social workers owing no duty of care to parents whom they suspected of child abuse).

59 *Barrett v Enfield London Borough Council* [2001] 2 AC 550, 568 per Lord Slynn.

60 Limitation Act 1980, sec. 28 and 38(2).

61 Limitation Act 1980, sec. 11.

62 Limitation Act 1980, sec. 11(4)(b) and 14.

63 Limitation Act 1980, sec. 33.

64 Limitation Act 1980, sec. 2.

65 [1993] AC 498. Noted by A. McGee (1993) 109 *Law Quarterly Review* (LQR) 356, M. Jones (1994) 110 LQR 31, and M. Lunney (1993–94) 4 *King's College Law Journal* (KCLJ) 79. See further A. Mullis, Compounding the Abuse? The House of Lords, Childhood Sexual Abuse and Limitation Periods, (1997) 5 *Medical Law Review* (Med L Rev) 22 and J. Conaghan, Tort Litigation in the Context of Intra-familial Abuse, (1998) 61 *Modern Law Review* (MLR) 132.

that the (extendable) three-year period applied even to the intentional infliction of personal injury,[66] but the House of Lords there took the contrary view. The claimant, then aged 30, commenced proceedings against her adoptive father and stepbrother in August 1987, claiming damages for sexual and physical abuse and rape amounting to trespass to the person. She claimed that the relevant incidents occurred when she was between the ages of two and 17. She sought to rely upon the latent injury provisions of the Limitation Act 1980 on the grounds that, although she knew she had been a victim of abuse, she did not know until September 1984 that certain psychological conditions from which she suffered were caused by the abuse. The House of Lords ruled that, as her claim was for trespass to the person, the six-year limitation period applied, and no extension was permitted by the legislation; the action was therefore statute-barred. The claimant subsequently brought proceedings before the European Court of Human Rights, but the Court found no violation of the Convention.[67] In *KR v Bryn Alyn Community (Holdings) Ltd*,[68] the Court of Appeal ruled that the six-year limitation period also applied where the claimant sought to hold the defendant vicariously liable for intentional injury caused by an employee in the scope of employment.

An anomaly resulting from the decision in *Stubbings v Webb* is that a claim for the negligent failure to stop child abuse may still be in time even though there is no longer any claim against the actual perpetrator of the abuse. In *S v W*,[69] the claimant sued her parents, alleging that her father had subjected her to sexual abuse, from which her mother had negligently failed to protect her. The action against the father was for battery and therefore governed by the six-year limitation period; as the writ had been issued too late, this claim was struck out. However, the action against the mother was negligence, and the latent injury provisions of the Limitation Act applied: The normal three-year period could therefore be extended, consequently this claim could proceed to trial. (There is no record of the action's subsequent fate.) The Law Commission has recently recommended reforms to the law of limitations that would have the effect of removing this anomaly by subjecting personal injury claims to the same limitation rules whether founded on an intentional tort or negligence.[70] 15

The application of the extendable three-year limitation period to cases of negligent failure to prevent childhood sexual abuse is frequently far from easy. In its Report on *Limitation of Actions*, the Law Commission noted that difficulties may arise because the victim may suffer both immediate injury and delayed psychiatric injury, the latter only manifesting itself several years later.[71] Disentangling the effects of the two injuries can be problematic. In *KR v Bryn* 16

[66] *Letang v Cooper* [1965] QB 232.
[67] *Stubbings v UK* [1997] 1 FLR 105.
[68] [2003] EWCA Civ 85, [2003] QB 1441.
[69] [1995] 1 FLR 862.
[70] Law Commission, *Limitation of Actions*, Law Com. no. 270 (2001), § 4.33.
[71] Law Commission (supra fn. 70), § 4.23.

Alyn Community (Holdings) Ltd,[72] the Court of Appeal observed that the immediate impact of the abuse may be to cause feelings of distress, humiliation and shame which have the effect of deterring or disabling the victim from bringing a claim within the limitation period. In the longer term, the victim of abuse may repress or mask memories of the abuse, whilst suffering from serious psychiatric injury. Such considerations may impact upon both the application of the latent injury provisions and the exercise of the court's discretion to hear claims out of time.[73] As regards the former, time only runs against the claimant from the date on which he has actual or imputed knowledge that (amongst other things) the injury in question was "significant".[74] In the *Bryn Alyn* case, the Court criticised the trial judge for addressing this issue only in respect of the immediate effects of the abuse. He ought to have asked "What is the action all about?" and the answer to that question in the present case was that it was all about long-term, post-traumatic, psychiatric injury. The Court noted that the test of "significance" was partly subjective, and its application to victims of childhood sexual abuse was often difficult because many of them were already damaged and vulnerable because of similar ill-treatment in other settings. The behaviour might appear to them as unpleasant but "normal"; it was committed by persons in authority, whom the children were powerless to stop; they may also have believed that, to some extent, they deserved it. The question for the court was whether and when such an already damaged person would have reasonably seen the significance of his injury so as to turn his mind to litigation as a solution to his problems.[75] This was in turn likely to be affected by the extent of public awareness of the phenomenon of childhood sexual abuse.[76] The Court also noted that, in considering the additional question of whether such a claimant also had knowledge that his injury was attributable to the act or omission in question, it might only be after the intervention of a psychiatrist that the claimant realises that there could have been a causal link between the childhood abuse and the psychiatric problems from which he was suffering as an adult.[77]

17 In considering the discretion to disapply the normal time limits in sec. 33 of the Limitation Act 1980, the Court observed that, in cases of childhood sexual abuse, the court was likely to be particularly sensitive to the prejudice that might be caused to the defence.[78] It had to be borne in mind that allegations of childhood sexual abuse could be easy to make but difficult to refute, and the danger of injustice therefore acute. For understandable reasons, the alleged

[72] [2003] QB 1441, § 18.

[73] The psychiatric injury may also amount to a "disability", allowing an extension of the limitation period by virtue of Limitation Act 1980, sec. 28. Cf. Law Commission (supra fn. 70), § 4.28.

[74] Limitation Act 1980, sec. 14(2).

[75] [2003] QB 1441, §§ 41–42.

[76] [2003] QB 1441, § 43.

[77] [2003] QB 1441, § 43. For consideration of some of the difficulties arising in a claim of childhood sexual abuse governed by earlier Limitation Acts, see *McDonnell v Congregation of Christian Brothers Trustees* [2003] UKHL 63, [2004] 1 AC 1101.

[78] [2003] QB 1441, § 80.

victims could be unreliable witnesses. On the particular facts, it was possible that some of the claims had been fabricated or exaggerated for financial gain in the wake of publicity about sexual abuse in care homes.[79] The Court also observed that, once the reasons for the claimant's delay had been taken into account in applying the latent injury provisions of the Limitation Act, the weight to be given to them in the exercise of the sec. 33 discretion should normally be limited.[80]

III. Contributory Negligence

5. Are there any special provisions concerning contributory negligence if the tortfeasor is a child?

There are no special provisions concerning contributory negligence where the tortfeasor is a child. In 1978, the Pearson Commission proposed a statutory rule prescribing that children under 12 should never have their damages reduced for contributory negligence when injured by a motor vehicle, submitting that this broadly reflected the existing practice of the courts,[81] but the proposal was never enacted. 18

6. What are the rules governing contributory negligence of the child? Do such principles follow the same lines as those governing the negligence issue itself (mirror-image)?

The question of contributory negligence is to be assessed on the basis of the degree of care and skill to be expected of an ordinarily prudent and reasonable child of the claimant's age.[82] In other respects, the rules governing the contributory negligence of a child are the same as those applicable to an adult. Where the claimant suffers injury as the result partly of his own fault and partly of the fault of another person, the damages recoverable "shall be reduced to such extent as the court thinks just and equitable having regard to the claimant's share in the responsibility for the damage."[83] Formally at least, these rules constitute a mirror-image of those governing the negligence issue itself, save that the claimant's fault resides in carelessness for his own safety rather than carelessness for the safety of others.[84] In practice, however, it has been suggested that "[t]he test of negligence as applied to the conduct of plaintiffs is more "subjective" than the test of negligence applied to defendants", and that "the courts are more prepared to acquit plaintiffs of negligence on grounds of their personal abilities and characteristics (and so avoid the need to reduce their damages) than they are to acquit defendants on such grounds (with the 19

[79] [2003] QB 1441, § 82.
[80] [2003] QB 1441, § 80.
[81] *Pearson Report* (supra fn. 5), vol. 1, § 1077.
[82] *Gough v Thorne* [1966] 1 WLR 1387.
[83] Law Reform (Contributory Negligence) Act 1945, sec. 1(1).
[84] *Davies v Swan Motor (Swansea) Ltd* [1949] 2 KB 291.

result that the plaintiff is deprived of compensation)."[85] No doubt these tendencies are particularly marked when a child is involved as claimant or defendant.

7. Does the fixed minimum age for children to be liable, if any exists, also apply to the contributory negligence of the child?

20 There is no fixed minimum age for children to be liable, nor any fixed minimum age below which, as a matter of law, a child is deemed to be incapable of contributory negligence. Whether or not a very young child is guilty of contributory negligence is a question of fact to be assessed in the circumstances of the individual case.[86] Still it is doubtless true, as a practical matter, that "[a] very young child cannot be guilty of contributory negligence."[87]

8. What is the standard of care governing the behaviour of children in the context of contributory negligence? Is such standard determined by the same principles and criteria which are relevant to the duty of care incumbent upon the child in the context of him or her being held liable?

21 We have already observed that the standard of care employed in assessing whether a child is guilty of contributory negligence is that of an ordinarily prudent and reasonable child of the claimant's age.[88] In the leading case, the claimant, a 13-year-old girl, was injured whilst crossing the street. She had been beckoned on by a lorry driver, who stopped his vehicle in the road and signalled for other traffic to wait. The defendant, driving too fast and failing to keep a proper lookout, did not see the lorry driver's signal and struck the claimant as he drove past. At trial, the claimant was found to have been one-third to blame for the accident, but the Court of Appeal overturned the finding of contributory negligence, having regard to the limited degree of road sense and experience to be expected of an "ordinary" child of the claimant's age, that is, one who was neither "a paragon of prudence" nor "scatterbrained".[89] It appears therefore that the standard is determined by the same principles which are relevant to the duty of care incumbent upon the child in the context of it being held liable. As noted in *Part I: Children as Tortfeasors*, there is some divergence of authority on the question of the extent to which the child's subjective intelligence and experience may be taken into account.[90] Additionally, as noted above,[91] there is a suspicion that, although the test of a child's contribu-

[85] P. Cane, *Atiyah's Accidents, Compensation and the Law* (6th edn. 1999), 46.
[86] *Speirs v Gorman* [1966] NZLR 897, 902 per Hardie Boys J.
[87] *Gough v Thorne* [1966] 1 WLR 1387, 1390 per Lord Denning.
[88] *Gough v Thorne* [1966] 1 WLR 1387. See also *C v Imperial Design Ltd* [2001] *Environmental Law Reports* (Env LR) 33. M. Moran, *Rethinking the Reasonable Person* (2003), chap. 3 suggests that girl and boy claimants are often treated differently because of the courts' stereotyped gender-based assumptions.
[89] *Gough v Thorne* [1966] 1 WLR 1387, 1391 per Salmon LJ.
[90] K. Oliphant, Children as Tortfeasors under the Law of England and Wales in: M. Martín-Casals (ed.), *Children in Tort Law Part I: Children as Tortfeasors* (2006), no. 15.
[91] No. 19.

tory negligence is formally the "mirror image" of that relating to its negligence to others, the former test is in practice made more "subjective" and hence more lenient to the child.

IV. Contribution in Equity

9. Is there a parallel (mirror-image) to liability in equity in the field of contributory negligence? If so, do the criteria determining liability in equity of the child also apply to the issue of holding him or her accountable for his or her contributory negligence?

10. If answered affirmatively: Is the fact that the child is privately or socially insured against the accident a factor to be considered? Is the existence of liability insurance of the tortfeasor to be taken into account? What factors have a bearing on the assessment of equitable contribution?

For the reasons stated in *Part I: Children as Tortfeasors*,[92] the issue does not arise in English law. 22

V. Miscellaneous

11. What are the rules for a situation in which the child is guilty of contributory negligence but the parents have also breached their duty to supervise? Is the child held accountable in any way for his or her parents' breach of the duty to supervise so that his or her claim for damages is reduced?

Where a child is guilty of contributory negligence but the parents have also breached their duty to supervise, the defendant may seek (a) a reduction in his liability in damages for the contributory negligence, and (b) contribution from the negligent parents. The child is not strictly accountable for his parents' breach of duty,[93] which does not affect the damages to which he is formally entitled, but the practical outcome (where the parents are not covered by insurance) will be a reduction in the family's wealth so the child may be indirectly disadvantaged as a result of his parents' negligence. 23

12. Do the rules of contributory negligence also apply in the area of strict liability?

The rules of contributory negligence do apply in the area of strict liability.[94] 24

[92] K. Oliphant in: M. Martín-Casals (supra fn. 90), no. 17.

[93] Cf. Congenital Disabilities (Civil Liability) Act, sec. 1(7) which requires a reduction in the damages recovered by a child in respect of a congenital disability where its parent shares responsibility for the disability with the defendant. See further no. 36 below.

[94] See, e.g., Consumer Protection Act 1987, sec. 6(4), corresponding to Council Directive 85/374/EEC, art. 8(2).

13. Do the rules of contributory negligence apply in the area of strict liability for traffic-accidents or other areas of tort liability?

25 There is no strict liability for traffic accidents under English law. Liability arises on the basis of fault and contributory negligence is a defence.

14. Are adults held to a higher standard of care in their interactions with children, or when children are or may be around?

26 Adults may be held to a higher standard of care – more accurately, more care may be demanded of them, though the standard remains that of the reasonable person – when they are dealing with children, or when children are or may be around. One express acknowledgement of this is in sec. 2(3)(a) of the Occupiers' Liability Act 1957 which provides that an occupier, in discharging his duty under the Act, "must be prepared for children to be less careful than adults."[95] It is generally accepted that the content of the duty under the Act is identical with that in negligence at common law.

VI. Insurance Matters

15. Are pupils covered by private or public accident (first-party) insurance?

27 Schools have no duty to provide personal accident insurance for their pupils, nor to advise parents of the advisability of such insurance if their children participate in potentially dangerous sports or pastimes.[96] So far as I have been able to ascertain, personal accident insurance is normally regarded as a matter for the parents, not the school. There have, however, been various initiatives to encourage schools to take out personal accident insurance for their pupils in respect of particular activities.[97]

16. Does this insurance cover any damage incurred on the way to school and back?

28 If such insurance were obtained, it is highly unlikely that it would cover damage occurring on the way to or from the school.

[95] Though, depending on the circumstances, he may be entitled to expect that children will be under parental supervision, which consideration may reduce the practical content of the occupier's duty of care (i.e. reduce the precautions he is actually required to take): *Phipps v Rochester Corporation* [1955] 1 QB 450.

[96] *Van Oppen v Clerk to the Bedford Charity Trustees* [1990] 1 WLR 235. *Aliter*, if the school has taken out a block policy for its pupils but negligently failed to renew it: [1990] 1 WLR 235, 268 per O'Connor LJ.

[97] The background to the *Van Oppen* case was a campaign by the Medical Officers of Schools Association to ensure that schools took out personal accident insurance for pupils playing rugby football (as was required of all clubs affiliated to the English Rugby Football Union).

17. Are there restrictions on damages recoverable by the child, e.g. with respect to loss of future earnings?

It is highly unlikely that any insurance policy would cover a child for the loss of future earnings which the child has never enjoyed. It is conceivable that such insurance might be available in exceptional cases where the child already has substantial earnings. 29

VII. Damage Issues

18. If damages for loss of earnings are available, what are the principles governing their assessment?

A child who suffers personal injury which is expected to affect his earning capacity in later life can, in principle, recover damages for loss of future earnings. Where a reasonable estimate can be made of what he would have earned if he had not been injured, the courts employ a multiplier/multiplicand method under which the assumed net annual loss (the multiplicand) is combined with a multiplier calculated by reference to the number of years for which the loss is expected to continue, but discounted for the vicissitudes of life and the fact of accelerated payment. As these latter factors are exaggerated where the claimant is a young child – the uncertainties are greater, as too is the element of acceleration – the discount is much larger than in the case of an adult.[98] Particular uncertainty may surround any claim made in respect of "lost years" (i.e. where the claimant's life expectancy is diminished by the injury, those years after his now-expected death), and the court may decline to award damages on the basis that this loss is too speculative,[99] or simply make a small adjustment in the multiplier applied to the full multiplicand rather than trying to calculate a separate figure,[100] but the latter approach may be justified in other cases, for example, where the claimant's post-injury life expectancy only just takes him to working age.[101] Where the injury is sustained when the child is very young, the multiplicand is normally assessed by reference to average national earnings,[102] though evidence that the child could have been expected to have higher or lower earnings than average may be taken into account. In one case of perinatal injury,[103] the Court of Appeal approved a multiplicand of al- 30

[98] *Croke v Wiseman* [1982] 1 WLR 71, 83 per Griffiths LJ. The claimant was expected to live till 40 but the court applied a multiplier of five.

[99] *Croke v Wiseman* [1982] 1 WLR 71, 82 per Griffiths LJ.

[100] *Housecroft v Burnett* [1986] 1 *All England Law Reports* (All ER) 332, 345 per O'Connor LJ. Where damages for the "lost years" are calculated separately, the claimant's expected personal expenditure whilst alive is deducted from the multiplicand.

[101] *Neale v Queen Mary's Sidcup NHS Trust* [2003] *England and Wales High Court Decisions* (EWHC) 1471, 13 June 2003, Cox J. The claimant, who suffered devastating injuries as a result of clinical negligence at the time of his birth, was expected to live to 19. Cox J assessed compensation for the lost years on the basis of a 50% deduction in the multiplicand in respect of living expenses and a discounted multiplier of 10.3 (§§ 83–84).

[102] See, e.g., *Croke v Wiseman* [1982] 1 WLR 71.

[103] *Cassel v Riverside Health Authority* [1992] *Personal Injuries and Quantum Reports* (PIQR) Q1 (Rose J) and Q168 (Court of Appeal).

most two and a half times national average earnings, calculated with reference to the claimant's favourable family circumstances (caring, close-knit, happy and well-to-do) and heredity – several of his forbears had achieved success in commerce, the arts and the professions, including an uncle, grandfather and great grandfather who all became Queen's Counsel, his parents both achieved several "O" and "A" Levels at school, and his father had increased his assets by prudent investment in property, as others in the family had done in the past. In all, it was reasonable to presume that the claimant possessed "legal, [...] artistic and entrepreneurial genes."[104] He would also have had as good an education as money could buy, and indeed had been put down for Eton (the famous private school) at or before birth. In these circumstances, taking neither too optimistic nor too pessimistic a view, it was reasonable to assume that he would have enjoyed earnings equivalent to the salary of a partner in a medium-sized City law firm. In the case of older children, calculation of the multiplicand will be assisted by the evidence of actual educational achievement.[105] Where there is simply too much uncertainty as to what the claimant would have earned in the absence of the tortious act, the court should depart from the multiplier/multiplicand method and calculate the damages on a lump-sum basis.[106] In exceptional cases where the child is already an earner (e.g. in what is sometimes called a "Shirley Temple" scenario) the damages will obviously reflect this fact.

19. Which of the child's non-material interests are protected in your jurisdiction? May the child, for example, sue for impairment of intellectual or social development, the onset of behavioural problems, or reduced employment prospects?

31 Where the claimant suffers a physical injury or an actionable interference with his physical integrity (e.g. a battery), he is in principle entitled to compensation for any non-pecuniary losses consequential thereupon, for example, his pain and suffering and loss of amenity. In the case of a severely-injured child, this may include an element reflecting his being deprived of "the innocent joys of childhood or the awkward pleasures of growing up."[107] However, the common law does not recognise tortious liability for free-standing mental injury falling short of a recognised psychiatric condition.[108] Even if there is such

[104] *Cassel v Riverside Health Authority* [1992] PIQR Q1, Q15 per Rose J.

[105] See, e.g., *Doyle v Wallace* [1998] PIQR Q146; *Herring v Ministry of Defence* [2003] EWCA Civ 528, [2004] 1 All ER 44, § 24 per Potter LJ.

[106] *Clarke v Devon County Council* [2005] EWCA Civ 266, [2005] 2 FLR 747 (failure to diagnose and treat dyslexia; uncertain what the claimant would have earned if he had received special education).

[107] *Croke v Wiseman* [1982] 1 WLR 71, 85 per Shaw LJ.

[108] *McLoughlin v O'Brian* [1983] 1 AC 410 (negligence); *Wong v Parkside Health NHS Trust* [2001] EWCA Civ 1721, [2003] 3 All ER 932 (intentional infliction of emotional distress). In *Wainwright v Home Office* [2003] UKHL 53, [2004] 2 AC 406, § 46 Lord Hoffmann expressly reserved his opinion on whether compensation should be recoverable for the intentional infliction of emotional distress. Lord Scott, although expressing his agreement with Lord Hoffmann, seems to have been less disposed to accept such claims (§ 62). Cf. the statutory claim for bereavement damages, considered below.

injury, liability is greatly restricted in "secondary victim" cases, where the claimant witnesses an accident involving someone else. The claimant must satisfy various "proximity" requirements and prove that his condition arose "by shock".[109] But most of the cases recognising a liability for a child's psychiatric injury involve a pre-existing relationship between the parties (e.g. school-pupil), or a defendant who has a statutory responsibility for the child's welfare (as in the case of a local authority), and here the damages may be awarded on the basis that the claimant was a "primary victim" of the tort (without the need to show a "shock" as is required of a secondary victim).[110] A typical example would be a claim relating to post-traumatic stress disorder caused by childhood sexual abuse.[111] Particular difficulties of classification have arisen regarding the nature of the loss in cases of educational malpractice. In several cases, the claimant has alleged that his school negligently failed to address his special educational needs (e.g. relating to dyslexia), or over-zealously addressed his special educational needs, with consequent impairment of his intellectual and social development. There is a strong case for regarding such loss as purely economic, and not as a personal injury, with damages to be awarded for the diminution of the claimant's employment prospects, and liability premised upon the school's assumption of responsibility for the child's development. In the leading case, however, it appears that the claimant recovered damages not just for loss of earnings but also for her non-pecuniary losses, including an element representing her loss of congenial employment.[112]

20. Are there special rules for the assessment of damages sustained by a child, e.g. with respect to pain and suffering?

Apart from those noted above, there are no special rules for the assessment of 32
damages sustained by a child, including those relating to pain and suffering. Where a child is entitled to damages for personal injury, the award in respect of pain and suffering is (in accordance with general principle) assessed subjectively and could in theory be reduced to nothing on the basis that the child, if very small, was not capable of feeling the loss. The issue could conceivably arise where the child suffers a diminution of life expectancy for which damages are in principle available under the head of pain and suffering,[113] but there would not seem to be any justification for reducing damages where the child experiences physical pain for it has not to my knowledge been suggested that even a small child is unable to experience pain to the same extent as an adult. It should be noted that damages for pain and suffering are normally part of a global award encompassing also damages for loss of amenity, which are as-

[109] *Alcock v Chief Constable of South Yorkshire* [1992] 1 AC 310. If the claimant is the child of the "primary victim", this *prima facie* satisfies the requirement of "proximity of relationship".
[110] *W v Essex County Council* [2001] 2 AC 592.
[111] *KR v Bryn Alyn Community (Holdings) Ltd* [2003] EWCA Civ 85, [2003] QB 1441.
[112] *Phelps v Hillingdon London Borough Council* [2001] 2 AC 619, restoring the order of Garland J [1997] 3 FCR 621.
[113] Administration of Justice Act 1982, sec. 1(1).

sessed objectively, that is, without regard to the claimant's awareness of the loss.[114]

21. Does a small child have a claim for damages for pain and suffering, if he or she is deprived of his or her parents by a tortious act? If so, may the claim be denied on the ground that the child does not feel the loss?

33 If a small child is deprived of its parents by a tortious act, and suffers mental distress as a consequence but not actionable psychiatric harm, there is no claim for pain and suffering at common law. The child may, however, have a claim for loss of dependency under the Fatal Accidents Act 1976, and this extends to the loss of non-financial support such as parental care.[115] But this does not strictly cover the child's distress, and it should be noted that the Act does not provide for the award of bereavement damages where a child loses its parents, though it does if the positions are reversed and the parents lose their child (provided s/he is unmarried and under the age of 18).[116] A Law Commission proposal[117] to extend the entitlement to bereavement damages to the child of the deceased has not yet been implemented. Where the child suffers a recognised psychiatric condition as a result of the parent's death (or, indeed, the parent's actual or even threatened injury) by a tortious act, a claim for "nervous shock" may arise. In accordance with general principle, the child must demonstrate the reasonable foreseeability of psychiatric illness in consequence of the defendant's negligence, a close tie of love and affection with the primary victim (which is presumed in the case of a parent-child relationship), and proximity to the accident in time and space.[118] The latter requirement is satisfied where the claimant, though not present at the time of the accident, comes upon its immediate aftermath.[119] Psychiatric injury arising merely from being told of the bereavement is not enough.

22. With respect to a damage claim for the costs of medical treatment: May the tortfeasor defend himself by pointing to the fact that the parents have a duty to maintain the child?

34 I am not aware of any case in which the tortfeasor has sought to reduce his liability for the cost of medical treatment by pointing to the fact that the parents have a duty to maintain the child. This would appear to go against the policy behind the rule that a claimant may opt for private medical care even where the same treatment can be provided at public expense.[120] Of course, if the parents actually maintain the child, the damages will not extend to nursing or other medical costs that might otherwise have been incurred. But, in accordance with general principle,[121] the child is entitled to recover the value of any care

[114] *Lim Poh Choo v Camden & Islington Area Health Authority* [1980] AC 174.
[115] *Regan v Williamson* [1976] 1 WLR 305.
[116] Fatal Accidents Act 1976, sec. 1A.
[117] Law Commission, *Damages for Wrongful Death*, Law Com. no. 269 (1999), § 6.31.
[118] *Alcock v Chief Constable of South Yorkshire* [1992] 1 AC 310. See also no. 31 above.
[119] *McLoughlin v O'Brian* [1983] 1 AC 410.
[120] Law Reform (Personal Injuries) Act 1948, sec. 2(4).
[121] *Hunt v Severs* [1994] 2 AC 350.

gratuitously rendered by the parents, at least where this goes distinctly beyond that which is part of the ordinary regime of family life, though not just in very serious cases.[122] If the parent giving the gratuitous care is the tortfeasor, however, its value is deducted from the damages.[123]

23. In case of wrongful life: Does the child have a damage claim against the physician or a health care institution?

English law has not so far recognised a child's claim for "wrongful life" against the physician or health care institution. In the leading case, *McKay v Essex Area Health Authority*,[124] the infant claimant was born disabled by rubella (German measles), her mother having been infected in early pregnancy. She claimed damages on the basis of the negligence of the mother's doctor and the health authority's testing laboratory in failing to diagnose the infection and (in the case of the doctor) in failing to advise the mother of the desirability of an abortion. The Court of Appeal ruled that the claim was contrary to public policy and disclosed no reasonable cause of action. Imposing a duty on the doctor to advise an abortion on grounds of the child's likely disability would "make a further inroad on the sanctity of human life [...] [and] would mean regarding the life of a handicapped child as not only less valuable than the life of a normal child, but so much less valuable that it was not worth preserving."[125] In addition, it was utterly impossible to put a value upon the child's loss in such a case, which required a comparison between life in the child's present condition and not being born at all,[126] and to determine the degree of disability that would entitle the child to bring such an action.[127] The decision accorded with earlier recommendations from the Law Commission and the Pearson Commission, both of which noted the concern that an action for wrongful life would place doctors under intolerable pressure to advise abortions in doubtful cases lest they subsequently be sued for damages.[128] Nevertheless, the Court's reasoning has attracted considerable academic criticism,[129] 35

[122] *Giambrone v JMC Holidays Ltd* [2004] EWCA Civ 158, [2004] 2 All ER 891.

[123] *Hunt v Severs* [1994] 2 AC 350.

[124] [1982] QB 1166.

[125] [1982] QB 1166, 1180 per Stephenson LJ (who conceded that the doctor might owe *the mother* a duty to allow her the opportunity to terminate the pregnancy). See also [1982] QB 1166, 1188 per Ackner LJ (sanctity of life).

[126] [1982] QB 1166, 1181–82 per Stephenson LJ, 1189 per Ackner LJ, and 1192–93 per Griffiths LJ.

[127] [1982] QB 1166, 1193 per Griffiths LJ. Cf. 1180–81 per Stephenson LJ and 1188 per Ackner LJ.

[128] Law Commission, *Report on Injuries to Unborn Children*, Law Com. no. 60 (1974), § 89; *Pearson Report* (supra fn. 5), §§ 1485–86. In *McKay v Essex Area Health Authority* [1982] QB 1166, 1192 Griffiths LJ expressed scepticism about this argument, observing that the final decision always rested with the pregnant woman, and the doctor's duty was only to advise of the pros and cons.

[129] See, e.g., T. Weir, Wrongful Life – Nipped in the Bud, [1982] *Cambridge Law Journal* (CLJ) 225; A. Grubb, "Wrongful Life" and Pre-Natal Injuries, (1993) 1 Med L Rev 261, 263–5; A. Grubb, Problems of Medical Law in: S. Deakin/A. Johnston/B. Markesinis, *Markesinis and Deakin's Tort Law* (5th edn. 2003), 308–9. Cf. T. Weir, *Tort Law* (2002), 186 (affirming that the decision was right).

with some commentators going so far as to call for the recognition of a cause of action for wrongful life in English law.[130] The facts of the case arose before the implementation of the Congenital Disabilities (Civil Liability) Act 1976, which supersedes all previously effective legal provisions governing liability to children in respect of their congenital disability,[131] and the Court noted that the Act's passage effectively precluded wrongful life claims relating to births from its in-force date in 1976 on.[132] It has been suggested,[133] however, that the subsequent extension of the Act to make specific provision for infertility treatments[134] has opened the door for wrongful life claims in a limited set of circumstances, namely, where the disability results from negligence in the selection of a damaged embryo to place in the mother, or damaged gametes to create the embryo, but this has yet to be tested in court. One anomaly in the present law is that the mother may have an action for "wrongful birth" in precisely the circumstances that a wrongful life action is refused.[135] Such actions – which may be distinguished from actions for "wrongful conception", where the defendant's negligence causes the pregnancy of a woman who does not wish to conceive[136] – are based on the mother being deprived of the opportunity to have an abortion by the defendant's negligence (e.g. in failing to detect an abnormality in the foetus), and hence raise policy considerations which overlap to a very great extent with those in the wrongful life scenario. As in wrongful conception cases, the successful mother recovers damages for losses, including pain and suffering, arising directly out of the birth, plus the additional costs of having to raise a disabled child, but not the ordinary costs of child-rearing.[137]

130 H. Teff, The Action for "Wrongful Life" in England and the United States, (1985) 34 *International and Comparative Law Quarterly* (ICLQ) 423; A. Morris/S. Saintier, To Be or Not to Be: Is That The Question? Wrongful Life and Misconceptions, (2003) 11 Med L Rev 167.

131 Sec. 4(5).

132 [1982] QB 1166, 1178 per Stephenson LJ, 1187 per Ackner LJ, and 1192 per Griffiths LJ.

133 A. Grubb (supra fn. 129), 264.

134 Congenital Disabilities (Civil Liability) Act 1976, sec. 1A, introduced by Human Fertilisation and Embryology Act 1990, sec. 44.

135 *Salih v Enfield Health Authority* [1991] 3 All ER 400, criticised by P. Glazebrook, Unseemliness compounded by injustice, [1992] CLJ 226. Cf. *Rance v Mid-Downs Health Authority* [1991] 1 QB 587 (public policy precluding the award of damages where the hypothetical abortion would have been illegal).

136 The distinction is not watertight because, in a wrongful conception action, it may be part of the claimant's case that the defendant's negligence meant that she did not remain as alert to the risk of pregnancy as she might otherwise have been, and deprived her of the opportunity (which she would have taken) to have an abortion. See, e.g., *Thake v Maurice* [1986] QB 644, 680–1.

137 *Groom v Selby* [2001] EWCA Civ 1522, [2002] PIQR P18. See also *Parkinson v St James and Seacroft University Hospital NHS Trust* [2001] EWCA Civ 530, [2002] QB 266 (wrongful conception). In *Rees v Darlington Memorial Hospital NHS Trust* [2003] UKHL 52, [2004] 1 AC 309 the House of Lords was evenly divided between those who thought it was right to allow recovery of the additional child-rearing costs attributable to the child's disability, and those who thought it was wrong, with one Law Lord declining to express an opinion. See K. Oliphant, England and Wales in: H. Koziol/B. Steininger (eds.), *European Tort Law 2003* (2004), 131.

24. Concerning liability for pre-natal injuries: Are third parties liable to the child? May the mother be liable to the child, for example for excessive consumption of alcohol or even for an omission to procure treatment?

As a general rule, a child born with a congenital disability may sue the person 36
responsible. The situation with regard to births before 22 July 1976 is governed by the common law, which sidesteps the foetus's lack of independent legal personality by treating the damage as suffered at the time of birth, and considers it irrelevant that the negligent act or omission preceded birth; it need only be shown that it was reasonably foreseeable that the negligence might result in the child being born damaged.[138] Births on or after that date are governed by the Congenital Disabilities (Civil Liability) Act 1976. The Act applies where the child is disabled as a result of an occurrence before its birth that affects either parent in his or her ability to have a normal, healthy child,[139] or affects the mother during pregnancy, or affects her or the child in the course of its birth, so that the child is born with disabilities which would not otherwise have been present,[140] or relates to an act or omission in the selection, keeping or use of an embryo placed in the mother, or of gametes used to bring about the creation of the embryo, in the course of infertility treatment.[141] The child's claim is derivative in that it requires the defendant to have been in breach of a legal duty to the parent such as, if accompanied by injury, would give rise to liability in tort, but it is not necessary that the parent actually suffer actionable injury.[142] The derivative nature of the claim is also evident in the statutory exclusion of claims where either or both parents knew of the risk of their child being born disabled,[143] the provision for the liability to the child to be excluded or limited by contract with the parent affected,[144] and the mandatory reduction of damages, to such extent as the court thinks just and equitable, where the parent affected shares the responsibility for the child being born disabled.[145] The mother is generally exempted from liability under the statutory regime,[146] and therefore cannot be held liable for her excessive consumption of alcohol or her omission to procure treatment, but the Act makes exceptional provision for women driving a motor vehicle when they know (or ought reasonably to know) that they are pregnant: they are deemed to owe the same duty to take care for the safety of their unborn child as the law imposes on them for the safety of other people, and may be held liable to the child if it is born with disabilities as a result of their breach of that duty.[147] The exception

[138] *Burton v Islington Health Authority* [1993] QB 204. See further A. Whitfield, Common Law Duties to Unborn Children, (1993) 1 Med L Rev 28.

[139] Congenital Disabilities (Civil Liability) Act 1976, sec. 1(1) and (2)(a).

[140] Congenital Disabilities (Civil Liability) Act 1976, sec. 1(2)(b).

[141] Congenital Disabilities (Civil Liability) Act 1976, sec. 1A(1).

[142] Congenital Disabilities (Civil Liability) Act 1976, sec. 1(3) and 1A(2).

[143] Congenital Disabilities (Civil Liability) Act 1976, sec. 1(4) (excepting cases where the father is the defendant and only he, and not the mother, knew of the risk) and sec. 1A(3).

[144] Congenital Disabilities (Civil Liability) Act 1976, sec. 1(6).

[145] Congenital Disabilities (Civil Liability) Act 1976, sec. 1(7).

[146] Congenital Disabilities (Civil Liability) Act 1976, sec. 1(1).

[147] Congenital Disabilities (Civil Liability) Act 1976, sec. 2.

is clearly-motivated by the independent legal requirement that users of motor vehicles be insured against third-party risks.[148] Whether the mother has any immunity at common law, however, is uncertain. The matter has not yet fallen for decision by an English court, and it now appears unlikely that it ever will (because the common law only applies to births before the passage of the 1976 Act), though it was suggested in the leading case that it was for Parliament, not the courts, to provide for such immunity if it should be deemed necessary.[149] This conforms with the position previously adopted in Australia,[150] but the Supreme Court of Canada has recently affirmed the contrary, primarily because it viewed the imposition of a duty of care as an undue interference with the pregnant woman's privacy and autonomy that could have a devastating effect on the family unit.[151] In the United States, some states recognise the immunity[152] while others do not,[153] and an intermediate position has also emerged whereby the mother can be held liable for negligence in her use of a motor vehicle, but only up to the limit of her liability insurance.[154]

148 Road Traffic Act 1988, sec. 143.

149 *Burton v Islington Health Authority* [1993] QB 204, 232 per Dillon LJ. For further analysis of parental liability for congenital disability, see A. Whitfield (supra fn. 138), 49–52.

150 *Watt v Rama* [1972] *Victorian Reports* (VR) 353 (Supreme Court of Victoria); *Lynch v Lynch* (1991) 25 *New South Wales Law Reports* (NSWLR) 411 (New South Wales Court of Appeal).

151 *Dobson v Dobson* [1999] 2 SCR 753, noted by M. McInnes (2000) 116 LQR 26. The Court expressly declined to recognise a "motor vehicle exception" as this could only be a matter for the legislature.

152 *Stallman v Youngquist* (1988) 531 *North Eastern Reporter, Second Series* (NE 2d) 355 (Supreme Court of Illinois); *Chenault v Huie* (1999) 989 *South Western Reporter, Second Series* (SW 2d) 474 (Texas Court of Appeals); *Remy v MacDonald* (2004) 801 NE 2d 260 (Supreme Judicial Court of Massachusetts).

153 *Grodin v Grodin* (1980) *North Western Reporter, Second Series* (NW 2d) 869 (Court of Appeals of Michigan) (mother's drug use in pregnancy); *Bonte v Bonte* (1992) 616 A 2d 464 (Supreme Court of New Hampshire) (mother's lack of care in crossing street).

154 *National Casualty Co v Northern Trust Bank* (2002) 807 *Southern Reporter, Second Series* (So 2d) 86 (District Court of Appeal of Florida).

Children as Victims under French Law

Laurence Francoz-Terminal, Fabien Lafay, Olivier Moréteau and Caroline Pellerin-Rugliano

I. Factual Introduction

1. What are the most common causes of injury to children in your jurisdiction? In what proportion of cases are actions brought for damages in tort? How many of these are successful? (Plus any other relevant factual data.)

1 In France, it is difficult to obtain figures on civil actions in general, let alone on those specifically involving children. What we can say is that in 2003, 4.2% of cases heard by the lower courts – the *tribunaux de grande instance* (district courts) or *Cours d'appel* (first-level appeal courts, CA) – involved matters relating to civil liability in general. To this we must add a significant number of cases where the civil action in damages was taken directly to the criminal court. Among the most usual causes of action, one finds countless accidents of all kinds, related to traffic, school and sports activities, many of them being caused by violence. Domestic violence is more and more in the spotlight these days but does not seem to generate much tort litigation.

2 A recent report caused quite a stir as it revealed that, in 1998–1999, one million children in France were living below the poverty line. (This figure was based on a purely "monetary" assessment or, in other words, on household incomes and not living standards.) This represented a full 8% of the country's child population. Recent studies also reveal that 300 to 600 children die every year as a consequence of child abuse. Due to the difficulty in assessing the phenomenon this is only a rough estimate. Out of every 200 children admitted to hospital, one is a victim of child abuse. 80% are less than three years old and 40% less than one year old.[1]

[1] D. Sibertin-Blanc/C. Vidailhet, *Maltraitance et enfant en danger*, <http://www.chu-rouen.fr/ssf/anthrop/enfantmaltraite.html> (accessed 5 July 2005).

II. Damage Caused by Parents and Other Specific Third Parties

2. In what circumstances may a parent be held liable for an injury sustained by his or her child?

3 The French system, at least in terms of civil law, makes no special provisions with regard to liability in cases where the tortfeasor is the victim's parent. A child's mother and father are treated as third parties in relation to the child victim; this means that the child can claim damages from them for injury caused.

4 As a consequence, no special standards for parental behaviour are set down in law, though the notion that the parent should behave as a *bon père de famille* – the *bonus pater familias* from Roman law – is cited with particular frequency in cases of this type.

5 In a domestic setting, parents are, of course, free to bring up their children as they see fit. Even so, they are subject to specific duties with respect to their children, being responsible for their development, well-being, safety, and moral welfare. When a parent fails in one of these duties, French law has at its disposal a variety of measures, ranging from the withdrawal of parental authority by the civil courts to criminal sanctions.

(a) In what circumstances may a parent be held liable for injury resulting from his or her intentional conduct? (Liability for intent.) In particular, in what circumstances may the parent be held liable for injury resulting from his or her physical chastisement of the child?

6 Intentional acts committed by a parent, including smacking and other forms of corporal punishment, have not been the subject of any specific legislation in France. While such acts – and indeed disciplinary acts of any variety – are covered by art. 1382 *Code civil* (French Civil Code, C. civ.), to the best of our knowledge no case of this kind has been brought before the civil courts. Such cases are more likely to be dealt with by criminal courts, where the victim may also bring a civil action in damages. This also reveals the traditional reluctance of French courts to get involved in "domestic" matters. Interestingly, however, there is no such reluctance when disciplinary acts involve teachers rather than parents, the matter no longer being domestic.

7 The only limitations on the right of parents to discipline their children are those imposed by criminal law, even though they are not specific. As a result, the criminal courts are often somewhat hesitant in their handling of cases of this type: while intentional violence is often involved,[2] assaults of this type tend not, all things being equal, to result in a criminal sentence. This may indicate that the right of parents to discipline their children is being interpreted as

[2] For one case where a father was found guilty of intentional violence, see *Chambre criminelle de la Cour de cassation* (Criminal Chamber of the *Cour de cassation*, Cass. Crim.), 4 November 1993, (unreported) <www.legifrance.fr>.

falling within what might be termed the "permission of the law" described in art. 122-2 *Code pénal* (French Criminal Code, C. pén.). This deals with circumstances in which a party cannot be found liable. On this point, criminal law considers that, "[even] if corporal punishment or even the traditional right of parents to discipline their children no longer accords with the moral standards of the day, parents and teachers still retain disciplinary powers in the context of raising or educating children. These may possibly be imposed on young children in the form of gentle smacks."[3] If, therefore, an individual is to be acquitted of a charge of intentional violence, it must be shown that any punishment imposed was "appropriate, proportional, and necessary for the good behaviour of pupils or for keeping order in the classroom."[4] Similarly, the basis for deciding whether an act constitutes an acceptable smack rather than intentional violence would seem to be the severity of that act.[5]

(b) In what circumstances may a parent be held liable for injury resulting from his or her unintentional conduct? (Liability for fault.) Are there special rules for liability of the parents? E.g. are parents liable only in case of gross negligence? Are parents held to a lower or higher standard of care? In what circumstances may a parent be held liable for injury resulting from his or her failure to protect the child from harm? (Liability for omissions.)

French laws relating to civil liability impose no special duties or standards of behaviour in respect of parents' treatment of their children. Furthermore, liability for negligence and liability for omission are subject to identical treatment under the terms of art. 1383 C. civ., which applies to any act that may result in damage or injury without there being deliberate intent to cause such damage or injury. 8

Sometimes falling halfway between gross negligence and intentional conduct (though most of the time intentional), child abuse has been the subject of renewed attention from legislators during the last few years.[6] This attention can be attributed in large part to the disturbing statistics emerging on children at risk of abuse or neglect: figures issued by the *Observatoire national de l'action sociale décentralisée* (ODAS – a research institute focusing on social affairs and policy), showed that the number of children falling into this category 9

[3] *Tribunal de Police* (T. Pol.) Bordeaux, 18 March 1981 in [1982] *Recueil Dalloz* (D.), 182, note D. Mayer.

[4] T. Pol. Sarlat, 11 September 1997 in [1998] *Bulletin d'information de la Cour de cassation* (BICC), 390.

[5] Cass. Crim., 31 January 1995 in *Bulletin des arrêts de la Cour de cassation chambre criminelle* (Bull. Crim.), 38; [1995] *Revue de Sciences Criminelles* (RSC), 814, note Y. Mayaud. The following is also a particularly relevant case: Cass. Crim., 4 November 1993, (unreported), <www.legifrance.gouv.fr>.

[6] This has led to the introduction of two new laws in this area in 2000. *Journal Officiel* (JO), 7 March 2000, 3536 and 3537; [2000] D., Lég., 183 and 185: the first of these instituted a *Défenseur des enfants* (children's ombudsman), while the second was intended to strengthen the role of schools in preventing and identifying neglect or abuse of children (Law no. 2000-197).

had risen slightly between 2000 and 2001, with 85,000 cases reported (18,000 of these involved reports of actual abuse,[7] while another 65,000 concerned children considered to be "at risk").[8] In addition, the national telephone help-line dealing with issues of child abuse and neglect (SNATEM), which provides a 24-hour counselling and information service, received a total of 1,962,861 calls in 2001. It passed on 5,415 reports of suspected or alleged abuse to the social services divisions of *Conseils Géneraux* (departmental councils). Finally, in the most shocking statistic contained within a government report published in that year,[9] a total of 122 children died as a result of abuse or neglect in 1998. According to the medical world, actual figures are much higher, somewhere between 300 and 600.[10]

10 Even so, this interest on the part of the authorities has focused not so much on the punishment of those responsible for abuse – a matter which in any case is subject to the provisions of criminal law – as on emergency measures, ways of halting abuse, mechanisms for moving children to safer hands, and particularly on better provision of information.[11] Furthermore, tort liability may not be the most appropriate option in cases of abuse, as it is difficult for a minor to sue for damages. The usual sanction is the withdrawal of parental authority. Yet, nothing prevents a child from suing as a civil party in instances where a criminal action is brought against the parent for inflicting psychological or physical harm on the child. In such circumstances, the child is assigned an *ad hoc* representative to fight his case.[12]

11 In cases of abuse or neglect, the French system does theoretically allow for civil action as well as criminal proceedings. However, matters tend generally to be left in the hands of social services, few cases being heard by the courts.[13]

[7] The term "abuse" (*maltraitance* in French) is used here to describe cases where a "child [is the] victim of physical violence, sexual abuse, psychological violence, [or] gross neglect that may have severe consequences for the child's physical and psychological development". (Definition from the *Guide méthodologique de l'ODAS*, June 2001).

[8] The term "at risk" refers to situations where a "child is living in conditions which may endanger his health, safety, moral welfare, education, or wellbeing, but is not actually suffering from abuse". (Definition from the *Guide méthodologique de l'ODAS*, June 2001).

[9] Report no. 10 by Jean-Louis Laurain covering the background to the 2004-1 Law (of 2 January 2004), which deals with the care and protection of children. Source: <www.legifrance.gouv.fr>.

[10] See fn. 1, above.

[11] For details of the current state of the system, see J. Rubellin-Devichi, Regards sur quelques incohérences en matière de droit de l'enfance, [2001] D., chron., 1323.

[12] F. Granet, Protection des enfants: deux nouvelles lois, [2000] D., chron., 343.

[13] For an overview of the situation in this area, see S. Nguyen-Guénée, Enfance maltraitée et action sociale, [1990] *Actualité législative du Recueil Dalloz* (ALD), Comm. Lég., 27.

3. In what circumstances may a third party (e.g. a school or local authority social services department) be held liable for failing to render a child positive assistance (e.g. by preventing parental abuse)?

Child protection in France was reorganised with the introduction of a new statute on 10 July 1989,[14] which established a system enabling authorities to intervene more effectively to prevent abuse or neglect of children. This was supplemented very recently by the adoption of the Law of 2 January 2004, dealing with the care and protection of children.[15] 12

As a preventive step, legislators gave a specific mandate to two institutions with the aim of centralising and improving the system for reporting cases of abuse or neglect to the legal authorities.[16] These were the *service de Protection maternelle et infantile* (PMI) (service for mother and child protection)[17] and the *service de l'Aide sociale à l'enfance* (ASE) (service for social protection to children).[18] These two bodies were placed under the stewardship of the *Conseils généraux* (departmental councils), whose presidents are directly charged under art. L. 226-3 *Code de l'action sociale et des familles* (Family and Social Assistance Code, CASF) with organising for their respective departments[19] "measures for keeping ongoing records on cases of child abuse and for responding to emergencies". As a result, any failure by these institutions to report cases of abuse or neglect to the judicial authorities may be interpreted as a failure in their public service duty of child protection. In such circumstances, the central government may be held liable for the actions of its local representatives, such cases being heard by the administrative courts. Medical doctors and social workers must also report directly to the *Procureur de la république* (public prosecutor) wherever a child is in danger.[20] The Procureur may then initiate criminal proceedings and refer the case to the *juge des enfants* ("children's judge").[21] 13

To clarify the circumstances in which a failure on the part of the administrative child protection services might be inferred, it may be useful to examine 14

[14] Law no. 89-487 of 10 July 1989 relating to abuse of children and child protection issues.

[15] Law no. 2004-1 of 2 January 2004 relating to issues of care and protection of children.

[16] Art. L. 226-1 *Code de l'action sociale et des familles* (Family and Social Assistance Code, CASF).

[17] Art. L. 2112-2 *Code de la santé publique* (Public Health Code, CSP).

[18] Art. L. 221-1 subs. 5 CASF.

[19] For administrative purposes France is divided into *régions* and *départements*, which are governed respectively by *Conseils régionaux* and *Conseils généraux*. These bodies, elected by local voters, are responsible for implementing government policy on a local level.

[20] It appears that the majority of direct referrals to the public prosecutor's office (i.e. those that do not pass through the social services overseen by the ASE) are made by either the state educational authority or by hospitals. On this point, see the 2002 report published by ODAS: *La décentralisation de la protection de l'enfance. Quelles réponses pour quels dangers*, 13.

[21] The *juge des enfants* (children's judge) is specifically authorised under art. 375 C. civ. to take all legal measures necessary to safeguard the health, safety, and moral welfare of the child when the circumstances in which the child is being raised are seriously compromised. In exceptional circumstances he may act on his own motion.

more closely the obligations incumbent on them in the performance of their duties. The tasks of preventing abuse and of providing protection for abused children are carried out "on the ground" by the social workers employed by the PMI or ASE. They are subject to a duty of professional confidentiality (*secret professionel*).[22] This means that, in practice, there may be a conflict between their duty to report abuse and their duty of confidentiality.

15 Art. 226-14 C. pén. expressly allows individuals to be released from their duty of professional confidentiality when reporting neglect, physical abuse, or sexual acts involving children of 15 years of age or younger. However, social workers remain free to make their own assessment of the situation and to decide not to report cases to the legal authorities.[23] Yet, most public prosecutors require the administrative services to report all cases of sexual abuse committed against children.

16 Reports to the judicial authorities are always made in the name of the president of the local *Conseil général*. As a result, social workers are required to respect the hierarchy and report cases to their supervisory body before making their report known to the legal authorities. If they fail to respect this obligation, they may be subject to disciplinary measures. Nevertheless, in an attempt to render the child protection system more effective, art. 313-24 CASF does offer a degree of protection to social workers in the following instance. It explicitly states that disciplinary action may not be taken against social workers who report – directly to judicial authorities, without informing their supervisory bodies – abuse or neglect occurring in public institutions that have specific responsibility for children's welfare. These provisions are intended to remove any professional obstacle that might discourage social workers from acting as "whistleblowers" in order to prevent or halt abuse of children in instances where their superiors fail to take action.

17 Even so, in spite of these different provisions a social worker, just like any citizen, is required to act when he might, by "acting immediately without any risk to him or others" prevent the commission of a crime or misdemeanour against a person, or else where he might, "either by taking action personally, or by causing help to be provided", render assistance to a person in danger.[24] As a consequence, in circumstances where a failure to report abuse of a child could be interpreted as a failure to render assistance, a social worker (just like any other citizen) may be held criminally liable for this failure. He will not, therefore, be able to invoke the duty of professional confidentiality as grounds

[22] Art. 221-6 CASF states that "any person participating in the tasks carried out by the ASE is subject to a duty of professional confidentiality". Art. 226-13 C. pén. stipulates that breaches of professional confidentiality may result in a sentence of one year in prison or a € 15,000 fine.

[23] In such circumstances, the child remains under the protection of the administrative services, and no judicial child protection process is initiated.

[24] Art. 223-6 C. pén. This states that failing to prevent a crime or render assistance to a victim may incur a sentence of five years' imprisonment or a fine of € 75,000.

for releasing himself from this obligation. The body for which he works (and by implication the government) may also be held liable by the administrative courts for failing to provide an adequate public child protection service.

Under the terms of art. 226-4 CASF, the president of the local *Conseil général* (and by implication the bodies of which he is in charge) remains subject to a duty to inform the legal authorities without delay when a child is or is suspected of being a victim of abuse and: 18

- when it is impossible for the social services to make an assessment of the situation or
- when the child's family refuses to allow the social services to take action.

Any failure or delay in reporting such cases to the judicial authorities may, therefore, render the bodies concerned liable under administrative law. 19

In circumstances other than those covered by art. 226-4 CASF, social workers are free to decide on the appropriate course of action. They are, therefore, totally free to decide whether or not to report to the judicial authorities instances of abuse of which they are aware, and run no risk of being held criminally liable for breaching professional confidentiality or for failing to report a crime or abuse inflicted on children of 15 years or younger or on individuals viewed as unable to protect themselves by virtue of their age.[25] 20

Staff employed by the *Éducation nationale* services (state education authority) and by healthcare services[26] have also been made aware of their role in preventing child abuse. They may report cases of abuse either to the administrative services of the ASE or directly to the local public prosecutor (*Procureur de la République*). Primary and secondary school teachers employed by the state education authority are, as might be expected, required to go through their superiors when reporting any abuse. It appears, however, that they (just like social workers) may also be held liable for any failure to inform the authorities, though they are not subject to a duty of professional confidentiality and could not, therefore, face charges on this basis. Those employed by the state education authority are also required, just like other citizens, to render assistance to victims of crime or individuals at risk, as stipulated by art. 223-6 C. pén. Again, a failure to report instances of abuse may be interpreted as a failure to provide assistance and may therefore render the teacher criminally liable and subject to possible criminal charges. Nevertheless, if a case is brought under civil law in circumstances where a teacher has been aware in 21

[25] This refers to crimes set down in artt. 434-1 and 434-3 C. pén., for which a prison sentence of three years or a fine of € 45,000 may be imposed.

[26] Law no. 2004-1 of 2 January 2004 relating to issues of child protection and welfare also sets down provisions concerning the duty of professional confidentiality incumbent on doctors. Specifically, doctors may no longer be subjected to disciplinary action – imposed by the *Ordre des médecins* (the French national medical association) – for failure to maintain professional confidentiality in instances where they report abuse of children to the authorities.

his professional capacity of possible abuse, it is the state educational authority that may be held liable by the administrative courts. This would not prevent the bodies found liable from bringing a claim against the teacher if a direct fault on his part were established.

4. What limitation periods are applied to a child's claim?

22 The French system imposes no specific limitation periods with regard to civil proceedings brought by children against their parents. Children's actions, however, must be brought before the courts by an adult person entrusted in that capacity. In French law, capacity to sue is not granted to children. As a consequence, in normal circumstances, parents act as their children's legal representatives. Therefore any proceedings brought against them by their minor child would require that the parents "sue themselves". This is, of course, a classic "Catch 22" situation.

23 Civil claims in general have to be pursued within a period of ten years starting from the point at which the damage occurs or worsens (art. 2270-1 C. civ). This could – in the light of the facts given above – have the effect of preventing an adult from pursuing a claim in respect of an injury he suffered as a child. In order to circumvent this difficulty, the Civil Code has stated that children below the age of majority are not subject to this limitation period. Indeed, where the victim is a minor, and where no action has previously been introduced by his/her legal representative, the limitation period always runs from the eighteenth birthday. Time is suspended for the benefit of the victim.[27]

24 When the damage suffered by the child is the consequence of acts amounting to torture or barbarity or the consequence of sexual abuse, art. 2270-1 C. civ. provides that the limitation period is extended to twenty years.

III. Contributory Negligence

5. Are there any special provisions concerning contributory negligence if the tortfeasor is a child?

25 Treatment of such cases is the same as for an adult tortfeasor. French law treats a child as if he were an adult in matters of personal liability.

[27] This practice accords with the regime in force in criminal law. This stipulates – most notably in cases of sexual abuse – that the limitation period will commence when the victim reaches the age of majority if he was below that age when the offence(s) occurred. See J. Castaignède, La prescription des agressions sexuelles dont sont victimes les mineurs, [1996] D., Jur., 238.

6. What are the rules governing contributory negligence of the child? Do such principles follow the same lines as those governing the negligence issue itself (mirror-image)?

No special provisions apply in the case of contributory negligence when the victim is a child. In general, just as in cases where the victim is an adult, the principles of fault-based liability are applied, except in cases involving road traffic accidents.[28] 26

Since the famous decisions of 1984,[29] the courts have tended to interpret contributory negligence on the part of child victims with considerable latitude. While rejecting any requirement for the child victim to be aware of the dangers involved, the courts have – in cases where the victim's behaviour has contributed to the subsequent damage or injury – at the same time accepted the notion of shared liability based on a simple causal link (implying neither fault nor, necessarily, any ill intent) between the victim's actions and their effects.[30] As one author has noted: "Clumsy reactions, being distracted, incorrectly assessing how far away an approaching vehicle is from the victim, movements that are too sudden or too slow […], these are just some of the faults customarily held against a victim for the purpose of reducing the level of compensation to be paid."[31] Others have gone even further, to criticise "this tendency to transform the slightest mistake or mishap on the part of the victim into a fault"[32] so as to reduce the compensation due to the aggrieved party. The concept of "fault" in its traditional sense (implying a certain level of awareness by the party at fault) has therefore been abandoned both for the victim and the tortfeasor. Similarly, the existence of a purely causal link between an act and an event is generally enough to establish contributory negligence on the part of a child victim and thus, by implication, to prevent him from receiving full compensation. 27

Cases are treated identically when the legal concept of *responsabilité du fait des choses* ("liability for damage or injury caused by things in one's care") is involved. Here, the *gardien* ("custodian") of those things may be granted full release from liability if it is shown that contributory negligence amounted to 28

[28] On the question of road traffic accidents, and contributory fault as applied to children, see below.

[29] *Assemblée Plenière de la Cour de cassation* (Ass. Plen.), 9 May 1984 in [1984] *La semaine juridique* (JCP), II, 20255, note N. Dejean de la Bâtie et 20256, note P. Jourdain et 20291, Rapport Fédou; [1984] D., 525, note F. Chabas; [1984] *Revue Trimestrielle de Droit civil* (RTD civ.), 508, obs. J. Huet.

[30] In the Lemaire case, a child was electrocuted while unscrewing a light bulb connected to an electrical circuit that had just been rewired by an electrician. Although the electrician was found liable by virtue of the defective nature of his work, the child was also held equally liable for the injury. Ass. Plen., 9 May 1984, 5th Lemaire case in *Bulletin de la Cour de cassation, Assemblée plénière* (Bull. Ass. Plen.), 4.

[31] G. Viney, La faute de la victime d'un accident corporel, le présent et l'avenir, [1984] JCP, I, 3155, 22.

[32] On this point, see M.-C. Lebreton, *L'enfant et la responsabilité civile* (1999), 312.

force majeure.[33] The same applies to *responsabilité du fait des bâtiments* ("liability for damage or injury caused by buildings in one's care", a concept similar to occupiers' liability in English law).[34]

29 Accordingly, the courts tend to handle fault on a child victim's part in a similar way to cases where the tortfeasor himself is a child, though perhaps with a higher degree of flexibility. As a consequence, contributory negligence is often accepted by the court and regularly leads to shared liability, releasing the tortfeasor from the full burden of providing compensation. One might, therefore, be tempted to conclude that the courts tend to treat fault on the victim's part rather harshly. In theory, as has been shown, this division of liability may even result in the tortfeasor gaining total exemption from liability if the victim's contributory negligence can be interpreted as *force majeure* or if, in road traffic accidents, it amounts to an inexcusable fault (*faute inexcusable*). However, while such a scenario is indeed quite feasible in the law books, in practice the courts have been largely unwilling to grant a total release from liability based simply on contributory negligence committed by the victim.[35] In fact, the records provide innumerable examples of cases where the tortfeasor could have been, but was not, released from liability on the basis of *force majeure*; generally, even the most serious or unpredictable negligence on the part of victims has not been enough to prevent them from being awarded compensation, whether in cases of *responsabilité du fait des choses*[36] or *responsabilité du fait des bâtiments*.[37] As regards admission of an "inexcusable fault" (*faute inexcusable*) in road traffic accident cases, the decisions of the court are often even more shocking, with judges displaying a similar degree of indulgence towards the victim.[38]

[33] F. Terré/Ph. Simler/Y. Lequette, *Droit civil, Les Obligations* (8th edn. 2002), 761.

[34] On *de iure* liability and contributory fault in such instances, see below.

[35] For an excellent analysis of this practice in recent years, see S. Hocquet-Berg, L'activité délictueuse de la victime, [2002] *Responsabilité civile et assurance* (RCA) 6, 8–9.

[36] For an example of a decision that is, to say the least, questionable, see *Cour de cassation 2ème Chambre civile* (Cass. Civ. 2ème), 8 June 1994 in [1994] *Bulletin des arrêts de la Cour de cassation. Chambres civiles* (Bull. Civ.) II, 151; [1995] RTD civ., 122, note P. Jourdain, who observed that, "judges in the lower courts failed to identify *force majeure*, stating that fault on the part of a child who lay down on a swing door of a garage after opening it was not an easily foreseeable scenario and that the safety measures [in place] were in accordance with the standards required."

[37] For a particularly interesting case of this type, see Cass. Civ. 2ème, 18 December 1995 in [1995] Bull. Civ. II, 315; [1997] D., Somm., 188, note A. Lacabarats. Here, "[a situation in which] fault on the part of a victim who ignored a sign forbidding access to private land and was then injured when a wooden bridge collapsed could not be viewed by the *gardien* (custodian) of the bridge as an unforeseeable and unavoidable scenario."

[38] For example, the court ruled that there was no "inexcusable fault" in the case of a pedestrian, who undertook in an area with very heavy traffic as night was falling and in rainy conditions, to cross a four-lane highway without using an underpass nearby (Cass. Civ. 2ème, 7 February 1996 in [1996] Bull. Civ. II, 33). Similar decisions were reached in the case of a cyclist who, ignoring a clearly visible stop sign, cycled straight onto a main road (Cass. Civ. 2ème, 24 February 1998 in [1998] Bull. Civ. II, 48 – 2nd decision) and in a situation where another cyclist, riding a bicycle at night without lights, emerged from a one-way street and cut in front of the car involved in the accident (Cass. Civ. 2ème, 28 March 1994 in [1994] Bull. Civ. II, 110).

The attitude of the courts could perhaps best be described as ambivalent: while tending to assign liability to both tortfeasor and victim, they are generally reluctant to go as far as releasing the former from any liability.

7. Does the fixed minimum age for children to be liable, if any exists, also apply to the contributory negligence of the child?

Since there is no minimum age in respect of civil liability in French law, the question of the victim's level of awareness (*capacité de discernement*) of the consequences of his actions may indeed be relevant. Just as with the issue of liability on the part of a child tortfeasor, the courts used to hold that a sufficient level of awareness on the part of a child victim was necessary if contributory negligence on his part was to be established.[39] Even after the 1968 ruling that those classed as insane could be held liable, the courts continued to treat cases involving children as they had done previously, requiring that "the existence of a sufficient level of awareness (*discernement*) be established on the child's part if he is to be found liable for part of the damage or injury resulting from a fault committed by him."[40] 30

However, the major changes in the courts' practice that occurred in 1984 did affect the treatment of children who had committed contributory negligence. In two such cases, the *Cour de cassation* for the first time solemnly affirmed the principle that a young child could be held liable; here, the court dismissed appeals against two *Cours d'appel* (local appeal courts) that had refused to share liability between tortfeasor and victim. The decision of the *Cour de cassation* was justified in the following terms: "The *Cour d'appel*, which was not required to verify whether the child had been capable of discerning the consequences of his act, could have found that, on the basis of art. 1382 C. civ., the victim had committed a negligence that had partly contributed […] to the injury caused."[41] 31

This ruling has since been reaffirmed on a number of occasions with a clarity that has rarely been questioned. Accordingly, in a recent case, the *Cour de cassation* found that, "fault on the part of a minor may be held against him even if [that minor] is incapable of discerning the consequences of his actions or the dangers inherent in a thing used by its custodian." (This constitutes a reference to the French legal concept of *garde de la chose* or "custody of the thing".)[42] 32

[39] Cass. Civ. 2ème, 12 November 1959 in [1959] Bull. Civ. II, 722.

[40] Cass. Civ. 2ème, 11 December 1974 in [1975] *Gazette du Palais* (Gaz. Pal.) 1, summary, 68; [1975] D., IR, 67; Cass. Civ. 2ème, 11 June 1980 in [1980] Bull. Civ. I, 140; [1980] JCP, IV, 323; [1983] D., IR., 323, note C. Larroumet.

[41] Derguini and Lemaire cases: Ass. Plen., 9 May 1984 in [1984] JCP, II, 20255, note N. Dejean de la Bâtie and 20256, note P. Jourdain and 20291, report by Fédou; [1984] D., 525, note F. Chabas; [1984] RTD civ., 508, note J. Huet; [1984] D., 525, concl. J. Cabannes, note F. Chabas; [1984] Bull. Ass. Plen., 4; F. Terré/Y. Lequette, *Les grands arrêts de la jurisprudence civile, tome 2* (11th edn. 2000), 197–199 (III); R. Legeais, [1984] D., Chron., 237; [1985] *Répertoire du notariat Defresnois (*Defrénois), 557; G. Viney, [1985] JCP, I, 3189.

[42] Cass. Civ. 2ème, 19 February 1997 in [1997] RCA, comm., 154. See also: Cass. Civ. 2ème, 28 February 1996 in [1996] Bull. Civ. II, 54; [1996] RCA, comm., 157.

8. What is the standard of care governing the behaviour of children in the context of contributory negligence? Is such standard determined by the same principles and criteria which are relevant to the the duty of care incumbent upon the child in the context of him or her being held liable?

33 Just as with the general laws governing personal liability (*responsabilité du fait personnel*), no particular standard of behaviour is incumbent upon child victims of tort. As a result, the courts tend to rely on solutions drawn from general law. Accordingly, the standard of behaviour required for the establishment of contributory negligence on the victim's part is, strictly speaking, identical to that required to establish fault on the part of the tortfeasor himself. Even for a child is found liable, this rule still holds.

34 Furthermore, this standard is assessed *in abstracto*, by comparison with the behaviour that might be expected in similar circumstances of a "normal" person showing average common sense. Such a comparison is all that is needed if contributory negligence is to be established on the part of the victim.[43]

IV. Contribution in Equity

9. Is there a parallel (mirror-image) to liability in equity in the field of contributory negligence? If so, do the criteria determining liability in equity of the child also apply to the issue of holding him or her accountable for his or her contributory negligence?

35 The courts consider contributory negligence to be a justification for reducing the level of compensation due to the victim. The fact that a child might willingly have played a part in causing or aggravating the injury caused to him may well lead the judges to treat such a victim rather harshly, viewing him perhaps not just as a victim but also as being responsible for the injury caused. This can certainly be considered a practice based on the principles of equity.[44]

10. If answered affirmatively: Is the fact that the child is privately or socially insured against the accident a factor to be considered? Is the existence of any liability insurance of the tortfeasor to be taken into account? What factors have a bearing on the assessment of equitable contribution?

36 Of relevance here is not so much the fact that the child is insured as the fact that his parents are. Generally speaking, parents in France hold a family liability insurance policy, though this is by no means obligatory.

37 In practice – as certain authors have noted[45] – the current trend for parents to be held liable for their children's actions follows the general tendency to seek

[43] J. Flour/J.-L. Aubert/E. Savaux, *Droit civil, les obligations – 2. Le fait juridique* (9th edn. 2001).

[44] See CA Nancy, 10 September 1996 in *jurisdata* no. 1996-049122.

[45] See especially F. Alt-Maes, La garde, fondement de la responsabilité du fait du mineur, [1998] JCP, I, 154 and S. Zeidenberg, A la recherche de la source de la responsabilité parentale, [2001] *Revue de la Recherche Juridique, Droit prospectif* (RRJ) 4, 1351 et seq.

out the party with the deepest pockets. Since the principles of fault-based liability are applied[46] in order to ensure that adequate compensation is available to victims, the courts tend to treat the tortfeasor's guarantor as the liable party.[47]

This practice seems to be based on the principle of always allowing the victim to locate a party with the ability to pay. The fact that it appears impossible for parents to benefit from a ruling of *force majeure* forms part of a similar trend. Parents thereby bear the risk associated with their children's actions. This is based not on fault or liability but on the risk generated *a priori* by a child (and, indeed, administrative law does allow for strict liability). As one author has noted, "the creation of this risk justifies [the parents'] liability by virtue of the inequality of their situation *vis-à-vis* that of the victim."[48] Nevertheless, this desire to insure against risk primarily in relation to the child, or simply in relation to fault, has led to a tendency to treat children as "commodities" in the eyes of the law. Anyone with responsibility for children is accordingly seen as "owning" them in the same way one might own a car. This has led to a situation where the need to have insurance for one's child – just like one has for one's car – is, perhaps sadly, becoming a fact of life for many French people. 38

In the final analysis, the only ones to benefit from this trend are the insurance companies. They, however, will surely be more likely to complain about the compensation costs incurred than admit the profit they might be making from this situation! 39

V. Miscellaneous

11. What are the rules for a situation in which the child is guilty of contributory negligence but the parents have also breached their duty to supervise? Is the child held accountable in any way for his or her parents' breach of the duty to supervise so that his or her claim for damages is reduced?

Historically, the courts have tended to find that a *faute de surveillance* ("fault" or "lack" of supervision) on the part of parents could be held against the child victim. In a case heard by the Meaux children's court (*tribunal pour enfants*),[49] it was ruled that a father "acting in his son's name would have no right to claim full compensation for damage or injury resulting from a prejudicial act to which he personally contributed through his own negligence." In effect, the court held that negligence on the part of the parents whose child caused the injury – in this 40

[46] S. Zeidenberg, [2001] RRJ 4, 1367.

[47] F. Alt-Maes, [1998] JCP, I, 154 quoted by S. Zeidenberg, [2001] RRJ 4, 1353.

[48] P. Kayzer, Le sentiment de justice et le développement de la responsabilité civile en France, [2000] RRJ 2, 445 et seq., particularly 460.

[49] *Tribunal pour enfants* Meaux, 28 May 1948 in [1948] Gaz. Pal. 2, 177. In this case, a six-year old boy had lost the sight of one eye as a result of a shot fired from a children's gun being used by D., a ten-year old child. Child D. had been given a nail instead of the rubber-tipped dart she normally used with the gun. The court assigned liability as follows: 2/3 to child D., 1/3 to the victim's father.

case, negligence in the form of a lack of supervision – could be held against the father of the victim: "[The father], for his part, showed a lack of care in allowing his son to mix with children several years older than him, without worrying about the games they were playing and in which his son was too young to participate." In this case, as in all others where the person who caused the injury was released from full liability on the basis of a *faute de surveillance* on the part of the victim's parents it is, noteworthy that such fault must be linked to another. As several authors have noted, it is the fault committed by the child, or at least his role in causing the damage or injury, that forms the basis for releasing the tortfeasor from part of the liability.[50] On this point, as one author has stated, "the main thing was that a causal link [between the child's action and the subsequent damage or injury] be proved that, once established, would allow a *faute de surveillance* on the part of the parents to be inferred, a fault which could then be held against the child in order to reduce his right to compensation."[51] The reason for this was the subjective assessment of fault used by the courts at this time, which meant that no contributory negligence could be assigned to the child by virtue of the lack of awareness (*discernement*) on his part. Since the fact that the child's act was a contributory factor could not, in itself, be considered a fault, the courts automatically sought to establish a fault on the part of the parents – in most cases a *faute de surveillance*. It is, however, the action of the child that forms the basis for releasing the tortfeasor from liability and reducing the amount of compensation the child might receive.[52]

41 This consistency in the courts' decisions has, however, been subject to some challenges. In a judgment handed down on 24 April 1964[53], the *Cour de cassation* upheld a ruling of the *Cour d'appel* that, while accepting that the parents of the child victim had committed a *faute de surveillance*, had refused to exempt the tortfeasor (the "custodian" of a motor-scooter) from liability, on the basis that there was no causal link between the injury and the parents' lack of supervision. At no point in its deliberations did the court seek to establish a causal relationship between the child's actions and the injury suffered. Accordingly, in this case the tortfeasor could only have been released from liability on the basis of a contributory *faute de surveillance* on the part of the child's parents. While this ruling raised some concerns that the courts would begin to take a tougher stand against child victims of tort,[54] it actually turned out to be a case stuck on the facts without general significance. Subsequently, the courts' former practice of linking the *faute de surveillance* committed by the parents with the child's actions – even if these showed no "fault" – was reaffirmed. In a 1967

[50] H. Vray, L'incidence de la faute de surveillance des parents sur la responsabilité du tiers étranger, impliqué dans un accident survenu à l'enfant, [1964] Gaz. Pal. 2, doctr., 99; M.-C. Lebreton (supra fn. 32), 298.

[51] H. Vray, [1964] Gaz. Pal. 2, doctr., 100.

[52] In the case referred to here (*Tribunal pour enfants* Meaux, 28 May 1948 (supra fn. 49)), the court felt it necessary to point out that "the accident occurred when child D. was attempting to prevent C. from joining A., who had climbed a tree".

[53] Cass. Civ. 2ème, 24 April 1964 in [1964] Bull. Civ. II, 328.

[54] On this point, see H. Vray, [1964] Gaz. Pal. 2, doctr., 100.

case,[55] for example, the Grenoble *Cour d'appel* found that, "since liability for the accident is shared by the child and the driver of the car that knocked him down, the driver is entitled to seek redress for his personal losses from the child's father on account of the *faute de surveillance* committed by the father. The driver may not, however, cite this *faute de surveillance* as grounds for having his own liability in respect of the child further reduced, since the fault of the father overlaps with that of the child, which was [only] made possible by the fault of the father." This case clearly demonstrated that a *faute de surveillance* does not exist automatically and cannot be used as a means of further reducing the compensation to which the child is eligible. Such a reduction may only be based on the existence of a fault committed by the child or of a causal relationship between the child's behaviour and the damage or injury by which he was affected.

Many scholars[56] and a majority of judges on the other benches of the *Cour de cassation* criticised the position of the Second Civil Chamber on this issue, in that it did not respect the principle of solidarity (obligation *in solidum*).[57] The only acceptable solution that accords with this principle consists in allowing the child to be fully compensated for his injury while allowing the tortfeasor to make a claim against the child's parents if they had committed a *faute de surveillance*. 42

The idea that a *faute de surveillance* on the parents' part may be opposed to a child victim's right to full compensation had, in fact, already been rejected by the courts.[58] Specifically, in two 1975 cases,[59] the Second Civil Chamber of the *Cour de cassation* expressly ruled that "where the child has not personally committed a fault, then any fault committed by his parents cannot be held against him." This situation has not, however, led to any improvement in the treatment of child victims. In two celebrated decisions handed down by the *Assemblée plénière* (the plenary session of the *Cour de cassation*) on 9 May 1984,[60] the court instituted a new regime of "objective fault" ("*faute objective*") as committed by a child, whether he be the victim or the tortfeasor in a case. This ruling has played a substantial part in releasing tortfeasors from liability and reducing the level of damages payable to a child. 43

[55] CA Grenoble, 23 January 1967 in [1970] Gaz. Pal., Tables 1966–1970/2, 788 and 789, p. 588.

[56] On this point, see M.-C. Lebreton (supra fn. 32), 310.

[57] A solidary (*in solidum*) obligation allows a victim to demand full compensation for his damage or injury from any one of the parties responsible for causing it on the basis that that the selected party may make a claim against the other responsible parties thereby allowing liability to be shared.

[58] This change was initiated by the Criminal Chamber of the *Cour de cassation* (Cass. Crim., 10 October 1963 in [1964] D., jur., 20). The second Civil Chamber of the court – a bastion of the view that a *faute de surveillance* could be held against the victim's claim – meekly came round to this position in a ruling of 15 May 1968 ([1968] Bull. Civ. II, 139) finding that the presumption of liability on the part of the child's parents could not be extended to the father of the victim in the case, and that, furthermore, in this case no *faute de surveillance* had been established. This overruling by the 2nd Civil Chamber was reinforced by two further rulings on 12 June 1975 and 27 November 1975.

[59] Cass. Civ. 2ème, 12 June 1975 and Cass. Civ. 2ème, 27 November 1975 in [1976] JCP, II, 18444.

[60] Ass. Plen., 9 May 1984, see supra fn. 29.

12. Do the rules of contributory negligence also apply in the area of strict liability?

44 A civil claim may be lodged either on the basis of art. 1382 C. civ., which instituted a regime of fault-based liability, or art. 1384 subs. 1 C. civ., which instituted a regime of strict liability[61] "for that which is caused by the acts of persons for whom [an individual] is responsible, or by things which are in his custody."

45 As regards the possibility of complete exemption from liability for the *gardien de la chose* ("custodian of the thing") in cases of strict liability, the courts have been consistent in their rulings. If a *gardien* is to be completely released from liability, the fault on the victim's part has to display the characteristics of *force majeure*: in other words, "externality", "unforeseeability", and "unavoidableness" (*extériorité*, *imprévisibilité*, and *irrésistibilité*).[62]

46 In respect of partial release from liability for the *gardien*, precedents were established with three rulings on 6 April 1987[63]: in one of these, the judges stated that "the gardien of the thing that caused the damage or injury may be partially released from liability if he proves that the fault of the victim contributed to [that] damage or injury."

47 As regards *responsabilité du fait des bâtiments* (liability for damage or injury caused by buildings in one's care), the courts have frequently had to deal with careless behaviour on the part of children who had gone to play in ruined buildings. In such instances, in spite of the often extreme seriousness of the injuries suffered by the child, the courts have stood by their "objectivising" practice established in the famous 1984 cases. Even when a child had suffered fatal injuries, the courts held, for example, that the victim had committed a fault that allowed the owner of the building to gain partial release from liability.[64]

[61] Cass. Civ 2ème, 20 November 1968 in [1970] JCP, II, 16567, note N. Dejean de la Bâtie, [1969] RTD civ., 337, note G. Durry. "The principle of *responsabilité du fait des choses inanimées* (liability for damage or injury caused by inanimate things in one's care) is based on the notion of *garde* (custody), *independent* of the intrinsic character of the thing and of *any fault committed personally by the gardien* (custodian)."

[62] See particularly Cass. Civ. 2ème, 11 January 2001 in [2001] Bull. Civ. II, 9.

[63] Cass. Civ. 2ème, 6 April 1987 in [1987] Bull. Civ. II, 86; [1987] JCP, II, 20828 note F. Chabas; [1987] Defrénois, 34049, 72, note J.-L. Aubert. In the Desmares case (Cass. Civ. 2ème, 21 July 1982 in [1982] D., jur., 449, conclusions Charbonnier, note C. Larroumet), the same court had ruled that "the behaviour of the victim, where this was not unforeseeable or unavoidable for the custodian, is insufficient to exempt [the custodian] from even partial liability." This departure from a well established rule was meant to press the legislature to adopt more protective legislation for victims of road traffic accidents, which was eventually done in 1985. The 1982 solution was overruled in 1987.

[64] In this case, the child was criticised for having trespassed on private property and for having struck with a stick part of the building that was not fenced off or maintained by the owners. Liability was shared between the parties, with one quarter assigned to the victim. CA Aix-en-Provence, 16 April 1991, Guiramand c. Trecat in *jurisdata* no. 048030.

Thus, whether liability is based on fault or not, the actions of the victim – even if a child – are likely to play a part in releasing the tortfeasor from some liability, and consequently reducing the compensation payable. 48

13. Do the rules of contributory negligence apply in the area of strict liability for traffic accidents or other areas of tort liability?

In response to the apparent unfairness of the courts' treatment of traffic accident victims and especially young children, the legislators felt it necessary to take action. This was because, since the Derguini case,[65] compensation paid to child victims had systematically been reduced on the basis of their contributory role in the accidents that had occurred. The law of 5 July 1985,[66] however, played a considerable role in improving the lot of road accident victims with its introduction of a clear right to compensation in such circumstances. This law provides very favourably for the needs of any victim who was not driving at the time of the accident, and especially for children in this category. 49

a) In respect of personal injury suffered by the victim[67]

Here, a distinction is made between victims who were driving a vehicle at the time of the accident and those who were not. 50

i) For a minor not driving the vehicle

Non-driving victims aged between 16 and 70 may have their fault held against them only where this is both "inexcusable" and the "exclusive cause of the accident."[68] "Inexcusable fault" is defined as a "voluntary fault of exceptional seriousness, exposing without valid reason the person causing it to a danger of which he should have been awar".[69] Being very limited in application, the notion of inexcusable fault as the exclusive cause of the injury means that the courts award compensation virtually as a matter of course. 51

The non-driving victim below 16 years of age falls within a special category of victims that has derived particular benefit[70] from this new law: Compensation for personal injury suffered by such victims can be claimed in practically every instance and, interestingly, the *Cour de cassation* has noted that full compensation may not be restricted even if the victim's behaviour might have 52

65 Ass. Plen., 9 May 1984 (see supra fn. 29).

66 Law no. 85-677 of 5 July 1985 relating to the improvement of the situation of road traffic accident victims and the acceleration of compensation procedures.

67 On the handling of road traffic accidents see: F. Chabas, *Les accidents de la circulation* (1995), 80 et seq.

68 Art. 3 of the law (supra fn. 66).

69 Cass. Civ 2ème, 20 July 1987 in [1987] Bull. Civ. II, 160 (10 cases); F. Terré/Y. Lequette, (supra fn. 41), 223; [1988] Gaz. Pal. 1, 26, note F. Chabas.

70 Art. 3 subs. 2 of the law (supra fn. 66) makes special provisions for children aged 15 or below, adults of 70 years or older, and, irrelevant of their age, to persons registered at the time of the accident as permanently disabled or at least 80% disabled.

constituted *force majeure*, or in the case of a child, even if he committed an inexcusable fault.[71]

53 However, for both categories of victims, including, therefore, those below 16 years of age, "a victim will not be compensated for injury resulting from injuries to his person where he has voluntarily sought out the injury suffered".[72] Any intentional fault on the part of such victims can therefore, at least in theory, be held against them in order to release the driver from liability. Nonetheless, the subjectivity of the court's assessment in such cases is particularly important, since – even if a victim has deliberately placed himself in a situation where an accident is very likely to occur – this is not in itself sufficient to constitute a "voluntary seeking out of the injury."[73] It goes without saying that the capacity of awareness (*discernement*) on the part of the victim plays a vital role here.[74]

ii) For a minor driving the vehicle

54 Any victim who was driving the vehicle at the time of an accident and who may, of course, be below the age of majority[75] is subject to particularly harsh treatment with regard to compensation. Art. 4 of the 1985 Law states: "any fault committed by [a] driver [...] will have the effect of reducing or removing any compensation [due to him] for the injury he has suffered". This means that any contributory fault committed by a driver below the age of majority may result in a reduction in the compensation he receives. However, while fault on the driver's part may constitute the exclusive cause of his injury, this does not necessarily indicate that the same fault was the exclusive cause of the accident. It is simply sufficient for the said fault to be "the sole cause of the injury."[76] The question of whether this fault needs to have the characteristics of an "external cause" (*cause étrangère*) has been the subject of much discussion.[77] With regard to reducing compensation, the courts are required to verify whether the fault committed by the victim contributed to the aggravation or realisa-

[71] See particularly Cass. Civ. 2ème, 19 February 1986 in [1986] JCP, IV, 121.

[72] Cass. Civ. 2ème, 31 May 2000 in [2001] JCP, II, 10577, note C. Butruille-Cardew.

[73] Most case-law in this area relates to the suicide or suicidal behaviour of the victim. See in particular Cass. Civ. 2ème, 17 February 1988 in [1988] Bull. Civ. II, 44; [1988] JCP, IV, 155; Cass. Civ. 2ème, 24 February 1988 in [1988] Bull. Civ. II, 49; Cass. Civ. 2ème, 21 June 1992 in [1992] Bull. Civ. II, 218; [1993] D., somm., 212, note J.-L. Aubert; Cass. Civ. 2ème, 31 May 2000 in [2000] Bull. Civ. II, 90; [2000] D., IR, 185; [2001] JCP, II, 10577, note C. Brutruille-Cardew.

[74] Even if children aged 15 or younger are held liable, they cannot be held to have committed an intentional fault, just as they cannot be denied compensation on the grounds that they might voluntarily have sought to suffer from the injury, since they cannot be considered to have such an intention in the first place. This has been pointed out by F. Duquesne, [1996] D., Jur., 603.

[75] A minor is allowed to drive a car from the age of 16 onwards for the purposes of learning to drive (artt. R. 211-3 and R. 211-5 *Code de la Route* (Highway Code)), and is also allowed to drive, unaccompanied, an agricultural vehicle (art. R. 167-1 *Code de la Route*). From the age of 14 onwards, a minor in possession of a road safety certificate may drive a motor-scooter (art. R. 200-1 *Code de la Route*).

[76] Cass. Crim., 22 May 1996 in [1997] D., 138, note F. Chabas; [1997] RTD civ., 153, obs. P. Jourdain; H. Groutel, Le conducteur rétabli dans ses droits, [1997] D., chron., 18 et seq.

[77] On this point, see F. Chabas, [1997] D., 138 and M.-C. Lebreton (supra fn. 32), 398 et seq.

tion of his injury, and are free to "make an independent assessment as to whether this fault has the effect of limiting or ruling out compensation."[78]

b) In respect of damage to the victim's property

In these cases, no distinction is made between different categories of victim: any contributory negligence on the victim's part can be held against him, thereby reducing his right to compensation.[79] Worse still, it is possible for the driver of a vehicle who has suffered material damage to make a claim against a child, even if this child is also the victim of physical injury. Accordingly, while the child may not have his fault held against him and will receive full compensation for his personal injury, this will not prevent him from being held personally liable for the material damage that his fault might have caused, for example, to the driver's car.[80] Furthermore, insurance for damage caused by a vehicle is not covered by family liability insurance policies. Instead, any damage or injury caused by a vehicle of which the child is the driver or is in charge is covered by the car insurance held by the vehicle's owner.[81] Art. L. 211-1 subs. 1 *Code des assurances* (Insurance Code, C. assur.) states that the owner of a vehicle is required to hold insurance for any damage or injury caused to third parties in the course of accidents in which his vehicle may be involved. § 2 of this article states that "insurance contracts covering the liability referred to in the first paragraph of this article must also cover the public liability of any person who has custody of the vehicle or who drives the vehicle, even if not so authorised." As regards the scenario where the vehicle has been used without the knowledge of the insured party, if theft or violence is involved, art. R. 211-10 1 C. assur. forbids insurance companies from including clauses that might allow them to reject claims "where at the time of the accident the driver is not of legal age or does not possess the appropriately valid certificates required by the laws governing driving of the vehicle." These provisions ensure that protection is provided for the acts of others, for example, when road traffic accidents are caused by a minor (in claims based on art. 1384 C. civ. subs. 1). Even so, these provisions do not cover damage or injury caused by a child driving the car where that child is held personally liable (i.e. where the claim is based on art. 1382 C.civ.). In this scenario, the child can be held personally liable for the damage or injury caused and have both his current and, more importantly, his future assets used as compensation for the victim.[82] 55

[78] *Chambre Mixte de la Cour de cassation* (Cass. Ch. Mixte), 28 March 1997 in [1997] *Bulletin de arrêts de la Cour de cassation chambre Mixte* (Bull. Ch. Mixte), 1; [1997] D., 294, note H. Groutel.

[79] Art. 5 of the law (supra fn. 66).

[80] For children under 16, see: Cass. Civ. 2ème, 4 March 1992 in [1992] JCP, II, 21941, note N. Dejean de la Bâtie; for children aged between 16 and 18, see: Cass. Civ. 2ème, 18 October 1989 in [1989] JCP, IV, 405.

[81] J.-C. Saint-Pau/F. Gonthier, L'enfant et l'assureur, [2000] *Droit et patrimoine* (Dr. et patr.) 87, 59.

[82] On this point, see J.-C. Saint-Pau/F. Gonthier, [2000] Dr. et patr. 87, 59. They point out that this practice of the courts does not really help to provide compensation for the victim. Accordingly, parents may be held liable if their child has, without their knowledge, driven their vehicle or a vehicle belonging to a third party.

14. Are adults held to a higher standard of care in their interactions with children, or when children are or may be around?

56 Any negligent (*fautif*) behaviour committed by a tortfeasor is assessed *in abstracto* in French law, with reference to the behaviour expected from a "reasonable person" or a *bon père de famille*[83]. The circumstances external to the tortfeasor are also taken into account when determining his liability. Reference is made to the behaviour that would be expected of a "reasonable person" in similar circumstances. Liability is not, therefore, assessed in overly subjective terms. As one author has noted, "to be precise, what is expected of a 'reasonable man' is an adjustment of his behaviour to the circumstances in which he finds himself at a given moment."[84] We can, therefore, only conclude that an adult interacting with a child is subject to the standards of behaviour of a "reasonable person" and is expected to adapt his behaviour in response to the child's actions. French law thus imposes no special standards (other than those of the *personne raisonnable*) in such circumstances, but simply requires that an adult take particular care when undertaking actions that may cause injury to a child. Accordingly, the courts have rarely stated expressly that adults are subject to a special duty of care in their interactions with children.

57 Similarly, another commentator has noted that the *Cour de cassation* seems "aware of the fact that a third party, particularly where this third party has custody (*garde*) of a thing that may cause damage or injury to others, must show particular care and attention to the reactions and behaviour of an unsupervised child, since these reactions and behaviour are not generally unforeseeable in view of the child's lack of awareness of the danger."[85] As a basis for this statement, however, the author makes reference to a case[86] where "the failure to exercise 'reasonable care' (*les précautions utiles de prudence*) for which a bus driver was criticised seemed to be explained more by the particularly dangerous layout of the junction where the accident occurred than by the failure of the driver to adapt to the child's behaviour."[87]

58 This lack of a more strict criterion for evaluating an adult's behaviour when interacting with a child is even more obvious in cases where liability is based

[83] For an interesting analysis of this point, see G. Viney/P. Jourdain, *Les conditions de la responsabilité civile* (2nd edn. 1998), 462 et seq. and 350 et seq. See also Ph. Le Tourneau/L. Cadiet, *Droit de la responsabilité et des contrats* (2002–2003), 6267 et seq. and 1213 et seq.

[84] G. Viney/P. Jourdain (supra fn. 83), 464.

[85] H. Vray, [1964] Gaz. Pal. 2, doctr., 100.

[86] Cass. Civ., 4 May 1949 in [1949] Bull. Civ., 156.

[87] The *Cour de cassation* in this case actually quashed the decision of the *Cour d'appel*, which had found that the injury had not been caused exclusively by the fault of the child, who had "run across the junction without taking due care". Instead, as the *Cour de cassation* found, the layout of the junction and the size of the vehicle that prevented the driver from keeping to the right should have made the child display the maximum degree of care when crossing the junction. The fact that the child victim had been left unsupervised in this place, where his action of crossing the junction could have been foreseen, seemed not to be the main factor in the deliberations of the *Cour de cassation*, whose statement could have applied equally to an adult or child.

on some "objective fault" (*faute objective*), the tortfeasor then gaining partial release even more easily. This is often inferred solely on the basis of a causal link between the child's actions and the damage or injury[88]. If the tortfeasor were held to a stricter standard of behaviour toward the child, it would be much more difficult for him to gain release from liability when a child victim is involved.

VI. Insurance Matters

15. Are pupils covered by private or public accident (first-party) insurance?

First-party insurance policies[89] are becoming more common in the French system[90] and are being promoted more and more heavily by insurance companies. There is still a discussion about the preferred term for these types of policies: the two main alternatives are "*contrat garantie des accidents de la vie*" ("everyday life accidents insurance policy")[91] and "*assurance contre les accidents corporels*" ("insurance against physical accidents").[92] 59

This type of insurance can be taken out by an individual[93] or else take the form of a collective insurance policy held by an institution.[94] When held by an individual, such a policy "also covers all of the people within the household of the policy holder."[95] This means that any accidental injuries suffered by dependent children of the insured party are also covered, parents often purchasing additional coverage for extra-curricular school activities. Public and private schools request parents to bring evidence of such coverage at the time of registration and usually propose special insurance policies for those parents who do not have adequate coverage. 60

[88] In a good number of cases, it seems that the child victim is held liable simply on the basis of having been in the wrong place at the wrong time. M.-C. Lebreton questions whether "fault on the victim's part does not lead as a matter of course to a ruling of strict liability against the child." (M.-C. Lebreton (supra fn. 32), 386).

[89] This type of policy is defined as "a contract in which, in exchange for a premium, the insurer commits in principle, in cases where during the period of cover the insured party is affected by physical injury, to pay the insured party or, in case of [the insured party's] death, to pay a nominated beneficiary, a specified sum and, in addition, to provide full or partial reimbursement for the medical and pharmaceutical costs incurred as a result of the said accident"; M. Picard/A. Besson, *Les assurances terrestres en droit français, Volume 1: Le contrat d'assurance* (3rd edn. 1970), 444.

[90] This new type of all-purpose insurance cover for general, non-work-related "accidents of life" (the *Contrat garantie des accidents de la vie*) was set up by the French federation of insurance companies 2000. On this point, see Y. Lambert-Faivre, *Droit des assurances* (11th edn. 2001), 997-1.

[91] Y. Lambert-Faivre (supra fn. 90), 997-1.

[92] Y. Lambert-Faivre (supra fn. 90), 817 et seq. and 995 et seq.

[93] Accordingly, Professeur Lambert-Faivre uses the term "individual accident" (Y. Lambert-Faivre (supra fn. 90), 817 and 995).

[94] Examples commonly cited include those of policies for companies or sporting associations and also for schools to cover pupils during extra-curricular activities.

[95] Y. Lambert-Faivre (supra fn. 90), 999.

61 As far as state health insurance is concerned, at least some of the medical costs incurred by dependent children of the insured party as a result of their illness or accident, are covered by the social welfare system.[96] In the great majority of cases, people supplement their state health insurance with a private health insurance policy. This is arranged directly by the individual or by the employer.[97] Such additional policies cover dependents and therefore children, who benefit in their capacity as beneficiaries. This combination of state-provided social security cover and private health insurance allows for complete coverage of any medical costs incurred by a child of the insured party as a result of injury.

16. Does this insurance cover any damage incurred on the way to school and back?

62 Comprehensive insurance policies covering both civil liability and household insurance provide protection for the consequences of acts caused by children of the policy-holder, particularly at school and during the journey to and from school.[98]

63 It is worth noting that in the case of an accident occurring during a journey when the child victim is travelling in a school bus, a number of different parties may be liable. Liability can, in fact, be assigned to the organiser of the school transportation service,[99] the company providing that service, the driver of the bus,[100] the representative of the police service, the public highways department, other drivers on the road, parents, and even the victim himself.[101] The allocation

[96] Art. L. 313-3 subs. 2 *Code de la sécurité sociale* (Social Security Code, CSS) states that the social security system will provide cover for dependent, unwaged children of the insured party or of his or her partner. The nature of or indeed the absence of any filial relationship between the child and the insured party plays no part here. (The article expressly refers to children who may be "*legitimate, natural, recognised or not, adopted, pupils within the state education system where the insured party is their teacher, or fostered children*"). There is, however, a specified age limit: the social security system covers only dependent, unwaged children below the age of 16. The coverage can, however, be extended to the age of 18 if the child is an apprentice (art. L. 313-3 subs. 3 lit. a CSS) or even 20 if the child is a student (art. L. 313-3 subs. 3 lit. b CSS). Thanks to the creation of the status of "autonomous beneficiary" (*ayant-droit autonome*), a child of 16 may, in his capacity as beneficiary, be personally reimbursed for his medical costs (art. L. 161-14-1 CSS).

[97] Art. 2 of the Law no. 89-1009 of 31 December 1989 stipulates that such supplementary insurance is obligatory: "*Employees [may be] covered collectively, either on the basis of an agreement or collective agreement or following ratification by the majority of those party to an agreement proposed by the head of the company or by the unilateral decision of the employer.*"

[98] See, for example, artt. 23 and 24 of the multi-risk (civil liability and household) policy provided by MATMUT (<http://www.matmut.fr>).

[99] Outside major towns in France, the individual *départements* are responsible for organising school bus or similar services: Law no. 83-663 of 22 July 1983.

[100] Law no. 85-677 of 5 July 1985.

[101] As set down in Law no. 83-663 of 22 July 1983, which places *départements* in charge of organising and operating school transport services outside urban transport areas, the *départements* are responsible for determining the routes, timetables, and frequency of school bus services, as well as the location and arrangement of the stops. Legislation designed to protect the state education

of liability is determined solely by the courts. With regard to the accidents occurring at a location where children are collected by the school bus, the local public authorities can also be held liable in their capacity as providers of the transportation service.[102]

It seems that there are only two limitations on cover: firstly, the degree to which the injury was accidental[103] and, secondly, the nature of the physical injury.[104] The place where the injury occurred seems to be irrelevant in determining whether the cover is effective. Extensive insurance coverage is therefore available. 64

17. Are there restrictions on damages recoverable by the child, e.g. with respect to loss of future earnings?

French law views a loss of future earnings for children in terms of the loss of a chance to achieve those earnings in future. The loss of a chance has been defined in case-law as "the disappearance of the probability of a favourable event."[105] The main difficulty here lies in assessing the level of compensation due to the victim in view of the fact that the loss has not yet occurred. The courts have held that only the loss of a chance may be considered in their assessment of compensation, and not "the full amount of what the opportunity, if it had been realised, might have brought for the victim."[106] When deciding whether the lost opportunity to achieve future earnings is eligible for compensation, the courts require that this loss should involve "the certain and direct continuation of a current state of affairs" and should be "capable of being estimated at the current time."[107] The courts have refused to provide compensation for loss of a purely hypothetical opportunity. In a ruling handed down on 9 November 1983,[108] the *Cour de cassation* quashed a decision whereby a nine- 65

service (*l'Education nationale*) from liability, as set down in Circular no. 97-178 of 18 September 1997, indicates that a teacher, when not teaching his pupils, is discharged from any duty of care with regard to them, particularly when they are being transported to or from school. He is not, therefore, liable in the case of any accident. Question no. 18488 asked by Deputy Mancel Jean-François (Union pour un Mouvement Populaire – Oise) to the Minister of Transport; question published in JO, 19 May 2003, 3809; answer published in JO, 4 August 2003, 6213.

[102] For an illustration of this, see: <www.legalnews.fr>, "*A qui incombe la responsabilité d'un accident survenu au cours d'un ramassage scolaire?*"

[103] Y. Lambert-Faivre notes that this type of insurance covers any "*physical injury not intentionally caused by the insured party and deriving from the sudden action of an external cause*", Y. Lambert-Faivre (supra fn. 90), 998. For similar statements recorded in case-law, see Ph. Le Tourneau/L. Cadiet (supra fn. 83), 2778.

[104] Internal injuries are not covered by this type of policy, since the cause of the lesion has to be external to the individual. On this point, see Ph. Le Tourneau/L. Cadiet (supra fn. 83), 2781.

[105] Cass. Crim., 6 June 1990 in [1990] Bull. Crim., 224; [1991] RTD civ., 121, note P. Jourdain

[106] On this point, see Ph. Le Tourneau/L. Cadiet (supra fn. 83), 1419.

[107] *Chambre des requêtes* (Cass. Req.), 1 June 1932 in [1933] *Recueil Sirey* (S.), 1, 49, note H. Mazeaud.

[108] Cass. Civ. 2ème, 9 November 1983 in [1984] Gaz. Pal. 2, pan., 237, note F. Chabas; [1985] JCP, II, 20360, note Y. Chartier.

year-old child had been awarded – in addition to compensation for the permanent partial disability caused by the accident – an allowance as compensation for his "lack of opportunity to progress to a well-paid job". The *Cour de cassation* criticised the judges in the lower court for not having demonstrated the manner in which "the loss of a chance [...] was certain and directly related to the act on which the claim was based". Since merely hypothetical losses may not be compensated, the loss of a chance to progress to a well-paid or better-paid job may be taken into account in the assessment of compensation only when "the candidate is very advanced in his studies [...] and is destined, on the basis of his qualities, for [future] success."[109] Needless to say, this situation hardly applies to a nine-year-old child at primary school who is injured in an accident, in spite of the fact that his educational achievements may be seriously affected as a result of this accident. A child's future career, can hardly be fixed or certain in character.

66 Accordingly, while restrictions are placed on the compensation due to a child for the loss of the chance to achieve future earnings, these are based on the difficulty of establishing that any such loss of opportunity is certain or that the accident definitely led to this loss. Thus, while the assessment of a loss of opportunity is monitored by the *Cour de cassation*, it remains a question of fact rather than of law. It is still theoretically possible that the courts might rule in favour of a child or adolescent in respect of his potential future earnings. This would, however, require evidence of a "real and serious"[110] loss of opportunity that was directly caused by the act on which the claim is based.[111]

VII. Damage Issues

18. If damages for loss of earnings are available, what are the principles governing their assessment?

67 Any damages would, as stated above, have to be based on a loss of the chance to achieve future earnings. The precise definition of such a loss has been given by the Criminal Chamber of the *Cour de cassation*, which stated that while such a loss may be established, the losses to the victim caused by the loss of

[109] F. Chabas notes on Cass. Civ 2ème, 9 November 1983 in [1984] Gaz. Pal. 2, pan., 237. In one case, involving a student about to obtain his diploma (second year of a vocational training certificate) and forced to abandon his studies following injuries suffered in a road traffic accident, the court did accept that there was a loss "of a serious opportunity to gain a better position than that which [the victim's] current faculties allow him to take up" (and accordingly of the corresponding earnings). (CA Pau, 27 October 1998 in *Cahier de Jurisprudence Aquitaine Midi Pyrénées* 1990/1175, note D. Krajeski)

[110] G. Viney/P. Jourdain (supra fn. 83), 283.

[111] Consider the example of an apprentice (below the age of majority) who is reaching the end of his apprenticeship and has the skills necessary to obtain his qualification, but who loses the use of his hands as a result of an injury. Since this incapacity has the effect of preventing him from practising his chosen trade and preventing him from achieving the corresponding earnings, the courts could indeed rule that he had suffered a compensable loss of opportunity to achieve future earnings.

chance must be "direct" and "certain."[112] Examples of this rule in case-law include that of a young child being unable to progress to the next class at school as a result of an accident[113] and of another child finding his career options severely restricted.[114]

There may be cases where a minor is employed as an apprentice. In these instances, tort law does not prevent a victim from suing his employer for damages in recompense for the economic loss incurred. However, there are very few examples of claims of this type made by minors. One may imagine the case of a child model who suffered injury and disfigurement before a planned photo shoot. A claim for economic loss resulting from the impossibility of continuing as planned with the photo shoot may then be envisaged, but there is no such case on record. 68

19. Which of the child's non-material interests are protected in your jurisdiction? May the child, for example, sue for impairment of intellectual or social development, the onset of behavioural problems, or reduced employment prospects?

In principle, children are represented by their parents in any court action. Children are subject to exactly the same legal rights and duties as adults. Accordingly, a child may make a claim based on civil liability and is entitled to claim damages in just the same way as an adult for a variety of losses or injuries. 69

A child may also recover in case of disfigurement (*préjudice esthétique*) and loss of amenity (*préjudice d'agrément*).[115] The latter refers to a decline in the victim's quality of life caused by the injury, for instance preventing the victim from practising certain sport or leisure activities.[116] This comes in addition to a possible psychological affliction affecting the victim's living conditions or his ability to work, which would be classed as a straightforward physical injury.[117] 70

Because the victim is a child, a claim based on loss of earnings may not be admissible, since such a loss would have to be "certain". Likewise, disfigurement and loss of amenity may be less obvious than in the case of an adult.[118] A re-evaluation of such losses may be carried out when the child reaches the age 71

[112] This is of course a "no-win" situation, as an opportunity cannot, by definition, be certain.

[113] CA Nîmes, 2 October 1996 in *jurisdata* no. 1996-030236.

[114] CA Poitiers, 28 January 1987 in *jurisdata* no. 1987-041397.

[115] Cass. Civ. 2ème, 10 December 1986 in [1986] Bull. Civ. II, 188. For details of a case involving a four-year-old, see *Chambre sociale de la Cour de cassation* (Cass. Soc.), 11 February 1981 in [1981] Bull. Civ. V, 129.

[116] The liable party is required to provide compensation not only for the physical injury caused to the victim but also, where appropriate, for the loss resulting from a reduction in his enjoyment of life, so to speak. This would generally involve the victim being incapable of or having difficulty in carrying out certain normal enjoyable activities. CA Paris, 2 December 1977 in [1978] D., 285, note Y. Lambert-Faivre.

[117] Cass. Soc., 16 November 1983 in [1983] Bull. Civ. V, 559.

[118] Cass. Crim., 10 May 1979 in [1979] Bull. Crim., 171; [1980] Gaz. Pal. 127.

of majority.[119] Claims for physical injury, pain and suffering (*préjudice moral*), and loss of a chance are also admissible, as well as for invasion of privacy.[120]

20. Are there special rules for the assessment of damages sustained by a child, e.g. with respect to pain and suffering?

72 As indicated above, all normal types of loss or injury are eligible for compensation, including physical injury, pain and suffering, disfigurement, loss of amenity, loss of a chance, etc. Fundamentally, the child is treated as if he were an adult,[121] yet with the qualifications made in no. 70 above.

73 In respect of economic loss, the Criminal Chamber of the *Cour de cassation* has accepted the possibility of compensation both for the financial losses incurred by a wife as a result of her husband's death and also directly for the child of the couple.[122] The fact that a child is undertaking a course of study is a major factor when the courts are setting the level of any such compensation.

74 A case has been found where a compensation fund offered minimal compensation. The court did not hesitate to increase the amount in a substantial manner.[123]

[119] Cass. Crim., 10 May 1979 (supra fn. 118).

[120] CA Paris, 6 November 2003 in [2004] Gaz. Pal. 16 and 17 January, 12–15. The case dealt with the right to claim for breach of a child's right to privacy. The proceedings were brought in the child's name by his parents, but personal compensation was awarded to the child.

[121] See G. Viney/P. Jourdain (supra fn. 83), 250 et seq., where no distinction is made between the adult or the child victim.

[122] Cass. Crim., 20 February 2001, unreported, appeal no. 00-83880.

[123] CA Douai, 10 April 2003, decision no. 2001/28, available at <www.legifrance.gouv.fr>: "In view of the fact that – in order to arrive at the aforementioned sum – the *Fonds de Garantie* claims that following the death of her father, Florecita would be deprived of the sum of FF 750 per month in the form of [her father's] *RMI* [minimum welfare payment] – and that, for his part, her father would have set aside only 10% for the maintenance of the child (equating to a monthly loss of FF 75); but in view of the fact that such a line of reasoning cannot be followed on account of the extremely low level of the income which Mr Bruno M. and Ms Annie S. were receiving for themselves and their two children; and, indeed, considering that in 1995, if all of their benefit payments are combined, they had a monthly income of FF 3,657.33; and while it is not unreasonable in these circumstances to consider, even while using the FF 750 *RMI* payment as a basis for our considerations, that as a result of the death of her father the child has been deprived of a monthly sum of FF 550 (corresponding to a proportion of the FF 750), there remaining FF 200 for the father's needs, or the equivalent of 15% of the total income received by the couple; [and] it being noted that the total of the monies being occasionally received by Mr Bruno M. as a result of his work is unknown; [in view of all the above, therefore], taking account of the value of benefits adjusted for inflation applicable in this case, i.e. FF 6,648, [we conclude that] the economic losses suffered by Florecita M. should be increased to FF 43,876.80 or € 6,688.98." It is indeed fortunate that the courts reassessed the losses suffered by the child in this case. It should be remembered that the courts' evaluations are not dictated by any legal considerations.

21. Does a small child have a claim for damages for pain and suffering if he or she is deprived of his or her parents by a tortious act? If so, may the claim be denied on the ground that the child does not feel the loss?

All normal types of loss or injury suffered by a child are eligible for compensation, and so is pain and suffering as a result of the accidental death of one of their parents.[124] The claim cannot be denied on the ground that the child does not experience the loss in the same ways as an adult might, indeed the child victim is treated as if he were an adult and, therefore, he is entitled to full compensation. However, it is not easy to assess losses in the case of young children and psychiatrists seem to agree that they deal with grief more quickly than adults.[125] 75

22. With respect to a damage claim for the costs of medical treatment: May the tortfeasor defend himself by pointing to the fact that the parents have a duty to maintain the child?

Since the law does not differentiate the heads of damage that may be compensated, the courts are often tempted to order an overall payment, without distinguishing between the different elements of loss or injury. Even so, many courts do make an effort to list the items for which compensation is payable,[126] which would, of course, include medical costs. The duty to maintain the child, provided for in art. 213 C. civ., offers no defense to the tortfeasor. 76

23. In case of wrongful life: Does the child have a damage claim against the physician or a health care institution?

While the *Conseil d'État* deems it inappropriate to institute compensation for this type of loss,[127] the Plenary Assembly of the *Cour de cassation* accepted it in 2000, in the famous Perruche case.[128] Early in her pregnancy, a mother had 77

[124] Cass. Crim., 4 February 2003, unreported, appeal no. 00-21428, <www.legifrance.gouv.fr>.

[125] On the *resilience* concept, see Boris Cyrulnik, *Un merveilleux malheur* (1999), or more recently B. Cyrulnik, *Le murmure des fantômes* (2002). Accordingly, any determination of pain and suffering based on the criteria applied to adults runs the risk of being incorrect. See Y. Lambert-Faivre (supra fn. 90), for details of how losses are determined by the courts.

[126] G. Viney/P. Jourdain (supra fn. 83), 200.

[127] *Conseil d'Etat* (CE), 14 February 1997 in [1997] JCP, II., 22828, note J. Moreau; [1997] D., somm., 323, note J. Penneau; [1997] *Revue française de droit administratif* (RFDA), 374.

[128] Ass. Plen., 17 November 2000, Perruche case in [2000] JCP, II, 10438, report P. Sargos, concl. J. Ste-Rose, note F. Chabas; [2001] D., jur., 332, note D. Mazeaud and 336, note P. Jourdain; [2000] *Les petites affiches* (Petites affiches), 8 December 2000, 9, note M. Gobert. Among the many articles on the case, see J. L. Aubert, Indemnisation d'une naissance handicapée qui, selon le choix de la mère, n'aurait pas dû être, [2001] D., chron., 489; L. Aynès, Préjudice de l'enfant né handicapé: la plainte de Job devant la Cour de cassation, [2001] D., chron., 492; P.-Y. Gauthier, A propos du débat éthique sur la responsabilité civile, [2001] JCP, I, 287; M. Gobert, La Cour de cassation méritait-elle le pilori?, [2000] Petites affiches, 8 December 2000, 4; F. Leduc, Handicap génétique ou congénital et responsabilité civile, [2001] RCA, chron., 4; B. Markesinis, Réflexions d'un comparatiste anglais sur et à partir de l'arrêt Perruche, [2001] RTD civ., 77; D. Mazeaud, Réflexions sur un malentendu, [2001] D., chron.,

contracted rubella (German measles), a condition that was misdiagnosed by her doctor and not picked up on by the medical analysis laboratory. Her child was born with severe deformities. The *Cour de cassation* was unsurprisingly – since similar decisions had been reached well before 2000 – ready to grant compensation to the parents on the basis that the faults committed by the laboratory and doctor had prevented them from exercising their right to terminate the pregnancy. However, the court also held that the child was entitled to compensation for his own losses resulting from his disability, ruling that such losses had been caused by the same faults. The ensuing discussion was unusually heated. It focused first on the question of whether there was indeed a causal relationship between the laboratory's and doctor's fault on the one hand and the child's disability on the other, and secondly on the issue of whether wrongful birth should be accepted as a loss worthy of compensation. In spite of the many ethical and legal barriers that might have been held to preclude such a decision, the *Cour de cassation* seemed willing to put aside any doubts with regard to both issues. The court held, somewhat elliptically, that the child was entitled to "compensation for the loss resulting from his disability".

78 This holding was confirmed and clarified by the Plenary Assembly of the *Cour de cassation* in three subsequent cases decided half a year later, where the claim was based on breach of contract.[129] The court explained that compensation could only be envisaged if the two following conditions were met:

79 1. A direct causal link must exist between the medical fault and the loss or injury suffered by the child. In all three cases, very similar to the Perruche case, it was held that there was no direct causation. Causation had been accepted in a rather loose way in the Perruche case.

80 2. That the conditions for termination of the pregnancy must be met (art. L. 2213-1 *Code de la santé publique*), namely, the pregnancy would have endangered the mother's life or there was a strong probability that the child would suffer from a particularly serious condition (recognised as being incurable at the time of the diagnosis). Again, in all three cases, this had not been established before the lower courts.

352; G. Mémeteau, L'action de vie dommageable, [2001] JCP, I, 279; C. Radé, Etre ou ne pas naître? Telle n'est pas la question!, [2001] RCA, chron., 1; G. Viney, Brèves remarques sur un arrêt qui affecte l'image de la justice, [2001] JCP, I, 286; A. Sériaux, Perruche et autres. La Cour de cassation entre mystère et mystification, [2002] D., chron., 1996 et seq.; C. Labrusse-Riou/B. Mathieu, [2000] D., III, point de vue; D. Fenouillet, Pour une humanité autrement fondée, [2001] *Revue droit de la famille* (Dr. Famille), April 2001, chron., 7; O. Cayla/Y. Thomas, *Du droit de ne pas naître, À propos de l'affaire Perruche, Le débat* (2001); F. Terré, Pitié pour les juristes!, [2002] RTD civ., 247 et seq.

129 Ass. Plen., 13 July 2001 in [2001] JCP, II, 10601, concl. J. Ste-Rose, note F. Chabas; [2001] D., jur., 2325, note P. Jourdain.

The Perruche case was most controversial and triggered a prompt legislative response. The law of 4 March 2002[130] provided that "no one may seek redress for an injury resulting merely from the fact of his birth". This represented a clear intention – though one perhaps doomed to failure – to put an end to the ongoing debate around the issue of wrongful life. In fact, the concept of wrongful life has never been expressly recognised by the *Cour de cassation*, which only recently reaffirmed that it is indeed the disability that constitutes the loss for the individual, and not the loss of any opportunity or the life itself. As regards the question of fault on the part of the healthcare professional, the law adds that "the person born with a disability due to a medical negligence may obtain compensation for his losses provided that the negligent act directly caused the disability or aggravated it or prevented measures from being taken that might have attenuated it." While this ruling is not much clearer than or significantly different from others made by the *Cour de cassation*, it at least has the virtue of making clear that "direct" causation should henceforward be interpreted more narrowly by the courts. In addition, the current state of medical knowledge enables only a few very rare congenital conditions to be treated or attenuated *in utero*,[131] a fact that further reduces the likelihood of a negligent doctor being held liable. In any case, this approach excludes any faults previously established, since it is clear that mistakes made in the diagnosis or detection of a condition are not the cause of the disability itself. 81

The person affected by the disability therefore has two possible courses of action: 82

If a fault can be established as having directly caused the disability, the child can sue the medical practitioner and obtain compensation. 83

If no fault on the part of the medical practitioner can be established or if such fault is not the direct cause of the disability, the child is not, however, left without remedy: The law states that "any disabled person, whatever the cause of his disability, is entitled to the full support of the State". Even so, while this noble intention is indeed laudable, the national body responsible for providing compensation to victims of medical accidents set up under the new law (the *Office national d'indemnisation des accidents médicaux* or *ONIAM*), is only authorised to compensate losses resulting from medical accidents where the level of disability exceeds a specified threshold. This means that many victims suffering from less serious conditions are excluded from its provisions. 84

Finally, it is noteworthy that while a child may not be granted compensation on the basis of wrongful life, the parents may still be entitled to compensation 85

[130] Law no. 2002-303 of 4 March 2002 relating to the rights of the sick or injured and the quality of the healthcare system, [2002] *Revue de droit sanitaire et social* (RDSS), *numéro special,* 641–844. Art. 1 was re-enacted by Law no. 2005-102 of 11 February 2005, art. 2, as art. L.114-5 of *Code de l'action sociale et des familles.*

[131] A. Dorsner-Dolivet, L'indemnisation des dommages médicaux après la loi Kouchner, [2003] *Revue générale de droit médical* (Rev. Gén. Dr. médical) 9, 47–62.

for their own losses resulting from the child's wrongful birth. This is considered quite separately from any payment due to them as a result of the child's own losses.

24. Concerning liability for pre-natal injuries: Are third parties liable to the child? May the mother be liable to the child, for example, for excessive consumption of alcohol or even for an omission to procure treatment?

86 In France, a distinction is made between third parties who are medical practitioners and those who are not.

87 1. In respect of healthcare professionals, the so-called "Anti-Perruche" law stipulates that compensation will be paid only where the pre-natal injury is directly caused by a fault committed by such a professional.[132] This approach is intended to apply in cases of a "wrongful life" type, though, as has been noted above, this concept is not explicitly recognised as a basis for compensation in French law. The healthcare professional remains *a priori* liable for any fault on his part that has resulted in a pre-natal injury that became apparent when the child was born.

88 There are, however, no clear rules to govern how civil law should deal with cases where pre-natal injury does not become evident at the time of birth – in other words, where the foetus is killed as a direct result of a fault on the part of a medical practitioner. Here, instead of being handled as a pre-natal injury causing long-term suffering to the victim, such cases could potentially be treated as an unintentional attempt on the victim's life. The main question in such a scenario would be whether the foetus could be classed as a child and, correspondingly, could be held to have suffered a damage or injury under tort law. The likely answer to this question can be found in criminal case-law. Governed by the principle of legality, the criminal courts have refused to consider the death of a foetus caused by a third party as homicide. The legal position on this issue was finally clarified, in a somewhat disturbing case,[133] in a decision handed down by the Criminal Chamber of the *Cour de cassation* on 25 June 2002. This has resulted in a situation in which both civil claims and criminal charges are ruled out if the child dies *in utero*. Cases will, therefore, only be accepted when the child has been born alive, for example, if injuries inflicted during the birth have led to the death of a new-born baby[134], since the

[132] See above, question no. 23.

[133] Cass. Crim., 25 June 2002 in [2002] JCP, II, 10155, note M.-L. Rassat. A pregnant woman who was over-term by seven days was taken to hospital and placed under observation. In the night, she noticed an abnormality in her unborn child's heartbeat and reported this to a midwife who neglected to inform the doctor. The patient restated her concerns the following morning and again no action was taken. Ninety minutes later the child died *in utero*, albeit without suffering from any deformity. Despite the fact that the pregnancy went to term and that negligence on the part of the healthcare professionals had resulted in the baby's death, the *Cour de cassation* refused to class the death as homicide since the child had not been born.

[134] Cass. Crim., 23 October 2001 in [2001] Bull. Crim., 217.

main criterion is that the child is no longer in its mother's womb at the time of its death.

The response of the criminal courts has, therefore, resulted in a rather narrow interpretation of the civil guidelines set down in the 2002 statute: compensation for the suffering of a child *in utero*, directly caused by a medical practitioner, is only possible if the child is born before dying. Third party liability towards a child could not, therefore, be extended to an unborn child.[135] This accords with the approach taken in the newly reformed laws on inheritance, which stipulate that in order to be eligible for any inheritance the child "exists at the moment that the will enters probate or, having been conceived, [is born] in a viable state."[136] 89

2. When dealing with fault committed by a third party outside the medical arena, the courts tend to proceed with care, since, for the time being, their only useful precedents are drawn from the criminal courts' handling of the "homicide" of a foetus. On 29 June 2001, the Plenary Assembly of the *Cour de cassation* had to decide a case where a pregnant woman had been run over by a drunk driver and consequently suffered a miscarriage.[137] The court ruled that there was no involuntary homicide according to art. 221-6 of the Criminal Code, since the child was not yet born. This ruling clarified the pre-existing case law. Thus, if a child dies in the womb during an accident – in other words, before being born – the child does not come to legal existence and has no claim for compensation. If, however, the child survives the accident in spite of the injuries suffered, it becomes eligible for compensation as soon as it is born.[138] 90

In conclusion, then, whether a healthcare professional or other third party is at fault, there is no liability to a child who was not born. Parents may, however, claim for their losses, including pain and suffering, resulting from the child's death. 91

Ordinarily, as far as civil liability is concerned, parents are simply treated as third parties in relation to their own child and may, therefore, be held liable for any injury they have caused to their child.[139] In theory, then, there is nothing to prevent a case being brought on behalf of a child against its mother if it can be proven that fault on her part is the direct cause of injury, but proving such cau- 92

[135] The present authors prefer the term "unborn child" to "embryo" or "foetus". In our view this represents a useful recognition of the interests of a baby who is not yet a child in that its interests are equated with those of a child. The concept of "interest of a foetus or embryo" is not, of course, accepted by the courts.

[136] The new art. 725 C. civ., added as a result of Law no. 2001-1135 of 3 December 2001.

[137] Ass. Plen., 29 June 2001 in [2001] JCP, II, 10569, report P. Sargos, concl. J. Ste-Rose, note M.-L. Rassat; [2001] D., 2917, note Y. Mayaud. See also: J. Pradel, La seconde mort de l'enfant conçu (à propos de l'arrêt d'Assemblée Plénière du 29 juin 2001), [2001] D., Chron., 2907.

[138] Cass. Crim., 9 January 1992 in [1993] RSC., 328, note G. Levasseur.

[139] *Jurisclasseur de droit civil*, artt. 1382 to 1386, fascicule 130-2, 37.

sation might be difficult, or even impossible. So far no case has been found where French courts had to deal with such a claim.

93 Closely related to the issues of pre-natal injury, liability of parents towards their children, and claims for "wrongful life" – a route now closed off following the "anti-Perruche" law discussed above – is the question of the liability of the rapist toward the child conceived as a result of the rape. For a number of years now, this has been the subject of much attention from scholars and legislators in France. Two years before the Perruche case, the *Cour de cassation* handed down an equally remarkable decision concerning wrongful life,[140] though in this case the defendant was not a healthcare provider or doctor, but the child's father himself. A father had raped his own daughter, an act that resulted in her giving birth to a child. This child later decided to sue the father on the basis of having been conceived as a result of the crime of incest. The Criminal Chamber accepted the child's claim and the father had to pay damages.

94 This ruling – considered unsatisfactory by many observers – represented a departure from previous case law. It raised the question of parental liability towards children living with disabilities or suffering as a result of a parent's criminal behaviour. Two main trends can be identified in the courts' treatment of this issue of parental liability:

95 1. Firstly, the courts have accepted that a father guilty of raping the child's mother may be held liable,[141] since the injury inflicted on the child's mother may be carried over to the child (*préjudice par ricochet*);

96 2. Secondly, a mother may not be held liable for the life of her child, on the same principle applied to the doctor in the Perruche case. At worst, she (or a doctor) could be held liable for the survival of her child and not for the child's disability. However, the mother can never be made liable for simply having decided to "keep" her child, since the *Cour de cassation* ruled that any losses suffered by a child in such circumstances are only indirectly related and occur subsequently to those suffered by the mother. The decision to terminate a pregnancy is always left up to the mother and may not be treated as a fault.[142] In respect of the potential liability of a mother who smokes during her pregnancy, in theory at least, a case could be brought against her by her child. It may be difficult to prove direct causal relationship between her smoking and the injury suffered by the child. The only instance where a court has had to deal with smoking by a parent was a custody case. A court once ruled that, for the sake of the child, custody should be transferred to the father, since the mother's excessive smoking was harming the child. This may be a first step towards holding smoking parents liable to their suffocating children.

[140] Cass. Crim., 4 February 1998 in [1998] Bull. Crim., 43.
[141] On this issue, see F. Garron, La responsabilité civile du géniteur, [1999] RRJ 2, 367–381.
[142] M. Iacub, *Penser les droits de la naissance* (2002), 20 et seq.

CHILDREN AS VICTIMS UNDER GERMAN LAW

Gerhard Wagner

I. Factual Introduction

1. What are the most common causes of injury to children in your jurisdiction?

Statistics concerning the sources of accidents involving children are very hard to come by. The German Federal Statistical Office (*Statistisches Bundesamt*) collects data on the number of fatal accidents per year and the sources of these accidents. The relevant numbers for the year 2002 show that children under the age of ten are most likely to suffer an accident at home. Whether these conclusions also apply to the area of accidents causing physical injury but not death, is open to question. However, it seems highly likely that there is some correlation between the sources of fatal accidents and those of accidents with less serious consequences. 1

Age	<10	10–15	15–20
Total Number of Fatal Accidents	330	174	962
Road Traffic	118	115	852
Home	98	13	17
Sports/Play	35	16	9
Other	79	30	84

Source: Statistisches Bundesamt, Todesursachenstatistik, Teil VIII a – Gesundheit,
© Statistisches Bundesamt, Bonn 2004

II. Damage Caused by Parents and Other Specific Third Parties

2. In what circumstances may a parent be held liable for an injury sustained by his or her child?

(a) In what circumstances may a parent be held liable for injury resulting from his or her intentional conduct? (Liability for intent.) In particular, in what circumstances may the parent be held liable for injury resulting from his or her physical chastisement of the child?

(b) In what circumstances may a parent be held liable for injury resulting from his or her unintentional conduct? (Liability for fault.) Are there special rules

for liability of the parents? E.g. are parents liable only in case of gross negligence? Are parents held to a lower or higher standard of care? In what circumstances may a parent be held liable for injury resulting from his or her failure to protect the child from harm? (Liability for omissions.)

2 § 1664 subs. 1 *Bürgerliches Gesetzbuch* (German Civil Code, BGB) provides a statutory basis for claims of the child against his parents for injuries suffered by the child at the hands of his parents.[1] On the other hand, this provision establishes a privilege and limits the parents' responsibility to the *diligentia quam in suis* in the sense of § 277 BGB. The parents merely have to observe the same level of care and diligence they follow in their own affairs,[2] as long as they do not act intentionally or recklessly.[3] The justification for this privilege is the protection of the family against *inter-se* lawsuits which aim at little more than a redistribution of wealth from one family member to another.

3 It is a matter of debate and controversy whether parents today still enjoy the right to chastise their child physically, i.e. to inflict corporeal punishment for misdemeanours. The practical impact of the controversy is slight, as evidenced by the total lack of court decisions dealing with this issue. The reason is that even the most generous of commentators limit the right of chastisement by imposing two requirements:[4] Firstly, any physical chastisement must be motivated by an educational purpose and not by the desire to take revenge or the impulse to inflict corporeal pain. Secondly, the right of chastisement is limited to injuries of minor gravity. At the most, it is permissible for the parent to beat the child with their hand, and in a way that inflicts pain without lasting injury. As of 2000, one of the reform acts transforming family law has introduced the provision § 1631 subs. 2 cl. 2 BGB which states explicitly that corporeal punishment of children is impermissible per se. From this one has to draw the conclusion that any right of physical chastisement that might have existed in German law was abolished in the year 2000.[5]

[1] § 1664 BGB: "(1) Die Eltern haben bei der Ausübung der elterlichen Sorge dem Kind gegenüber nur für die Sorgfalt einzustehen, die sie in eigenen Angelegenheiten anzuwenden pflegen." § 1664 subs. 1 BGB provides at the same time a legal basis for claims of third parties against the child in cases where the child causes damage due to a violation of the parental custody, U. Diederichsen in: Palandt, *Kommentar zum Bürgerlichen Gesetzbuch* (65th edn. 2005), § 1664 no. 1.

[2] L. Michalski in: Erman, *Kommentar zum Bürgerlichen Gesetzbuch*, vol. II (11th edn. 2004), § 1664 no. 3.

[3] § 277 BGB: "Wer nur für diejenige Sorgfalt einzustehen hat, welche er in eigenen Angelegenheiten anzuwenden pflegt, ist von der Haftung wegen grober Fahrlässigkeit nicht befreit."

[4] Cf. A. Eser in: Schönke/Schröder, *Kommentar zum Strafgesetzbuch* (26th edn. 2001), § 223 no. 17.

[5] U. Diederichsen in: Palandt (supra fn. 1), § 1631 no. 11; P. Huber in: *Münchener Kommentar zum Bürgerlichen Gesetzbuch*, vol. VII (4th edn. 2002), § 1631 nos. 21 et seq.

3. In what circumstances may a third party (e.g. a school or local authority social services department) be held liable for failing to prevent a parent from harming his or her child?

4 The liability of a public authority, including the public school board, for any damages arising from the mistreatment of the child by his parents is a matter for the liability of public bodies under § 839 BGB, art. 34 *Grundgesetz* (German Constitution, GG). Court decisions concerning the liability of a social worker or other employee of a school or a public youth welfare office are not available. However, there has been a criminal trial in a case where social workers employed by a children's home have been held accountable for the death of a three-year-old child who had been mistreated by her mentally retarded mother during her whole short life.[6] The criminal court held that given that the social workers knew of the mother's mental state and the mistreatments committed in the past, they were under an obligation to take all the necessary steps to ensure that mother and child would not be left to themselves, to separate the child from her dangerous mother and to remove the mother's right of custody.

5 If transferred to the area of private tort law, these principles would support a damage claim brought by a mistreated child against the public youth authority. Under art. 34 GG it is the authority itself that would be liable, not the employee in person.[7]

4. What limitation periods are applied to a child's claim?

6 The regular limitation period is three years (§ 195 BGB) and runs from the end of the year in which the claim arose and in which the creditor learns or ought to have learned of the circumstances underlying the claim and of the identity of the tortfeasor, § 199 subs. 1 BGB.[8] In addition, there is another limitation period which runs irrespective of the knowledge of the victim from the day of injury. This second period, the so-called "long stop" cuts off claims brought after too long a time has lapsed since the acts complained of occurred. In the case of damage claims for injuries to life, body, health or personal freedom, the cut-off period is thirty years after occurrence of the act which caused the injury complained of, § 199 subs. 2 BGB.[9]

[6] *Oberlandesgericht* (State High Court, OLG) Stuttgart (28 May 1998), [1998] *Neue juristische Wochenschrift* (NJW), 3131 et seq.; P. Bringewat, Kommunale Jugendhilfe und strafrechtliche Garantenhaftung, [1998] NJW, 945 et seq.

[7] For details see G. Wagner, Children as Tortfeasors under German Law in: M. Martín-Casals (ed.), *Children in Tort Law Part I: Children as Tortfeasors* (2006), no. 92.

[8] § 195 BGB: "Die regelmäßige Verjährungsfrist beträgt drei Jahre."; § 199 subs. 1: "Die regelmäßige Verjährung beginnt mit dem Schluss des Jahres, in dem 1. der Anspruch entstanden ist und 2. der Gläubiger von den den Anspruch begründenden Umständen und der Person des Schuldners Kenntnis erlangt oder ohne grobe Fahrlässigkeit erlangen müsste."

[9] § 199 subs. 2 BGB: "Schadensersatzansprüche, die auf der Verletzung des Lebens, des Körpers, der Gesundheit oder der Freiheit beruhen, verjähren ohne Rücksicht auf ihre Entstehung und die Kenntnis oder grob fahrlässige Unkenntnis in 30 Jahren von der Begehung der Handlung, der Pflichtverletzung oder dem sonstigen, den Schaden auslösenden Ereignis an."

7 If the creditor (i.e. the victim) is a child, the relevant person to obtain the information required by § 199 subs. 1 BGB is not the child itself but its legal agent, i.e. the parents.[10] As this rule would frustrate most claims of the child against its parents, in this case the start of the limitation period is delayed until the child has reached full age, § 207 subs. 1 cl. 2 no. 2 BGB.[11]

8 § 208 cl. 1 BGB establishes a similar delay for claims relating to violations of the right to sexual self-determination. Here, the limitation period does not start running until the creditor has reached the age of twenty-one at the least.[12] If the victim continues to live together with the perpetrator in the same household even beyond the age of twenty-one, the limitation period remains put on hold and only starts running once the victim moves out, § 208 cl. 2 BGB.[13] These provisions guarantee that the claim does not become time-barred while the victim is living together under one roof with her or his tormentor.

III. Contributory Negligence

5. Are there any special provisions concerning contributory negligence if the tortfeasor is a child?

9 No. The contributory negligence of both children and adults is governed by § 254 BGB.[14]

[10] *Bundesgerichtshof* (Federal Supreme Court, BGH) (23.1.1962), [1993] *Versicherungsrecht* (VersR), 161, 162; BGH (8.7.1969), [1969] VersR, 906; BGH (16.5.1989), [1989] NJW, 2323, 2324; BGH (23.4.1991), [1991] NJW, 2350; OLG Frankfurt (15.11.1990), [1992] VersR, 708; OLG Celle (2.11.2000), *Verkehrsrechts-Sammlung* (VRS) 100, 250, 252 et seq.; K. Budewig in: Budewig/Gehrlein, *Das Haftpflichtrecht nach der Reform* (2002), 109 no. 5; E. Scheffen/F. Pardey, *Schadensersatz bei Unfällen mit Kindern* (2nd edn. 2002), no. 1016.

[11] § 207 subs. 1 BGB: "Die Verjährung von Ansprüchen zwischen Ehegatten ist gehemmt, solange die Ehe besteht. Das Gleiche gilt für Ansprüche zwischen … 2. Eltern und Kindern und den Ehegatten eines Elternteils und dessen Kindern während der Minderjährigkeit der Kinder …".

[12] § 208 cl. 1 BGB: "Die Verjährung von Ansprüchen wegen Verletzung der sexuellen Selbstbestimmung ist bis zur Vollendung des 21. Lebensjahres des Gläubigers gehemmt."

[13] § 208 cl. 2 BGB: "Lebt der Gläubiger von Ansprüchen wegen Verletzung der sexuellen Selbstbestimmung bei Beginn der Verjährung mit dem Schuldner in häuslicher Gemeinschaft, so ist die Verjährung auch bis zur Beendigung der häuslichen Gemeinschaft gehemmt."

[14] § 254 BGB: "Mitverschulden. (1) Hat bei der Entstehung eines Schadens ein Verschulden des Beschädigten mitgewirkt, so hängt die Verpflichtung zum Ersatz sowie der Umfang des zu leistenden Ersatzes von den Umständen, insbesondere davon ab, inwieweit der Schaden vorwiegend von dem einen oder dem anderen Teil verursacht worden ist. (2) Dies gilt auch dann, wenn sich das Verschulden des Beschädigten darauf beschränkt, dass er unterlassen hat, den Schuldner auf die Gefahr eines ungewöhnlich hohen Schadens aufmerksam zu machen, die der Schuldner weder kannte noch kennen musste, oder dass er unterlassen hat, den Schaden abzuwenden oder zu mindern. Die Vorschrift des § 278 findet entsprechende Anwendung."

6. What are the rules governing contributory negligence of the child? Do such principles follow the same lines as those governing the negligence issue itself (mirror-image)?

Contributory negligence follows the same rules as those governing the negligence issue itself: The provisions regarding the fixed minimum age and the capacity to act reasonably in § 828 BGB[15] and the standard of care applicable to children under § 276 subs. 2 BGB[16] apply *per analogiam* to the child's contributory negligence.[17] 10

7. Does the fixed minimum age for children to be liable, if any exists, also apply to the contributory negligence of the child?

A child under the age of seven cannot be held accountable for contributory negligence, § 828 subs. 1 BGB. This minimum age is raised to ten years if the damage was sustained in an accident involving a motor vehicle, a railway, or a cable car, § 828 subs. 2 cl. 1 BGB. If the child is older than seven or ten, respectively, but younger than eighteen years, the finding of contributory negligence depends on the child's capacity to understand his responsibilities, § 828 subs. 3 BGB. In the context of the child's liability for his own tortious acts, this provision stipulates that the minor has the necessary capacity only if his intellectual maturity allows him to understand that he acted wrongfully and that this wrongful conduct may result in civil liability.[18] When applying § 828 subs. 3 BGB in the context of the child's contributory negligence, the relevant criterion is whether the child had the intellectual maturity to understand that he is under a duty to protect himself from damage.[19] The intellectual maturity to appraise this duty may develop sooner or later than the aforementioned capacity to act wrongfully.[20] 11

[15] Cf. G. Wagner in: M. Martín-Casals (supra fn. 7), nos. 1–8.

[16] Cf. G. Wagner in: M. Martín-Casals (supra fn. 7), nos. 9–13.

[17] *Reichsgericht* (RG) (5.5.1902), *Entscheidungen des deutschen Reichsgerichts in Zivilsachen* (RGZ) 51, 275, 276; BGH (29.4.1953), *Entscheidungen des deutschen Bundesgerichtshofs in Zivilsachen* (BGHZ) 9, 316, 317; BGH (28.5.1957) BGHZ 24, 325, 327; R. Alff in: Reichsgerichtsrätekommentar, *Das bürgerliche Gesetzbuch mit besonderer Berücksichtigung der Rechtsprechung des Reichsgerichtshofes und des Bundesgerichtshofes* (RGRK), vol. II/1 (12th edn. 1976), § 254 no. 16; H.-J. Mertens in: Soergel, *Kommentar zum Bürgerlichen Gesetzbuch* (12th edn. 1990), § 254 no. 29; C. Grüneberg in: Bamberger/Roth, *Kommentar zum Bürgerlichen Gesetzbuch*, vol. I (2003), § 254 no. 10; H. Oetker in: *Münchener Kommentar zum Bürgerlichen Gesetzbuch*, vol. IIa (4th edn. 2003), § 254 no. 34; H. Heinrichs in: Palandt, *Kommentar zum Bürgerlichen Gesetzbuch* (65th edn. 2005) § 254 no. 13; G. Schiemann in: J. von Staudinger, *Kommentar zum Bürgerlichen Gesetzbuch – §§ 249–254 Schadensersatzrecht* (13th edn. 2005), § 254 no. 42.

[18] Cf. G. Wagner in: M. Martín-Casals (supra fn. 7), no. 4.

[19] OLG München (13.7.1998), [2000] VersR, 1030, 1032; H. Oetker in: Münchener Kommentar (supra fn. 15), § 254 no. 34; H.-J. Mertens in Soergel (supra fn. 15), § 254 no. 29; G. Schiemann in: Staudinger (supra fn. 17), § 254 no. 39.

[20] OLG Celle (20.6.1968), [1968] NJW, 2146, 2147; OLG Celle (8.2.1995), [1996] VersR, 1511, 1513; H. Oetker in: Münchener Kommentar (supra fn. 17), § 254 no. 34; H.-J. Mertens in Soergel (supra fn. 17), § 254 no. 29.

8. What is the standard of care governing the behaviour of children in the context of contributory negligence? Is such standard determined by the same principles and criteria which are relevant to the duty of care incumbent upon the child in the context of him or her being held liable?

12 The objective standard of care in § 276 subs. 2 BGB is violated if the child does not observe the level of care and diligence which a reasonable child of the same age would observe to protect himself from damage. See G. Wagner in: M. Martín-Casals (supra fn. 7), § 276 BGB nos. 9–12.

13 If the child did not take reasonable care to protect himself, the tortfeasor is liable in proportion to his fault, balanced against the victim's negligence. However, § 254 subs. 1 BGB specifically provides that liability must be assessed with due consideration to all the circumstances of the individual case. The primary factor in this respect is not fault but *causation*: It is thought to be relevant to which extent the loss has been *caused* by the tortfeasor or the victim.[21] Of course, causation in the strict sense of the term is a matter of either/or; the concept does not allow for degrees. What is really meant when it is said that the "extent" of causation must be taken into account is that the "weight" of the several causes must be determined. If the damage has not predominantly been caused by either party, the quantum of liability is determined upon consideration of the degree to which one or the other party was at *fault*.[22] The dominant view here is that the objective standard of care applies, or rather: the mixture of objective and subjective elements enshrined in the general standard of care.[23] Thus, to the extent that the behaviour of children is held to the standard of the prudent child of the same age, a subjective element is allowed in. The same semi-subjective standard also applies in the area of contributory negligence.

IV. Contribution in Equity

9. Is there a parallel (mirror-image) to liability in equity in the field of contributory negligence? If so, do the criteria determining liability in equity of the child also apply to the issue of holding him or her accountable for his or her contributory negligence?

14 If the child lacks the necessary capacity to be held accountable for contributory negligence under § 828 BGB, the child's claim for damages may nevertheless be reduced by a mirror-image-like application of § 829 BGB within the context of § 254 subs. 1 BGB.[24] Accordingly, even a child *without* the intellec-

[21] H. Oetker in: Münchener Kommentar (supra fn. 17), § 254 nos. 108 et seq.

[22] BGH (29.1.1969), [1969] NJW, 789, 790.

[23] BGH (12.2.1990), [1990] NJW, 1483, 1484; E. Deutsch, *Fahrlässigkeit und erforderliche Sorgfalt* (2nd edn. 1995), 365; G. Schiemann in: Staudinger (supra fn. 17), § 254 no. 39, 115; H.-J. Mertens in: Soergel (supra fn. 17), § 254 no. 112; cf. also G. Wagner in: M. Martín-Casals (supra fn. 7), no. 11.

[24] BGH (10.4.1962), BGHZ 37, 102, 106; G. Wagner in: *Münchener Kommentar zum Bürgerlichen Gesetzbuch*, vol. V (4th edn. 2004), § 829 no. 12; G. Schiemann in: Staudinger (supra fn. 17),

tual maturity to understand his obligation to protect himself from damage may be subjected to the operation of § 254 subs. 1 BGB if equity so requires. § 829 BGB is likewise applicable if the child has the necessary capacity in the sense of § 828 BGB but did not act negligently because an ordinary child of the same age would not have been able to act more diligently.[25]

The high barrier that has to be overcome to establish a liability in equity under § 829 BGB, namely that compensation not merely corresponds to but is required by equity[26], cautions against too lenient an application of this provision.[27] Accordingly, the courts construe § 829 BGB narrowly when applying it within § 254 subs. 1 BGB: Equity must *require* the exemption of the tortfeasor from that share of the damages attributable to the victim; the mere fact that equity *allows* that the child be made to shoulder the consequences of his own contribution is not sufficient to trigger an application of § 829 BGB within the context of § 254 subs. 1 BGB.[28] 15

10. If answered affirmatively: Is the fact that the child is privately or socially insured against the accident a factor to be considered? Is the existence of liability insurance of the tortfeasor to be taken into account? What factors have a bearing on the assessment of equitable contribution?

On the insurance issues see G. Wagner in: M. Martín-Casals (supra fn. 7), nos. 21 et seq. 16

On the general elements of equity see G. Wagner in: M. Martín-Casals (supra fn. 7), nos. 18 et seq. 17

§ 254 no. 44; J. Oechsler in: J. von Staudinger, *Kommentar zum Bürgerlichen Gesetzbuch – §§ 826–829* (13th edn. 1998), § 829 no. 66; G. Kuckuk in: Erman, *Kommentar zum Bürgerlichen Gesetzbuch*, vol. I, (11th edn. 2004), § 254 no. 26.

[25] BGH (21.5.1963), BGHZ 39, 281, 285 et seq.; J. Oechsler in: Staudinger (supra fn. 24), § 829 nos. 33, 67; A. Zeuner in: Soergel, (supra fn. 17), § 829 no. 11; G. Wagner in: Münchener Kommentar (supra fn. 24), § 829 no. 8; E. Steffen in: Reichsgerichtsrätekommentar, *Das bürgerliche Gesetzbuch mit besonderer Berücksichtigung der Rechtsprechung des Reichsgerichtshofes und des Bundesgerichtshofes* (RGRK), vol. II/5 (12th edn. 1989), § 829 no. 9.

[26] See G. Wagner in: M. Martín-Casals (supra fn. 7), no. 18.

[27] BGH (24.6.1969), [1969] NJW, 1762; BGH (26.6.1973), [1973] NJW, 1795; *Kammergericht* (KG) (31.10.1994), [1996] VersR, 235, 236.

[28] BGH (24.6.1969), [1969] NJW, 1762; BGH (26.6.1973), [1973] NJW, 1795; G. Wagner in: Münchener Kommentar (supra fn. 24), § 829 no. 17.

V. Miscellaneous

11. What are the rules for a situation in which the child is guilty of contributory negligence but the parents have also breached their duty to supervise? Is the child held accountable in any way for his or her parents' breach of the duty to supervise so that his or her claim for damages is reduced?

18 The child is held accountable for his parents' breach of the duty to supervise only under the strict conditions of § 254 subs. 2 cl. 2, 278 BGB. Pursuant to these provisions, the fault of a third party may only be attributed to the victim if the third party is the victim's legal agent[29] and if there was a contractual relationship between the child and the tortfeasor at the time the tort was committed.[30] However, even legal obligations like *negotiorum gestio* are thought to be sufficient for the application of § 254 subs. 2 cl. 2, 278 BGB.[31] Tortious conduct usually occurs outside contractual or statutory relationships between the tortfeasor and the victim. For practical purposes, it may well be said that the child is never held accountable for the parents' breach of the duty to supervise.[32]

19 Even if the stringent requirements of § 254 subs. 2 cl. 2 BGB are not met, the claim of the child may still be reduced with respect to the contributory fault of a parent. Under the principle of *Haftungseinheit*, the tortious conduct of several tortfeasors can be integrated into one if each party is responsible for one and the same cause of injury, and if the tortious acts have merged before the injury was caused so that they can be considered as one source of harm.[33] Likewise, the victim's conduct may have merged with the conduct of one of the several tortfeasors, i.e. the child's conduct with the parent's violation of their duty to supervise if the parents' fault allowed for the child's self-damaging act (*Zurechnungseinheit*).[34] Then, parent and child are held responsible for an aggregated quota of the damage with the result that the child can hold the second tortfeasor accountable only for the rest of the damage.[35] This rule operates

[29] The child's legal agents are in particular the parents (§§ 1626 subs. 1, 1631 subs. 1 BGB) and the legal guardian (*Vormund* – §§ 1793 subs. 1, 1800, 1631 subs. 1 BGB).

[30] BGH (9.2.1982), [1982] VersR, 441, 442; BGH (1.3.1988), BGHZ 103, 338, 342; H. Oetker in: Münchener Kommentar (supra fn. 17), § 254 no. 129; H. Heinrichs in: Palandt (supra fn. 17), § 254 no. 60; R. Alff in: RGRK (supra fn. 17), § 254 no. 67; H.-J. Mertens in: Soergel (supra fn. 17), § 254 no. 94; W. Kürschner, Mitverursachung und Mitverschulden in: W. Wussow (ed.), *Unfallhaftpflichtrecht* (15th edn. 2002), ch. 55 no. 15.

[31] H. Oetker in: Münchener Kommentar (supra fn. 17), § 254 no. 130; H. Heinrichs in: Palandt (supra fn. 15), § 254 no. 60.

[32] H. Oetker in: Münchener Kommentar (supra fn. 17), § 254 no. 128.

[33] BGH (16.4.1996), [1996] NJW, 2023, 2024; G. Wagner in: Münchener Kommentar (supra fn. 24), § 840 no. 26.

[34] BGH (16.4.1996), [1996] NJW, 2023, 2024; BGH (18.9.1973), BGHZ 61, 213, 218; BGH (18.4.1978), [1978] VersR, 735, 736.

[35] BGH (16.4.1996), [1996] NJW, 2023, 2024 et seq.; BGH (18.9.1973), [1974] VersR, 34, 35; H. Roth, *Haftungseinheiten bei § 254* (1982), 99; H. Messer, Haftungseinheit und Mitverschulden, [1979] *Juristenzeitung* (JZ), 385, 386; M. Gehrlein in: Bamberger/Roth, (supra fn. 17), § 426 no. 10.

only if the child has the necessary capacity under § 828 BGB.[36] In the case of traffic accidents, for example, the courts refuse to reduce the damage claim of the child in the light of contributory negligence of his parent who failed to guard it through the traffic with the relevant care.[37]

There is a third possibility to reduce the victim's claim against one of several tortfeasors. If several tortfeasors are responsible for the same damage, they are jointly and severally liable, § 840 subs. 1 BGB. The victim may claim full compensation from the tortfeasor of his choice (§ 421 cl. 1 BGB), who may then enforce rights of recourse against the other tortfeasors in the amount of their share of the damages, § 426 subs. 1 cl. 1 BGB. Problems arise if one of the tortfeasors enjoys a legal privilege protecting him from liability, like parents do vis-à-vis their children under § 1664 subs. 1 BGB. According to this provision, the parents, in exercising their parental duties, only have to observe the level of care they apply in their own affairs (*diligentia quam in suis*). Some commentators argue that the child must accept the reduction of his damage claim against the third-party tortfeasor in the amount of the fraction of damages his parents would be liable for if the shield of § 1664 subs. 1 BGB were removed.[38] The Supreme Court, however, does not follow this proposal in order to make the third-party tortfeasor answerable for the full amount of damages and to exclude his right of recourse against the parents. Accordingly, the Supreme Court allowed for full compensation in a case where a child was injured on a public playground due to both a dangerous condition of the playground premises *and* the inattentiveness of his father. It allowed the child to hold the city operating the playground accountable for the entire damage and denied the city the right to obtain a contribution from the negligent parent.[39] 20

12. Do the rules of contributory negligence also apply in the area of strict liability?

As a general rule, § 254 BGB applies in the area of strict liability *per analogiam*: If the responsibility for fault allows for a reduction of the claim, strict liability must allow for this reduction per *argumentum a maiore ad minus*.[40] 21

[36] BGH (18.9.1973), BGHZ 61, 213, 218; BGH (1.3.1988), [1988] NJW, 2667, 2668; OLG Düsseldorf (12.1.1981), [1982] VersR, 300, 301; KG (31.10.1994), [1995] *Neue Zeitschrift für Verkehrsrecht* (NZV), 109, 110; OLG Hamm (27.8.1990), [1991] NZV, 152, 154; OLG Hamm (15.12.1997), [1998] *Neue juristische Wochenschrift – Rechtsprechungsreport* (NJW-RR), 1181, 1182; G. Wagner in: Münchener Kommentar (supra fn. 24), § 840 no. 27.

[37] G. Wagner in: Münchener Kommentar (supra fn. 24), § 840 no. 27.

[38] Cf. G. Wagner in: Münchener Kommentar (supra fn. 24), § 840 no. 33; G. Spindler in: Bamberger/Roth, *Kommentar zum BGB*, vol. II (2003), § 840 no. 13.

[39] BGH (1.3.1988), BGHZ 103, 338, 344 et seq.

[40] BGH (4.4.1977), BGHZ 68, 281, 288; G. Schiemann (supra fn. 17), § 254 no. 6; H.-J. Mertens in: Soergel (supra fn. 17), § 254 no. 9.

13. Do the rules of contributory negligence apply in the area of strict liability for traffic-accidents or other areas of tort liability?

22 Some of the statutes establishing strict liability explicitly provide for the application of the general rules on comparative negligence contained in § 254 BGB. A pertinent example is § 9 *Straßenverkehrsgesetz*[41] (German Road Traffic Act, StVG) with respect to the liability of the keeper of a car. Accordingly, the rules of comparative negligence expounded elsewhere[42] also apply in the area of strict liability for road traffic accidents.

23 However, it must be borne in mind that children enjoy special protection under the rules of the road, as embodied in the *Straßenverkehrsordnung* (German Road Traffic Code, StVO). Pursuant to § 3 subs. 2a StVO, drivers have to be particularly careful in the vicinity of children, as minors are less able to control their conduct and to behave prudently.[43] To compensate for the diminished capacities of children, drivers have to reduce their speed, prepare for having to apply the brakes instantaneously at any given moment, etc. From this provision, the BGH derived the rule that the child's contribution to the accident must not reduce his damage claim insofar as the child's behaviour merely reflects his inability to behave as prudently as an adult in road traffic.[44] That may even be the case if the child's conduct – seen as the conduct of an adult – was reckless. A different result only obtains if the child behaved in a reproachable way even by the standards applicable to children of the same age.[45]

24 Reduction of the victim's claim for damages with respect to contributory negligence is ruled out as a matter of law if the child has not yet reached the age of ten, § 828 subs. 2 BGB. An exception to this privilege is carved out by cl. 2 of § 828 subs. 2 BGB if the child harmed itself intentionally. The BGH has added another exception in cases where the child harmed itself by running or driving into a car that was parked in a lawful manner in a parking lot or on the street.[46] This category involves situations where children chase each other

[41] § 9 StVG: "Mitverschulden. Hat bei der Entstehung des Schadens ein Verschulden des Verletzten mitgewirkt, so finden die Vorschriften des § 254 des Bürgerlichen Gesetzbuches mit der Maßgabe Anwendung, dass im Fall der Beschädigung einer Sache das Verschulden desjenigen, welcher die tatsächliche Gewalt über die Sache ausübt, dem Verschulden des Verletzten gleichsteht."

[42] Cf. G. Wagner in: M. Martín-Casals (supra fn. 7), nos. 120–125.

[43] § 3 subs. 2a StVO: "Die Fahrzeugführer müssen sich gegenüber Kindern, Hilfsbedürftigen und älteren Menschen, insbesondere durch Verminderung der Fahrgeschwindigkeit und durch Bremsbereitschaft, so verhalten, dass eine Gefährdung dieser Verkehrsteilnehmer ausgeschlossen ist."

[44] BGH (13.2.1990), [1990] VersR, 535, 536.

[45] BGH (13.2.1990), [1990] VersR, 535, 536.

[46] BGH (21.12.2004), [2005] NJW-RR, 327, 328 et seq.; BGH (30.11.2004), [2005] NJW, 354; BGH (30.11.2004), [2005] NJW, 356; for details see H. Kötz/G. Wagner, *Deliktsrecht* (10th edn. 2005), nos. 558 et seq.; for another view see G. Wagner in: Münchener Kommentar (supra fn. 24), § 828 no. 6.

with kickboards or bicycles or where a single child driving a bicycle on the pavement loses control and scratches a car parked on the curb. Here, it is said the accident was not due to the inability of the child to adapt to the unavoidable dangers of motor traffic.[47] Rather, the child inflicted the injury upon itself as evidenced by the fact that the same damage would have been sustained had the collision been with a tree or a wall.

14. Are adults held to a higher standard of care in their interactions with children, or when children are or may be around?

According to § 276 subs. 2 BGB, a person is held to the standard of care and diligence a reasonable person of the same social group as the tortfeasor would observe.[48] As a general rule, the level of care required of an individual is contingent upon the level of care other individuals are expected to observe: In choosing the level of care, everyone may rely on his neighbour to take the appropriate measures of safety himself. There are, however, several exceptions to this so-called *principle of reliance* (*Vertrauensgrundsatz*), one being the interaction with children. As they cannot be expected to live up to the same safety level as adults, adults have to adjust their behaviour when interacting with children.[49] Adults have to compensate for the reduced capacities of children to cope with dangers by adhering to a stricter standard of care and by taking specific safety measures aimed at the protection of minors. The less care a child is perceivably able to exercise, the more care do others interacting with him have to apply. This principle has been codified for road traffic accidents in § 3 subs. 2a StVO, see supra no. 10. 25

VI. Insurance Matters

15. Are pupils covered by private or public accident (first-party) insurance?

Pupils at public and private general and vocational schools (*allgemein- und berufsbildende Schulen*) are covered by public accident (first-party) insurance (*Gesetzliche Unfallversicherung*). Under § 2 subs. 1 no. 8 lit. b *Sozialgesetzbuch VII* (German Social Laws Vol. VII, SGB VII), school accidents are insured against if they occur during school attendance or during the attendance of supervisory measures organised by or together with the school, as long as they take place immediately before or after school.[50] The concept of "school attendance" comprises school lessons and recesses as well as breaks between 26

[47] Supra fn. 46.

[48] Cf. G. Wagner in: M. Martín-Casals (supra fn. 7), no. 11.

[49] BGH (5.5.1964), [1964] VersR, 825; BGH (22.10.1974), [1975] VersR, 87; BGH (30.1.1968), [1968] VersR, 470, 471; BGH (21.2.1978), [1978] VersR, 561; KG (9.11.1978), [1979] VersR, 137,138; BGH (29.1.1980), [1980] VersR, 863, 865; G. Wagner in: Münchener Kommentar (supra fn. 24), § 823 nos. 257 et seq.

[50] § 2 subs. 1 no. 8 lit. b SGB VII: "Kraft Gesetzes sind versichert Schüler während des Besuches von allgemein- oder berufsbildenden Schulen und während der Teilnahme an unmittelbar vor oder nach dem Unterricht von der Schule oder im Zusammenwirken mit ihr durchgeführten Betreuungsmaßnahmen".

lessons, and all other official events inside and outside the school premises, such as walking-tours, sojourns in school-holiday homes and practical trainings.

27 To the extent that children are covered by public accident insurance, the question of liability and of liability insurance on the part of schools and the communities that run them becomes moot. The reason is that §§ 104 et seq. SGB VII isolate the school from liability for the consequences of personal injury suffered by a pupil during school attendance.

16. Does this insurance cover any damage occurred on the way to school and back?

28 Public accident insurance covers accidents that occur during the way to school and back, § 8 subs. 2 no. 1 SGB VII.[51] Although this provision mandates that only the *direct* way (*unmittelbarer Weg*) from home to school and back is insured, accidents that occur during detours are nevertheless still covered if the detour was motivated by infantile curiosity or playfulness.[52] Damage that occurred on the way from school to an official event and back is covered by § 2 subs. 1 no. 8 lit. b SGB VII,[53] cf. supra no. 13.

17. Are there restrictions on damages recoverable by the child, e.g. with respect to loss of future earnings?

29 No. As children are typically not yet employed, the impairment of the child's professional development will usually not result in a loss of *current* earnings but in a retardation of the entrance into the work force and the loss of professional advancement and occupational prospects.[54] § 842 BGB explicitly stipulates that the tortfeasor's obligation to compensate the victim extends to these losses. As the damage in the sense of this provision consists of the reduction in *future* earnings[55] and not of the impairment of the ability to work in the abstract,[56] the child has to sue the tortfeasor in court and motion for a declaratory judgment that confirms the tortfeasor's duty to compensate for the loss of future earnings.[57]

[51] § 8 subs. 2 no. 1 SGB VII: "Versicherte Tätigkeiten sind auch das Zurücklegen des mit der versicherten Tätigkeit zusammenhängenden unmittelbaren Weges nach und von dem Ort der Tätigkeit."

[52] B. Schulin/R. Schlegel, *Handbuch des Sozialversicherungsrechts*, vol. II (1996), § 18 no. 73.

[53] B. Schulin/R. Schlegel (supra fn. 52), § 18 no. 72; J. Schmitt, *Kommentar zum Sozialgesetzbuch VII – Gesetzliche Unfallversicherung* (1998), § 8 no. 142.

[54] W.-D. Dressler, „Verdienstausfall" (noch) nicht Erwerbstätiger in: W. Wussow (ed.), *Unfallhaftpflichtrecht* (15th edn. 2002), ch. 34 no. 4; G. Wagner in: Münchener Kommentar (supra fn. 24), §§ 842, 843 no. 49; BGH (6.6.2000), [2000] NJW, 3287, 3288.

[55] BGH (2.2.1965), [1965] VersR, 489, 491; BGH (25.1.1968), [1968] VersR, 396, 398; BGH (26.10.1976), [1977] VersR, 130, 131; BGH (24.10.1978), [1978] VersR, 1170; BGH (20.3.1984), [1984] VersR, 639, 640.

[56] BGH (5.5.1970), [1970] VersR, 766, 768; BGH (7.12.1976), [1977] VersR, 282.

[57] R. Rixecker in: R. Geigel (ed.), *Der Haftpflichtprozess* (22nd edn. 1997), ch. 4 no. 154.

VII. Damage Issues

18. If damages for loss of earnings are available, what are the principles governing their assessment?

Pursuant to § 287 *Zivilprozessordnung* (German Code of Civil Procedure, ZPO), the burden upon the claimant to prove the amount of the damages sustained at the hand of the defendant is lessened as the court enjoys broad discretion to fix the amount of loss.[58] § 252 cl. 2 BGB further facilitates the assessment of the loss of future earnings by establishing a rebuttable presumption that these earnings consist of the monies the child could have reasonably been expected to earn later in his life. Due regard has to be given to the development of the job market and the circumstances of the individual case, in particular the dispositions and arrangements the child or his parents have made for his professional life.[59] 30

As the child is not yet employed and, depending on his age, will continue to be unemployed during the near future, only rough estimates can be made. The younger the child, the more difficult is the assessment.[60] The courts try to accommodate these difficulties working from the basis of § 287 ZPO. In the absence of special circumstances, it must be assumed that a child has a chance to be welcomed by the job market and that it would take such chances instead of remaining idle.[61] If the child's professional development is already foreseeable, the lost earnings have to be estimated on the basis of an ordinary advancement on the particular career path the child most probably would have chosen.[62] If the child has had to abandon his education due to the tort, the court has to examine whether he would have been able to finish it successfully, with due regard to be given to the child's intellectual capacities and personal talents. If these capacities and talents have not yet become apparent, the court has to draw on the educational and professional development of sisters and brothers, the occupation of the parents and – as a last resort – the average income of children from families living in the same social environment.[63] 31

[58] See G. Wagner in: Münchener Kommentar (supra fn. 24), §§ 842, 843 no. 20 with further references.

[59] BGH (2.2.1965), [1965] VersR, 489, 490.

[60] G. Wagner in: Münchener Kommentar (supra fn. 24), §§ 842, 843 no. 49.

[61] BGH (17.1.1995), [1995] NJW, 1023, 1024; BGH (14.1.1997), [1997] NJW, 937, 938; BGH (3.3.1998), [1998] NJW, 1634, 1636.

[62] E. Scheffen/F. Pardey (supra fn. 10), no. 894; G. Wagner in: Münchener Kommentar (supra fn. 24), § 843 no. 49.

[63] OLG Hamm (26.11.1997), [2000] VersR, 234, 235; cf. also OLG Frankfurt (28.10.1987), [1989] VersR, 48; OLG Karlsruhe (25.11.1988), [1989] VersR, 1101, 1102; W.-D. Dressler (supra fn. 54), ch. 34 no. 7; R. Rixecker in: R. Geigel (supra fn. 57), ch. 4 no. 155; G. Wagner in: Münchener Kommentar (supra fn. 24), § 843 no. 49; E. Scheffen, Erwerbsausfallschaden bei verletzten und getöteten Personen (§§ 842 bis 844 BGB), [1990] VersR, 926, 928; D. Medicus, Schadensersatz bei Verletzung vor Eintritt in das Erwerbsleben, [1994] *Deutsches Autorecht* (DAR), 442, 447.

32 The Supreme Court generally allows for a discount on the amount of damages if the prediction of the future appears to be particularly uncertain.[64] Likewise, if several scenarios are probable, the lost earnings should be calculated for each scenario and aggregated with due regard to the respective degrees of probability.[65] If, by way of example, it is equally probable that the daughter of a successful attorney would have earned an annual income of € 100,000 or € 50,000, she ought to be compensated with an annuity of € 75,000.

19. Which of the child's non-material interests are protected in your jurisdiction? May the child, for example, sue for impairment of intellectual or social development, the onset of behavioural problems, or reduced employment prospects?

33 German law makes compensation for non-pecuniary losses contingent upon the infringement of health, bodily integrity, personal liberty and sexual self-determination (§ 253 BGB). Where a child has sustained personal injury and suffered a permanent disability, damages for non-pecuniary losses such as pain and suffering and loss of amenities of life will easily be awarded. As far as loss of amenities is concerned, it is even thought that the amount awarded should be increased for the simple reason that a person injured at a young age will have a long time to live with the handicap.[66]

34 Educational malpractice has not been developed as a category of case, let alone a separate tort in German law. If such a case were brought before the German courts, it may be predicted with some confidence that, regardless of the determination of the liability issue, damages for non-pecuniary loss would not be awarded. Failure to develop one's abilities is a different category of loss to personal injury, i.e. damage to health or bodily integrity. Although the German courts have been prepared to grant compensation for infringements of the general right of personality[67] it is highly unlikely that educational malpractice will be developed into another compartment of the general right of personality.

20. Are there special rules for the assessment of damages sustained by a child, e.g. with respect to pain and suffering?

35 No. Significant for the assessment of damages for pain and suffering are for both adults and children the gravity of the injury, the severity and length of the

[64] BGH (17.1.1995), [1995] NJW, 1023, 1024; BGH (24.1.1995), [1995] NJW, 2227, 2228; BGH (17.2.1998), [1998] NJW, 1633, 1634; BGH (6.6.2000), [2000] NJW, 3287, 3288; BGH (6.2.2001), [2001] NJW, 1640, 1641.

[65] G. Wagner in: Münchener Kommentar (supra fn. 24), §§ 842, 843 no. 49.

[66] H. Oetker in: Münchener Kommentar (supra fn. 17), § 253 no. 43.

[67] BGH (14.2.1958), BGHZ 26, 349 = [1958] NJW, 827 with a note by K. Larenz = [1958] JZ, 571 with approving article by H. Coing; cf. also G. Wagner, Germany in: H. Koziol/A. Warzilek (eds.), *The Protection of Personality Rights against Invasions by Mass Media* (2005), nos. 11 et seq.

suffering, the extent of the victim's perception of the injury and finally the degree of the tortfeasor's fault.[68] The perception of the victim is the relevant point of view. A nine year old child, whose intellectual capacity had not been impaired by the injury, was deemed to have grasped the core consequences of the injury, in particular his own imminent death and thus was awarded damages for the psychological strains that had been sustained.[69]

Damages for pain and suffering may even be awarded if the tortfeasor and the victim are members of the same family. However, when calculating the damages, due regard must be paid to the monies needed to support the family in everyday life.[70] The latter restriction is removed if the victim is of full age and no longer living in the same household with his parents.[71] 36

21. Does a small child have a claim for damages for pain and suffering, if he or she is deprived of his or her parents by a tortious act? If so, may the claim be denied on the ground that the child does not feel the loss?

§ 253 subs. 2 BGB limits the award of damages for pain and suffering to infringements of body, health, freedom and the right of sexual self-determination.[72] The victim's life is deliberately not mentioned in this provision; the death of the victim does not by itself establish a right to damages for pain and suffering.[73] Such a claim may mature, however, where the victim initially survived the injury in order to die after some period of agony and mortal fear. In such cases, a damage claim for pain and suffering arises in the person of the deceased, which becomes part of his estate upon death.[74] This claim, however, compensates for the suffering of the primary *victim*, not for that of the child in its role as an heir, and is therefore usually not substantial, in particular if the victim did not long survive the injury or if he did not regain consciousness after the time of infliction of the injury and therefore never was aware of his condition.[75] 37

German law does not recognise a remedy for bereavement, i.e. damages for the loss of a loved person.[76] For practical purposes an exception is made where 38

[68] BGH (12.5.1998), [1998] NJW, 2741, 2743; H. Heinrichs in: Palandt (supra fn. 17), § 253 no. 16.

[69] OLG Köln (9.1.2002), [2003] NJW-RR, 308, 309.

[70] BGH (18.6.1973), [1973] VersR, 941, 943 et seq.; BGH (8.7.1988), [1989] VersR, 1056.

[71] E. Scheffen/F. Pardey (supra fn. 10), no. 940.

[72] § 253 subs. 2 BGB: "Ist wegen einer Verletzung des Körpers, der Gesundheit, der Freiheit oder der sexuellen Selbstbestimmung Schadensersatz zu leisten, kann auch wegen des Schadens, der nicht Vermögensschaden ist, eine billige Entschädigung in Geld gefordert werden."

[73] BGH (12.5.1998), BGHZ 138, 388, 391 et seq.; E. Deutsch/H.-J. Ahrens, *Deliktsrecht* (4th edn. 2002), no. 469; G. Wagner in: Münchener Kommentar (supra fn. 24), § 844 no. 4.

[74] BGH (6.12.1994), [1995] VersR, 353, 354.

[75] BGH (12.5.1998), BGHZ 138, 388. See supra no. 19 for the victim's perception of the injury as the relevant point of view.

[76] G. Wagner, Ersatz immaterieller Schäden: Bestandsaufnahme und europäische Perspektiven, [2004] JZ, 319, 325 et seq.

the child suffered an injury to his own health in the form of a "shock" upon watching the death of a parent or upon learning from this incident, so-called *Schockschaden.*[77] Damages for mental shock are not granted lightly, however, but only upon a showing of a mental condition that not only exceeds mere sadness, however intense, but is pathological. Although premised on an injury of the child himself, the child must accept reduction of his damage claim in the amount of the contributory negligence of the deceased: Given that the close relationship between the deceased and the relative works to establish the causal link between the death of the parent and the impairment of the child's health, the same consideration justifies the attribution of the deceased's contributory conduct to the child as secondary victim.[78]

22. With respect to a damage claim for the costs of medical treatment: May the tortfeasor defend himself by pointing to the fact that the parents have a duty to maintain the child?

39 No. It is a general principle that the tortfeasor shall not be released from liability and that his obligation to compensate the victim shall not be diminished at the expense of those that are under an obligation to pay alimony, § 843 subs. 4 BGB.[79] Accordingly, the parent's obligation to support the child must be ignored when determining the tortfeasor's duty to pay damages, as the purpose of the parent's obligation is to benefit the child, not the tortfeasor.[80] This principle applies to the costs of medical treatment as well, i.e. the tortfeasor has to compensate for these losses even if the parents have already paid for the treatment.[81] The child's claim is only reduced to the extent the parents saved the costs of support during the time their child spent in hospital.[82]

40 This principle even applies where the child has been adopted after the death of its biological parent(s) and the adoptive parent(s) are providing support. The adoption does not curtail the child's claim for an annuity against the tortfeasor under § 844 subs. 2 BGB.[83]

[77] BGH (11.5.1971), [1971] NJW, 1883, 1884; BGH (4.4.1989), [1989] NJW, 2317, 2318; OLG Nürnberg (27.2.1998), [1998] NJW, 2293; G. Wagner in: Münchener Kommentar (supra fn. 24), § 823 nos. 76 et seq.

[78] BGH (11.5.1971), [1971] NJW, 1885; E. Scheffen/F. Pardey (supra fn. 10), no. 956.

[79] Cf. G. Wagner in: Münchener Kommentar (supra fn. 24), §§ 842, 843 no. 79.

[80] OLG Celle (16.12.1968), [1969] NJW, 1765, 1766; BGH (22.9.1970), [1970] NJW, 2061, 2063; OLG Frankfurt/M. (22.1.1998), [1998] *Monatsschrift für Deutsches Recht* (MDR), 1228; G. Spindler in: Bamberger/Roth (supra fn. 38), § 843 no. 35.

[81] H. Sprau in: Palandt, (supra fn. 1), § 843 no. 22; G. Spindler in: Bamberger/Roth (supra fn. 38), § 843 no. 36.

[82] OLG Celle (16.12.1968), [1969] NJW, 1765, 1766.

[83] BGH (22.9.1970), [1970] NJW, 2061, 2063.

23. In case of wrongful life: Does the child have a damage claim against the physician or a health care institution?

The term *wrongful life* refers to cases where a *child* claims damages for being born with a mental or physical disability that has been caused prior to birth or could have been detected during prenatal diagnostic investigation. The particular feature of these wrongful life cases is that the disability could not have been cured, even when detected, the only alternative solution being an abortion. Outside the area of this narrowly defined category it is well accepted that the foetus enjoys the full protection of the law of delict.[84] 41

Where the fault of the doctor is that he negligently failed to diagnose a congenital disability of the child during pregnancy and thus prevented his parents from considering an abortion, the BGH denies the child any claim for damages, be it grounded in tort law or derived from the contractual relationship between the mother and the doctor.[85] The child is held not to have a claim for damages under § 823 subs. 1 BGB since the doctor was not under a duty to prevent the life of a disabled child. In the eyes of the court, such a duty would run afoul of the core idea of tort law which is to protect the integrity of personal rights, with the right to life being the most solemn of all. Neither can the child derive a claim for damages from the contractual relationship between the mother and the doctor. As statutory law vests the right of abortion in the mother alone and for her own interest, the court held that the contract cannot be constructed to confer an implied right of abortion on the child as third party beneficiary.[86] Ultimately, every human being has to accept his life as given to him and has no claim against others to prevent or destroy it.[87] 42

Commentators have criticized this jurisprudence, arguing that only a claim for damages vested in the child would guarantee him sufficient financial means after the death of the parents. It is thought to be contradictory to deny the child a claim for damages under reference to respect for human life, and on the other hand put the dignity of the child's life into peril by disallowing him the necessary funds.[88] In the absence of a claim in his own right, the child would have to rely on social aid in that situation where the need is the greatest, i.e. upon the parents' death.[89] Other commentators add that the doctor should be re- 43

[84] G. Wagner in: Münchener Kommentar (supra fn. 24), § 823 nos. 87 et seq.; for details see below nos. 49 et seq.

[85] BGH (18.1.1983), BGHZ 86, 240, 251 et seq.

[86] BGH (18.1.1983), BGHZ 86, 240, 251 et seq.

[87] BGH (18.1.1983), BGHZ 86, 240, 251 et seq.

[88] E. Deutsch, Das behindert geborene Kind als Anspruchsberechtigter, [2003] NJW, 26, 27; A. Reinhart, "Wrongful life" – Gibt es ein Recht auf Nichtexistenz?, [2001] VersR, 1081, 1084; T. Winter, Leben als Schaden? Vom Ende des französischen Sonderwegs, [2002] JZ, 330, 331; G. Schiemann in: Erman (supra fn. 17), § 823 no. 22.

[89] A. Reinhart, [2001] VersR, 1081, 1087; M. Fuchs, Die zivilrechtliche Haftung des Arztes aus der Aufklärung über Genschäden, [1981] NJW, 610, 613; E. Deutsch, Unerwünschte Empfängnis, unerwünschte Geburt und unerwünschtes Leben, verglichen mit wrongful conception, wrongful birth und wrongful life des anglo-amerikanischen Rechts, [1984] MDR, 793, 795.

sponsible for his professional failure,[90] and that there are no reasons to release him from this burden at the expense of the tax-payers.[91] Finally, the acknowledgement of a liability in tort would not only provide for compensation but would also allow professional standards of care to be determined.[92] These arguments, however, have not convinced the BGH, which continues to deny the child any claim for damages.[93] The discussion is heavily influenced by the personal attitude of judges and commentators towards the divisive issue of abortion.

44 The term *wrongful birth* refers to cases where an unwanted child is born and the *parents* claim damages as a compensation for their obligation to render child support. The BGH acknowledged a right to damages in cases where a healthy child was born due to a failed sterilisation,[94] and where a child was born disabled but could have been lawfully aborted, had the prenatal investigation been conducted at all or with the necessary care.[95] The core argument was that the damage inflicted upon the parents was not the "child" as a human being but the obligation to pay alimony. The second Senate of the *Bundesverfassungsgericht* (German Constitutional Court, BVerfG) rejected this argument later on in an *obiter dictum*, arguing that the qualification of the child as cause for damage violated the guarantee of human dignity in art. 1 subs. 1 GG.[96] The BGH did not follow suit and insisted that the calculation of the damages based upon the amount of alimony does not put the child's dignity into question.[97] The first Senate of the *Bundesverfassungsgericht* finally confirmed this jurisprudence for cases where the medical treatment promised by the doctor was lawful.[98]

45 The doctor's contractual duty to compensate for the alimony payments of the mother hinges on the contract for medical treatment with the purpose of preventing the birth of an unwanted child in the interest of avoiding the associated obligation to support the child.[99] Further requirements are that the medical treatment was lawful and that the doctor acted negligently.[100] If the doctor omit-

[90] G. Wagner in: Münchener Kommentar (supra fn. 24), § 823 no. 91.
[91] A. Reinhart, [2001] VersR, 1081, 1086.
[92] M. Fuchs, [1981] NJW, 610, 613; E. Deutsch, Das Kind oder sein Unterhalt als Schaden – Eine Methode, Grundfrage des geltenden Rechts, [1995] VersR, 609, 613 et seq.
[93] BGH (22.11.1983), [1984] NJW, 658; BGH (6.1.2001), [2002] VersR, 192.
[94] BGH (18.3.1980), [1980] NJW, 1450, 1451.
[95] BGH (18.1.1983), [1983] NJW, 1371, 1372.
[96] BVerfG (28.5.1993), [1993] NJW, 1751, 1764.
[97] BGH (16.11.1993), [1994] NJW, 788, 791.
[98] BVerfG (12.11.1997), [1998] NJW, 519, 522.
[99] BGH (22.11.1983), [1984] NJW, 658, 660; BGH (9.7.1985), [1985] NJW, 2752, 2755; H. Oetker in: Münchener Kommentar (supra fn. 17), § 249 no. 35.
[100] BGH (18.1.1982), [1983] NJW, 1371, 1372; BGH (22.11.1983), [1984] NJW, 658, 660; BGH (27.11.1984), [1985] NJW, 671, 672; BGH (9.7.1985), [1985] NJW, 2752, 2754; BGH (28.3.1995), [1995] NJW, 1609, 1610; BGH (4.12.2001), [2002] NJW, 886, 888; BGH (19.2.2002), [2002] NJW, 1489, 1490; BGH (18.6.2002), [2002] NJW, 2636, 2637; BGH (24.6.2003), [2003] *Zeitschrift für das gesamte Familienrecht* (FamRZ), 1378, 1379; H. Oetker in: Münchener Kommentar (supra fn. 17), § 249 no. 34.

ted or misconducted the prenatal investigation, the mother has to prove that the proper diagnosis would have induced her to decide for an abortion. In determining whether sufficient evidence has been supplied, the court has to bear in mind the difficulties involved in proving *ex post* that the mother would have decided in favour of an abortion *ex ante* had she known the correct diagnosis.[101]

While contraceptive measures[102] and the provision of genetic information together with medical advice prior to procreation[103] are lawful without doubt, the lawfulness of abortion is a difficult and much contested issue. Might a doctor be held liable for a failure to inform the mother about congenital disabilities of the embryo that would allow her to terminate the pregnancy? Here, the lawfulness of the doctor's conduct is a matter of criminal law. Under the relevant German statutes, abortion is *lawful* if the pregnancy puts the potential mother's life or her physical or mental health into danger and *interuptio* is the only possible solution to avert the danger to her life or health, § 218a subs. 2 *Strafgesetzbuch* (German Criminal Code, StGB). Of course, the consent of the pregnant woman is also required; there may never be an abortion against the mother's will. A second prong of justification concerns women who have been sexually abused, when it seems likely that the child was fathered by the rapist, § 218a subs. 3 StGB. The mere fact that the child is likely to be born disabled is no basis in itself to make abortion lawful.[104] Even in these cases, the decisive factor remains the health of the potential mother; if her physical or mental health is put in jeopardy by the prospect of having a severely disabled child, an abortion is legal under § 218a subs. 2 StGB.[105] However, German criminal law is much more complex in that it not only operates on the basis of the distinction between lawful and wrongful abortion but distinguishes once more within the latter category. Even a "wrongful" abortion will *not* be punished if the pregnant woman participates in a counselling session aimed at encouraging her to continue the pregnancy, and provided that the abortion takes place less than twelve weeks after conception, § 218a subs. 1 StGB. If these requirements are not fulfilled an abortion is not only wrongful but will also be punishable. 46

This set of complicated distinctions forms the basis on which the BGH has built its jurisprudence in wrongful birth cases involving abortion. A damage claim brought by the mother is allowed provided that abortion would have been a lawful means for interrupting the pregnancy; the mere fact that it 47

[101] BGH (15.7.2003), [2003] NJW, 3411, 3412.

[102] BGH (29.6.1976), [1976] NJW, 1790; BGH (16.11.1993), [1994] NJW, 788, 790 (sterilisation); S. Hauberichs, *Haftung für neues Leben im deutschen und englischen Recht,* (1998), 1417; G. Müller, Fortpflanzung und ärztliche Haftung in: *Festschrift für E. Steffen* (1995), 355, 356.

[103] BVerfG (12.11.1998), [1998] NJW, 519, 521; BGH (16.11.1993), [1994] NJW, 788, 790.

[104] This justification for an abortion was abolished in 1995 by the Pregnancy and Family Aid Reform Act, *Bundesgesetzblatt I* (BGBl.) 1995, 1050. The purpose of this rule change was to clarify that the child's disability may by itself never justify an abortion, cf. the Reform Bill in BT-Dr. 13/1850, 26.

[105] BGH (18.6.2002), [2002] NJW, 2636, 2637 = BGHZ 151, 133; BGH (15.7.2003), [2003] NJW, 3411, 3412.

would not have been punishable does not suffice.[106] Provided that abortion would have been legal and the exercise of this choice has been frustrated through the negligence of the doctor, both the mother *and* her husband are entitled to damages as both of them are creditors of the doctor's contractual duty to take reasonable care in exercising his professional tasks.[107] These principles also apply if the parents are divorced,[108] but not to unmarried couples.[109] Where a doctor violated duties of care in the course of prenatal treatment of the pregnant woman, but an abortion would have been wrongful anyway – whether it be punishable or not – no damage claim lies.[110]

48 The BGH does not limit the damage award to the additional funds necessary to support a *disabled* child but grants the *entire* alimony: The point of reference for computation of damages is the situation of the parents without a child, not their life with a healthy one.[111] Otherwise, the damages would indeed amount to assessing the handicap of the child; this is thought to be irreconcilable with the guarantee of human dignity in art. 1 subs. 1 GG.[112] As a result, the doctor has to indemnify the parents in an amount that reflects the average needs of a child of the same age.[113] Any additional monies needed to allow for the elevated living standard of the parents will not be covered.[114] If the child has been born healthy, the claim for damages is limited to when the child has reached the age of maturity, i.e. eighteen years.[115] In order to avoid a crushing tort liability, the courts decided that the doctor's duty to compensate does not comprise the loss of earnings the parents sustain while taking care of their child.[116]

24. Concerning the liability for pre-natal injuries: Are third parties liable to the child? May the mother be liable to the child, for example, for excessive consumption of alcohol or even for an omission to procure treatment?

49 The *nasciturus* is not a legal person, as the concept of legal person is tied to the consummation of delivery, § 1 BGB. However, this limitation does not en-

[106] For details see G. Wagner in: Münchener Kommentar (supra fn. 24), § 823 no. 84.

[107] BGH (18.6.2002), [2002] NJW, 2636, 2637 = BGHZ 151, 133; BGH (18.1.1983), [1983] NJW, 1371, 1373; BGH (18.3.1980), [1980] NJW, 1452, 1455 et seq. (sterilisation).

[108] BGH (2.12.1980), [1981] NJW, 630, 632.

[109] Explicitly left open in BGH (27.11.1984), [1985] NJW, 671, 672. The jurisprudence also denies the inclusion of the male partner into the contract if he is not of full age, BGH (19.2.2002), [2002] NJW, 1489, 1490.

[110] BGH (24.6.2003), [2003] FamRZ, 1378, 1379; BGH (19.2.2002), [2002] NJW, 1489, 1490; BGH (18.6.2002), [2002] NJW, 2636, 2637 = BGHZ 151, 133.

[111] BGH (18.3.1980), [1980] NJW, 1452, 1455; BGH (22.11.1983), [1984] NJW, 658, 660; BGH (16.11.1993), [1994] NJW, 788, 793; BGH (4.3.1997), [1997] NJW, 1638, 1640; BGH (18.6.2002), [2002] NJW, 2636, 2637.

[112] BGH (16.11.1993), [1994] NJW, 788, 793.

[113] BGH (16.11.1993), [1994] NJW, 788, 792; BGH (4.3.1997), [1997] NJW, 1638, 1640.

[114] BGH (18.3.1980), [1980] NJW, 1452, 1455.

[115] G. Müller, Unterhalt für ein Kind als Schaden, [2003] NJW, 697, 706; BGH (18.3.1980), [1980] NJW, 1452, 1456. If the child is born disabled the duty to pay damages may continue until the end of the child's life, BGH (22.11.1983), [1984] NJW, 658, 660.

[116] BGH (2.12.1980), [1981] VersR, 278, 280; BGH (4.3.1997), [1997] NJW, 1638, 1640.

tail that the embryo lacks protection under § 823 subs. 1 BGB against prenatal injuries.[117] Accordingly, the Supreme Court has awarded damages to a child in a case where the mother was injured and the embryo suffered with her.[118] According to the same theory, a car driver who severely injured an unborn child's father was held liable to compensate the child who was born with disabilities after the mother suffered a shock with subsequent labour of 48 hours duration upon learning of the harm suffered by her husband.[119] Damages have even been awarded in cases where the injury occurred *prior* to conception, for example where the mother was infected with lues and transmitted this infection to the child.[120] The child may also claim damages for injuries that occurred shortly before or after the birth due to the misconduct of an obstetrician[121] or due to an improper abortion.[122] Those claims for *perinatal injuries* do not necessarily sound in tort, since the *nasciturus* is a creditor of the obstetrician's contractual duty to take reasonable care in exercising his professional task.[123]

Highly disputed is the liability of the *mother* towards her child for injuries caused by the mother's lifestyle, like the exercise of high-risk sport activities or the excessive consumption of alcohol, pharmaceuticals or other drugs. Some commentators reject any liability in this regard,[124] arguing that the pregnancy is part of the mother's sphere of privacy protected by art. 2 subs. 1, art. 1 subs. 1 GG[125] so that the mother's duty of care towards the child is subject to different rules than those governing the liability of third parties.[126] Other commentators counsel against the complete exemption of the mother from 50

117 BGH (11.1.1972), [1972] NJW, 1126; BGH (18.1.1983), [1983] NJW, 1371, 1374; BGH (6.12.1988), [1989] NJW, 1538, 1539; OLG Celle (2.11.2000), VRS 100, 250; G. Wagner in: Münchener Kommentar (supra fn. 24), § 823 no. 87; J. Hager in: J. von Staudinger, *Kommentar zum Bürgerlichen Gesetzbuch – §§ 823–825* (13th edn. 1999), § 823 no. B 42; A. Zeuner in: Soergel (supra. fn. 25), § 823 no. 21; K. Larenz/C.-W.Canaris, *Lehrbuch des Schuldrechts*, vol. II/2 (13th edn. 1994), § 76 II 1 h, 385.

118 BGH (11.1.1972), BGHZ 58, 48.

119 BGH (5.2.1985), BGHZ 93, 351.

120 BGH (20.12.1952), [1953] NJW, 417, 418; K. Larenz/C.-W.Canaris (supra fn. 117), § 76 II 1 h, 385.

121 BGH (11.1.1972), [1972] NJW, 1126, 1127; BGH (6.12.1988), [1989] NJW, 1538, 1539 et seq.; K. Larenz/C.-W.Canaris (supra fn. 117), § 76 II 1 h, 385; J. Hager in: Staudinger (supra fn. 117), § 823 no. B 42; A. Zeuner in: Soergel (supra. fn. 25), § 823 no. 21; H. Franzki, Neue Dimension in der Arzthaftung: Schäden bei der Geburtshilfe und Wrongful life als Exponenten einer Entwicklung?, [1990] VersR, 1181, 1184.

122 BVerfG (28.5.1993), [1993] NJW, 1751, 1764.

123 BGH (10.11.1970), [1971] NJW, 241, 242; KG (24.4.1980), [1981] VersR, 681, 682; Schmitt in: *Münchener Kommentar zum Bürgerlichen Gesetzbuch*, vol. I (4th edn. 2001), § 1 no. 36; H. Franzki, [1990] VersR, 1181, 1184.

124 H. Stoll, Zur Deliktshaftung für vorgeburtliche Gesundheitsschäden in: *Festschrift H. C. Nipperdey I* (1965), 739, 758 et seq.; J. Hager in: Staudinger (supra fn. 117), § 823 no. B 49.

125 Cf. for the pregnancy as part of the mother's sphere of privacy, BVerfG (25.2.1975), *Entscheidungen des Bundesverfassungsgerichts* (BVerfGE) 39, 1 (43); G. Spindler in: Bamberger/Roth (supra fn. 38), § 823 no. 761.

126 G. Fischer, "Wrongful life" Haftung für die Geburt eines behinderten Kindes, [1984] *Juristische Schulung* (JuS), 434, 439; W. Selb, Schädigung des Menschen vor Geburt – ein Problem der Rechtsfähigkeit, [1966] *Archiv für die civilistische Praxis* (AcP) 166, 76, 118; H. Stoll (supra fn. 124), 739, 758; E. Steffen in: RGRK (supra fn. 25), § 823 no. 13.

any duty of care,[127] arguing that the right to abortion enshrined in § 218a StGB shows that the mother's right to dispose of the child's life is not without limits.[128] Of course, the mother enjoys the benefits of the privilege defined in § 1664 subs. 1 BGB in relation to her unborn child, i.e. liability is limited to intentional or reckless acts.[129] For details see supra no. 2. Ultimately the interests of mother and child have to be balanced in order to protect the child and by the same token allow the mother a lifestyle that is not subjected to exaggerated exigencies.[130]

[127] G. Wagner in: Münchener Kommentar (supra fn. 24), § 823 no. 88; W. Selb, [1966] AcP 166, 76, 118.

[128] G. Wagner in: Münchener Kommentar (supra fn. 24), § 823 no. 88.

[129] G. Spindler in: Bamberger/Roth (supra fn. 35), § 823 no. 761; D. Coester-Waltjen, Der nasciturus in der hirntoten Mutter in: *Festschrift für J. Gernhuber* (1993), 837, 847 et seq.; W. Selb, [1966] AcP 166, 76, 127; G. Wagner in: Münchener Kommentar (supra fn. 24), § 823 no. 88.

[130] G. Wagner in: Münchener Kommentar (supra fn. 24), § 823 no. 88.

CHILDREN AS VICTIMS UNDER ITALIAN LAW

Giovanni Comandé and Luca Nocco

I. Factual Introduction

1. What are the most common causes of injury to children in your jurisdiction? In what proportion of cases are actions brought for damages in tort? How many of these are successful? (Plus any other relevant factual data.)

In Italy, the most frequent causes of damage to those under the age of majority arise out of the special characteristics and limitations which are a feature of youth, and can therefore be partially distinguished from those applicable to people in general. Broadly speaking, we can identify six areas of interest. 1

In the first place, there is an injury rate arising out of road accidents which differs from the data concerning people over the age of majority, first and foremost because those who have not reached the age of eighteen are not permitted to hold a driving licence. As regards motorcycles, the legislative trend over recent years has been consistently to equate the duties involved to those applicable to car driving (see *Decreto Legislativo* (D. Lgs.) of 30 April 1992 (*Nuovo codice della strada*: the new road traffic code)). 2

It is important to stress that deaths caused by road accidents among minors have greatly decreased in the last quarter of a century. A report by ISTAT (Italian National Institute of Statistics) points out that in 1998 5,857 minors were killed compared to 9,511 in 1975. 3

The sexual abuse of minors is undoubtedly also an important aspect, so that long-awaited legislative action was finally taken with the issue of *legge* (act, L.) no. 66 of 15 February 1996 (*Norme contro la violenza sessuale*: law against sexual violence). The most recent statistical data – provided by the *Centro Nazionale di documentazione e analisi per l'infanzia e l'adolescenza*, established by the Welfare Ministry – shows a 43% decrease in reported sexual abuse of minors in Italy in 2001 compared to 2000. According to this report, most cases of abuse are reported in southern Italy, and the risk increases significantly if the child is female (67% of cases). 4

5 Furthermore the assaults committed within the home in the exercise of so-called parental right of chastisement (*ius corrigendi*) should be mentioned (on this point, see art. 571 of the criminal code, *Abuso dei mezzi di correzione o di disciplina*: abuse of methods of correction),[1] as well as every other kind of maltreatment of minors by those who have a relationship involving their *educazione, istruzione, cura, vigilanza o custodia*: upbringing, education, care, supervision or custody (art. 572 of the criminal code, *Maltrattamenti in famiglia o verso fanciulli*: abuse in the family environment or of children). It should be recalled that the commission of such abuse of family members, among other acts, can result in the loss of parental authority (art. 34 of the criminal code and art. 330 of the *Codice civile* (Italian civil code, c.c.); and see art. 333 of the civil code for penalties in the case of conduct which is not so serious as to bring about the loss of parental authority, but sufficiently so for other measures to be adopted).[2] Still in the context of assaults within the home environment, imprisonment, as an alternative sanction to financial penalties, should be mentioned; this is provided for under art. 570 of the criminal code in cases of infringement of the duty to provide for the family, and under art. 591 of the criminal code in the case of the abandonment of minors or those under an incapacity.[3] The statistical data demonstrate a degree of domestic violence which, although quite probably lessened as a result of change in the socio-cultural climate, still persists as a problem which should be more effectively addressed. As ISTAT has shown, there are still, although not many, cases of infanticide (5 in 1998), while there has been a dramatic increase in abandonments of minors and persons under an incapacity, from 163 in 1990 to 456 in 1998. The cases of infringement of the duty to provide for the family, on the other hand, are fewer than in the past (5,673 in 1986 and 4,631 in 1998), while there is an increase in the domestic violence cases (2,225 cases in 1986 compared to 2,829 in 1998).

6 Another context in which the number of offences against minors (with resulting disadvantage to them) is particularly high, is to be found in the practice of taking minors from developing countries to Western countries to be sold to

[1] However, given the different cultural and social environment, legal scholarship today recommends the abrogation of this rule, of which it is stressed that little use is made by the courts. See nos. 13 et seq. See also N. Zanini, Il maltrattamento dei minori in: P. Cendon (ed.), *Trattato breve dei nuovi danni* (2001), II, 1458.

[2] See P. Zatti, Rapporto educativo e intervento del giudice in: M. De Cristofaro/A. Belvedere (eds.), *L'autonomia dei minori tra famiglia e società* (1980), 277 et seq. for an explanation of the cultural and social background of the rules concerning the civil sanctions for parents.

[3] On this issue see, among others, A. Fraternale, L'abbandono di soggetti deboli: minori e anziani in: P. Cendon (supra fn. 1), II, 957 et seq., in which there is also an explanation of the possibilities of damages compensation. See also art. 8 of L. no. 149 of 28 March 2001 about child abandonment as a condition for adoption. For legal scholarship, see A. Fraternale, L'abbandono di soggetti deboli: minori e anziani in: P. Cendon (supra fn. 1), II, 960 et seq. and G. Salito, Della dichiarazione di adottabilità in: G. Autorino/P. Stanzione (eds.), *Le adozioni nella nuova disciplina* (2001), 152 et seq. For case law, see *Corte di Cassazione* (Italian Supreme Court, Cass.) 20 January 1998, no. 482, [1998] *Giurisprudenza italiana* (Giur. it.), 2266, with comments by M. De Robertis and Cass. 5 December 1991, no. 13110, [1991] *Massimario della Giustizia civile* (Giust. civ., Mass.), fasc. 12.

couples who are unable to adopt legitimately. It was not by chance that this was the main motivation behind the first Italian adoption regulations (L. no. 184 of 4 May 1983), as well as current legislation in this field (art. 35 L. no. 149 of 28 March 2001).[4]

A large area where, theoretically, there are few injuries suffered by children concerns accidents at work and job-related illnesses, owing to the prohibition on putting children under 15 to work and also further limitations concerning arduous and dangerous work for minors over 15 (see below, nos. 52 et seq.). Happily, the improved economic situation nowadays has reduced the once particularly common application of criminal sanctions for preventing minors from attending compulsory education (*omesso avviamento dei minori all'istruzione obbligatoria*),[5] because parents generally need no longer put their minor sons and daughters to work to contribute to the maintenance of the family. Hence the repeal of art. 732 of the criminal code *omesso avviamento dei minori al lavoro*, (effected by L. no. 205 of 25 June 1999) and the little use made of art. 731 of the criminal code, *Inosservanza dell'obbligo dell'istruzione elementare dei minori* (failure to fulfil the duty to provide elementary education for minors).[6] It should, however, be noted that the failure to send minor children to elementary and middle school, which is compulsory, remains a phenomenon of great current relevance in certain impoverished areas of this country, in particular amongst immigrants from outside the EU, either present illegally or legally or with families, and among groups in the nomadic communities.[7] This leads to great uncertainties regarding statistical data. The most recent investigation, led by ISTAT, shows that about 15% of children under 15 have worked at least once, more male (18.8%) than female (10.4%). Not all work experience, however, should be considered, so to say, as a "trauma", as the report points out, since in most cases it is education rather than exploitation of minors. 7

Lastly, accidents at work and job-related illnesses, which may be suffered by minors over 15 who are working regularly and, one might add, openly, should be considered. 8

Another sector where case law instances are not lacking is the exploitation of persons under an incapacity (art. 643 of the criminal code) where the victim is a minor.[8] In this regard, criminal case law precedents emphasise that the safe- 9

[4] On which see G.M. Riccio, Norme finali, penali e transitorie in: G. Autorino/P.Stanzione (supra fn. 3), 437 et seq.

[5] Note the duty to educate children imposed by art. 30, para. 1 of the Constitution and by art. 147 of the civil code. Furthermore, please note that school is compulsory and free for at least eight years (art. 34, para. 2 of the Constitution).

[6] Cass. 26 February 1990, [1991] *Cassazione penale* (Cass. pen.), I, 1368 is one of the last applications of this rule.

[7] For some data, see F. Fierro, Lavoro minorile in: P. Cendon (supra fn. 1), III, 2193 et seq.

[8] For compensation profiles see, above all, C. Schenardi, La circonvenzione di persone incapaci in: P. Cendon (supra fn. 1), I, 447 et seq.

guard offered by the criminal law provision is not confined to financial aspects, but includes the autonomy of the minor.[9]

10 For the sake of completeness, the broad area of fertility treatments which involve minors should be included,[10] where legal scholarship, with a large element of imagination and looking to the future, has conceived of a damage arising from the knowledge that one was conceived by means of artificial insemination.[11]

11 In certain areas, however, such as those involving violence to minors (not just of a sexual kind), case numbers remain very low, probably due to the notoriety arising from publicising such unpleasant facts (see nos. 13 et seq.).[12]

12 Finally, a field in which at the moment there is litigation but recoverability is denied by the Supreme Court is the area of wrongful life (see nos. 84 et seq.).

II. Damage Caused by Parents and Other Specific Third Parties

2. In what circumstances may a parent be held liable for an injury sustained by his or her child?

(a) In what circumstances may a parent be held liable for injury resulting from his or her intentional conduct? (Liability for intent.) In particular, in what circumstances may the parent be held liable for injury resulting from his or her physical chastisement of the child?

(b) In what circumstances may a parent be held liable for injury resulting from his or her unintentional conduct? (Liability for fault.) Are there special rules for liability of the parents, e.g. are parents liable only in case of gross negligence? Are parents held to a lower or higher standard of care? In what circumstances may a parent be held liable for injury resulting from his or her failure to protect the child from harm? (Liability for omissions.)

13 There are no legal rules in Italy which provide a special scheme of liability for unlawful acts committed within the nuclear family.[13] However, this apparent lack of differentiation from the normal rules has for a long time had more to

[9] *Tribunale di Lecce* (Court of first instance, Trib.) 13 May 1991, [1993] *Rivista italiana di diritto e procedura penale* (RIDPP), 412, with comments by R. Pezzano, referred to the "*libertà del minore intesa come determinazione non condizionata in vista del perseguimento di un fine*".

[10] See, for further details, nos. 66–71 and 77–83.

[11] See G. Tornesello/M. Mancarella, La procreazione assistita in: P. Cendon (supra fn. 1), II, 1165.

[12] An example could be incest, on which see R. Bailo, L'incesto in: P. Cendon (supra fn. 1), II, 1477.

[13] On this topic, see S. Patti, *Famiglia e responsabilità civile* (1984), 31 et seq. and S. Patti, Il declino dell'immunity doctrine nei rapporti familiari in: F.D. Busnelli/S. Patti, *Danno e responsabilità civile* (1997), 257 et seq. and 271 et seq.

do with the fact that these rules were not applied in the first place, probably more for socio-cultural reasons, broadly speaking, than strictly technical-legal ones,[14] together with an equal degree of indifference on the part of legal science.[15]

Indeed, judicial intervention in domestic affairs[16] has for a long time been confined to only the most extreme cases, involving criminal aspects. The classic example arises from acts constituting the exercise of the *ius corrigendi* (the right of chastisement) which, until the reform of family law brought about by L. no. 151 of 19 May 1975, was considered justifiable in terms of the paternal requirement to *frenare la cattiva condotta del figlio* (to stop the bad behaviour of the child) (former art. 319 of the civil code).[17] In fact, legal scholarship has referred to "a power of the parent, in the past practically absolute and uncontrolled".[18] 14

Another area of practically total immunity concerned unlawful acts which, while unconnected to the exercise or abuse of the right of chastisement, nevertheless were not covered by any compensatory regime in the courts because of the conviction that any potential sum awarded in damages to the minor would be taken up by the authors of the tort themselves, the parents.[19] Clearly such a prospect left little room for compensation, either for *danno biologico* (bodily harm) or mental suffering sustained by the child. 15

The coming into force of the Republican Constitution in 1948 brought about changes in this sector too; art. 2 of the Constitution, which "recognises and guarantees the inviolable rights of man, both as individuals and in the social organisation where personality is fulfilled", in fact has inevitably necessitated the increase of safeguards in relation to damage originating in the domestic environment, which is a social organisation to the same extent as any other,[20] even without taking into account the equality principle under art. 3 of the Constitution. 16

[14] On this issue see M. Giorgianni, Problemi attuali di diritto familiare, [1956] *Rivista trimestrale di diritto e procedura civile* (RTDPC), 772, who excludes "at least in Italy" the possibility that spouses could take action against each other during the marriage and S. Patti in: F.D. Busnelli/S. Patti (supra fn. 13), 104.

[15] S. Patti in: F.D. Busnelli/S. Patti (supra fn. 13), 2.

[16] On this topic, see V. Roppo, *Il giudice nel conflitto coniugale* (1981), passim.

[17] See P. Rescigno, Immunità e privilegio, [1961] *Rivista di diritto civile* (RDC), I, 439 (now in [1999] *Persona e comunità*) and S. Patti in: F.D. Busnelli/S. Patti (supra fn. 13), 281 et seq. The decisions which declare such violence illegal, even if carried out with an "educational" aim, are, not surprisingly, all recent. See Cass. 18 March 1996, no. 4904, [1996] *Foro italiano* (FI), II, 1130.

[18] "Potere del genitore, per il passato pressochè assoluto e incontrollato". See M. Dogliotti, Intervento pubblico e diritti del minore. Assistenza, giustizia, emarginazione in: M. De Cristofaro/A. Belvedere (supra fn. 2), 141.

[19] S. Patti in: F.D. Busnelli/S. Patti (supra fn. 13), 105 et seq.

[20] In argument, see above all P. Rescigno, La tutela della personalità nella famiglia, nella scuola, nelle associazioni in: *Studi in onore di Chiarelli,* IV (1974), 4003 et seq.

17 Thus, it is possible to say that there are both internal and external limits to parental authority. The former derive from the very definition of it given by art. 30 of the Constitution, in particular from the use of expressions such as *mantenere*, *istruire* and *educare* regarding the offspring, which are references to support and psychophysical integrity. The latter consist in the parents' acceptance of the so-called principles of "auto-responsibility" and "auto-upbringing" of the minor or, in other words, the freedom for children to express their political and social ideas.[21]

18 Notwithstanding this, it would still be difficult to assert today that a mother could be sanctioned for her lifestyle (for example, for abusing alcohol or drugs);[22] equally improbable is the possibility of obtaining a judgment for the award of damages against parents for having generally influenced (or attempted to influence) the male or female child in an inappropriate way and, to a greater or lesser degree, to have insisted on certain sexual preferences.[23] In general, we can say that it is permissible to influence the minor's personality, since this is connatural with the parents' educational power, but only as long as it does not lead to a distortion of the parental authority.[24]

19 Abandonment is one of the most frequent causes of harm to minors.[25] Provision is made in numerous legal measures, tending first and foremost to govern matters of moral and financial support (see art. 403 of the civil code; L. no. 1972 of 17 July 1890; Royal Decree no. 12 of 1 January 1905), as well as the effects upon the possibility of adoption (L. no. 149 of 28 March 2001). The regime in criminal law governing the abandonment of minors and persons under an incapacity (art. 591 of the criminal code) should also be kept in mind, as well as the infringement of the duty to maintain the family (art. 570 of the criminal code), closely connected to art. 30, para. 1 of the Constitution and art. 147 of the civil code, which imposes the duty upon parents to bring up, maintain and educate their offspring, including children who have been legally recognised (*figli riconosciuti*) (artt. 258 and 277 of the civil code). In the past, this duty upon parents also included children who could not be legally recognised (*figli non riconoscibili*) (artt. 251 and 278 of the civil code). In 2002, the Constitutional Court[26] held that

[21] P. Cavalieri/M. Pedrazza Gorlero/G. Sciullo, Libertà politiche del minore e potestà educativa dei genitori nella dialettica del rapporto educativo familiare in: M. De Cristofaro/A. Belvedere (supra fn. 2), 109.

[22] On this topic, see D. Nordici, La tossicodipendenza in: P. Cendon (supra fn. 1), II, 1789 et seq. and here under no. 89 et seq.

[23] For a discussion of future development in this direction, see E. Menzione/M. Manna, Omosessualità: torti e discriminazioni in: P. Cendon (supra fn 1), I, 798 et seq.

[24] P. Zatti, Rapporto educativo e intervento del giudice in: M. De Cristofaro/A. Belvedere (supra fn. 2), 199.

[25] See F. Piccaluga, Famiglia, malattia, abbandono e responsabilità civile, [2003] *Famiglia e diritto* (Fam. dir.), 198 et seq. and M. Dogliotti, La responsabilità civile entra nel diritto di famiglia, [2002] *Il Diritto di famiglia e delle persone* (Dir. fam. pers.), 60 et seq.

[26] *Corte Costituzionale* (Constitutional Court, Corte Cost.) 28 November 2002, no. 494, [2004] Giur. it., 15, with comments by L. De Grazia, *I diritti dei "figli incestuosi" al vaglio della Corte Costituzionale. Osservazioni a margine della sentenza n. 494/2002.*

artt. 251 and 178 of the civil code were illegitimate insofar as they excluded the possibility of incestuous children being legally recognised. This removed, an unjustified limitation of the rights of the person, which had derived from the traditional privilege for the family based on marriage (so called legitimate family), but was in contrast with the Constitution and with the New York Convention on children's rights of 20 November 1989, introduced in Italy through L. no. 176 of 27 May 1991.

Whereas tortious liability for abandonment in the past was generally held to exist exclusively where there had been an unlawful act punishable under criminal law,[27] more recently compensation has been held to be recoverable for so-called "existential damage or damage to social life" (*danno esistenziale od alla vita di relazione*), a further and in any case distinct head of damage with respect to economic loss suffered as a consequence of the consistent failure by a parent to provide the child with means of subsistence. In the case in point a father, adjudged as such as a result of affiliation proceedings, had for a considerable time failed to make the maintenance payments ordered by the court in respect of his natural child.[28] The award of damages for non-economic loss was made solely on the basis that the father had failed over a long period to make maintenance payments for the child, demonstrative of the fact that the interest which deserved safeguarding was not strictly an economic one, but rather was founded on "the person's fundamental rights, inherent in the fact of being a child and a minor" (*fondamentali diritti della persona, inerenti alla qualità di figlio e di minore*).[29] Actually, this head of damage seems more like punitive damage, as in the American legal experience, rather than the compensation of a loss effectively suffered by the victim. 20

However, recent decisions rendered by the Italian Supreme Court and Constitutional Court[30] have changed the scenario regarding non-pecuniary damages 21

[27] See F. Piccaluga, [2003] Fam. dir., 202.

[28] On the parents' continuing duty to provide children with a means of subsistence after the age of majority, see A. Natucci, L'obbligo di mantenimento del figlio maggiorenne in: M. De Cristofaro/A. Belvedere (supra fn. 2), 381 et seq. For the case law, see, among others, Cass. 18 February 1999, no. 1353, [1999] Fam. dir., 457, with comments by D. Morello Di Giovanni, *Figli maggiorenni non autosufficienti: diritto al mantenimento e sua indisponibilità.*

[29] Cass. 6 June 2000, no. 7713, [2002] Fam. dir., 159, and, for legal scholarship, A. Gabrielli, Mantenimento e alimenti: la violazione degli obblighi in: P. Cendon (supra fn. 1), II, 1381 et seq. and R. Castiglioni, Lesioni neurologiche in: P. Cendon (supra fn. 1), I, 170 et seq. See also A. Fraternale, L'abbandono di soggetti deboli: minori e anziani in: P. Cendon (supra fn. 1), 853 et seq.; M. Cerato, Gli abusi della potestà dei genitori in: P. Cendon (supra fn. 1), II, 1413 et seq.; N. Zanini, Il maltrattamento dei in: P. Cendon (supra fn. 1), II, 1445 et seq.; R. Bailo, L'incesto in: P. Cendon (supra fn. 1), II, 1475 et seq. For a "sociologic" evaluation of the legal effects of some crimes in which minors are victims, see A. Liberati, La pedofilia in: P. Cendon (supra fn. 1), II, 1684 et seq. and S. Masucci, Abusi sessuali sui minori in: P. Cendon (supra fn. 1), II, 1717. For a sharp critique of the proliferation of the heads of damage see F.D. Busnelli, La parabola della responsabilità civile, [1988] *Rivista critica del diritto privato* (RCDP), 663 et seq.

[30] Cass. 31 May 2003, no. 8827 and no. 8828, [2003] *Danno e responsabilità* (DR), 816 et seq., with comments by F.D. Busnelli, *Chiaroscuri d'estate. La Corte di Cassazione e il danno alla*

recoverable, since it has been affirmed that art. 2059 of the civil code applies in each case in which an inviolable right of the person is involved and infringed.

3. In what circumstances may a third party (e.g. a school or local authority social services department) be held liable for failing to render a child positive assistance (e.g. by preventing parental abuse)?

22 There are no case law precedents in this field, probably because the law founding the social services department (L. no. 1085 of 16 July 1962), provides that the staff of social workers are subordinate to the judicial authorities[31] and, so far as it is concerned, the law on the tortious liability of magistrates (L. no. 117 of 13 April 1988) limits liability to cases of intent and gross negligence. To this must be added the intrinsic difficulty experienced by the social services department in taking action in domestic or family situations in which most individuals involved are disadvantaged and where there is difficulty in coping. This should not, however, lead to the conclusion that in respect of minors the social services (currently governed by L. no. 285 of 28 August 1997), provide an efficient or efficacious means for effectively helping so-called "children at risk". Indeed, the examples of clear incapacity are frequent, even if they only occasionally capture the newspaper headlines.[32]

23 So far as the liability of schools and educational institutions is concerned, we should recall (*cf.* D. Lgs. no. 297 of 16 April 1994) that social intervention on behalf of children in need is not one of their tasks.[33] Nevertheless, potential liability cannot be excluded where staff members, intentionally or negligently, have created the conditions for instability in a young person which have led him/her to commit suicide, nor, where clear reasons exist to presuppose the existence of suicidal tendencies and they have failed to provide any help.[34]

24 The issue of failure to supervise mentally ill minors deserves a chapter to itself, particularly concerning those with suicidal tendencies who harm themselves.

persona, G. Ponzanelli, *Ricomposizione dell'universo non patrimoniale: le scelte della Corte di Cassazione* and A. Procida Mirabelli Di Lauro, *L'art. 2059 c.c. va in paradiso* and Corte Cost. 11 July 2003, no. 233, [2003] DR, 939 et seq. with comments by G. Ponzanelli, *La corte costituzionale si allinea alla Corte di cassazione* and A. Procida Mirabelli Di lauro, *Il sistema della responsabilità civile dopo la sentenza della Corte Costituzionale n. 233/03.*

31 On this issue, see P. Tony, Percorsi di tutela giudiziaria dei minori. Dal d.p.r. n. 616 del 1977 ad oggi. I cambiamenti processuali e le prospettive, [2002] FI, V, 13.

32 For an evaluation of these problems, see F. Milanese-Mellina/M. Bares, Le inefficienze dei servizi minorili in: P. Cendon (supra fn. 1), 1493 et seq.

33 On the role of the school as a means of preventing suicide among youngsters, see G. Iorio, Il suicidio del congiunto in: P. Cendon (supra fn. 1), II, 1249 et seq.

34 Both these possibilities are treated in G. Iorio, Il suicidio del congiunto in: P. Cendon (supra fn. 1), II, 1255 et seq. See also S. Iapoce/F. Omero, La scuola in: P. Cendon (supra fn. 1), III, 1847 et seq. and C. Liverziani, Primi anni scolastici: "malpractice" educativa in: P. Cendon (supra fn. 1), III, 1883 et seq.

Case law only provides precedents concerning suicides among those who have reached majority, whether legally capable or not,[35] but clearly, if the same assumptions apply, the same considerations could be applied to cases concerning minors. 25

4. What limitations periods are applied to a child's claim?

The limitation periods applicable to unlawful acts within the nuclear family do not differ from those under the ordinary provisions (artt. 2946 et seq. of the civil code). However, the limitation period is suspended in situations existing between those who exercise parental authority or the powers inherent in it and the persons who are subject to it and between a legal guardian and the minor under guardianship (art. 2941, nos. 1 and 2 of the civil code). The obvious reasoning behind this rule is to avoid time running under the limitation period in all cases in which the person with a right to sue cannot do so because they are legally incapable of taking action, and the parents or guardian do not take action for them and find themselves in a situation of conflict of interest.[36] 26

The day from which the limitation period runs is the one when the damage occurred (*dies a quo*, according to the Latin expression). Although there is no case law on the specific matter, it is possible to say that, if the damage is latent (and as long as it remains latent), the limitation period does not even start (in other words, it is not a case of suspension). The Italian Supreme Court[37] stated this principle – which is the rule still applied nowadays – in a case of medical liability, reasoning on the basis that art. 24 of the Constitution recognises the right to sue in order to protect the rights of each person, and guarantees the effectiveness of this right as well. 27

It is important to stress that the unanimous case law has stated that it is irrelevant whether there is an ongoing criminal trial on the same facts which constitute the object of the civil process.[38] In such a case, the suspension of the limitation period is not applicable. 28

The hypothesis of temporary natural incapacity of the subject of itself does not imply automatically the suspension of the limitation period, since the cases of suspension are expressly set down by the law.[39] 29

Since at the end of the custody period the guardian has a duty to make a report, the suspension ends only after this duty has been fulfilled.[40] 30

[35] Cass. 10 November 1997, no. 11038, [1998] DR, 388; Trib. Trieste 30 April 1993, [1994] *Responsabilità civile e previdenza* (Resp. civ. prev.), 302, with comments by F. Pontonio.

[36] See, among others, F. Gazzoni, *Manuale di diritto privato* (8th edn. 2000), 114 et seq. and A. Iannaccone in: P. Vitucci (ed.), *Commento sub art. 2941, Commentario al codice civile Schlesinger* (1999), 10 et seq.

[37] Cass. 24 March 1979, no. 1716, [1979] *Giustizia civile* (Giust. civ.), I, 1440.

[38] See, among others, Cass. 11 December 2001, no. 15622, [2001] Giust. civ., Mass., 2127 and Cass. 6 October 2000, no. 13310, [2000] Giust. civ., Mass., 2100.

[39] Cass. 6 May 1975, no. 1751, [1976] FI, I, 153.

[40] A. Iannaccone in: P. Vitucci (supra fn. 36), 24 et seq.

31 Another case of suspension of the limitation period is provided for by art. 2942 of the civil code if the minor is without guardian and for the six months following the end of the incapacity or the appointment of a guardian. Hence, in this case the suspension of the limitation period applies not only to specific types of obligation or relationship, but applies to each right of the minor[41]. The Constitutional Court[42] has upheld the legitimacy of this rule notwithstanding the fact that it does not provide the same protection in the case of gross negligence of the parents or the guardian.

III. Contributory Negligence

5. Are there any special provisions concerning contributory negligence if the tortfeasor is a child?

32 Please refer to the next answer.

6. What are the rules governing contributory negligence of the child? Do such principles follow the same lines as those governing the negligence issue itself (mirror-image)?

33 Both case law and academic commentators have traditionally affirmed that the general rule of contributory negligence does not apply where the victim is under age or under an incapacity.[43]

34 Currently prevailing attitudes tend to be more severe towards minors. Indeed, case law has confirmed the existence of contributory negligence independent of the particular mental condition of the minor,[44] obviously as long as there is a causal nexus between the child's negligence and the aggravation of the damage sustained by him/her. Therefore, when someone who is unable to understand and intend suffers damage caused in part by him/herself, case law has

[41] A. Iannaccone in: P. Vitucci (supra fn. 36), 39.

[42] Corte Cost. 4 November 1987, no. 374, [1988] Dir. fam. pers., 39.

[43] Among several, see Cass. 24 March 1947, no. 421, [1947] *Repertorio del Foro italiano, voce Responsabilità civile* (Foro it., Rep.), no. 42. For legal literature, F. Corsi, Concorso di colpa di minore incapace di intendere e di volere e riduzione del risarcimento dei danni, [1960] *Giurisprudenza toscana* (Giur. tosc.), 217. For an analysis of case law see M. Comporti, Fatti illeciti: le responsabilità presunte. Commento sub artt. 2044–2048 in: *Commentario al codice civile Schlesinger-Busnelli* (2002), 77 et seq.

[44] Cass., sez. un., 17 February 1964, no. 351, with comments by G. Gentile, *Ancora sul concorso di colpa dell'incapace*; Cass. 15 June 1973, no. 1753, [1974] Giur. it., I, 1399, with comments by A. M. Marchio, *Concorso di colpa del minore incapace danneggiato nella produzione dell'evento dannoso (e questioni relative alla liquidazione del danno)*; Cass. 12 July 1974, no. 2110, [1975] Giur. it., I, 1, 70. More recently Cass. 29 April 1993, no. 5024, [1994] Resp. civ. prev., 472 and Cass. 3 March 1995, no. 2466, [1996] Giur. it., I, 91, with comments by D. Carusi, *Responsabilità del medico, diligenza professionale, inadeguata dotazione della struttura ospedaliera*; Trib. Genova 13 January 1995, [1995] Giur. it., I, 2, 554, with comments by A. Pinori, holding that provocation cannot reduce the amount of damages; contra: Cass. 29 January 1988, [1990] *Giustizia penale* (Giust. pen.), II, 405 and Cass. 2 February 1982, [1983] Giur. it., II, 158. For more details in English see F.D. Busnelli/G. Comandé, Italian Report in: B.A. Koch/H. Koziol (eds.), *Compensation for Personal Injuries in a Comparative Perspective* (2003), 194 et seq.

confined the issue to establishing the existence of a causal link between the damage sustained by the person under an incapacity and his/her conduct; the fault to be attributed to the incapable person, or to his/her guardian, is not a relevant consideration.[45]

The main reasoning used by the courts reflects the right of the tortfeasor to limit his/her own liability. The general rule is to be found in art. 1227 of the civil code,[46] which applies to non-contractual damage by virtue of the reference under art. 2056 of the civil code. The Constitutional Court[47] has affirmed the constitutional validity of this provision (and, *de facto*, the constitutional legitimacy of this tendency in case law) although a regime governing wrongful acts where the victim is a minor is not specifically provided. In this regard, it should be recalled that the judicial trend now prevailing excludes the special liability regime under art. 2048 of the civil code from being applicable in the case of conduct by the minor which causes damage to him/herself,[48] and in- 35

[45] Cass. 5 May 1994, no. 4332, [1994] *Archivio giuridico della circolazione e dei sinistri* (Arch. giur. circol. e sinistri), 953.

[46] Art. 1227 of the civil code "Se il fatto colposo del creditore ha concorso a cagionare il danno, il risarcimento è diminuito secondo la gravità della colpa e l'entità delle conseguenze che ne sono derivate".

[47] Corte Cost. ord. 23 January 1985, no. 14, [1985] FI, I, 934, with comments by R. Pardolesi.

[48] Cass. 10 February 1999, no. 1135, [2000] Giur. it., 507, with comments by V. Pandolfini, *Sulla responsabilità dei precettori e dell'ente scolastico per il danno cagionato dall'allievo a sé medesimo*; Cass 28 July 1967, no. 2012, [1968] *Rivista giuridica della circolazione e dei trasporti* (Riv. circol. trasp.), 390; Cass. 12 July 1974, no. 2110 (supra fn. 44); Cass. 13 May 1995, no. 5268, [1996] *Nuova giurisprudenza civile commentata* (NGCC), I, 239, with comments by A. Zaccaria, *Sulla responsabilità civile del personale scolastico per i danni sofferti dal minore*; *Corte d'appello* (Court of appeal, App.) Firenze 17 April 1964, [1964] Giur. tosc., 748; App. Milano, 22 March 1974, [1974] *Archivio civile* (Arch. civ.), 258; Trib. Roma 2 October 1997, [1998] *Giurisprudenza romana* (Giur. Rom), 1, 27; Trib. Roma 24 April 2002, [2003] *Gius*, 375. For legal literature, see M. Franzoni, Dei fatti illeciti, artt. 2043–2059 in: F. Galgano (ed.), *Commentario al codice civile Scialoja-Branca* (1993), 351; M. Franzoni, Illecito dello scolaro e responsabilità del maestro elementare, [1997] *Danno e responsabilitá* (DR), 454; L. Corsaro, Sulla natura giuridica della responsabilità del precettore, [1967] *Rivista di diritto commerciale* (Riv. dir. comm.), I, 38; S. Patti in: F.D. Busnelli/S. Patti (supra fn. 13), 258; F. Di Ciommo, L'illiceità (o antigiuridicità) del fatto del minore (o dell'incapace) come presupposto per l'applicazione dell'art. 2048 c.c., [2001] FI, I, 3100.
Contra*:* C. M. Bianca, *Diritto civile,* v, *La responsabilità* (1994), 701; M. Comporti in: *Commentario al codice civile Schlesinger-Busnelli* (supra fn. 43), 262 et seq.; Cass. 3 February 1972, no. 260, [1972] FI, I, 3522, with comments by M. Grossi; Cass., sez. un., 11 August 1997, no. 7454 [1998] Resp. civ. prev., 1071, with comments by R. Settesoldi, *La responsabilità civile degli insegnanti statali: l'obiter dictum delle Sezioni unite segna definitivamente il tramonto della presunzione di colpa prevista dall'art. 2048, comma 2 c.c.?* and [1998] DR, 260, with comments by M. Rossetti; Cass. 26 June 1998, no. 6331, [1999] FI, I, 1574, with comments by F. Di Ciommo, *Danno "allo" scolaro e responsabilità "quasi oggettiva" della scuola*; Trib. Messina 28 November 2001, [2002] FI, I, 602.
On this issue see also N. Daniele, La responsabilità dell'amministrazione scolastica per i danni recati dall'alunno a sé stesso, [2000] *Rivista giuridica della scuola* (Riv. giur. scuola), 157; V. Di Spirito, La responsabilità del personale della scuola per gli infortuni degli alunni, [1998] *Lavoro e Previdenza Oggi* (Lav. Prev. Oggi), 1934; S. Masala, Sulla applicabilità della disciplina dell'art. 2048 c.c. (relativa alla responsabilità degli insegnanti per il fatto illecito degli allievi) nel caso in cui l'allievo procuri un danno a sé stesso, [2000] *Rivista giuridica sarda* (Riv. giur. sarda), 59.

stead makes use of the general rule of liability for fault under art. 2043 of the civil code,[49] or contractual liability under art. 1218 of the civil code.[50]

7. Does the fixed minimum age for children to be liable, if any exists, also apply to the contributory negligence of the child?

36 No minimum age for the liability of children is provided for by law. Please refer to nos. 33 et seq. for the application of the rule on contributory negligence.

8. What is the standard of care governing the behaviour of children in the context of contributory negligence? Is such standard determined by the same principles and criteria which are relevant to the duty of care incumbent upon the child in the context of him or her being held liable?

37 There are no precedents on this topic. However, the standard of care used to establish the contributory negligence of minors is the same as that used to determine their liability. Once contributory negligence on the part of the minor has been found, there is in fact no further reason to attach importance to the fact that s/he is under an incapacity, since reference is made exclusively to the failure to respect an objective standard of conduct.[51]

IV. Contribution in Equity

9. Is there a parallel (mirror-image) to liability in equity in the field of contributory negligence? If so, do the criteria determining liability in equity of the child also apply to the issue of holding him or her accountable for his or her contributory negligence?

38 There is no need for the rules of equity to be applied to contributory negligence, since the present trend in case law demonstrates that the ordinary rules of law are applied where minors are concerned. Please refer to no. 37.

10. If answered affirmatively: Is the fact that the child is privately or socially insured against the accident a factor to be considered? Is the existence of liability insurance of the tortfeasor to be taken into account? What factors have a bearing on the assessment of equitable contribution?

39 Not applicable.

[49] Cass. 10 February 1999, no. 1135 (supra fn. 48).

[50] Cass. 27 June 2002, no. 9346, [2002] FI, I, 2636, with comments by F. Di Ciommo, *La responsabilità contrattuale della scuola (pubblica) per il danno che il minore si procura da sé: verso il ridimensionamento dell'art. 2048 c.c.* and [2003] DR, 46, with comments by A. Lanotte, *Condotta autolesiva dell'allievo: non risponde l'insegnante.*

[51] S. Patti in: F.D. Busnelli/S. Patti (supra fn. 13), 175.

V. Miscellaneous

11. What are the rules for a situation in which the child is guilty of contributory negligence but the parents have also breached their duty to supervise? Is the child held accountable in any way for his or her parents' breach of the duty to supervise so that his or her damage is reduced?

If the parents have failed to perform their duty of supervision, the defendant is not permitted to raise his/her their own breach of duty as a defence against the child.[52] However, it would be useful as well to draw attention to two conflicting judgments, which respectively affirm the possibility and the impossibility of taking the parents' contributory negligence into account.[53] 40

12. Do the rules of contributory negligence apply as well in the area of strict liability?

Yes.[54] 41

13. Do the rules of contributory negligence apply in the area of strict liability for traffic-accidents or other areas of tort liability?

Yes.[55] 42

14. Are adults held to a higher standard of care in their interactions with children, or when children are or may be around?

Although there are no specific rulings on the point, it can be said that the degree of care on the part of adults when children are nearby, or otherwise involved in activities of the former, is higher than normally required. Indeed, as has been widely noted, the degree of care must be established in the light of the prevailing circumstances. 43

We can recall 6 examples regarding this point. 44

The case of an adult driving a car near school premises where some children were playing, offers an illustrative example, as case law has referred to "the particular care required in such circumstances, since abnormal movements by users who are youngsters are foreseeable".[56] Therefore, in this type of case, 45

[52] Cass. 24 May 1997, no. 4633, [1997] Giust. civ., Mass., 834.

[53] Cass. 4 February 1988, [1988] *Rivista Giuridica della Circolazione e dei Trasporti* (Riv. giur. circol. trasp.), 823 and Cass. 7 March 1991, no. 2384, [1993] FI, I, 1974, with comments by A. Zampolli.

[54] Cass. 4 February 1988 (supra fn. 53).

[55] Cass. 4 February 1988 (supra fn. 53).

[56] App. Milano 1 October 1991, [1992] Arch. giur. circol. e sinistri, 359 and, more recently, Cass. 3 March 2004, no. 4359, [2004] *Guida al Diritto-Il Sole 24 Ore,* 16, 58. Cass., sez. un., 20 April 1991 no. 4290, [1991] Giur. it., I, 1, 1326, hold that the public administration is obliged to organise itself in order to avoid any damage to the users: "La pubblica amministrazione,

the assessment of fault should not be carried out with exclusive reference to the conduct of the tortfeasor, and should not exclude questions of relativity, in that the conduct of the victim himself must also be taken into account.[57]

46 Another case regarding this point concerns the clinical testing of medicines, given that the *Decreto Ministeriale* (Ministerial Decree, DM:) of 15 July 1997 requires the consent of the legal representative of any testing person who is under an incapacity, the consent – within the limits of his/her own capacity of understanding – of the person who is under the incapacity, and the signatures of these persons on the form providing informed consent. A similar provision, making explicit reference to minors, can be found later in the DM of 18 March 1998. In the light of these legal instances, it can be stated that Italian law requires researchers conducting the experiments to exercise a higher degree of care when minors are involved, such as ascertaining that the testing does not involve a degree of risk which is greater than s/he would meet in normal daily life. Indeed, as has been rightly emphasised, the informed consent given by the legal representative where the subject of the testing is under an incapacity is "only partially"[58] valid, since, at least with regard to experiments involving a higher degree of risk, the possibility of using persons under an incapacity and minors of tender age in particular, should be considered as being excluded.[59] In addition, in order to avoid the whole responsibility for the choice and respecting of test protocol falling upon one individual research doctor, and to assist such doctors in undertaking experimental research, it seems that recourse should be had to the professional collegiate bodies, such as the ethics committees.[60]

la quale istituisca ed organizzi un servizio di autotrasporto riservato agli alunni di scuola, è tenuta, in osservanza del principio del «neminem laedere», ad adottare le cautele occorrenti per tutelare la sicurezza e l'incolumità di detti utenti, anche nel tragitto dalla scuola al punto di partenza degli automezzi, senza poter invocare, quali ragioni di esonero, economie di spese o vincoli di bilancio". It is important to remember the opposite trend of criminal decisions which, while recognising the duty of particular diligence of the driver, excludes his or her liability for damages caused by the victim itself ("quelle situazioni di pericolo che nelle fasi precedenti o successive al trasporto siano determinate da causa diversa attribuibile alla vittima o a terzi non ricollegabile causalmente (ma solo occasionalmente) all'attività del conducente medesimo"). See Cass. 9 June 1987, [1988] Cass. pen., 1940. Contra: Trib. Isernia 22 April 1983, [1983] Riv. giur. scuola, 1401 and Cass. 21 November 1983, [1984] Arch. giur. circol. e sinistri, 747. For legal scholarship, see C. Salvi, Responsabilità per trasporto di minori con scuolabus, [1988] *Nuova rassegna,* 2066, A. Flores, La responsabilità nel trasporto degli alunni di scuola materna, [1983] Riv. giur. scuola, 1401 and A. Flores, Il principio di continuità nel dovere di vigilanza verso gli alunni, [1987] Riv. giur. scuola, 403. On this issue, see also nos. 56 et seq.

57 We must remember the study of F. Cafaggi, *Profili di relazionalità della colpa* (1996).

58 L. Canavacci, *I confini del consenso. Un'indagine sui limiti e l'efficacia del consenso informato* (1999), 88.

59 L. Canavacci (supra fn. 58), 90, and see also M. Barni, *Diritti doveri responsabilità del medico dalla bioetica al biodiritto* (1999), 103.

60 L. Canavacci (supra fn. 58), 92 and 139 et seq. and L. Nocco, Diritti fondamentali e tecniche di tutela degli incapaci: le esperienze USA e italiana a confronto sul ruolo dei comitati etici, [2004] *Rivista italiana di medicina legale* (Riv. it. med. leg.), 1103–1160.

An area of particular complexity in the relations between adults and children occurs in the field of medical intervention, where the issue of respect for the minor's wishes and safeguarding the legal representative's prerogatives may be difficult to reconcile (see more extensively nos. 66 et seq.). 47

Another example concerns instances from case law involving the prohibition on the use of lifts and goods-lifting equipment by unaccompanied persons under eighteen (L. no. 1415 of 24 October 1942, now repealed and replaced by *Decreto del Presidente della Repubblica* (Presidential Decree, D.P.R) no. 162 of 30 April 1999). In this regard, it is worth noting that case law precedents[61] show that the mere accompanying of the child by another minor, albeit one over twelve years old, is an insufficient safeguard, and instead the law requires the presence of someone able to protect the child effectively if the equipment malfunctions. Conversely, if the minor sustains injury, liability lies with the owners of the lift. This represents a further example of the standard of care imposed where minors are involved, which is above that ordinarily required by the law. 48

Regarding sports instructors, the need to adapt the degree of care to the "level of learning capability, the indispensable physical capacities needed to cope with certain tasks when undertaking activity [...], the level of assessment by the learner of the risks associated with undertaking sporting activity",[62] has a consequent effect on the degree of care required, particularly when the learner is a minor. 49

Purely by way of example, another context where the fact of minor age has consequences for the degree of care to be observed by third parties, concerns the mass media, where there are different legislative requirements specifically governing the relationship with children, with a view to their protection.[63] 50

In the light of these examples, it can be said that a general principle exists in Italian law which imposes a higher duty of care on adults in relation to children and, in general, when children are involved in their activities, even if on a quite occasional and/or incidental basis. 51

[61] Cass. 5 May 1982, no. 2826, [1982] FI, I, 2499.

[62] S. Di Paola, La responsabilità civile dell'istruttore subacqueo, [2004] DR, 16 et seq. See also P.G. Monateri/M. Bona/A. Castelnuovo, *La responsabilità civile nello sport* (2002), 85 et seq.

[63] See R. Capo, Bambini e mass media in: P. Cendon (supra fn. 1), II, 995 et seq. (particularly 1008 et seq. for the analysis of some legal rules on this topic); L. Buono, Tutela del minore e mass media, [1993] *Minori e giustizia*, 3, 139 et seq.; I. Cividali, Minori sbattuti in prima pagina. Prime sanzioni contro i giornalisti, [1994] *Minori e giustizia*, 1, 139 et seq.; A. Vaccaro, Stampa e minori: una storia semplice, [1996] *Minori e giustizia*, 4, 134 et seq.; G. Sergio, Libertà d'informazione e tutela dei soggetti deboli, [2000] Dir. fam. pers., 805 et seq. and AA.VV. (Various Authors), Tutela dei minori e responsabilità dell'emittente televisiva, [1986] *Diritto dell'informazione e dell'informatica* (Dir. inf.), 214 et seq. (particularly 219 et seq. for the protection granted to infancy by criminal law). On this topic see also nos. 66 et seq.

VI. Insurance Matters

15. Are pupils covered by private or public accident (first-party) insurance?

52 There is no compulsory system of first party insurance for personal injury in Italy.[64] Indeed, protection is limited to minors who are engaged in employment. In addition, although there is a general prohibition on employing minors under fifteen years of age in any kind of job, minors working in contravention of this rule are nonetheless covered by insurance against accidents in the workplace.[65]

53 In particular because of the general principle of Italian law, the so-called "automatic provision of cover" ("*dell'automaticità delle prestazioni*"), the provision of insurance cover is a duty owed to the employee even when the premiums have not been paid by the employer (see art. 2116 of the civil code), which is a very common occurrence, almost taken for granted where the illegal employment of minors is concerned.[66]

54 One should bear in mind, however, "that the presence of a national health system and of public legislation against disablement limits the forms of first-party insurance".[67] On the other hand, it is necessary to mention the increasing interest of insurance to Italian consumers, which highlights the inadequacy of Italian regime for this kind of contract[68].

55 Even though there is not a system of compulsory insurance, schools are usually (third-party) insured against accidents happening to their students and the normal rules on insurance contracts are applicable to them.[69] Particularly in

[64] For a careful analysis of the impact of first party insurance in the personal injuries field, see G. Comandé, *Risarcimento del danno alla persona e alternative istituzionali* (1999), 370 et seq.

[65] D. lgs. 30 June 1965 (so-called "*Testo unico degli infortuni sul lavoro e malattie professionali*"), L. 17 October 1967, no. 977 and D. lgs. 4 August 1999, no. 345; art. 6 of this act allows the engagement of children in the areas of culture, arts, sports and advertising ("*attività lavorative di carattere culturale, artistico, sportivo o pubblicitario e nel settore dello spettacolo*"), with the consent of the local work agency ("*direzione provinciale del lavoro*") and the written consent of parents/guardians. However, the job should warrant the development, the psycho-physical integrity and the safety of the child and should not be an obstacle to his/her education. For legal literature on this topic, see, for the former rules, L. De Cristofaro, voce Minori (lavoro dei) in: *Enciclopedia del Diritto* (E.d.D.), IX, 473 et seq. and, for the present regime, F. Di Cerbo, La protezione del lavoro minorile e le prescrizioni dell'Unione Europea, [2000] Lav. prev. oggi, 1 et seq. and M. Romano, Sulla rilevanza del d. lgs. 4 agosto 1999, n. 345 in tema di lavoro dei minori alla luce dei principi generali, [2001] *Familia*, 671 et seq. For the damages caused by children working illegally, see F. Fierro, Lavoro minorile in: P. Cendon (supra fn. 1), III, 2189 et seq.

[66] For academic comment, see G. Terzago, *Rapporto giuridico previdenziale ed automaticità delle prestazioni* (1971), and G. Canavesi, Contribuzione prescritta e automaticità delle prestazioni nell'ordinamento italiano e nella dimensione cominitaria, [1992] *Rivista giuridica del lavoro* (Riv. giur. lav.), I, 465 et seq.

[67] On this point: G. Comandé/D. Poletti, Italian Report in: U. Magnus (ed.), *The Impact of Social Security Law on Tort Law* (2003), 137.

[68] For an overview, see G. Volpe Putzolu, *Le assicurazioni. Produzione e distribuzione* (1992), passim.

[69] G. Comandé/L. Nocco, Children as Tortfeasors under Italian Law in: M. Martín-Casals (ed.), *Children in Tort Law Part I: Children as Tortfeasors* (2006), no. 71.

the sector of nurseries and primary schools, it is common also to have first-party insurance coverage in favour of the pupils, of which applicability is limited to the activities engaged in at school, including journeys.

16. Does this insurance cover any damage occurred on the way to school and back?

See nos. 52 et seq. Note that the school bus service is counted as a school activity. However, the rules of liability provided for teachers and schools apply. Liability persists even when minors are left at a bus stop and no one comes to collect them. In such a case, the driver must take all possible steps in the light of the circumstances of time and place. In case of injury, the driver's liability is of a tortious kind,[70] even where it was the parent him/herself who requested that the minor be left unsupervised in a particular place,[71] given that "the relationship between the school and the minor's parents [is] governed and predetermined in all its aspects, with no contribution being made by the will of those using the service".[72] 56

In general, we can say that the indemnity really depends upon the specific clauses of the contract. An overview of the contracts used in the insurance market has shown that the cover (and its contractual exclusion) is influenced more by the pre-existent health conditions of the person, than by his/her age. Anyway, it is more common to find insurance indemnifying all the damages suffered by any member of the family than only covering the children. 57

If during the way to and/or back from school an accident happens and there is insurance cover, the "principle of indemnity" ("*principio indennitario*") applies. It limits the compensation to the loss suffered by the victim but at the same time provides for recovery of the full damage.[73] It is necessary that the damage is due to an accidental, violent and external cause, which means a 58

[70] Cass. 5 September 1986, no. 5424, [1987] *Nuova giurisprudenza civile commentata* (Nuova giur. civ. comm.), I, 493, with comments by G. Amenta; Cass. 30 December 1997, no. 13125, [1998] DR, 389, with comments by A. Palmieri, *Scuolabus e sorveglianza dei minori*, 462; Cass. 19 February 2002, no. 2380, [2002] FI, I, 2438, with comments by F. Ronconi. See also D.M. 31 January 1997, *"Nuove disposizioni in materia di trasporto scolastico"* and D.M. 18 April 1977 *"Caratteristiche costruttive degli autobus"*.

[71] This provokes sharp critique by P.G. Monateri, Responsabilità extracontrattuale. Fattispecie (Sintesi di informazione 1986–1989), [1989] *Rivista di diritto civile* (Riv. dir. civ.), 491. Contra: E. Bucciante, La potestà dei genitori, la tutela e l'emancipazione in: *Trattato di diritto privato diretto da Rescigno* (2nd edn. 1997), 4, *Persone e famiglia*, III, 517 et seq.

[72] Cass. 14 April 1993, no. 4410, [1993] Giust. civ., Mass., 660 ("il rapporto tra la scuola ed i genitori del minore [è] regolato e predeterminato in tutti i suoi aspetti, senza alcun concorso della volontà del fruitore del servizio").

[73] See M. A. Bianchi Pitter, Commento sub art. 1905 in: G. Cian/A. Trabucchi (eds.), *Commentario breve al codice civile* (1997), 1798 and G. Gallone, Commento sub art. 1905 in: P. Rescigno (ed.), *Codice civile* (1992), 2043 et seq.

cause not depending on the will of the insured, produced by a third party or by an object and not linked to the existing health conditions of the victim.[74]

17. Are there restrictions on damages recoverable by the child, e.g. with respect to loss of future earnings?

59 There are no limitations on the damages recoverable by minors. However, the criteria for the quantum of damages may differ from those applicable to adults (see nos. 60 et seq.). To this end, judges may make certain presumptions.

VII. Damage Issues

18. If damages for loss of earnings are available, what are the principles governing their assessment?

60 The principles which apply in respect of damages suffered by minors are the same as those in all other cases.[75] However, the existence of specific features should be born in mind, when damages for personal injury are to be assessed in respect of a minor.[76] In the first place, the main difficulty consists in assessing the quantum of damages for loss of future earnings;[77] however, in practice, presumptions are applied in the light of the factual circumstances. In fact, when the effective loss cannot be quantified (as in cases concerning minors), judges calculate damages by considering the damage to health together with the reduction in working capacity due to the permanent state of invalidity, which is calculated taking studies and work experience (if any) into account. On the other hand, compensation is not allowed for the temporary reduction of work capacity.[78] Damages for loss or reduction of the economic contribution made by the minor to the family, based on the duty of children to "contribute to the maintenance of the family, on the basis of their means and income, while they continue to live at home" (art. 315 of the civil code) are normally

[74] See G. Scalfi *Manuale delle assicurazioni private* (1994), 203 et seq., who recalls the requisites posed by D. lgs. 30 June 1965 (so-called "*Testo unico degli infortuni sul lavoro e malattie professionali*"), for the compensation of job-related damages and A. De Senibus, I prodotti danni alle cose in: S. Miani (ed.), *I prodotti assicurativi e* previdenziali (2002), 183 et seq.

[75] See art. 1223 of the civil code: "Il risarcimento del danno per l'inadempimento o per il ritardo deve comprendere così la perdita subita dal creditore come il mancato guadagno, in quanto ne siano conseguenza immediata e diretta". This rule is applicable to tort liability by means of the reference made by art. 2056 of the civil code. For an outline of the Italian compensation system see F.D. Busnelli/G. Comandé in: B.A. Koch/H. Koziol (supra fn. 44), 177 et seq.

[76] For a clear description of general aspects of compensation for personal injuries in Italy see F.D. Busnelli/G. Comandé in: B.A. Koch/H. Koziol (supra fn. 44). For the specific case of chidren, see F. Giardina, Le dommage corporel chez l'enfant. Aspects juridiques in: *Actes du XXXIX Congrès international de langue française de médecine légale et de médecine sociale*, Siena 25–28 October 1989.

[77] See also F.D. Busnelli/G. Comandé, Damages in the Italian Legal System in: U. Magnus (ed.), *Unification of Tort Law: Damages* (2001), 117 et seq.; F.D. Busnelli/G. Comandé, Non-Pecuniary Loss under Italian Law in: H. Rogers (ed.), *Damages for Non-Pecuniary Loss in a Comparative Perspective* (2001), 135 et seq.

[78] A. Segreto, *Le assicurazioni* (2000), 862.

confined to the support which the minor would have provided, according to criteria of normality or probability.[79]

So far as damage to health is concerned, some precedents apply by analogy the criterion under art. 4 Decreto Legge (D.L.) no. 857 of 23 December 1976 and L. no. 39 of 26 February 1977 for injury arising out of road traffic accidents:[80] The annual income to be taken into account may not be less than three times the amount of the state welfare pension (*pensione sociale*),[81] a sum of money normally given monthly to all people in need, in the presence of certain conditions. 61

[79] See Trib. Verona 21 March 1978, [1979] Arch. giur. circol. e sinistri, 85; Cass. 11 January 1988, no. 23, [1988] Giust. civ., Mass., fasc. 1; App. Bologna 7 October 1995, [1996] Resp. civ. prev., 1217, with comments by M. Pogliani, *Il reddito virtuale del minore e quello dei genitori in caso di sua uccisione*; Cass. 12 October 1998, no. 10085, [1999] Resp. civ. prev., 752, with comments by P. Ziviz, *Il turbamento emotivo come fonte di danno biologico*; Cass. 17 November 1999, no. 12756, [1999] Giust. civ., Mass., 2280; Cass. 7 November 2002, no. 15641, [2003] DR, 618, with comments by L. Gremigni Francini, *Ipotesi particolari di danno alla persona e onere della prova*. The same criterion based on foreseeable future job of the child is used in Cass. 3 September 1998, no. 8769, [1999] Resp. civ. prev., 763, with comments by S. Bastianon, *Risarcimento del danno patrimoniale e riduzione della c.d. capacità lavorativa generica*, to calculate the amount of economic damages suffered by the minor. For a clear description of the different case law trends, see S. Patti in: F.D. Busnelli/S. Patti (supra fn. 13), 192 et seq.

[80] See, for instance, Trib. Palermo 26 January 1991, [1991] Arch. giur. circol. e sinistri, 588; Trib. Milano 17 February 1986, [1986] Resp. civ. prev., 323; Trib. Napoli 29 January 1986, [1987] *Assicurazioni* (Ass.), I, 2, 32; contra: M. Pogliani [1996] Resp. civ. prev., 1217; Cass. 3 September 1998, no. 8769 (supra fn. 79), excludes the possibility of using the quoted rule to recover the "*danno biologico*". For a sharp critique on the use of criteria such as natural skills and abilities or the familiar and social conditions, see Trib. Firenze 5 March 1990, [1991] Arch. giur. circol. e sinistri, 42. Actually, indeed, they can lead to an infringement of the equality principle, as in the famous case treated by Trib. Milano 18 January 1971, [1971] *Giurisprudenza di merito* (Giur. mer.), 209 (for a comment see A.M. Galoppini, *Il caso Gennarino, ovvero quanto vale il figlio dell'operaio*, [1971] *Democrazia e diritto*, 255). On that occasion, the court awarded damages on the basis of the foreseeable future job of the minor. They presumed he would have done the same job as his father, an unskilled worker. Nowadays, after the achievement of *"danno biologico"*, this problem of discrimination has lost most of its interest. For an outline of the evolution of the case law in the matter of *"danno biologico"*, over the last thirty years, see F.D. Busnelli, Il danno biologico: dal "diritto vivente" al "diritto vigente" (2001).

[81] This trend was originally supported by the "*Tribunale di Genova*" (*inter alia*, see Trib. Genova 9 March 1989, [1989] Giur. it., I, 2, 938) and accepted by the "*Corte di Cassazione*" (Cass. 16 January 1985, no. 102, [1985] Arch. giur. circol. e sinistri, 397). Later, the Supreme Court, however, changed opinion (Cass. 13 January 1993, no. 357, [1995] *Rivista italiana di medicina legale* (Riv. it. med. leg.), 247 and Cass. 18 February 1993, no. 2009, [1993] Resp. civ. prev., 47, with comments by G. Comandé), stressing the absolute irrelevance of the victim's earning capacity (*"capacità di produzione del reddito che aveva il danneggiato"*). Finally, the criterion of the triple of the welfare state pension has also been abandoned by the court which created it. See Trib. Genova 28 September 1998, [1999] FI, I, 684, with comments by A. Lanotte, *Criteri di liquidazione del danno biologico. Il "revirement" dei giudici genovesi: dalla "livella" alle "barèmes" milanesi.* See also F.D. Busnelli, Danno biologico e danno alla salute in: M. Bargagna/F.D. Busnelli, *La valutazione del danno alla salute* (2nd edn. 1988), 9 et seq. and F.D. Busnelli, Diritto alla salute e tutela risarcitoria in: F.D. Busnelli/U. Breccia (eds.), *Tutela della salute e diritto privato* (1978), 565 et seq.

62 In connection with this, a brief review of the quantum criteria on *danno biologico* which has traditionally been applied in case law precedents may be useful.[82] Besides the criterion of three times the state pension, which has just been mentioned, we should recall the criterion of the average national income[83], as well as the purely equitable criterion, which is characterised by very uncertain and unpredictable features.[84]

63 Currently, the system normally adopted is a calculation based on variable points, ("*calcolo a punto variabile*") which was developed by case law precedent in Pisa,[85] the main features of which are the importance given to the age of the injured person and the kind of damage sustained:[86] each of these is given a value which increases with the type of injury and decreases with the age of the injured party; and the damages recoverable are derived from the point of intersection of these values, with a power of adjustment reserved for the judge to adapt the quantum to the circumstances of the particular case. The main problem arises from the proliferation of tables by the individual Courts;[87] to obviate this, academic commentators have proposed that a national reference table ("*tabellazione indicativa nazionale*") should be developed, to be used in the same way as now happens with respect to the tables of the individual courts.[88]

64 In general, case law precedents tend to award compensation for psychophysical injury and mental suffering, even when there is no recoverable economic loss.[89]

65 A similar subject is damages for economic loss sustained by minor children as a result of the violent death of the parent(s) caused by another person's (or persons') wrongful act; in this case, in assessing the damages which are recov-

[82] On this issue, see also G. Comandé (supra fn. 64), 254 et seq. and G. Alpa, Sulle tecniche di liquidazione del danno biologico, [1984] Riv. giur. circol. trasp., 14. More recently, A. Negro, *Quantum debeatur: la liquidazione del danno biologico*, part II (2003).

[83] Trib. Genova 25 November 1974, [1975] Giur. it., I, 2, 74 and, for legal literature, V. Monetti/ G. Pellegrino, Proposte per un metodo di liquidazione del danno alla persona, [1974] FI, IV, 159. Also this criterion has been later abandoned for the strong influence of patrimonial aspects.

[84] Neverthless, this criterion has been applied by the Supreme Court in one decision (Cass. 11 February 1985, no. 1130, [1985] Resp. civ. prev., 210).

[85] Trib. Pisa 16 January 1985, [1985] Riv. giur. circol. trasp., 543.

[86] This opinion is supported, *inter alia*, by F.D. Busnelli in: F.D. Busnelli/U. Breccia (supra fn. 81), 569 et seq. and G. Ponzanelli, Fermenti giurisprudenziali toscani in tema di valutazione del danno alla persona, [1979] Resp. civ. prev., 357 et seq.

[87] On this topic, see G. Comandé (supra fn. 64), 258; G. Comandé, Verso una moltiplicazione delle tabelle? Il "sistema" del Tribunale di Massa Carrara per la liquidazione del danno alla persona, [1997] DR, 368 et seq.

[88] On this topic, see G. Comandé, La sperimentazione di una tabellazione indicativa nazionale fra esigenze di prevedibilità ex ante del danno e di liquidazione equitativa ex post in: *Rapporto sullo stato della giurisprudenza in tema di danno alla salute del Gruppo di ricerca C.N.R. sul danno alla salute coordinato e diretto da Bargagna F.D. Busnelli* (1996), 201 et seq.

[89] Cass. 6 December 1995, no. 12569, [1998] Riv. it. med. leg., 1163.

erable, the fact of the victim reaching the age of majority does not end the entitlement to damages, given the expectation of being able to enjoy the economic support of parents in the period immediately following (at the least).[90]

19. Which of the child's non-material interests are protected in your jurisdiction? May the child, for example, sue for impairment of intellectual or social development, the onset of behavioural problems or reduced employment prospects?

There are many heads of damage, not of a strictly economic kind, which con- 66
cern minors and which are protected by the Italian legal system. Reference may be made first and foremost to the protection of personality rights ("*diritti della personalità*"), starting with the right to a name and one's own likeness (artt. 6 et seq. of the civil code),[91] which are extended to copyright (L. no. 633 of 22 April 1941).[92] As far as other prejudicial matters are concerned, such as damage to intellectual development, the reader is referred to the issues raised in the preceding question, since in order for there to be a right to compensation, damage must have been sustained. In this regard, mention could be made of a case which is close to the point under consideration, in which the judgment[93] spoke of loss of future earnings because of reduced employment prospects concerning the conduct of a bank which, having failed to deal properly with a bank cheque payment, caused the plaintiff (a person over eighteen) to lose the chance of attending a Master's degree course in the United States.[94]

[90] Cass. 25 June 1981, no. 4137, [1981] Giust. civ., I, 2213;. Trib. Treviso 27 December 1994, [1995] Resp. civ. prev., 617, with comments by F. Cassella, *Le sentenze interpretative di rigetto della Corte Costituzionale: la loro efficacia nei giudizi successivi e il limite del diritto vivente (a proposito di C. Cost. n. 372/1994)*, restricted this period until the twenty first year of age. In Cass. 22 July 2002, no. 10898, [2003] DR, 186, with comments by A.L. Bitetto, *Loss of parents: risarcimento solo ai nonni se si occupano dei nipoti!* and [2003] Resp. civ. prev., 113, with comments by S. Bastianon, *Il danno patrimoniale, la Cassazione e i nonni*, since the compensation of out-of-pocket expenses had been awarded to the grandparents, nothing was awarded to the victims' sons. The aim was to avoid a sort of collateral source rule, because the damages awarded in the actual case, were only the expenses suffered by the grandparents after the death of the parents for the maintenance of the grandchildren.

[91] On which P. Perlingieri, I diritti del singolo quale appartenente al gruppo familiare, [1982] *Rassegna di diritto civile* (Rass. dir. civ.), 75 et seq. and S. Patti in: F.D. Busnelli/S. Patti (supra fn. 13), 168 et seq.

[92] On which, for an introduction, see V. De Sanctis, voce Autore (diritto di), [1959] E.d.D., IV, 413 et seq. and U. Breccia, Delle persone fisiche in: *Commentario al codice civile Scialoja-Branca* (1988).

[93] See Cass. 15 October 1999, no. 11629, [2000] DR, 1215, with comments by F. Alonzo, *Il nesso causale e la lesione di aspettative future: un master mancato.*

[94] On the loss of a chance see R. Partisani, Lesione di un interesse legittimo e danno risarcibile: la perdita della chance, [2000] Resp. civ. prev., 566 et seq. For the case law, see Cass. 19 July 1982, no. 4236, [1983] Resp. civ. prev., 451, with comments by P.G. Monateri, *Nesso causale e determinazione della responsabilità* and, more recently, Cass. 14 December 2001, no. 15810, [2002] *Diritto & Giustizia* (D. & G.), 2, 53, with comments by S. Evangelista, *Perdita di chance: non c'è danno senza la prova sulle possibilità di promozione (la dimostrazione può basarsi sul calcolo delle probabilità).*

67 A famous case law precedent to do with the protection of a minor's image concerned a child who was unable to wear any kind of clothing because of a particular type of allergy[95] and who, for this reason, was subjected to severe harassment by the mass media.[96]

68 Significantly, it was not purely and simply economic loss from loss of earnings which was held to be recoverable, as found by the judges at first instance, but the *danno biologico* as well, "namely damage to social life due to the considerable limitation of movement and the resulting diminution in the outlook for self-affirmation in human society, both in an educational ambit and outside the family context in general".[97]

69 An area which up to now has not been contentious, but in which an increase in importance is foreseeable owing to the phenomenon of immigration which is a feature of present-day Italy, concerns female circumcision. This is a field which is as yet unregulated, although at one time two draft acts had been put forward (respectively those of 29 May and 16 October 1997) which linked this conduct with the penalties provided for offences against the person under art. 582 of the criminal code. There is only one precedent, in which the accused, an Egyptian father of the Muslim faith who had subjected both his children to genital mutilation, was sentenced following a plea bargain offered on his behalf to a lenient sentence of two years' imprisonment in addition to an order for compensation for damage.[98] In such a case, the impact of the father's conduct on the dignity of the children is evident, including hindering the harmonious development of the personality and a healthy attitude to one's own body, which could give rise to behavioural disturbances.

70 It is also necessary to mention the complex issues surrounding the issue of minors and medical treatment. The problem is worsened, rather than resolved, by the clarity with which the civil code expresses itself on this point, given that art. 2 of the civil code lays down that only upon reaching the age of eighteen does a person "acquire the capacity to undertake all acts, unless a different

[95] App. Trieste 13 January 1999, [1993] Giur. it., I, 267 and, for the legal literature, M. T. Annecca, Il diritto all'immagine in: P. Cendon (supra fn. 1), I, 558 et seq. and A. Pierucci, Il diritto alla riservatezza in: P. Cendon (supra fn. 1), I, 653 et seq.

[96] On the relationship between children and mass media, see question no. 14 and, for the scholarship, R. Capo, Bambini e mass media in: P. Cendon (supra fn. 1), II, 995 et seq.; L. Buono, [1993] *Minori e giustizia*, 3, 139 et seq.; I. Cividali, [1994] *Minori e giustizia*, 1, 139 et seq.; A. Vaccaio, [1996] *Minori e giustizia*, 4, 134 et seq.; G. Sergio, [2000] Dir. fam. pers., 805 et seq. and AA.VV., Dir. inf., 214 et seq. As rightly remarked by A. Liberati, La pedofilia in: P. Cendon (supra fn. 1), II, 1705 and 1713, the damage in case of paedophilia can be of two kinds: the one, obviously, is the act *in se*. The other is provoked by the mass media. For the casuistry regarding children in the "case law" of the "*Giurì di autodisciplina pubblicitaria*" (an organ with the aim of assuring certain ethical, but also legal, standards in advertisements) and of the "*Autorità garante della concorrenza e del mercato*" (the antitrust authority), see F. Unnia, La pubblicità illecita in: P. Cendon (supra fn. 1), III, 2670 et seq.

[97] App. Trieste 13 January 1999 (supra fn. 95).

[98] On this, see A. Minunni, Bambine islamiche e mutilazioni sessuali in: P. Cendon (supra fn. 1), I, 293 et seq.

age-limit has been established in respect of such acts". In the light of this provision, an old academic commentator[99] concluded that "in outlining a conflict between a person who is incapable in law, although otherwise naturally perfectly capable, and the legal representative or parent exercising paternal authority or guardian, the latter's will must prevail". Nowadays the preferred solution is, while respecting the constitutional provision, to allow minors broader areas of independence,[100] so long as s/he has the capacity to understand and to form intention, particularly when they are very near to majority age. In this way the law avoids challenging reality, by taking into consideration the fact that a minor's mental and physical maturity is reached at the end of a process of steady evolution and not normally by leaps and bounds.[101]

Taking a longer term view, it is possible to foresee the beginnings of another line of litigation which could potentially involve minors, as well as adults. This concerns the issues relating to non-economic loss deriving from huge environmental disasters, which have already involved the Italian Supreme Court (*Corte di Cassazione*) in the so-called "Seveso case".[102] 71

20. Are there special rules for the assessment of damages sustained by a child, e.g. with respect to pain and suffering?

As regards mental suffering, the precedents show that courts believe that children, regardless of their age, are well aware of the effects which the damage they have sustained has caused to their mental and physical well-being, as 72

[99] See C. Pedrazzi, voce Consenso dell'avente diritto, [1961] E.d.D., IX, 151.

[100] See F.D. Busnelli/F. Giardina, La protezione del minore nel diritto di famiglia italiano, [1980] Giur. it., IV, 203; F.D. Busnelli, Capacità ed incapacità d'agire del minore, [1982] Dir. fam. pers., 54 et seq.; F. Giardina, *La condizione giuridica del minore* (1984), 58 et seq.; M. Marcoccia, I diritti dei morenti in: P. Cendon (supra fn. 1), II, 911 et seq.; L. Nocco, Autodeterminazione dei soggetti a capacità "ridotta" e tecniche di "sostegno" della volontà in: G. Comandé (ed.), *Diritto Privato Europeo e Diritti Fondamentali* (2004), 111–148.

[101] See R. Fresa, *Il consenso informato in odontoiatria. Legislazione e guida pratica* (1998), 119 et seq. On this topic see also the advice of Italian National Bioethics Committee ("*Comitato Nazionale di Bioetica*") about information and consent to medical treatment (*"Informazione e consenso all'atto medico"*) of 20 June 1992, about bioethics and childhood (*"Bioetica con l'infanzia"*) of 22 January 1994 and about organ transplantation in the infancy (*"Trapianti di organi nell'infanzia"*) of 21 January 1994. Lastly, see art. 28 of the code of ethics for the medical profession ("*codice di deontologia medica*") of 1998 which, even if lacking mandatory effect in Italy plays an important role in everyday medical practice: in exercising his/her profession, the physician should guarantee the child [...] and should do his/her best to satisfy the need of the minor for an adequate psycho-physical development ("Nell'esercizio della professione, il medico deve impegnarsi a tutelare il minore [...] deve in particolare adoperarsi perché il minore possa usufruire di quanto necessario ad un armonico sviluppo psico-fisico [...]". For useful advice on medical treatment of the legally or naturally incapable, see P. Cendon, *I malati terminali e i loro diritti* (2003), 265 et seq.

[102] Cass., sez. un., 21 February 2002, no. 2515, [2002] DR, 499, with comments by G. Ponzanelli, *Una "nuova" stagione del danno non patrimoniale? Le Sezioni Unite e il caso Seveso*; [2002] *Corriere giuridico* (Corr. giur.), 461, with comments by G. De Marzo, *Il danno morale nel caso Seveso: l'intervento delle Sezioni Unite.* On electromagnetic pollution, see I. Barbagallo, L'inquinamento elettromagnetico in: P. Cendon (supra fn. 1), III, 2385 et seq.

they are of their personal handicaps and also that they are even fully aware of the imminent death of a relative.[103] Consequently, damages for mental suffering are also usually awarded.[104] The exception allowed (with respect to the normal rule) is that the damages are usually tailored to fit the particular case, that is, the judge usually increases or diminishes the award or selects specific forms of compensation,[105] in the light of the particular facts.

73 In this connection, it may be helpful to recall the recent judicial trend to extend the area of damages recoverable for non-economic loss, which could lead to a broadening of the context of damages for mental suffering, including cases involving victims who are minors. In fact, the *Corte di Cassazione* has recently held that "it is not necessary to show fault in case of strict presumed liability, in order to obtain compensation for non economic losses".[106] Thus, the conviction that there can be no award of damages for mental suffering which requires the fault of the tortfeasor in cases of strict liability should be overcome.

74 In addition, a further contribution to extending the sphere of recoverable damages could be made by another recent series of rulings from the *Corte di Cassazione* and the Constitutional Court, which resulted with the effect that damages for mental suffering should be awarded in cases of violation of an inalienable right, notwithstanding the limitation imposed by art. 2059 of the civil code.[107]

[103] See P. Cendon (supra fn. 1), 127.

[104] See Trib. Spoleto 7 June 1996, [1996] *Rassegna giuridica umbra* (Rass. giur. umbra), 665; Trib. Terni 15 December 1995, [1996] Rass. giur. umbra, 664; Trib. Napoli 16 January 1995, [1995] Resp. civ. prev., 617, with comments by F. Cassella, *Le sentenze interpretative di rigetto della Corte Costituzionale: la loro efficacia nei giudizi successivi e il limite del diritto vivente (a proposito di C. Cost. n. 372/1994);* App. Milano 15 April 1994, [1995] Resp. civ. prev., 136, with comments by D. Feola, *Il caso "Seveso" e la risarcibilità dei danni non patrimoniali alla collettività vittima di un disastro ambientale*; Trib. Milano 16 July 1992, [1995] Riv. it. med. leg., 280. On this topic see also E. Navarretta, *Diritti inviolabili e risarcimento del danno* (1996), 352. For a case in which the "damage caused by spoiled holiday" ("*danno da vacanza rovinata*") was awarded to a child, see Trib. Roma 3 March 2003, [2003] DR, 901.

[105] See M. Rossetti, *Il danno da lesione della salute* (2001), 676.

[106] "Alla risarcibilità del danno non patrimoniale ex artt. 2059 c.c. e 185 c.p. non osta il mancato positivo accertamento della colpa dell'autore del danno se essa, come nei casi dell'art. 2054 c.c., debba ritenersi sussistente in base ad una presunzione di legge e se, ricorrendo la colpa, il fatto sarebbe qualificabile come reato". Cass. 12 May 2003, no. 7283, [2003] DR, 2003, 713, with comments by G. Ponzanelli, *Danno non patrimoniale: responsabilità presunta e nuova posizione del giudice civile*, Cass. 12 May 2003, no. 7281 (applying art. 2051 of the civil code), [2004] Giust. civ., 2379 et seq., with comments by A. Carrino, *Danno morale e presunzione di colpa: una convivenza ormai possibile*, and Cass. 17 May 2003, no. 7282, [2003] Giust. civ., I, 1480 et seq.

[107] Cass. 31 May 2003, no. 8827 and Cass. 31 May 2003, no. 8828 (supra fn. 30); Corte Cost. 11 July 2003, no. 233 (supra fn. 30). On this issue see also E. Navarretta (supra fn. 104), 320 et seq.

21. Does a small child have a claim for damages for pain and suffering, he or she is deprived of his parents by a tortious act? If so, may the claim be denied on the ground that the child does not feel the loss?

The claim for damages by a small child against the killer of his/her parent(s) has provoked a wide debate within the Italian legal system. Some precedents concern the damage caused by the death of the father prior to the minor's birth. There is considerable divergence between these case law precedents. While one court will award compensation,[108] another will deny it.[109] 75

Courts have also held that the right to receive a balanced upbringing by both parents is violated where one parent has been killed. This gives rise to a further claim for damages against the tortfeasor.[110] 76

22. With respect to a damage claim for the costs of medical treatment: May the tortfeasor defend himself by pointing to the fact that the parents have the duty to maintain the child?

No, since the expenses would have been of a different kind, or completely non-existent.[111] 77

In certain wrongful birth cases, damages for the birth of a child have been held to be recoverable, bearing in mind the expense which the parents are bound to incur in terms of upbringing and maintenance,[112] but also in view of a couple's right to self-determination on the issue of having children.[113] 78

[108] Cass. 22 November 1993, no. 11503, [1994] NGCC, I, 690, with comments by V. Zeno-Zencovich, *"Il danno al nascituro"*; Cass. 9 May 2000, [2001] DR, 172 et seq., with comments by A. D'Angelo, *Limitata prospettiva di vita e qualificazione del danno*; Trib. Monza 8 May 1998, [1998] Resp. civ. prev., 1101. For the legal scholarship, S. Patti in: F.D. Busnelli/S. Patti (supra fn. 13), 208 et seq. and I. Merzagora Betsos/M. Mantero, Il lutto in: P. Cendon (supra fn. 1), II, 1208 et seq. Please remember that these damages have necessarily effects also on the future (see F.D. Busnelli in: F.D. Busnelli/U. Breccia (supra fn. 81), 538, fn. 79).

[109] Trib. Monza 28 October 1997, [1998] Resp. civ. prev., 1102; Trib. Casale Monferrato 11 November 1998, [1999] Arch. giur. circol., 132.

[110] Cass. 17 September 1996, no. 8305, [1997] DR, 251.

[111] Trib. Napoli 22 October 1980, [1981] Arch. giur. circol. e sinistri, 59 and, more recently, Trib. Venezia 10 September 2002, [2003] DR, 406, with comments by A.L. Bitetto, *Bambino inatteso ... paga il medico consapevole della possibilità del suo arrivo!* Please note that a recent decision of the *Corte di Cassazione* (Cass. 16 February 2001, no. 2335, [2002] DR, 409, with comments by B. Sieff, *Danno neurologico da parto al neonato: nesso di causalità ed alternative indennitarie no-fault*) did not reduce the damages proportionally to the effect of the natural causes. This is also the opinion of the majority of the scholarship. See L. Nocco, Il nesso di causalità ed il concorso di cause nella responsabilità sanitaria in Italia ed in Francia in: G. Comandé (ed.), *Persona e tutele giuridiche* (2003), 281 et seq.

[112] Trib. Padova 9 August 1985, [1986] Riv. it. med. leg., 871, with comments by M. Tantalo, *Responsabilità civile del sanitario in caso di gravidanza indesiderata;* App. Venezia 23 July 1990, [1991] Riv. it. med. leg., 1320, with comments by M. Zanchetti, *Il "danno giusto" conseguente alla mancata interruzione di una gravidanza per colpa dei sanitari;* App. Bologna 19 December 1991, [1993] Dir fam. pers., 1081, with comments by L. Cei, *La tutela della salute ed il padre del concepito;* Trib. Roma 13 December 1994, [1995] Dir. fam. pers., 662,

79 In these circumstances, the liability of doctors and the health authority is fairly obvious, mainly because the instruments currently used in gynaecological investigations usually provide quite reliable diagnostic results[114]. What we are witnessing here, in any case, is apparent uncertainty as to the nature and amount of the recoverable damage.[115]

80 In any event, a proportion of the maintenance and treatment costs can be awarded to the parents, since this can be based on both contractual and tortious liability, in conformity with the accepted way of resolving medical negligence cases.[116]

with comments by M. Conte, *Dovere d'informazione e danno biologico: uno strano connubio* and by M. Dogliotti, *"Diritto a non nascere" e responsabilità civile*, 1474. For a case of wrongful birth as a consequence of a failed male sterilization intervention, see Trib. Milano 20 October 1997, [1998] Resp. civ. prev., 1144, with comments by M. Gorgoni, *Intervento di vasectomia non riuscito e genitorialità indesiderata: problemi di qualificazione della responsabilità e quantificazione dei danni connessi alla nascita del figlio*; Trib. S. Maria Capua Vetere 9 September 1999, [2000] *Giurisprudenza di merito* (Giur. mer.), 307, with comments by S.M. Guarriello, *Diritto alla procreazione cosciente e responsabile e dovere di informazione*; Trib. Locri 6 October 2000, [2001] DR, 393, with comments by F. Bilotta, *Il danno esistenziale: l'isola che non c'era.* For legal literature on the subject, see G. Cassano, Intervento di sterilizzazione, nascite indesiderate e danni incidenti nella sfera "esistenziale", [2001] Fam. dir., 106. In general on this topic, see A. D'Angelo (ed.), *Un bambino non voluto è un danno risarcibile?* (1999), G. Smorto, La responsabilità sanitaria per concepimento non voluto. Note comparatistiche, [1999] Dir. fam. pers., 910 et seq. and E. Bellisario, Nascita indesiderata e vita non voluta: esperienze europee a confronto, [2001] *Familia*, 824.

113 See C. Favilli, Il danno dei genitori in caso di nascita "indesiderata": profili di comparazione in: G. Comandé (supra fn. 111), 347. For the case law, Trib. Busto Arsizio 17 July 2001, [2002] Resp. civ. prev., 2002, 440, with comments by F. Bilotta, *La nascita non programmata di un figlio e il conseguente danno esistenziale.* On the notion of planned parenthood, see F. Mantovani, Il c.d. diritto del feto a nascere sano, [1980] Riv. it. med. leg., 244. Non-economic types of loss sustained by victims of medical negligence should also not be overlooked, damage which is often referred to as "secondary sterility", or the inability of a woman to conceive, even though no gynaecological or hormonal problem of any kind has been diagnosed. In other words, it clearly concerns a type of psychological disturbance which in fact hinders conception. On these issues, see above all R. Castiglioni, False diagnosi in: P. Cendon (supra fn. 1), I, 418 et seq.

114 See G. Sebastio, Le malformazioni del feto in: P. Cendon (supra fn. 1), I, 120 and G. Nicolais/ M. Silvietti, La nascita indesiderata in: P. Cendon (supra fn. 1), I, 1080.

115 See C. Favilli, Il danno dei genitori in caso di nascita "indesiderata": profili di comparazione in: G. Comandé (supra fn. 111), 353 et seq. and R. Castiglioni in: P. Cendon (supra fn. 1), 424 et seq.

116 Trib. Padova 9 August 1985, [1986] NGCC, I, 115, with comments by P. Zatti; [1986] FI, I, 1995, with comments by V. Zeno-Zencovich, *Responsabilità e risarcimento per mancata interruzione della gravidanza*; on this issue also R. Simone, Danno alla persona per nascita indesiderata, [2002] DR, 473. The solution generally adopted, anyway, is contractual liability (see Trib. Cagliari 23 February 1995, [1995] Resp. civ. prev., 599, with comments by M. Gorgoni, *Sul danno in caso di non riuscito intervento di interruzione della gravidanza: un'anarchica decisione di merito;* Cass. 22 January 1999, no. 589, [1999] DR, 294, with comments by V. Carbone, *La responsabilità del medico ospedaliero come responsabilità da contatto*; Trib. Monza 26 October 2000, [2001] Resp. civ. prev., 580, with comments by E. Guerinoni, *«Vecchio» e «nuovo» nella responsabilità del medico: un campionario di soluzioni e questioni;* App. Milano 6 February 2002, [2003] *I Contratti*, 23 with comments by E. Guerinoni, *«Contratto sociale» e nesso causale nella responsabilità del medico dipendente;* Cass. 10 May 2003, no. 6735, [2002] Giust. civ., I, 1490).

The main issues in cases concerning unwanted births can therefore be summarised with reference to two aspects, namely establishing a *causal nexus* between the doctor's negligent conduct and the birth, and ascertaining that informed consent about the limits of the treatment has been given by the patient.[117] 81

Another trend can be contrasted with this line of case law, which, placing importance exclusively on the physical well-being of the pregnant woman, excludes any other head of damage from being recoverable unless it concerns physical damage to the organism (*danno biologico*).[118] The main reason is that the birth of a child is a physiological event of ordinary life.[119] 82

In certain cases involving the death of a minor, damages awarded to the parents by the court are reduced by the application of the principle of so-called "*compensatio lucri cum damno*", namely a proportionate award of damages for the loss sustained by the parents – economic losses, *danno biologico* and mental suffering – balanced by the amount that would no longer be expended on the education and maintenance of the deceased child.[120] 83

23. In case of wrongful life: Does the child have a damage claim against the physician or a health care institution?

The answer may be significantly different in cases where the doctor or the health authority has caused (or aggravated) the damage to the child. In such a 84

[117] On these topics, see S. Cacace, Ancora a proposito di nascite indesiderate, [2003] DR, 1230 et seq.; F. Maschio, I diritti del malato in: P. Cendon (supra fn. 1), II, 882 et seq.; G. Nicolais/M. Silvietti, La nascita indesiderata in: P. Cendon (supra fn. 1), II, 1079 et seq. and C. Favilli, Il danno dei genitori in caso di nascita "indesiderata": profili di comparazione in: G. Comandé (supra fn. 111), 341 et seq. According to a judicial trend, the right to recovery of damages in case of wrongful birth exists only if there were the conditions to have an abortion (see Cass. 24 March 1999, no. 2793, [1999] DR, 766, with comments by M. Gorgoni, *Interruzione volontaria della gravidanza tra omessa informazione e pericolo per la salute (psichica) della partoriente*) and if the woman shows she would have actually had an abortion (Cass. 1 December 1995, no. 12195, [1999] DR, 522, with comments by E. Filograna, *"Se avessi potuto scegliere ...": la diagnosi prenatale e il diritto all'autodeterminazione*). Contra: Trib. Bergamo 2 November 1995, [1996] DR, 249, with comments by C. Palumbo, *Errore diagnostico e mancata interruzione della gravidanza; circa l'effettuazione di un'erronea diagnosi prenatale.*

[118] Cass. 8 July 1994, no. 6464, [1996] Rass. dir. civ., 342 et seq., with comments by D. Carusi, *Fallito intervento d'interruzione di gravidanza e responsabilità medica per omessa informazione: il "danno da procreazione" nella giurisprudenza della Cassazione italiana e nelle esperienze straniere;* Cass. 24 March 1999, no. 2793 (supra fn. 117). On the matter, see also C. Favilli, Il danno dei genitori in caso di nascita "indesiderata": profili di comparazione in: G. Comandé (supra fn. 111), 352 et seq.

[119] F.D. Busnelli, Wrongful birth, wrongful life in: F.D. Busnelli, *Bioetica e diritto privato* (2001), 301.

[120] In accordance with that, see Cass. 7 May 1996, no. 4242, [1996] Resp. civ. prev., 1176 and App. Napoli 10 July 2000, [2000] Riv. giur. circol. trasp., 946, and, for legal scholarship, S. Patti in: F.D. Busnelli/S. Patti (supra fn. 13), 197. In general about *"compensatio lucri cum damno"*, G. Gallizioli, Note critiche in tema di compensatio lucri cum damno, [1977] Riv. dir. civ., II, 333 et seq.

case, the child has a cause of action in negligence against both the doctor and the health authority, under the ordinary rules of liability.

85 If the case is that the minor is asserting that s/he should never have been born at all, because a potential alternative choice was available to the parents, s/he does not have a direct cause of action against the doctor or the health authority.[121]

86 Finally, the Italian Supreme Court[122] has confirmed the non-existence of a right not to be born, arguing in the light of the principle of solidarity established by art. 2 of the Constitution and the general principle of article 5 of the civil code, which prohibits acts causing a permanent reduction or loss of psycho-physical integrity. We should bear in mind the restriction on the use of abortion (L. 194/78), excluding it if there is no danger for the health of the mother, but also establishing the duty of the doctor to save the life of the viable foetus, independently from the subsistence of any pathology (art. 7 L. 194/78). Lastly, another decision[123], without any consideration about the legal acceptability of the wrongful life cases, awarded a sum equal to the usual compensation for non-pecuniary losses in the case of death of a relative.

87 Some opinions draw attention to "the need to re-examine the complex issue of liability in the area of reproduction",[124] in the light of the "new safeguard" conferred on the act of reproduction by L. no. 194 of 22 May 1978, but also in view of the progress made in medical technology and scientific techniques, which permits particularly serious defects to be detected in advance with a considerable degree of success, and the birth of individuals affected by such defects to be prevented. Finally, mention should be made of the shock which the knowledge of being the result of an unwanted pregnancy could produce in the child. According to this line of academic thought, all this should lead to the recognition of a potential "right not to be born".

88 On the other side, however, legal scholarship has pointed out the inconsistency between the Italian legal system and the possibility of having systematic abor-

[121] In Trib. Brescia 13 May 2003, [2003] DR, 1222, with comments by S. Cacace, *Ancora a proposito di nascite indesiderate*, the judge declined to award damages to the parents as legal representatives of the child, but only because of time running. A case of express rejection of this request is Trib. Palermo 3 March 2003, [2003] DR, 671. According to S. Chiessi, Diagnosi prenatale e risarcimento del danno a favore del bambino nato handicappato, [2003] *Familia*, 190, the dignity of the person is inconsistent with the right not to be born.

[122] Cass. 29 July 2004, no. 14488, [2005] Fam. dir., 559, with comments by G. Facci, *Wrongful life: a chi spetta il risarcimento del danno?* and [2005] Giust. civ., 121, with comments by E. Giacobbe, *Wrongful life e problematiche connesse*. In the same direction see Trib. Roma 9 March 2004, [2005] DR, 2005, 197, with comments by S. Cacace, *Perruche et alii: un bambino e i suoi danni*.

[123] Trib. Reggio Calabria 31 March 2004, [2005] DR, 179, with comments by A.L. Bitetto, *«Wrongful birth»: diritti dei genitori e assistenza tempestiva al figlio disabile*.

[124] See G. Nicolais/M. Silvietti, La nascita indesiderata in: P. Cendon (supra fn. 1), I, 1091 et seq. and M. Feola, Violazione degli obblighi d'informazione e responsabilità del medico per il danno prenatale, [2004] *Rivista critica diritto privato* (Riv. crit. dir. priv.), 617 et seq.

tions or euthanasia for handicapped foetuses or newborns. To some extent, it can be said that the maintenance in life of these people is not an act of discrimination but of beneficence.[125] Furthermore, the absence of a "biological" causal link between the hypothetical damage to the child and the medical misconduct has been stressed.[126]

24. Concerning the liability for pre-natal injuries: Are third parties liable to the child? May the mother be liable to the child, for example for the excessive consumption of alcohol or even for an omission to procure treatment?

A foetus has the right to life and to physical and mental integrity[127]. 89

In the case of medical negligence, a minor can claim compensation for damage sustained[128] and "the courts will find doctors liable where they have not taken all suitable precautions to prevent damage to the unborn child".[129] 90

On this point, the issue of the restrictive formulation of article 1 of the civil code, by which "legal capacity is acquired at birth", is overcome by reference to art. 1 of L. no. 405 of 29 July 1975 which created the family assistance services, which lists "the protection of the health […] of the embryo" among the objectives of the family and maternity assistance services, as well as art. 1 of L. no. 194 of 22 May 1978 on the intentional interruption of pregnancy, which guarantees the "protection of human life from its beginnings".[130] In this way, satisfactory protection of the unborn child is achieved, without venturing into the dangerous territory of conferring legal rights, in the fullest sense, on the embryo/foetus.[131] 91

[125] V. Carbone, Sviluppi ed orientamenti della responsabilità professionale medica nei confronti dell'embrione, [2000] DR, 1173 and C. Cortesi, Il diritto del minore a conoscere il proprio patrimonio genetico, [2003] Fam. dir., 513 et seq. On these issues, see also G. Cassano, *Le nuove frontiere del diritto di famiglia* (2000).

[126] G. Facci, La legittimazione al risarcimento in caso di danno da vita indesiderata, [2005] Resp. civ. prev., 335. Contra: M. Feola (supra fn. 124), 617 et seq.

[127] See App. Trento 18 October 1996, [1999] Dir. fam. pers., 1999, 633 speaks about the legitimate expectation of the foetus to be born safe.

[128] Trib. Verona 31 January 1994, [1994] FI, I, 2532; Trib. Nocera Inferiore 7 March 1996, [1997] Giur. mer., 527; Trib. Monza 8 May 1998, [1998] DR, 927; Cass. 5 December 1995, no. 12505, [1996] FI, I, 2494, with comments by V. Lenoci, *Diritto a nascere sani e responsabilità del medico per l'attività di assistenza al parto.*

[129] See G. Sebastio, Le malformazioni del feto in: P. Cendon (supra fn. 1), I, 121, regarding the judicial case (Cass. 13 March 1998, no. 2750, [1998] FI, I, 3521) in which the failed auscultation of the foetus' heart made it impossible to notice his distress.

[130] On this topic P.G. Giammaria, Cenni sul danno al concepito, [1992] Giur. mer., 1, 337 et seq. For the case law, see App. Trento 18 October 1996 (supra fn. 127); Trib. Verona 15 October 1990, [1991] Arch. Civ., 716 et seq. with comments by P. Morelli, *La responsabilità civile in campo medico: appunti e riflessioni*; App. Torino 8 February 1988, [1989] Giur. it., I, 2, 690; Trib. Milano 13 May 1982, [1982] Riv. it. med. leg., 1011.

[131] See G. Sebastio, Le malformazioni del feto in: P. Cendon (supra fn. 1), I, 140 et seq. On this issue see also F.D. Busnelli, Lo statuto del concepito, [1988] Democrazia e diritto (Dem. dir.), 213 et seq., and P. Perlingieri, *Il diritto civile nella legalità costituzionale* (1991), 289.

92 Nonetheless, there is debate as to whether a contract in favour of a third party can exist between the expectant mother and the hospital, where the third party is, obviously, the unborn child. Such a hypothesis, adopted by one decision of the *Tribunale di Verona*,[132] was later rejected by the Supreme Court, which preferred as a theoretical basis the so-called "contract with protective effects for third parties" (*contratto con effetti protettivi a favore di terzo*), characterised by "a plurality of contractual duties in which, alongside the principle obligation, a further right is guaranteed. Third parties outside the contract must not sustain damage".[133] Some academic commentators[134] have expressed perplexity on this point. Indeed, the beneficiary is not simply any third party, but a particular individual. Hence, it is not clear how "authoritative" legal effects can be produced in the context of a third party who is not a party to the contract if it does not come under the category of contracts in favour of a third party.

93 However, if the doctor did not cause the illness, and it is congenital, the mere fact that there was a mistaken diagnosis will not provide the child with a cause of action in negligence.[135]

94 In general, it can be said that the duty to maintain a child is very different in the case of a child needing special medical treatment: This difference constitutes the damage sustained.

95 If the parents or legal guardian(s) are taking the action on behalf of the minor, the long-term medical expenses are treated as out-of-pocket expenses until the minor reaches eighteen years of age. From then on, any potential expenses are awarded directly to the injured party.[136]

96 The possibility for a child to take legal action in tort against his/her parents was introduced for the first time as long ago as the Fifties[137]. It concerned a case in which the sexual act that caused the pregnancy, simultaneously trans-

[132] Trib. Verona 15 October 1990 (supra fn. 130).

[133] Cass. 22 November 1993, no. 11503 (supra fn. 108): "una pluralità di prestazioni, in cui, accanto ed oltre alla prestazione principale, è garantito e rimane esigibile un ulteriore diritto a che non siano arrecati danni a terzi estranei al contratto".

[134] See A.R. Venneri, Diritto del nascituro a nascere sano, obbligo di prestazione del medico e sua responsabilità contrattuale, [1995] Rass. dir. civ., 916 et seq.

[135] See Trib. Roma 13 December 1994, [1995] Dir. fam. pers., 662: the right not to be born is inconsistent with the Italian legal system recognising life as a supreme and indisposable good. On this topic, G. Nicolais/M. Silvietti, La nascita indesiderata in: P. Cendon (supra fn. 1), I, 1090 et seq.

[136] Among others, Trib. Genova 29 April 1995, [1995] Giur. it., I, 2, 555, with comments by A. Pinori.

[137] Trib. Piacenza 31 July 1950, [1951] FI, 987, with comments by F. Carnelutti. The same theory was supported, in the literature, by P. Rescigno, Il danno da procreazione in: *Studi Vassalli*, II (1960), 1158 et seq. Please note, however, that for S. Patti in: F.D. Busnelli/S. Patti (supra fn. 13), 114 et seq. there still cannot be any liability in that case because the damage coincides with the conception. For profiles of responsibility for sex-related AIDS transmission, see F. Bilotta, Dalla sieropositività all'AIDS in: P. Cendon (supra fn. 1), I, 275 et seq.

mitted a disease to the woman and the foetus. The judgment provoked bitter debate among jurists, who were split between its supporters[138] and those opposing the new trend.[139] What is more, one cannot do otherwise than assert that this ruling is fully in line with the law in force at the time (and still in force): In fact, it was ahead of its time in that it foreshadowed future developments. Indeed, it should be recalled that, at that time, damage to health or *danno biologico* was still not treated as an independent category of damage, or even that, until quite recently, there were those who maintained[140] that there was no recoverable damage.[141]

138 G. Cofano, Intangibile la libertà sessuale?, [1952] FI, IV, 12 et seq.

139 S. Lener, Mero delitto la paternità?, [1952] FI, IV, 18 et seq.

140 A. Candian, Temi, [1980] *Rivista giuridica italiana* (Riv. giur. it.), 119.

141 More recently the discussion in F. Mantovani, [1980] Riv. it. med. leg, 237 et seq. and G. Sebastio, Le malformazioni del feto in: P. Cendon (supra fn. 1), I, 113 et seq., especially 123 et seq.

Children as Victims under Dutch Law

Willem H. van Boom and Melissa Moncada Castillo

I. Factual Introduction

According to a *European Child Safety Alliance* report, injuries are the leading 1
cause of death and disability for children in the European Union.[1] An international study shows that the child injury death rate for The Netherlands is 6.6. Although this is a relatively low score, it is outscored nonetheless by the performance of Sweden, the UK and Italy.[2] Moreover, the Dutch Consumer Safety Institute has calculated the following accident figures.[3]

Road accidents	3.10
Drowning	1.17
Burns and scalds	0.24
Falls	0.28
Poisoning	0.02

Figure 1. Child mortality rate per 100,000 population.

As far as risk perception with regard to children is concerned, the following 2
may be of interest. International study[4] shows that parents feel they personally take a number of relevant precautionary measures to avoid accidents. Parents perceive traffic to be the most serious danger to their children's lives. Accident statistics support this perception. Parents also consider the fact that they cannot guard their children all the time as a major difficulty in protecting their

[1] "Priorities for Child Safety in the European Union: Agenda for Action", report published by the European Child Safety Alliance, Amsterdam: ECOSA 2001, available from <www.childsafety-europe.org>.

[2] Source: UNICEF. A League Table of Child Deaths by Injury in Rich Nations, Innocenti Report Card, Issue no. 2, February 2001, quoted in Parents' Perceptions of Child Safety, report published by the European Child Safety Alliance, Amsterdam: ECOSA, available from <www.childsafetyeurope.org>.

[3] Source: supra fn. 1.

[4] Source: "Parents' Perceptions of Child Safety", report published by the European Child Safety Alliance, Amsterdam: ECOSA, available from <www.childsafetyeurope.org>.

offspring from having accidents. Parents also seem to believe that the majority of accidents involving children can be prevented.[5]

3 Precautionary measures that have been implemented by several European countries to reduce the number of casualties include compulsory safety belt and safety seats use. Three of these popular safety measures have not (yet?) been implemented in the Netherlands: the compulsory use of bicycle helmets by children, fencing of domestic swimming pools and a ban from riding and driving farm tractors.

4 As far as intentional injuries are concerned, no precise figures are available. It is estimated that in the Netherlands some 50,000 children per year are the victim of physical, mental or sexual abuse.[6]

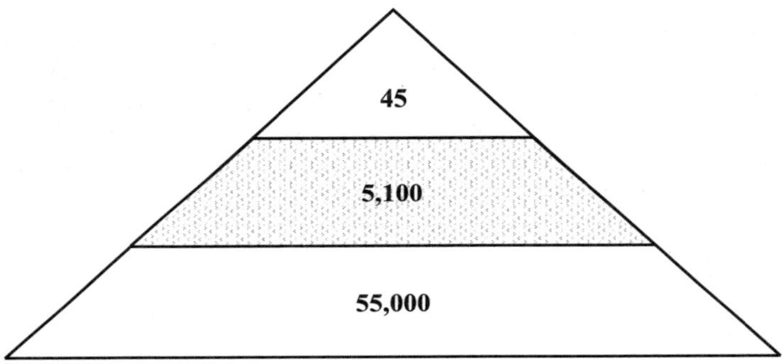

Figure 2. Pyramid private accidents 0-4 yrs. (death/hospital admittance/first aid). Source: Consument en Veiligheid.

II. Damage Caused by Parents and Other Specific Third Parties

2. In what circumstances may a parent be held liable for an injury sustained by his or her child?

(a) In what circumstances may a parent be held liable for injury resulting from his or her intentional conduct? (Liability for intent.) In particular, in what circumstances may the parent be held liable for injury resulting from his or her physical chastisement of the child?

5 As a rule, the infliction of physical harm or the infliction of mental harm – resulting in a psychiatric condition – is unlawful and will give rise to tortious liability. There are no specific statutory rules or immunities for the benefit of

[5] For an overview of European legislation relevant for child safety regulations, see "A Guide to Child Safety Regulations and Standards in Europe", Amsterdam: ECOSA 2003 (available from <www.childsafetyeurope.org>), 13 et seq.

[6] Source: <www.kindermishandeling.info>.

parents, which basically means that the general rules of tort law apply. Every case should be judged on its own merits, but there is no doubt that there is a fundamental difference between the occasional parental slap on the one hand, and frequent and intense harassment or beating on the other. Although there is hardly any case law on the subject, it seems fair to say that there is no liability in the former case and there will certainly be liability in the latter. Between these two opposites, there is undoubtedly a grey area of cases. In judging the parental behaviour, the court will leave some room for parental autonomy.[7]

Presumably, most cases do not reach the courts. The ones that do reach the 6
courts are generally the cases of (long-term) sexual, physical, or mental abuse.[8] In these cases intent or severe fault bordering on intent is almost always presumed. In the absence of fault – for instance, in cases of abusive parents that are mentally retarded – tortious liability can also be established. The Dutch Civil Code does not require *fault* for the imputation of wrongful acts: art. 6:162 of the Civil Code also allows the imputation of wrongful acts committed by incapacitated individuals.[9]

(b) In what circumstances may a parent be held liable for injury resulting from his or her unintentional conduct? (Liability for fault.) Are there special rules for liability of the parents? E.g. are parents liable only in case of gross negligence? Are parents held to a lower or higher standard of care? In what circumstances may a parent be held liable for injury resulting from his or her failure to protect the child from harm? (Liability for omissions.)

There are no special thresholds for parental liability *vis-a-vis* their children. 7
The common standards of conduct apply, although there is no rule against taking the family situation into account when assessing the applicable standard of care. There is hardly any case law on parents' liability for unintentional harm. The case law that is available seems always to involve a liability insurer that can bear the financial consequences of liability. For example, it has been decided that the standard of care owed by a motor vehicle driver to the passengers is not lowered if the passengers happen to be close relatives.[10]

Again, most cases do not seem to reach the courts. The cases that do reach the 8
courts are recourse claims by (health) insurance companies issued against either the parent in person or the parent's liability insurance company.[11] Perhaps, the fact that the claim does or does not involve the parent and child in

[7] C.C. Van Dam, *Aansprakelijkheidsrecht* (2000), no. 1504; District Court Arnhem 1 February 1973, [1973] *Nederlandse Jurisprudentie* (NJ), 143. See also T. Hartlief and R.P.J.L. Tjittes, *Verzekering en aansprakelijkheid* (2nd edn. 2002), 85.

[8] The majority of these cases are criminal court cases in which the victims file accessory claims for pain and suffering.

[9] See Wilhelm H. van Bloom, Children as Tortfeasors under Dutch Law in: M. Martín-Casals (ed.), *Children in Tort Law Part I: Children as Tortfeasors* (2006), no. 1.

[10] *Hoge Raad* (Supreme Court, HR) 11 April 1975, NJ 1975, 373.

[11] E.g. Hof Leeuwarden 25 September 1996, [1997] Verkeersrecht (VR), 208.

person may be of influence on the outcome. There is no hard evidence, however, to support this.

3. In what circumstances may a third party (e.g. a school or local authority social services department) be held liable for failing to render a child positive assistance (e.g. by preventing parental abuse)?

1. There are no specific statutory rules governing the liability of schools or local authorities with a statutory supervisory task. Therefore, the general rules of tort law apply. These rules leave a good deal of room for policy by the courts. Although there is hardly any case law that can be applied directly, there seems to be good sense in applying the relevant standard of care of supervisors. Supervisors should take reasonable care that the person under supervision will not cause unlawful harm to others. If there is a concrete danger of such harm, and the supervisor has or should have knowledge of this danger, it should act upon this information and use its supervisory powers to prevent this danger from materialising.[12] Therefore, if a school or authority has information that should give it reason to seriously suspect abuse, it should act upon this information. If necessary, it should use its powers to prevent damage from occurring, e.g. by informing the relevant public authorities.

4. What limitations periods are applied to a child's claim?

9 Claims of children against their parents are time-barred according to the general rules. In general, the limitation period is two-fold: first, there is a five year period running from the moment that the victim has knowledge of his damage and the identity of the tortfeasor. Second, the claim is barred in any case after twenty years, running from the moment of the tortious act. With respect to tortious acts committed after 1 January 2004, resulting in death or personal injury, the five year period is the exclusively relevant period.[13]

10 However, it should be noted that as a rule a time-barred claim is extended by six months after the ending of the parental authority (e.g. six months after coming of age at 18).[14] Moreover, according to Supreme Court case law, claims for abuse are not barred during the period that the abused child was unable to submit its claim as a direct or indirect consequence of the abuse. This period may include a number of years of adulthood, if the abuse resulted in a semi-permanent state of denial or mental block. The Supreme Court has ruled that it would be against the basic norms of reasonableness and fairness to hold that the five year prescription period would commence irrespective of the

[12] Further on this subject of supervisors' tortious liability, see I. Giesen, Aansprakelijkheid voor gebrekkig toezicht, Een beschouwing over de grondslagen en achtergronden van de aansprakelijkheid van (financiële) toezichthouders jegens gedupeerde derden, [2002] *Aansprakelijkheid, Verzekering en Schade* (AV&S) 4, 97–110.

[13] Act of 27 November 2003, *Staatsblad* 2003, 495.

[14] Art. 3:321 (1) (b) *Burgerlijk Wetboek* (BW).

abuse that prevents the victim physically or psychologically from filing his claim.[15]

In addition, there is a specific statutory rule on convergence of the civil and criminal prescription period: As long as criminal charges can be brought against the perpetrator, the civil claim cannot be time-barred.[16] 11

III. Contributory Negligence

5. Are there any special provisions concerning contributory negligence if the tortfeasor is a child?

There are no special provisions concerning contributory negligence if the child is the tortfeasor. However, it cannot be ruled out that in specific circumstances the age of the tortfeasor has some bearing on the equitable adjustment of art. 6:101 BW (on that article, see infra, no. 13). 12

6. What are the rules governing contributory negligence of the child? Do such principles follow the same lines as those governing the negligence issue itself (mirror-image)?

The rules that govern contributory negligence of children are laid down in art. 6:101 BW. Art. 6:101 BW provides: 13

> "When the damage is partly caused by an occurrence that can be imputed to the injured party, the obligation to pay compensation is reduced by apportioning the damage between the injured party and the liable party in proportion to the degree in which the occurrences that can be imputed to the parties have contributed to the damage, provided that account is taken of the disparity in the seriousness of the respective faults, or other circumstances of the case, to decide whether equity demands that an alternative apportionment or full recovery takes place or that the obligation to pay lapses."

This article leaves room for adjustment between the tortfeasor and the injured party who is contributorily negligent on a double basis: a causal and an equitable adjustment. Equity may come into play when either tortfeasor or injured party is a child. 14

Contributory negligence of the child is clearly not the mirror image of tortious liability of the child, because in that case there would have been no room for a contributory negligence defence. Children up to 14 years are not considered to 15

[15] HR 23 October 1998, [2000] NJ, 15; HR 25 June 1999, [2000] NJ, 16 (ruling that the twenty year period – as it then was in force – cannot be stopped or prevented from commencing by the physical or psychological forces that impede the victim from filing his or her claim); 11 October 2002, [2002] NJ, 558 (ruling that if the five year period has not commenced due to the exception based on reasonableness and fairness, there cannot be a statutory extension of the period either).

[16] Art. 3:310 subs. 4 BW.

be capable of being liable in tort, as follows from art. 6:164 BW.[17] In legal doctrine the mirror image theory has been put forward in the sense that some authors hold the view that children up to 14 years should never be held contributorily negligent at all.[18] This theory does not reflect the law as it stands.

7. Does the fixed minimum age for children to be liable, if any exists, also apply to the contributory negligence of the child?

16 The short answer to this question would be: generally speaking, the fixed minimum age for a child to be liable (14 yrs.) is not reflected in contributory negligence. There is no statutory rule to that effect. A more elaborate answer would be that there does seem to be a strong tendency to this effect, both in case law and the Civil Code itself. As far as the Civil Code itself is concerned, a strong suggestion against contributory negligence of children is found in art. 6:164 BW. If a tortious act is committed by a child under the age of fourteen, the child himself is immune from liability (art. 6:164 BW); instead his parents can be held (strictly) liable, provided that the child would himself have been liable, had he been 14 years or older (art. 6:169, para. 1, BW). It is sometimes argued that the legislature's objective of children's immunity is best served by excluding their contributory negligence as well. As the law stands, however, there is no explicit statutory exclusion to this effect.

17 As far as case law is concerned, the Hoge Raad (Supreme Court) has led the way in a number of decisions. In a landmark 1989 ruling, the Court had to decide on contributory negligence of a ten-year-old boy, whose hand had been caught in a revolving, unshielded part of a mechanical milking device. The farmer was held liable for failing to protect the boy, who had been helping him milk the cows, against the clear dangers of the milking device. The appellate court decided that the boy was 50 percent contributorily negligent. The Supreme Court quashed this decision, ruling that – although from a causal perspective, the boy's conduct might indeed have been 50 percent contributory – the court in fact should have applied an equitable adjustment, because children have a minimal understanding of the dangers surrounding them and they cannot be expected to act in full accordance with these dangers. In the Supreme Court's opinion, in cases like these children should in principle be awarded full recovery, and if the lower court would wish to deviate from this principle, it should state its motives thoroughly.[19]

[17] See the previous report for more details.

[18] See, e.g., C.J.H. Brunner, case note [1990] NJ, 778 and C.C. van Dam, [1990] *Kwartaalbericht Nieuw BW*, 3, 93. Cf. A.R. Bloembergen in: A.J.O. van Wassenaer, *Eigen schuld bij onrechtmatige daad: de verdeelsleutel zoals neergelegd in art. 6:101 BW: inleidingen, gehouden op het symposion van de vereniging van letselschadeadvocaten* (1997) [LSA-proceedings no. 8], 5 et seq., and contra: T. Hartlief, 'Eigen schuld en letselschade' in: *Festschrift Miscellanea – Jurisconsulto vero Dedicata* (1997), 129 et seq.

[19] HR 8 December 1989, [1990] NJ, 778. See also C.C. van Dam, Onrechtmatige daad. Eigen schuld van een kind. Billijkheidscorrectie, [1990] *Kwartaalbericht Nieuw BW*, 90 et seq. Cf. also HR 30 June 1978, [1978] NJ, 685, and *Asser-Hartkamp (Verbintenissenrecht)* I, no. 451 et seq.

In two far-reaching decisions, issued in the early 1990s, the Supreme Court has stretched the limits of its judicial powers even further by *completely* excluding contributory negligence of children up to 14 years in case of traffic accidents involving motor vehicles.[20] Essentially, children up to 14 years are granted a fixed 100 percent compensation award where they are hit (while cycling or walking) by a motor vehicle. In these cases, the Supreme Court reasons that children are in special need of legal protection against the consequences of traffic accidents, because they cannot be expected to act in accordance with the serious dangers they are exposed to when participating in traffic. The resulting high level of protection ensures that a child that is injured when riding a bicycle or participating in traffic as a pedestrian, can claim full damages, even if he heavily contributed (in a causal sense) to the occurrence of the accident. An exception is left open where the child acts with intent or wilful recklessness.[21] 18

In short, most legal authors hold the view, based on the quoted Supreme Court decisions, that children up to fourteen years can only be held contributorily negligent if their intent or their act of wilful recklessness contributed to their injury.[22] Possibly, this is in accordance with case law. 19

It should be stressed that the result of full recovery for children is a matter of equitable adjustment. With respect to children, art. 6:101 BW probably works as follows: first, it must be ascertained whether the injured person has acted negligently – that is, from an objective perspective, and therefore without regard to his age. If this is the case, then a causal apportionment should be applied. And finally, this causal apportionment is fully equitably adjusted, having regard to the young age of the injured person. Although taking the second step seems futile, given the final adjustment, in practice this second step is most relevant whenever the claimant is not the injured child himself, but a subrogated insurance company. 20

8. What is the standard of care governing the behaviour of children in the context of contributory negligence? Is such standard determined by the same principles and criteria which are relevant to the duty of care incumbent upon the child in the context of him or her being held liable?

It seems that similar standards apply that would apply to liability of the child himself (save for the statutory exclusion in art. 6:164 BW). Note, however, that the standard of care is in itself not decisive when it comes to setting the percentage of the damage that the injured child has to bear by himself. Within the framework of art. 6:101 BW, the contributory *negligence* is a first yard- 21

[20] HR 1 June 1990, [1991] NJ, 720; HR 31 May 1991, [1991] NJ, 721; The Supreme Court has resisted the temptation of stretching the age limit of 14 years; see HR 24 December 1993, [1995] NJ, 236.

[21] Which will hardly ever be the case, given the strict interpretation of both intent and wilful recklessness.

[22] Cf. *Schadevergoeding* (loose-leaf), art. 101, no. 17.2, with further references.

stick and the *equitable adjustment* the second, according to which the young age may play a role in setting the percentage.[23]

IV. Contribution in Equity

9. Is there a parallel (mirror-image) to liability in equity in the field of contributory negligence? If so, do the criteria determining liability in equity of the child also apply to the issue of holding it accountable for his or her contributory negligence?

22 In principle, there is no equivalent to the 'liability in equity' under Dutch tort law.[24] However, the principles of equitable adjustment in case of contributory negligence indeed allow equitable reduction of the child's claim. The fact that the child is insured against the injuries it sustained, plays a major role in the legal administration of traffic accidents. See supra nos. III.18 et seq.

10. If answered affirmatively: Is the fact that the child is privately or socially insured against the accident a factor to be considered? Is the existence of liability insurance of the tortfeasor to be taken into account? What factors have a bearing on the assessment of equitable contribution?

23 If the child can claim from a social security agency or a private insurer, his or her contributory negligence is taken into consideration when a recourse claim is exercised by the agency or insurance company.[25] The recourse claim is treated differently in this respect than the child's claim itself would have been treated (had he not been insured).[26] The existence of liability insurance is also considered to be a factor that should be taken into account when weighing the respective circumstances that decide the assessment.[27]

V. Miscellaneous

11. What are the rules for a situation in which the child is guilty of contributory negligence but the parents have also breached their duty to supervise? Is the child held accountable in any way for his or her parents' breach of the duty to supervise so that his or her claim for damages is reduced?

24 Children are not "identified", for the purpose of establishing contributory negligence, with their supervisors (parents, legal guardians). This was decided in a 1985 Supreme Court decision.[28] In that case, a four-year-old girl was severely injured by a dog bite. The dog owner was held strictly liable, but he alleged

[23] See H. van Bloom in: M. Martín-Casals (supra fn. 9), nos. 5–6.
[24] See H. van Bloom in: M. Martín-Casals (supra fn. 9), passim.
[25] See on this topic T. Hartlief and R.P.J.L. Tjittes, *Verzekering en Aansprakelijkheid* (2nd edn. 1999).
[26] Further on this topic, see C.E. du Perron and W.H. van Boom in: U. Magnus (ed.), *The Impact of Social Security Law on Tort Law* (2003), 156 et seq.
[27] See, e.g., HR 4 May 2001, [2002] NJ, 214 (Chan/Maalsté).
[28] HR 31 May 1985, [1986] NJ, 690.

that the accident was in part caused by negligence of the victim's father. The Supreme Court held that even if the father – who, at the time of the accident, no longer had parental control over his daughter – had indeed been negligent, his negligence would not be imputed to the victim as contributory negligence. The Supreme Court stated that the mere existence of a family relationship between the victim and one of the negligent originators, was not a valid reason for deviating from the principle that concurrent tortfeasors are liable as joint and several debtors. The Court stressed that children are not vicariously liable for the faults of their parents, and that imputation of parental negligence would lead to the undesirable side-effect that the child would be forced to claim from two tortfeasors in two separate actions, and, moreover, that the child would bear the risk of insolvency of either – although it had done nothing wrong. Finally, the Court did not see any solid reason for discerning relatives living together from those living apart. Conclusively, the dog owner was held to pay damages in full.

12. Do the rules of contributory negligence apply also in the area of strict liability?

The general provision on contributory negligence (art. 6:101 BW, see supra no. III.13) include strict liability. Consequently, not only negligent acts of the injured party himself can constitute contributory negligence (as dealt with in art. 6:101 BW), but also the acts of persons for whom the injured party bears vicarious responsibility (e.g. employer's liability, parental liability for wrongful conduct of children up to fourteen years). Moreover, the injured party generally bears the risk of strict liabilities: if the occurrence is caused in part by the act of an animal in possession of the injured party, or by the defectiveness of a tangible object in possession of the injured party, this will give rise to application of art. 6:101 BW.[29] However, as far as children up to 14 years is concerned, art. 6:183 BW shifts most strict liability to *the parents*. 25

This could lead to the conclusion that a child of ten years who walks his dog and is injured in a fight between his dog and someone else's, is not partially responsible for his own injuries. If this is true, he could claim in full from the owner of the other dog, which in turn might address the parents for contribution. No case on this topic has yet been decided. 26

13. Do the rules of contributory negligence apply in the area of strict liability for traffic-accidents or other areas of tort liability?

In principle the general rules apply. However, in a number of Supreme Court decisions, a more subtle system of contributory negligence has been developed for children – that is, bicyclists and pedestrians up to 14 years – that fall prey to the dangers of motorized traffic. See supra no. III.18. 27

[29] See A.J.O. van Wassenaer van Catwijck/R.H.C. Jongeneel, *Eigen schuld en medeaansprakelijkheid* (2nd edn. 1995), 8–10.

14. Are adults held to a higher standard of care in their interactions with children, or when children are or may be around?

28 There is ample proof that children are better protected by tort law than adults. The case law on traffic accidents involving children bears witness to this policy.[30] Case law on duties of care to mitigate dangerous situations is also strong indication of this judicial policy.[31]

VI. Insurance Matters

15. Are pupils covered by private or public accident (first-party) insurance?

29 Although some schools take out first-party accident policies to the benefit of their pupils, there is no compulsory scheme to that effect.

16. Does this insurance cover any damage incurred on the way to school and back?

30 Not applicable.

17. Are there restrictions on damages recoverable by the child, e.g. with respect to loss of future earnings?

31 Not applicable.

VII. Damage Issues

18. If damages for loss of earnings are available, what are the principles governing their assessment?

32 With regard to personal injury, the aim of the law of damages is *full* compensation of the damage suffered, both in respect of pecuniary loss and non-pecuniary loss. This implies that the actual damage must be compensated, no more and no less. Effectively, all *pecuniary* loss is to be compensated, including the cost of medical treatment, reasonable cost of supplemental care, increased expenses due to the physical impairment, actual loss of income, loss of future increase of income (e.g. if the injuries cancel possible career prospects), and other (future) damage.

33 As far as future damages are concerned, the courts are allowed to award damages either as a lump sum or as a periodic allowance (art. 6:105 BW). In personal injury legal practice, both injurer and injured party generally prefer the payment of a lump sum (partly for purposes of avoiding income tax). The payment for future damages by means of a lump sum is calculated on the basis of reason-

[30] See supra nos. 18 et seq.

[31] E.g. HR 25 September 1981, [1982] NJ, 254 (Martin Smit/Royal); HR 8 December 1989, [1990] NJ, 778, dealt with supra no. III.17.

able projections of how the future would have evolved if the injury had not occurred.[32]

19. Which of the child's non-material interests are protected in your jurisdiction? May the child, for example, sue for impairment of intellectual or social development, the onset of behavioural problems, or reduced employment prospects?

It is quite difficult to ascertain whether Dutch tort law does in fact protect the child's non-material interests. For example, the impairment of development can result in a claim for *material* damages, e.g. the loss of future earning capacities or the loss of future job opportunities. Although in theory these claims may be brought into court, in most cases the damage will be too hypothetical to value. Having said that, in theory both the direct material consequences of impairment as well as the non-pecuniary consequences (loss of enjoyment and prospects) can be the subject of compensation. "Infringement of the person" is a type of tort that can be compensated under the heading of non-pecuniary loss. The amount is assessed in accordance with the principles of fairness (art. 6:106 BW). 34

20. Are there special rules for the assessment of damages sustained by a child, e.g. with respect to pain and suffering?

There are no specific rules with regard to the assessment of damages of children. 35

21. Does a small child have a claim for damages for pain and suffering if he or she is deprived of his or her parents by a tortious act? If so, may the claim be denied on the ground that the child does not feel the loss?

No specific case law seems to address this question, and although a claim for pain and suffering is dependent upon the actual experience of this pain and suffering, it does not seem plausible that a child can claim the immaterial loss of parental affection and guidance. In cases of death of the parents, art. 6:108 allows certain persons who were dependent on the deceased to claim material damages as a result of the loss of maintenance. Minor children are included.[33] 36

Art. 6:108 BW bars claims for non-pecuniary loss of parental consortium because an award for these third party damages would be inconsistent with the exhaustive nature of the regime on third-party claims. A proposal for a statute amending this regime is currently pending before parliament, which would en- 37

[32] The Civil Code calls this the *afweging van goede en kwade kansen* ("taking into account good and adverse chances"; art. 6:105 BW). See for this process "in action" HR 15 May 1998, [1998] NJ, no. 624; HR 14 January 2000, [2000] NJ, no. 437.

[33] This includes a claim for the compensation for loss of services by the deceased who maintained the common household.

title the child to a fixed amount of € 10,000 in non-pecuniary damages for bereavement.[34]

22. With respect to a damage claim for the costs of medical treatment: May the tortfeasor defend himself by pointing to the fact that the parents have a duty to maintain the child?

38 The tortfeasor cannot raise the defence that he should not bear the cost of medical treatment because the parents are obliged to maintain and provide for their child. This was explicitly decided by the Supreme Court.[35]

23. In case of wrongful life: Does the child have a damage claim against the physician or a health care institution?

39 The Supreme Court has recently decided in the Baby Kelly-case[36] to allow claims concerning wrongful life. 'Wrongful life' arises when a child is born that would have been aborted had the parents known that the child was going to be severely disabled. In essence, the negligence of the doctor is not the cause of the injury (the injury has a congenital origin), but the negligence interferes with the parents' right of self-determination and therefore violates the interests of child, mother and father. In the Kelly-case, the obstetrician had negligently refused to apply prenatal diagnostics. As a result Kelly was born with severe congenital defects. Kelly and her parents sued for material and non-pecuniary losses, including the non-pecuniary loss suffered by the severely disabled Kelly herself.

40 There were a number of very difficult issues in the Kelly-case. To sustain the claim of the child, she would have to be party to the medical treatment contract. The Supreme Court pointed out that an unborn child is not self-evidently party to such a contract. In theory the child can, but due to the nature of this contract, in principle the mother enters into the contract on her own behalf. The mere fact that the child benefits from the contract is not enough justification to be considered a party to the contract. However, irrespective of the uncertainty of whether the child is party or not, the hospital (the LUMC) can be held liable by the child on the basis of tortious liability, as we shall see later on.

41 The Supreme Court was faced with the difficult task of determining whether the child had a right of non-existence or not. The Supreme Court answered this question in the negative. Only the mother has this right of self-determination. Moreover, according to Dutch civil law the child obtains legal rights just after being born, namely on the basis of retrospection. Thus, the unborn child

[34] See memorandum by the Minister of Justice, 20 June 2001, *Kamerstukken* II, 27.400 VI, no. 70.

[35] HR 28 May 1999, [1999] NJ, 564 (Johanna Kruidhof).

[36] HR 18 March 2005, [2005] RVDW, 42 (Baby Kelly).

has patrimonial rights, but it obtains these rights retrospectively at the moment of birth. This reasoning could have required the court to decide that Kelly did not have the right not to live before she was born. The dogmatic problem that thus arises was in a sense by-passed by the Court by arguing that the right to non-existence was the mother's prerogative rather than the child's.

The Court also held that it is irrelevant for the liability of the LUMC whether the child is or is not a party to the contract. In both cases the medical health-care institution has the obligation to care for the benefit of both the parents and the child itself. The child can accordingly claim compensation. The Court awarded the claim of the child and convicted the LUMC to compensate all heads of damage caused by the hospital's negligence. This claim not only concerned medical costs, but also maintenance costs (even after Kelly's 21st birthday). The Court also awarded immaterial damage. The Court did not acknowledge the right of non-existence of the child. However, this does not mean that she had no claim for compensation. 42

Concerning the determination of the size of the compensation award, a comparison has to be made between the state of affairs after the negligent omission of the obstetrician (existence) and the state in which the child would have been if negligence had not been committed (i.e. non-existence). Obviously, this comparison is almost impossible, not only practically, but also ethically. From an ethical perspective, by allowing this type of claim the court would implicitly hold that non-existence is to be preferred over a disabled existence. It would also imply that physically and/or mentally disabled persons are inferior. This line of reasoning is the main objection against allowing this type of claim. 43

There still is discussion going on about this issue, notably in Parliament. Intuitively, people tend not to accept that by allowing the claim the courts accepts non-existence to be a better option than existence. The Supreme Court anticipated these arguments by stating that the claim is allowed not because non-existence is better than living with a severe disability, but because Kelly (and every other severely disabled child) has a right to compensation if a third party has acted negligently with respect to her well-being. This decision, or so the court stressed, should in no way be constructed as holding the disabled child to be inferior, but rather as making her life more bearable. 44

Moreover, there were two more policy objections the Supreme Court had to deal with. The first is called the slippery-slope argument. This argument claims that by allowing this claim, the courts would have to allow every child with congenital defects to sue his or her parents for not having aborted the child. The Supreme Court explicitly rejects this argument, by stating that the right of non-existence has not been sustained, so the child cannot sue his parents. The other objection is the "defensive medicine" argument. This argument boils down to the fear that gynaecologists and obstetricians would have to practice their profession more defensively to avoid liability. The Supreme 45

Court rejects this argument. According to the Supreme Court doctors will not behave differently because of the decision because the liability of the physician and the hospital lies in the fact that they did not act in accordance with the expected standard which was held to be good standing practice within the medical community. In other words: As the standards of conduct that were applied by the court originated from the medical profession itself, there was no ground for fear of defensive medicine.

24. Concerning liability for pre-natal injuries: Are third parties liable to the child? May the mother be liable to the child, for example for excessive consumption of alcohol or even for an omission to procure treatment?

46 The answer to this question depends on what we consider to be "prenatal injuries". If we leave 'wrongful life' cases aside, we understand 'prenatal injuries' to be injuries caused by the obstetrician or by others during the pregnancy. The liability of physicians is governed by the common rules of contract breach. However, first we must determine whether there is a contract between the child (because it is the child who claims) and the obstetrician. In this respect we refer to our answer to the previous question.

47 If the child cannot claim in contract, it can possibly sue in tort. For a successful claim against the obstetrician or gynaecologist, the usual requirements apply. There are three categories of tortious acts:[37] violation of a subjective right, acts or omissions contrary to a statutory duty, and acts or omissions contrary to the standard of conduct seemly in society.[38] The obstetrician can be held accountable for the tortious act either on the basis of subjective "*fault*" or the objective "*imputation on the basis of an unwritten source of legal and moral opinion*".

48 In cases of pre-natal injury the causation requirement may stand in the way of liability. To determine whether there is causality, a two-fold test is applied: Firstly, the *condicio sine qua non* test is used. It is clear that this theory takes causality too far. Therefore, the second test used is the so-called "*leer van de toerekenbaarheid naar redelijkheid*" (the theory of reasonable imputation of causes). With this theory the court can decide, by looking at all circumstances of the case, whether there is a reasonable ground for imputing the damage to the tortious behaviour.

49 With regard to parties other than the physician treating the mother, the usual rules apply. As far as the second question is concerned, there is no case law on

[37] Art. 6:162 subs. 2 BW.

[38] Many claims in tort are based on this latter category. The reason is simple: The openness of this category makes it possible to base almost every tort claim, even if the claim can also be based on one of the other two categories. If the claim can be based on one of these categories, the action is not per se wrongful. There can be a 'rechtvaardigingsgrond' (justification; viz. self-defence).

the maternal liability for pre-natal injuries. In the legal writing it has been suggested that such liability can in fact arise in case of drug abuse or excessive alcohol consumption.[39]

[39] See, e.g., D.I. Levine & C.J.J.M. Stolker, Een onrechtmatig bestaan in Nederland; Een stand van zaken, [1997] *Aansprakelijkheid en Verzekering* (A&V), 38–45; S.D. Lindenbergh, Schadevergoeding wegens wrongful birth en wrongful life, [2003] *Ars Aequi* (AA), 365–374.

Children as Victims under Portuguese Law

Maria Manuel Veloso

I. Factual Introduction

1. What are the most common causes of injury to children in your jurisdiction? In what proportion of cases are actions brought for damages in tort? How many of these are successful?

The most common causes of injury to children concern: 1

- domestic accidents, one third of them being with children under 14,[1] they concern mainly falls, ingestion of toxic liquids, or the misuse of matches,
- accidents attributable to other children, at home or at school or when playing games (mainly football),
- accidents when launching fire rockets, fireworks or carnival bombs – these accidents represent around 42% of the most serious accidents,[2]
- accidents occurring in abandoned places or in the vicinity of construction sites,
- accidents occurring in amusement parks[3] and when playing sports (with sports equipment);[4]

[1] According to the *Observatório Nacional de Saúde*, these are the data for 2003, taking into consideration the registration of cases by the ADÉLIA system (*Acidentes domésticos e de lazer-Informação adequada*). Mortality is nevertheless low in domestic accidents. The *Associação Portuguesa de apoio à vítima* (APAV) registered, in the year 2004, 310 crimes against minors.

[2] J.C.B. Proença, Responsabilidade pelo risco do detentor do veículo e conduta do lesado: a lógica do "tudo ou nada", [2004] *Cadernos de Direito Privado*, 11–15.

[3] One of the most commented upon cases was an accident in an water park that resulted in the death of a child. The State was held liable for the omission of regulations on safety measures. See on this case, J.G. Canotilho, Responsabilidade civil do Estado pelos danos decorrentes do não exercício da função legislativa. Anotação ao Acórdão do Tribunal da Relação de Lisboa de 7 de Maio de 2002, [2002] *Revista de Legislação e de Jurisprudência* (RLJ), 202. On "parques infantis", see Decree-Law 379/97, 27 December 1997; in the Preamble of this Decree, a number of 4.000 accidents per year in children's parks is mentioned.

[4] On the cases involving a fall of football goals (a very typical cause of minors' injuries), see J.A. Dias, *Dano corporal-quadro epistemológico e aspectos ressarcitórios* (2001), 304, who endorsed the applicability of the Products Liability Act, Decree-Law 385/99, 28 September 1999. Nowadays, special provisions strengthen the duty to supervise sport equipment; see, Decree-Law 100/2003, 23 May 20003, reviewed by Decree-Law 82/2004, 14 April 2004, and Portaria 1049/2004, 19 August 2004, which regulates the compulsory insurance connected with the use of such devices.

- traffic accidents,[5]
- chastisement.

The number of cases and the seriousness of the injuries caused led to a protective effort on the part of the legislature, which was particularly evident in the late 1990s.

2 I also would like to add injuries deriving from medical malpractice. They are not probably seen as a common case of damage to children, since there are not so many cases on the subject. Hitherto, nevertheless, the few cases which have arisen play an important role since they are embedded in the common obstacles to holding physicians (and nursery professionals or even professionals in general) liable. This can be illustrated by way of several examples.

3 a) *Supremo Tribunal de Justiça* (Supreme Court, STJ) 5 November 1997, <www.dgsi.pt>: A pregnant woman of 36 weeks and 4 days dies in the hospital from sepsis. The child was stillborn, after suffering tachycardia before the delivery. The Court exempted the hospital from liability. However, a remarkable dissenting vote, stating that the hospital ought to have acted with urgency even if the cause of sepsis was not known, was lodged.

4 b) *Supremo Tribunal Admnistrativo* (Supreme Administrative Court, STA) 9 March 1999 ([1999] BMJ, 485, 155): The court recognized that there had been a wrongful delay in the timing of the delivery of a baby (ignoring the indications of the gynaecologist), but drew the conclusion that there was no causal link between that fact and the death of the baby. An autopsy was not ordered by the hospital and, therefore, it was not possible to determine the cause of death.

5 c) STA 5 February 2003, <www.dgsi.pt>: There was a proven delay of 15 minutes in calling the obstetrician to a risky delivery, although the gynaecologist was called after detecting the foetus' bradycardia. The child was not being observed by the CTG/RCT method as he should. The fact that 15 minutes would also be the time required to prepare for a caesarean, and that it was not proven that the untoward result would be different had the CTG been operative, lent weight to the court's rejection of the appeal.

6 d) STA 20 February 2002, <www.dgsi.pt>: A 7-year-old minor with meningococcemia died in the hospital. His parents accused the hospital of lack of observation during the night. The Administrative Supreme Court quashed the decision of the lower court, imposing a new judgment, requiring proof of causation between the alleged breach of duty and the death of the child.

[5] In 1998, 2.000 children under the age of 14 were knocked down by cars; see J.C.B. Proença, *Ainda sobre o tratamento mais favorável dos lesados culpados no âmbito dos danos corporais*, *Estudos em homenagem ao Professor Doutor Almeida Costa* (2000), 822, fn. 52. According to a UNICEF study in 2001 on infant mortality, in Portugal around 7% of the deaths result from a traffic accident.

Only a few of these cases have come before the courts. The main field is represented by traffic accidents' liability. 7

Many of the above situations do not fulfil liability requirements, due to the absence of fault. 8

The most successful amongst them are cases involving children playing inside fire-rocket factories or stores (some of them abandoned). Since the activity (and connected acts) of dealing with fire rockets is regarded as dangerous, the presumption of fault under art. 493, 2 *Código Civil Português* (Portuguese Civil Code, CC) applies. 9

II. Damage Caused by Parents and Other Specific Third Parties

2. In what circumstances may a parent be held liable for an injury sustained by his or her child?

(a) In what circumstances may a parent be held liable for injury resulting from his or her intentional conduct? (Liability for intent.) In particular, in what circumstances may the parent be held liable for injury resulting from his or her physical chastisement of the child?

(b) In what circumstances may a parent be held liable for injury resulting from his or her unintentional conduct? (Liability for fault.) Are there special rules for liability of the parents? E.g. are parents liable only in case of gross negligence? Are parents held to a lower or higher standard of care? In what circumstances may a parent be held liable for injury resulting from his or her failure to protect the child from harm? (Liability for omissions.)

There is no special provision on this matter. 10

Art. 1897 CC, nevertheless, prescribes that parents must administrate their children's patrimony as if they were administrating their own patrimony. This rule is an exception, since it deviates from the general yardstick in the fulfilment of parental statutory duties (in the Family Law Book of the Portuguese Civil Code), not only because it specifies the duty of care, but also because it curtails the common standard of care (of *bonus pater familiae*, according to art. 487, 2 CC). At the outset, this ruling could be seen as a basis for parental liability (although confined to pecuniary concerns), but legal scholarship has never recognized that role. The breach of duty simply implies the adoption of judicial measures in order to preserve the children's assets. 11

Decisions on parental civil liability are not common in Portugal. It would be difficult to reconcile their existence with the principle of the maintenance of the family relationship[6]. But this does not happen in criminal law, where hypo- 12

[6] Similar arguments tried to justify the *interspousal immunity*. On its decay in the Portuguese system, see A. Cerdeira, *Da responsabilidade civil dos cônjuges entre si* (2000).

thetically it could be argued that a criminal action should not be tried as it would also violate the principle of the maintenance of the family relationship. Probably the deciding argument relates both to the fact that in most civil cases the declaration of unfitness of parents suffices[7] and to the economic dependency (and benefits) of children towards their parents.

13 According to art. 152 Criminal Code, he who, when taking care of, or supervising the education or work of, a person particularly needed of protection on account of her age, causes physical or psychological damage or treats her cruelly or employs her in dangerous activities or demands excessive work can be convicted and imprisoned for between one and five years (if the same fact is not covered by art. 144, on crimes violating physical integrity).[8]

14 In *Relação do Porto* (Oporto Court of Appeal, RP) 13 October 1993, <www.dgsi.pt>, the court had to deal with the following situation: a two-year-old child was chastised by her mother and her mother's partner, by leaving the child alone for long periods of time. Both were convicted.

15 In STJ 30 October 1996, <www.dgsi.pt>, the Court dealt with the limits of the power of correction of parents. The father of a child used, almost daily and for futile reasons, a belt to punish him. It was a clear case of abuse of his power.

3. In what circumstances may a third party (e.g. a school or local authority social services department) be held liable for failing to render a child positive assistance (e.g. by preventing parental abuse)?

a) Private school

16 A private school can assume the duty to protect the child against one of the parents, deprived of his parental duty due to his violent character. Both the child and the contracting party (the other parent) could claim for damages if such a duty is infringed.

17 If the private school acknowledges that the child is a victim of parental abuse, there is a duty to inform the competent authorities. But this duty cannot be taken as absolute. By complying with that kind of duty, the school (or a neighbour) is not really abiding to a "norm of protection" (under art. 483, 1 CC, whose breach is classified as an unlawful act).[9]

[7] See, on the limitation of parental care, artt. 1913–1974 CC.

[8] J.F. Dias (ed.) *Comentário Conibricense ao Código Penal* (2001). On chastisement of minors, see J.A.G. Cruz, *Maus tratos à criança* (1994); A.N. Almeida/I.M. André/H.N. Almeida, Sombras e marcos: os maus tratos às crianças na família, [1999] *Análise social*, 34, 91–121. On the limits of a parental "right to punish", F.S. Monteiro, *O direito de castigo ou o direito de os pais baterem nos filhos* (2002).

[9] J.S. Monteiro, *Responsabilidade por conselhos, recomendações e informações* (1989), 237–271.

b) Public school

In RP 3 November 2001, <www.dgsi.pt>, a teacher threatened a child of 5 years old with a knife (to the neck), in order to re-establish order in the classroom. The child was scared and traumatized by the incident and resisted rejoining the classmates after the threat. The court held there was a serious degree of blameworthiness, because the teacher was supposed to educate the children and take good care of them. Moreover the behaviour was deemed blameworthy as teachers themselves should play the part of guardians, preventing, for instance, injuries from classmates. 18

A different view of the educational role of teachers (and schools in general) has resulted in the abolishment of punishments in classrooms. Parents are critical of traditional methods of physical punishment. 19

Other questions concern the power of public schools to prevent or denounce parental abuse. Decisions on the liability of schools for omitting to do so do not exist. 20

c) Social Services/Courts

There is a general feeling in Portuguese public opinion (without significant reflection on legal scholarship) that social services (*assistentes sociais*, for instance) and courts should be liable where a child is adopted, or is returned to his family after a previous recognition of the parents' lack of fitness, and there is subsequent parental abuse. 21

A number of notable cases came to light recently which revealed that whilst the later behaviour of the foster parents in question was in many cases unpredictable, it was tenable that the reports of social services on the foster families and parents in whose custody children were placed, and subsequently subjected to abuse, were prepared without the requisite care. 22

The State will also probably play the role of defendant due to the fact that the child may suffer psychological disorders when after some time she must leave the foster family and return to the biological family. The emotional links (sometimes strengthened by the wrongful belief that this situation is a stage before adoption proceedings) between the child and the family that replace his own ought to have some legal protection. Other potential cases of damage caused to children due to the actions of authorities concern the power to authorize the minor's participation in spectacles (such as circus) and other activities (e.g. participation in advertisements) by the *Comissão de Protecção de crianças e adolescentes*.[10] Could personal injuries of the child or privacy in- 23

[10] See art. 143 *Código do Trabalho* (Labour Law Code). In 27 September 2005 a new self-regulatory code was adopted – *Código de Boas Práticas na Comunicação Comercial para Menores* – in order to make more effective the protection of minors in advertisements. As an example of this protection, a pecuniary sanction for broadcasting a piece with violent images and

fringements be seen as a result of a careless decision of the *Comissão*? Portuguese courts would probably conclude that the causation requirement is lacking.

24 Due to many scandalous cases of sexual abuse of children living in orphanages and similar public institutions, calls were made for the imposing of state liability for the lack of supervising these institutions. An arbitration Court (established by *Resolução de Conselho de Ministros* 104/2004, 29 June 2004, DR- I Série-B 21 July 2004, regulated by *Despacho conjunto* 63/2005, 30 December 2004, DR II Série 19 January 2005), decided in 2006 that the State should compensate children victims of sexual abuse during their stay in "Casa Pia" (a foster public institution). Almost all the victims were compensated in € 50,000 (being € 50,000 the cap, according to art. 8 of the *Resolução*).

d) Health Services

25 Health authorities are in a privileged position to denounce parental abuse where the child requires their services. Still, there are no decisions on the civil liability of health staffs for failing to act.

26 Where, on the opposite side, health services are the offenders, can parents sue the hospital due to severe injuries caused to their child? In STJ 25 November 1999,[11] parents sought compensation for non-pecuniary loss in a case where their child (of a few months) was severely injured due to the careless omission of a nurse who used an electric blanket. The court bypassed the obstacle of art. 496, 2 CC, that enables the victim's relatives to claim for non-pecuniary loss only in case of death, by classifying parental care as an absolute right, protected under art. 483, 1 CC. The line taken by the court was original,[12] but

sounds (linked to sexual abuse) was made against a television channel in *Relação de Lisboa* (Lisbon Court of Appeal, RL) 22 June 2004, <www.dgsi.pt>. In RL 21 February 2002, the Volvo company was not held liable for using the image of a child in the "security campaign", although there had been a claim alleging breach of art. 14. 3 of the Publicity Code. According to the rule, children can appear as the main character in advertisements if there is a direct link between them and the product advertised. The Court accepted that their image in that campaign fulfilled a relevant interest beyond the commercial scope of advertising.

[11] STJ 25 November 1999, [1999] *Boletim do Ministério da Justiça* (BMJ), 481, 470. On parental care, see L.C. Gonçalves, *Tratado de direito civil em comentário ao código civil português* II (1930), 347 et seq.; J.C. Mendes, *Direito da família* (1990/1991), 338–340; A. Leandro, Poder paternal: natureza, conteúdo, exercício e limitação. Algumas reflexões de prática judiciária in: *Temas de direito da família* (1986), 121; M.F.A. Duarte, *O poder paternal. Contributo para o estudo do seu actual regime* (reprint, 1994); D.L. de Campos, *Lições de direito da família e das sucessões* (2nd edn. 1997), 370–372; J.A. Varela, *Direito da família* I (1999), 79–83 (where the author professed his agreement on the nature of parental care as an absolute subjective right, against the majority of scholarly opinion) and F.P. Coelho/G. de Oliveira, *Curso de direito da família* I (2001), 40 et seq.

[12] Strongly defending the compensation for pain and suffering of parents in case of (serious) personal injuries caused to their child, A.V. Serra, Anotação, [1971–1972] RLJ, 104, 14. See also the notes (in favour) on the case of A.A. Geraldes, *Temas da responsabilidade civil. Indemnização dos danos reflexos* II (2005), 71, 81–85, particularly at 82 fn. 120 and H.S. Antunes,

the same solution is not unfortunately followed by the (large) majority of courts.

4. What limitation periods are applied to the child's claim?

There are no specific rules on limitation periods applied to children's claims. 27

According to art. 498 CC, the limitation period is three years, starting from the moment the victim acknowledges the right to demand of the tortfeasor, regardless of the fact that she might not know the identity of the tortfeasor and the full extent of the damages. The general limitation period (twenty years, as prescribed in art. 309 CC) also applies, starting from the day of the tortious act. An important derogation from the three year period is regulated in art. 498, 3 CC. If the act is criminal in nature, the limitation period of the compensation claim follows the criminal code rule on the limitation period for that specific act, if the latter is longer. 28

Still, the legislature, following the solution of the previous code (Código de Seabra de 1867, in its art. 549), deviated from the general rules on time limitation where minors' interests might be affected. The solution provided for in art. 320, 1 CC is that prescription does not start or run against minors lacking legal representatives (unless the right or the act concerns the limited sphere of capacity of the minor – art. 127 CC). Even where the minor has legal representatives (or even administrators), prescription will only extinguish his right after a complete year has passed following his coming of age. 29

Legal writers and case law agree on the fact that the scope of the article aims at the protection of minors against a possible *omissio* of parents in defending their rights. But the child is probably not protected if the denial of compensation was due not to the omission of the parents (not suing the tortfeasor), but to a different kind of behaviour (e.g. not being present in court). In that case, the reticent position of the case law in respect of lawsuits within the family will most probably bar the child's compensation claim. 30

In RL (*Relação de Lisboa*, Lisbon Court of Appeal) 27 January 2005, in a case of injuries caused to a minor by the workers of a boat who infringed safety measures when docking at the harbour, the court decided that prescription might be interrupted, even if it is suspended. The recognition of liability of the tortfeasor (by assuming some of the minor's health expenses) replaced the initial date of prescription; therefore there is an actual extension of the limitation 31

Responsabilidade civil dos obrigados à vigilância de pessoa naturalmente incapaz (2000), 342 fn. 995. As an example of the traditional negative answer, see STJ 8 May 1991, <www.dgsi.pt>, where parents' failure to lodge their claim for pain and suffering flowed from their child's own suffering due to a fall at the hospital where he was staying.

period[13]. It seemed reasonable to balance the minor's position with the adult's defences. Therefore, if an adult victim can benefit from the prescription's interruption, so can the minor (despite having a special deadline).

32 Rules such as that in art. 320 confirm the remarks of Menezes Cordeiro, for whom the law on minors does not confine itself to the problem of incapacities. The historical evolution of this branch shows that the Portuguese legislature intended to create a range of solutions concerning the peculiarities of minors.[14]

33 In a wrongful life action (STJ 19 June 2001),[15] the Supreme Court seems to accept the idea that personal rights should be considered separate from legal representation. This approach would undermine the application of art. 320 CC in the field of protection of *direitos puramente pessoais* (strictly connected with the personality). Hence, the distinction between *capacidade jurídica de gozo* (on the question of legitimacy) and *capacidade de exercício* (on the question of handling one's own rights) seems to have no practical effect in personality rights.[16]

III. Contributory Negligence

5. Are there any special provisions concerning contributory negligence if the tortfeasor is a child?

34 There are no special provisions expressly concerning contributory negligence of the child.

35 According to art. 571 CC, contributory negligence of representatives and tutors[17] is similar to contributory negligence of the tortfeasor. That rule considered in tandem with art. 570 CC, where fault on the part of the victim allows

[13] That is the reason why in STJ 11 May 1993 the limitation period of one year after coming of age was described as the *minimum* deadline applying to the minor.

[14] A.M. Cordeiro, *Tratado de direito civil português* I, Parte geral, III (2004), 391–395. See also L. Furtado/P. Guerra, *O novo direito das crianças e jovens: um recomeço* (2004); A.R. Monteiro (ed.), *Direitos das crianças* (2004); A.G. Leandro, Direito e direitos dos menores: síntese da situação em Portugal no domínio civil e no domínio para-penal e penal, [1990] *Infância e juventude*, 9–34; R. Clemente, Um novo olhar sobre a criança: um direito novo de promoção de direitos, [1998] *Intervenção social*, 19–26 and J.M. Vidal (ed.), *O direito dos menores: reforma ou revolução* (1998).

[15] See F. P. Monteiro, Direito à não existência, direito a não nascer, *Comemorações dos 35 anos do Código Civil e dos 25 anos da reforma de 1977* II (2006), 131–138. See, also infra question 23.

[16] The same conclusion had been drawn on the topic of fundamental rights legitimacy; see, for all, R. Martins, *Menoridade. (In)capacidade e cuidado parental* (2003), 47 et seq. As to minors over 14 years of age, it seems representation hinders the development of the personality of the child. Therefore, the idea of replacing *representação* with *assistência* is quite convincing, where the minor acts by himself, but the parents give their consent or participate in the child's acts. Further developments, R. Martins, Poder paternal vs. autonomia da criança e do adolescente, [2004] *Lex familiae*, 1, 71–74.

[17] Art. 571 CC also includes "[...] those *employed* by the victim".

the judge to exclude compensation or limit it, would render the protection of minors/victims less effective.

Legal scholarship[18] accepts that fault of the legal representatives (for failure in their duty to supervise) is equivalent to fault of the victim. Also, in the case law, that idea is accepted without restrictions.[19] 36

A sector of the legal scholarship endorses the fact that the rule cannot be seen as "the mirror-image" of art. 491 CC, since that would represent a weakening of the protection of the child. 37

The main reasoning under art. 571 CC has regard to the aim of an equitable allocation of damages.[20] The restrictive interpretation of art. 571 CC conditions its application only where the victim would be liable for damages caused by representatives and when they were chosen by the victim. This theory is most prominently espoused by B. Proença[21] who has also suggested that in cases of minors, as victims, there should be joint liability of the tortfeasor and the supervisor. 38

Furthermore, another argument has also given weight to the inapplicability of art. 471 where parents fail in their duty to supervise. In fact, they ought to supervise not because they were the legal representatives[22], but because the minor was lacking natural capacity and parental care includes the duty to supervise. 39

6. What are the rules governing contributory negligence of the child? Do such principles follow the same lines as those governing the negligence issue itself (mirror-image)?

There are no specific legal rules. 40

[18] F. Pires de Lima/J.A. Varela, *Código civil anotado* I (1987), 588; M.J.A. Costa, *Direito das obrigações* (2000), 673; M.O. Matos, *Código da estrada anotado* (6th edn. 1991), 562. Nevertheless, since the damage is not caused to third parties but to the child, the presumption of fault on the part of parents (art. 491 CC) does not apply.

[19] RL 3 May 1978, [1978] *Colectânea de Jurisprudência* (CJ) III, 913 (where there is contributory negligence on the part of the victim's grandmother, letting the child leave the tram before assuring safety conditions in the street were met); STJ 26 March 1980, [1980] BMJ, 295, 408 (a child was run over by a car although holding hands with her parents); RP 20 May 1986, [1986] CJ, III, 196 (hunting accident) apud J.C.B. Proença, *A conduta do lesado como pressuposto e critério de imputação do dano extracontratual* (1997), 719 fn. 2444. See also STJ 10 February 1992, [1992] BMJ, 414, 564 and RP 10 April 1996, [1996] CJ, 240.

[20] J.C.B.Proença (supra fn.19), 720.

[21] J.C.B.Proença (supra fn.19), 730–732. The solution is considered to be aimed at protecting minors without capacity (J.C.B.Proença (supra fn.19), 729). The author does not take into consideration cases of minors with capacity that must be supervised due to the lack of natural capacity.

[22] H.S. Antunes (supra fn.12), 336.

41 Legal scholarship accepts the idea that contributory negligence has as its basis the principle of self-responsibility.[23] The victim that caused or aggravated damages has not acted unlawfully, she simply deviated from a burden.

42 If the victim is not imputable (i.e. is without tortious capacity), her contributory negligence will reduce compensation or even rule out compensation. It is important to establish the degree of fault of both the tortfeasor and the victim, since the amount of compensation might be reduced taking into account the degree of fault and the contribution to damage (the consequences that flowed from each act), according to art. 570, 1 CC.

43 If the minor does not have tortious capacity, he cannot self-determine or restrain from acting in order to avoid damages.[24] As the principle of self-responsibility does not therefore apply, contributory negligence should probably be if the child does not have capacity. See also no. 7.

7. Does the fixed minimum age for children to be liable, if any exists, also apply to the contributory negligence of the child?

44 The majority of legal scholarship considers imputability as a requirement of contributory negligence (in fault-liability cases)[25]. In case law, a consensus has not been reached[26].

45 The wording of art. 570 CC is not the decisive argument to require imputability. Still, it mentions expressly the "fault of the victim" and it is feasible to trust in the idea of a single concept of fault. The legislature would not use the same word in the context of tort liability with two different meanings. Therefore, only those whose actions can be blameworthy because they could have acted differently are regarded as having acted with contributory negligence.

46 The aim of protecting the victim and the incapable also helps to explain the dominant approach.

47 Antunes Varela, however, endorsed that the victim without capacity can act with contributory negligence if she did not fulfil the minimum standard of care or attention or expertise of a normal person.[27]

[23] J.C.B. Proença (supra fn.19), 414 et seq.
[24] J.C.B.Proença (supra fn.19), 527–559, in particular 555.
[25] A.V. Serra, Conculpabilidade do prejudicado, [1959] BMJ, 86, 153; J. Ribeiro de Faria, *Direito das obrigações* I (1990), 524 and J. Calvão da Silva, *Responsabilidade civil do produtor* (1990), 732–733.
[26] Disregarding the fact that the victim did not have capacity (either natural capacity or tortious capacity): RL 28 February 1975, [1975] BMJ, 244, 306 and *Relação de Evora* (Evora Court of Appeal, RE) 9 December 1981, [1981] BMJ, 314, 382 apud J.C.B. Proença (supra fn. 19), 539 fn. 1814.
[27] J.A. Varela, Anotação-Acordão do STJ de 9 de Fevereiro de 1968, [1969–1970] RLJ, 102, 61, Anotação-Acordão do STJ de 5 de Dezembro de 1967, [1968–1969] RLJ, 101, 254 fn. 2.

8. What is the standard of care governing the behaviour of children in the context of contributory negligence? Is such standard determined by the same principles and criteria which are relevant to the duty of care incumbent upon the child in the context of him or her being held liable?

The general standard of care is the abstract standard (*critério objectivo*[28] or *abstracto*), which is related to the behaviour of a careful and wise person. According to art. 482, 2 CC (where the general standard of care is regulated, expressly admitting that other rules[29] may adopt another solution), the circumstances of the case must also be taken into consideration; amongst them is the minority of the tortfeasor or the victim (in contributory negligence). 48

Some authors accept this starting point, but they subject the criterion to some flexibility, as far as the subjective state of the victim is concerned, mainly in cases of minors or disabled persons.[30] 49

Amongst the situations that could excuse the minor's behaviour, a minor's lack of experience or of expertise, or a situation of fear or hastiness stand out. 50

Usually doctrine isolates, from the general standard of care, the rule on medical treatments. Some refusals of medical treatment (after a personal injury), where the minor is over fourteen years of age, may be regarded as irrelevant[31] (art. 38, 3 Criminal Code).[32] 51

IV. Contribution in Equity

9. Is there a parallel (mirror-image) to liability in equity in the field of contributory negligence? If so, do the criteria determining liability in equity of the child also apply to the issue of holding him or her accountable for his or her contributory negligence?

No, there is no parallel ruling. 52

[28] Followed by the case law, as in RP 20 March 1984; STJ 16 February 1993; STJ 15 June 1988 apud J.C.B. Proença (supra fn. 19), 573 fn. 1949.

[29] Even if there is not another legal criterion ("na falta de outro critério legal", as said in art. 487, 2 CC), parties can come to an agreement on the content of the standard of care. See, inter alia, A.P. Monteiro, *Cláusulas limitativas e de exclusão da responsabilidade* (2003-reprint).

[30] J.C.B. Proença (supra fn. 19), 581–599.

[31] A.P. Monteiro (supra fn. 29), 79 et seq. Also J.C.B. Proença (supra fn.19), 684–688 (the author deals with this problem having regard only to where the victim's act aggravated the initial damages).

[32] A. Pereira, O consentimento informado na relação médico-paciente, *Esboço de direito civil* (2004), 320–322. and idem, A capacidade para consentir: um novo ramo da capacidade jurídica, *Comemorações dos 35 anos do Código Civil e dos 25 anos da reforma de 1977* II (2006), 242–248. See also G. de Oliveira, O acesso dos menores aos cuidados de saúde, [1994] RLJ, 16–18 and R. Martins, A criança, o adolescente e o acto médico in: *Comemorações dos 35 anos do código civil e dos 25 anos da reforma de 1977* (2004), 791–831.

53 Nevertheless, in the legal writing we can see a different approach.[33] Arguments of liability in equity have the same meaning in the field of contributory negligence. The protection of the unimputable has some limits. On the one hand, he is not liable, in principle. On the other, his lack of capacity also protects him against a possible reduction or exclusion of compensation, due to some personal participation in the wrongful event, *unless* reasons of equity furnish the legal ground for a different solution.

54 B. Proença accepts contributory negligence in equity as a factor of art. 494 CC (that provides for a possible moderation of compensation, on account of the slight degree of fault – *mera culpa*, non-intentional fault).[34] Nevertheless, the author is critical of the use of art. 489 (liability in equity), by way of analogy, to provide for contributory negligence.[35]

10. If answered affirmatively: Is the fact that the child is privately or socially insured against the accident a factor to be considered? Is the existence of liability insurance of the tortfeasor to be taken into account? What factors have a bearing on the assessment of equitable contribution?

55 The existence of liability insurance is not usually taken into account.[36] The exception might arise where there is a decision in equity. But Portuguese law seems to refuse the idea of "contribution in equity".

V. Miscellaneous

11. What are the rules for a situation in which the child is guilty of contributory negligence but the parents have also breached their duty to supervise? Is the child held accountable in any way for his or her parents' breach of the duty to supervise so that his or her claim for damages is reduced?

56 If the child is imputable, and there is contributory negligence on the part of either the child or his/her parents, compensation may be reduced or even excluded, on account of both acts (the child's act and the parents' act).

57 According to some authors,[37] one should avoid a literal interpretation of art. 571 CC, under which parents' contributory negligence has the same effect as the victim's contributory negligence. Otherwise, it would lead to a disadvantageous result to the minor (see supra no. 37).

[33] A.V. Serra, [1959] BMJ, 154 and H.S. Antunes (supra fn. 12), 335.

[34] As H.S. Antunes (supra fn. 12), 335 fn. 974, reminds, with that solution only reduction would be possible, whilst in applying art. 570 CC exclusion is also feasible, at least in theory.

[35] J.C.B. Proença (supra fn. 19), 558.

[36] On the irrelevance of the existence of insurance (STJ 10 October 2002, <www.dgsi.pt>).

[37] J.C.B. Proença (supra fn.19), 714 et seq. and 722 et seq. and H.S. Antunes (supra fn.12), 336.

Decisions finding both the parents and the direct tortfeasor liable seem rare. There are no redress claims against the parents on account of their own fault and contribution to damages. 58

This "right of redress" of the tortfeasor should be regulated, according to B. Proença, taking into account the degree of blameworthiness of the several tortfeasors, the nature of the damage, the economic situation and the existing insurances.[38] 59

12. Do the rules of contributory negligence also apply in the area of strict liability?

According to art. 505 CC (ground for strict liability for damages in traffic accidents), the *fact* of the victim excludes liability. The traditional interpretation of the article did not distinguish a faulty act from acts without fault (sometimes even facts not controlled by the victim's will, such as fainting). Both situations would lead to the exclusion of liability.[39] 60

The evolving understanding of the article pointed at another direction. Fact of the victim should be interpreted as an act with fault and as the exclusive (i.e. the only) cause of the accident.[40] 61

In fact, in the Products Liability Act, the solution provided for in art. 7 encompasses the exclusion (and even the reduction) of damages in cases of a faulty act on the part of the victim. After other recent laws on strict liability, the coexistence between fault (contributory negligence) and risk of the agent is no longer *ius in fieri*. 62

13. Do the rules of contributory negligence apply in the area of strict liability for traffic-accidents or other areas of tort liability?

The rule on contributory negligence in the area of strict liability for traffic accidents (art. 505) is the only rule in the section on strict liability in the Portu- 63

[38] J.C.B. Proença, Ainda sobre o tratamento mais favorável dos lesados culpados no âmbito dos danos corporais por acidente de viação, *Estudos em homenagem ao Prof. Mário Júlio Almeida Costa* (2003), 115.

[39] The fact of a child or other unimputable excludes strict liability; RE 16 September 1974, [1974] BMJ, 358; RL, 28 February 1975, [1975] BMJ, 306; STJ, 31 October 1978, [1978] BMJ, 280; STJ 1 March 1979, <www.dgsi.pt>, RE, 9 December 1981, [1981] BMJ, 382, following the opinion of J.A. Varela, Anotação 5 December 1967, 253 (justifies the solution because the accident is uslly due to the lack of supervising of parents). Recognizing this outcome as the result of legal interpretation, but strongly defending the idea of serious fault as an exclusion of liability, R. Alarcão, *Direito das Obrigações* (1983), 278. See also J. Ribeiro de Faria (supra fn. 25), 72.

[40] J.S. Monteiro, *Estudos sobre responsabilidade civil* (1983), 73, fn. 206bis, 198, where the author endorses the idea that only a serious and unforgivable fault should lead to the exclusion of strict liability. See, more recently, J. Calvão da Silva, Anotação ao Acordão do Supremo Tribunal de Justiça de 1.3.2001, RLJ, 134, 115 and L.M. Leitão, *Direito das obrigações* I (2000), 331.

guese Civil Code (from art. 499 to art. 510 CC) Previously, in the case law the extension of that ruling to other areas of tort liability was taken into consideration. But many decisions were made based on the exceptionality of that rule, the major obstacle to any extension.

64 Due to that viewpoint, a child that provokes an animal and suffers injuries due to an attack can still ask for compensation, since the holder of the animal is strictly liable, under art. 502 CC, where there are no references to the exclusion of the fact of the victim. A more recent approach, however, allows compensation in cases of victims who are at fault, if the act of the victim was the real cause of the damage. "The specific danger of the animal" (as expressed in art. 502 CC) might be irrelevant to the case.

65 In STJ 31 March 1993, <www.dgsi.pt>, the driver was not held liable due to the (non-faulty act) of the three-year-old victim. The outcome is no different from the vast majority of the case law.

66 But in the legal scholarship the *fragility argument* is being enhanced.[41] Acts of minors under ten years should not, in principle, determine the exclusion of liability, due to their incapacity to react as adults and realize the danger in traffic. The minor would not be protected if he had acted with intent. The solution is important in the area of personal injuries where the scope of protection is even more acute.

67 Also in the field of strict liability for traffic accidents, one may wonder if the rule that provides that the unimputable driver is liable in equity (art. 503, 2 CC) has some symmetry in cases of victims without capacity. An answer in the negative is more common.

68 Apart from the cases of traffic accidents, the case law on contributory negligence in strict liability cases is rare. One of these few cases is STJ 6 May 1987, <www.dgsi.pt>, where the court stated that if there is contributory negligence or a *fact* of a third person, the person who exploits the electric installation (art. 409 CC)[42] does not have to prove that technical rules were fulfilled (either when it was installed or as far as duties of maintenance are concerned).[43]

[41] J.C.B. Proença, Acidentes de viação e fragilidade por menoridade (para uma nova conformação normativa) in: *Iuris et de iure. Nos 20 anos da Faculdade de Direito do Porto* (1998); idem, Ainda sobre o tratamento mais favorável dos lesados culpados no âmbito dos danos corporais por acidene de viação, *Estudos em homenagem ao Prof. Mario Júlio Almeida Costa* (2003); J.C.B. Proença, Responsabilidade pelo risco do detentor do veículo e conduta do lesado: a lógica do "tudo ou nada", [2004] *Cadernos de Direito Privado*, 7 et seq.

[42] See also the interesting case of STA 15 June 1982 (a case of causation and the fact of parents).

[43] In a different sense, holding the corporation liable, STJ 15 June 1982 apud A.M. Cordeiro, *Da responsabilidade dos administradores das sociedades comerciais* (1997), 544 and fn. 280 (electrocution of a child who entered in a hole of the wall of the installation).

14. Are adults held to a higher standard of care in their interactions with children, or when children are or may be around?

The general standard of fault applies: The agent must act as a *bonus pater familae*, but according to the circumstances of the case (art. 487, 2 CC). The circumstance of the vicinity of children demands a considerable degree of attention and care. That is particularly evident where there is an accident in front of a school or when the driver could realize the presence of children not far from the road/street[44]. 69

The line taken by the courts can probably be summarized by the words of the following decision of Coimbra Court of Appeal[45] that found the driver not liable for running over a child that escaped from her parent's hands: "The careful driver has only to take into account the typical or normal behaviours of the other users of the road". Still, unusual conducts, such as crossing the street unexpectedly, can be predictable; that is the case with a child walking alone or playing with a ball, but is not the case with a child holding hands with an adult. This is in accordance with the "reliance principle" which allows one to rely on the behaviours of others.[46] 70

In Guimarães Court of Appeal 9 February 2004[47], the court highlighted the *special* duty of care of the owner of a dog when going out with it if children are around. 71

Both the legislature and case law are sensitive to the problem of injuries caused to minors at work. But it has already been accepted by the *Supremo Tribunal de Justiça* that the presumption of fault in cases of non-fulfilment of statutory duties (the case in point involved breach of the law applicable on the contracting of a fourteen-year-old minor) might not entail the employer's liability, if the non-fulfilment of the duty was not the cause of injury. 72

The special duty of care of the State was considered by Relação do Porto of 24 September 2001, when due to the lack of safety and supervision a child fell while playing on the wall of the school. Similar duties of supervision occur in swimming pools open to the public (STJ 8 March 2005, <www.dgsi.pt>). In this last case, the court qualified the activity of exploring a swimming pool as a dangerous activity. The victims can take advantage of the presumption of fault under art. 493, 2 CC, and the tortfeasor will be exempt from liability if he proves he adopted all the measures required to avoid the damage. 73

[44] J.A. Varela (supra fn. 27), 151.

[45] RCoimbra 1 November 2000, <www.dgsi.pt>. See also RCoimbra 19 December 2000, <www.dgsi.pt>, where the court decided that adults must count on the normality of children's abnormal acts.

[46] On the reliance principle in Portuguese law, see A. Carneiro da Frada, *Teoria da confiança e responsabilidade civil* (2004).

[47] RGuimarães 9 February 2004, [2004] CJ, I, 296.

74 The lack of (effective) signs in buildings or in the vicinity of construction sites or industrial premises is usually not enough to ascertain liability of workers or the owner of the building or premises.[48] This is probably one of the most problematic set of cases, since the defence of having adopted the legal measures does not take into consideration that children are prone to disregard them (the signs) or misunderstand their importance.[49]

75 Selling carnival bombs to minors is not only qualified as an unlawful act, but it can be also be seen as the cause of injuries caused due to the unexpected explosion of the device (even if a defect was not detected). The *Relação de Guimarães* (12 March 2003, <www.dgsi.pt>) held the seller liable for the injuries caused to the minor, calling upon the scope of the protection of the law that is to avoid that minors use dangerous objects without realizing that particular feature. But as the minor ought to have realised that the object was dangerous, due to the fact he was over fifteen years of age, the court admitted there had been contributory negligence.

VI. Insurance Matters

15. Are pupils covered by private or public accident (first-party) insurance?

a) Private accident insurance

76 Since the "*seguro escolar*" (see infra question no. 15 section b)) also encompasses students of private schools, it is not common to contract private insurance, unless of course parents or private educational centres feel the need of an extension of the damages covered by the "*seguro escolar*".

77 That is precisely the case of the insurance policy "*Protecção e sucesso escolar*" offered by the Portuguese insurer Global. Under the item "extraordinary expenditures of education", this insurance covers the costs of employing a tutor, in order to recover time spent in hospitals or at home. Costs of special means of transport (ambulance, adaptation of the family vehicle) are also covered. These heads of damages, as explained subsequently, are not covered by the "*seguro escolar*".

78 Private accident insurances depend on the contractual frame (since they are not compulsory, there is no need of approval of the *Instituto de Seguros de Portugal*). Some of the standard clauses that might be of interest are those connected with the existence of caps and the exclusion of compensation where there is contributory negligence on the part of the child.

[48] Denying causation between lack of signalisation and damages caused to an 8 year-old child, see RCoimbra 5 June 2001, <www.dgsi.pt>.

[49] A recent decision of Lisbon Court of Appeal (July 2005, unpublished) dealt with the death of two children, drowned in a small swamp inside industrial premises. The media cover of cases like this one reflected a critical viewpoint of public opinion against the courts that tend to deny liability in similar cases.

b) Non-private (first-party) accident insurance

The "*seguro escolar*" (school insurance) is regulated by Portaria no. 413/99, of 8 of July 1999, as one of the measures of the so-called "acção social escolar" (as defined in Decree-Law 35/90, of 25 January 1990), in order to protect students during some of their years of learning. It covers children of pre-university schools (from pre-elementary schools or kindergartens until secondary schools – it corresponds to an average age of 18 years). Students of private schools are also protected. 79

It is a compulsory insurance (art. 27 of Portaria), although it is free for children of pre-elementary schools, handicapped children and students frequenting what is called "*escolaridade obrigatória*" (after that it is no longer compulsory to attend classes), under art. 28, 4 Portaria. 80

Apart from the accidents that occur at school (being more frequent in the playground than in the classroom), also damage caused where the child is staying in an OTL (*organização dos tempos livres* – activities before or after the classes) organized by the school and excursions (or more precisely any activity under the responsibility of school or authorized by it) are covered by the "*seguro escolar*". 81

One of the most important exclusions under the "*seguro escolar*" concerns the case of refusal of medical treatment (even if due to the child's parents), according art. 26, 1 a Portaria. But contributory negligence of the child is not a general defence. 82

The nature of such an insurance has already been the subject of discussion in the courts: 83

i) In RC 7 January 2001,[50] the court classified the school insurance as a social insurance. There is no contract between the parents and the State, therefore the State cannot be ordered to pay all the damages caused to the victim and subrogate the victim's rights (as happens in private insurance, pursuant to art. 422 Commercial Code). State liability depends upon the extent of the liability of the tortfeasor/student.[51] 84

ii) In RP 18 November 2003[52], the parents of a child who was the victim of an accident sued the State for breach of its duty to offer a preventive programme and social assistance, through the "social insurance" and preventive measures (such as educational programs about traffic safety). The court refused jurisdiction over the case on account of this being a matter of administrative law (and therefore to be judged by administrative courts). 85

[50] RCoimbra 7 January 2001, [2001] CJ, V, 12–14.

[51] Being a complementary scheme, the *seguro escolar* does not preclude the intervention of "National Health System" (Art, 1, 2 Portaria).

[52] RP 18 November 2003, [2003] CJ, III, 196.

86 iii) The differences between insurance and compensation for civil liability were scrutinized in STA 7 April 2005[53]. Amongst them, the court stressed three points: the irrelevance of fault on the part of the victim, the irrelevance of damage caused to parents (which is rather controversial in tort liability) and the irrelevance of damage due to rehabilitation.

87 There are other insurances related to children (although the status of pupil is irrelevant)[54]:

88 i) Decree-Law 304/2003, 9 December 2003, for damage caused to children between the ages of six and eighteen in a holiday camp.

89 ii) Decree-Law 190/92, 3 September 1992 that mentions an accident insurance for children covered by programs of "*acolhimento familiar*" (staying with foster families), programs that had their beginnings in Decree-Law 288/79, 13 August 1979).

16. Does this insurance cover any damage incurred on the way to school and back?

90 The "*seguro escolar*" covers damage incurred on the way to school/home under certain conditions mentioned in artt. 21 and 22 of Portaria.[55]

91 According to art. 21, accidents occurring on the normal way to school/home, and in a period immediately before or after the classes (within the average period of time required to walk) are covered. Nevertheless it only covers *minors* that are not being accompanied by an adult that, by law, is obliged to supervise the child in question.

92 Conditions are stricter where the child is run over by a car. In this case, the accident must be imputable to the child and the accident must be denounced to the authorities in 15 days (even if due to the child).[56]

17. Are there restrictions on damages recoverable by the child, e.g. with respect to loss of future earnings?

93 Specific heads of damage and criteria of assessment are envisaged by the Portaria.

[53] STA 7 April 2005, <www.dgsi.pt>.

[54] Also compulsory insurance for playing sports (Decree-Law 146/93, 26 April 1993) should be mentioned, with the remark that there are no specific regulations for children.

[55] Since with accidents *in itinere* there is an important extension of the scope of protection, the legislature only takes into consideration "minors".

[56] If a teacher or other member of the school is walking with the child the insurance covers the accident. This is not the case if the company is another adult, burdened with the duty to supervise the child.

The insurance covers medical expenses, transport and accommodation (also alimentation), in accordance with art. 6. 94

It also covers, by virtue of art. 10, non-pecuniary losses, compensation for temporary loss of earning capacity (but only if the student was actually paid and if the amount of damages is "specifically" proved) and permanent incapacity. Non-pecuniary losses were not covered before this Portaria.[57] 95

As a curiosity, non-pecuniary losses may be assessed *in abstract.* In fact, according to art. 11, 4, by request of the victim and with the consent of the regional director for education, non-pecuniary losses can be fixed in the amount corresponding to 30% of compensation for incapacity. 96

As far as assessment of pecuniary damages is concerned, the degree of incapacity is taken into consideration as well as the minimum income. The amount of the minimum income (around € 300) is multiplied by 300, corresponding to an incapacity of 100%. 97

The lump sum will be deposited in an account of the victim. If the victim is a minor, the guardian (parents or others) can use a percentage of the lump sum per year, if needed for the welfare of the child (but the amount cannot surpass 5% of the sum deposited). 98

VII. Damage Issues

18. If damages for loss of earnings are available, what are the principles governing their assessment?

"The irreversible damage caused to a baby of seven months, involving severe facial scars and crippled hands, causes an important deprivation in future earning capacity, and damages are available, and it is not worthy to suggest that it represents a mere exercise in futurology", due to the uncertainty of such damages, decided the Supreme Court in STJ 25 November 1998.[58] 99

Apart from specific regulations, the general rules apply.[59] 100

The courts must follow the general principle of *restitutio in integrum* (art. 562 CC). 101

[57] See, for instance, RE 27 May 1999, [1999] CJ, III, 261. In the Preamble of the Portaria, the change is deemed as one of the most significant changes.

[58] STJ 25 November 1998, [1998] BMJ, 481, 471.

[59] J.S. Dinis, Dano corporal em acidentes de viação.Cálculo da indemnização. Situações de agravamento, [1997] *Colectânea de Jurisprudência do Supremo Tribunal da Justiça* (CJ/STJ), 1 and Dano corporal, [2001] CJ/STJ, 6 et seq. I.G. Telles, *Direito das obrigações* (6th edn. 1989), 387–394; J.A.Varela, *Das obrigações em geral* I (2000), 903–909 and P.R. Martinez, *Direito da obrigações. Aditamentos* (2003), 117–120.

102 In cases of long-lasting damage, the court may award periodical payments, instead of awarding a lump sum, but only at the request of the victim (art. 564 CC). Some legal commentators have highlighted the fact that this solution might have a negative effect on the protection of certain victims (severely disabled persons and children). Cases of parents who decided, for instance, to use all the compensation in order to improve their own house, instead of paying a special assistance for their disabled child are well-known. Also, insurers criticise the fact there is not a flexible approach allowing judges, regardless of the wishes of the victim, to opt for the periodical payment.

103 Future losses are awarded if foreseeable (art. 566, 2). As to *lucrum cessans*, the legislature does not seem to treat them differently from "current damage". In fact, the wording of art. 564 is quite explicit: both heads of damage (*dano emergente* and *lucro cessante*) are taken into account. In many decisions, however, future losses (or loss of profits) and *lucrum cessans* are not treated separately. That was not the case of STJ 2 November 1995, where the court, in a case of a seven-year–old child who lost an eye due to an accident with a bullet, drew the line between the two concepts. Future damages are compensable in equity (therefore close to non-pecuniary damages), whilst *lucrum cessans* refers to the loss of monetary values, of inevitable gain, because they would become real, had the damage not occurred.[60]

104 In order to assess pecuniary damages (loss of earnings), the courts adopt the following steps. Firstly, the percentage of disability is established, as well as its nature (permanent or temporary). There are no civil law tables (barèmes), but it is not unusual to see decisions based on experts views grounded in the *Tabela Nacional de Incapacidades* (applied in labour accidents). Secondly, the courts determine the impact of the disability on the earning capacity (and on the actual professional capacity). In a representative number of cases, the degree of impairment of earning capacity is estimated equal to the degree of disability.[61] The next step concerns the calculation[62] of the amount of money (capital) and appropriate interest[63] which corresponds to the lost wages up until retirement age of the victim.[64]

[60] Similar situation in STJ 19 November 2002, <www.dgsi.pt>.

[61] This is probably one of the weak points of the Portuguese method of assessing loss of earnings. To avoid the fallacy of believing that both the mentioned degrees coincide (accepted as problematic by some courts) it was already suggested to adopt the "theory of the extra-effort" on performing professional and non-professional activities. The difficulties on assessing the degree of extra-effort rendered the criteria scarcely efficient.

[62] See, for all, the mathematic formula adopted by RCoimbra 12 July 1999, probably the most followed method. The same Court of Appeal pointed out afterwards that this method is neither compulsory, nor shall equity reasons be set apart (RCoimbra 4 May 2004, <www.dgsi.pt>). Stressing that equity should prevail in relation with methods of capitalization, STJ 25 November 1998, <www.dgsi.pt>.

[63] The rate of interest has been decreasing. In the late 1990s it was around 5%, while more recent decisions apply an interest rate of 3%.

[64] Sixty-five years or seventy years. Recent decisions replaced this factor by life expectancy (sometimes taking into account the average life expectancy, other times regarding particular features of the victim from which it is feasible to infer a difference from the average life expectancy).

The discretional power of the judge is particularly evident where some correctional factors are introduced. One of these concerns a reduction factor that tries to neutralize the advantage of obtaining the award immediately and in a once-off payment. In practical terms, the judge will reduce the amount by one-third or one-fourth. Also predictable changes in the professional career of the victim are taken into account. 105

The last step, a complex one, concerns the calculation of interest.[65] 106

The described method does not fit with the assessment of loss of earning of children[66] since this kind of consequence will only be known several years afterwards. Nonetheless, some objective factors can be detected in the legal scholarship and the case law: 107

a) Students who lose financial support, like scholarships, suffer a present damage.[67] 108

b) If there is a proved professional option, the courts can take into consideration how difficult it is to get such a job and what is the corresponding average income. 109

c) In any case the intelligence of the victim and her persistence in her studies, as well as her success at school, are factors from which one can infer a predictable successful career. 110

d) Either combined with the previous factors or standing alone, taking the average national income seems to be the fairest solution[68]. There are a significant range of decisions which have adopted the criteria of the father's income or the minimum income (taking into account the humble condition of parents). Both these approaches have been severely reproved by the Supreme Court.[69] 111

[65] See *Acordão uniformizador de Jurisprudência* 4/02, 9 May 2002.

[66] Even where the minor is working, since her current income depends, in a large extent, on the fact of being a minor. It would be, therefore unfair to use as a starting point the amount of wages granted in an early stage of professional life. See, for instance, STJ 3 February 2005, <www.dgsi.pt>: a 16-year-old minor, with a salary of € 300 and an IPP (*Incapacidade permanente parcial* – partial permanent incapacity) of 10% (reduced mobility of knees) obtained € 13,000. According to RP 9 July 1998, equity should prevail due to the unpredictability of minor's *lucrum cessans*.

[67] See, for further details, J.A. Dias (supra fn. 4), 291 et seq.

[68] See also, J.A. Dias (supra fn. 4), 297.

[69] See, for instance, STJ 18 December 2003, <www.dgsi.pt>, on the unfairness of taking as basis (exclusive basis) the minimum income to compensate a 17-year-old victim. Adopting the minimum income criteria, see RP 29 January 1997, <www.dgsi.pt>.

112 The final amount is reached by also balancing the protection of the victim and the protection against unjust enrichment of the victim. Therefore, some of the so-called factors of correction are applied. Amongst them, the idea that the victim is awarded once and for all prevails.

113 In case of "relational torts", the death or personal injury of the direct victim will affect the right to maintenance of any children. The children can claim compensation from the tortfeasor (art. 495, 3 CC[70]). The assessment of these particular losses of *income* is complex and different approaches have already been adopted by the case law. The prevailing tendency is to assess damages according to what was actually given by the parent in terms of right of maintenance.

19. Which of the child's non-material interests are protected in your jurisdiction? May the child, for example, sue for impairment of intellectual or social development, the onset of behavioural problem, or reduced employment prospects?

114 Non-pecuniary damages, insofar as they are serious, are compensated (art. 496, 1 CC). The impairment of intellectual or social developments and the onset of behavioural problems are taken into account in the head of damage "*prejuízo de afirmação pessoal*". This head of damage encompasses the negative effect of damage on social life (e.g. the fact that the minor can no longer play football with his classmates) and also the effect on one's self-confidence, in particular the feeling of inferiority usually associated with handicaps.

115 As to the problem of reduced employment prospects, the legal scholarship does not deal with it in the frame of a possible "*perte de chance*".

116 Professional ambitions are not protected as such. Still, if the victim was a good student and was finishing high school, some courts regard that situation as a factor of equity, mainly in assessment of loss of earnings. In that case, the victim's professional future is highly predictable and the judge will resolve the problem by taking into account the average income of the kind of profession the victim would have chosen but for the accident.[71]

117 In many of these cases of "employment prospects", the main bar is the proof of damage. However, it is feasible, but only in a non-representative number of

[70] M.J.A. Costa (supra fn.18), 547–548, J.A.Varela (supra fn. 59), 647; A.V. Serra, O dever de indemnizar e o interesse de terceiros, [1959] BMJ, 86, 103–125.

[71] In the decision held by the Supreme Court of Justice of 7 October 1997, [1997] BMJ, 470, 569, the victim, studying at university, changed professional orientation. The difference of incomes between the two professions and the fact that the market usually requires professionals of the area she gave up were regarded as determinant factors for the assessment of pecuniary damages (regarded as actual damages).

cases, to sue for this last head of damage, especially if the victim had already started some kind of "professional" activity (in the field of sports or arts).

In STJ 3 June 2004[72], the court accepted as pecuniary damages (loss of profit) those which arose from the delay in graduating and entering the professional market. The victim had lost the vision in one eye.[73] 118

20. Are there special rules for the assessment of damages sustained by a child, e.g. with respect to pain and suffering?

There are no special legal rules on non-pecuniary losses sustained by a child. 119

The general rules on non-pecuniary loss apply. The seriousness of non-pecuniary loss is the only condition for compensation (art. 496, 1 CC)[74]. The judge will have to assess the damages taking into consideration the legal criteria: Compensation of non-pecuniary loss is subject to equity judgements that are given according to the degree of fault of the tortfeasor, the economic situation of the tortfeasor and the victim and other circumstances of the case (art. 494 *ex vi* art. 496, 3CC). 120

Usually the courts give a total award without distinguishing the different heads of non-pecuniary loss (*prejuízo de afirmação pessoal*/loss of amenities, *dor*/pain and suffering, *prejuízo estético*/aesthetic loss and, for some courts, also the *prejuízo functional*/personal injury *per se*). In STJ 17 December 2002, however, the court drew a line between "*danos líquidos*" (actual suffering) and future non-pecuniary losses (eventual future assessment, eventual need of psychiatric support, eventual surgery), in a case concerning injuries caused to a three-year-old child, burnt by the hot soup that an employee of the kindergarten was carrying. The distinction is the ground on which the requirements of different standards of proof are explained. 121

21. Does a small child have a claim for damages for pain and suffering if he or she is deprived of his or her parents by a tortious act? If so, may the claim be denied on the ground that the child does not feel the loss?

According to art. 496, 2 CC, descendents can claim compensation for pain and suffering when deprived of their parents (or even grandparents, if parents are no longer alive). This article enables the relatives (only those mentioned in the 122

[72] STJ 3 June 2004, <www.dgsi.pt>. In RCoimbra 29 January 2003, the judges qualified the effort of the student to recover his studies and the loss of two years as a non-pecuniary loss. Also in RP 29 April 1997, the effort to join the classmates and avoid a lost year in the studies had the same treatment.

[73] See also for a 10-year-old child, with an IPP of 22.5%, STJ 8 June 1993, [1993] CJ/STJ, II, 138.

[74] M.M. Veloso, *A compensação do dano contratual não patrimonial (em especial no direito de autor)* (1998), 208.

article and by the order established in the article)[75] to claim damages[76] in case of bereavement, including damages for their own suffering, the pain and suffering of the victim until the moment of death and the damage to life (*dano da morte*).[77]

123 Also, children older than eighteen can claim compensation, but more delicate questions arise when *minors* are deprived of their parents. In case law, for bereavement there is an unwritten rule: "the younger the child, the bigger the compensation".

124 As far as the first head of damage is concerned, the courts cannot deny the claim on the ground that the child did not feel the loss.[78] In fact the courts have also bypassed the obstacles of the argument of the lack of "*personalidade juridica*" (art. 66; see also infra question no. 24) where the child was born after the death of one of the parents (or both).

125 One of the most interesting decisions is RP 30 March 2000.[79] The court relied on the teachings of A. Damásio, the world famous neurologist, which proffer that the capacity to feel and suffer depends on the capacity to feel emotions. The *nasciturus,* and the same certainly applies to small children, does not have secondary emotion. They have nothing other than primary, basic emotions.

[75] Certainty and safety values prevailed in the question of legitimacy, as recognized A.J.M. Costa (supra fn. 18), 549. The solution also relates to rules of life experience (bereavement usually occurs within the family) and with the rules on successors, where there is no will. Hence, one might suspect that third parties not mentioned in the article are *ab initio* excluded. The controversy on bereavement of a more uxorio partner forced another conclusion. In *Tribunal Constituçional* (TC) 275/02, *Diário da República*, 2, 24 July 2002, the Constitutional Court held the article unconstitutional for not protecting the interests in cohabitation. Denied such compensation taking into consideration the literal wording of the Article and the aim of not spreading the loss, STJ 4 November 2003, [2003] CJ/STJ, III, 133.

[76] On the discussion if the compensation is *iure sucessorio* (L.M. Leitão, supra fn. 40, 301; in the case law, for instance, STJ 17 June 1997, <www.dgsi.pt>) or *iure proprio* as defended by J.A. Varela (supra 59), 333; amongst many, see STJ 4 October 2000, [2000] BMJ, 500, 300.

[77] As to their own suffering, one must bear in mind that the courts also accept claims on *Schockschaden* (usually as a head of damage for bereavement). See RL 29 September 2004, <www.dgsi.pt>, where the court awarded a different amount to one of the victim's children who was also a victim of the accident. About "*dano da morte*", see D. Leite de Campos, A indemnização do dano da morte, [1974] *Boletim da Faculdade de Direito da Universidade de Coimbra* (BFD), 66; J.A. Dias (supra fn. 4), 350–364; J.A.Varela (supra fn. 59), 608–617 and L.M. Leitão (supra fn. 40), 299–302. There are different approaches on the way to compensate that damage: the uniform (the same amount for all regardless of age) or differentiated approaches (in the last sense, STJ 25 March 2004, [2004] CJ/STJ, I, 140: in this case the differentiating factors were: age, health, social interaction, and function in society).

[78] RP 13 April 1989, [1989] CJ, II, 221, denied compensation to a child whose parent died when she was still a *nasciturus*, but admitted that, being born alive, as an heir of the victim she could obtain compensation for the damage to life and pain and suffering before the death of the parent. Ten years later, the same court in RP 21 April 1999, granted bereavement loss to a child by the same token as the predominant case law.

[79] RP 30 March 2000, [2000] CJ, II, 209. See also RE 10 January 2006 <www.dgsi.pt>, where the court decided, according to the reports of experts on Psychology, that a nine months baby should be compensated for the loss of his father.

They might sense their parents' warmth, but they have no feelings. Only gradually might they acknowledge the absence of parents and suffer accordingly. Therefore, according to the court, the *future foreseeable damage* is the feeling flowing from secondary emotions.

The acceptance of a punitive function[80] of non-pecuniary loss is also a strong argument against a restrictive solution where conscience is a requisite of compensation.[81] 126

The additional criteria on assessing damages (probably referred to in *obiter dicta* as "other circumstances of the case")[82] are: 127

a) Usually the courts give a higher amount to small children in comparison to the widows and widowers.[83] 128

b) As a general rule, damages are equal for all the children, regardless of the age or the fact of living with the victim at the time of death. But in STJ 18 March 2003,[84] the court decided that the amount for non-pecuniary losses of a baby would be higher than the amount of her brothers (who were children of a previous marriage). 129

c) In some decisions, we can read that the fact that there is insurance (life insurance) might be taken into consideration. In favour of regarding also the economic situation of the insurer, some decisions are out of line with common opinion (amongst legal scholars and in the case law). 130

22. With respect to a damage claim for the costs of medical treatment: May the tortfeasor defend himself by pointing to the fact that the parents have a duty to maintain the child?

Parents' maintenance duties cannot be used by the tortfeasor as a valid defence. It was the action of the tortfeasor that caused the particular kind of expense. The duty to maintain the child[85] does not extend to the expenses accrued due to the injury. 131

The tortfeasor can, nevertheless, defend himself by pointing to the fact that he has already "compensated" those who, by trying to save the victim, had suf- 132

[80] Punitive damages are, nevertheless, frowned upon by most Portuguese commentators.

[81] The same "functional approach" (where lack of knowledge is less relevant than the preventive function of tort liability) is not followed in the compensation of non-pecuniary damages for victims in vegetative states. There are however a few decisions awarding this head of damages.

[82] See supra question no. 20.

[83] STJ 18 July 1985, [1985] BMJ, 349, 499.

[84] STJ 18 March 2003, <www.dgsi.pt>. In the same sense, awarding a higher amount to the 10-year-old child with respect to his brothers (older than 16 years), RP 16 March 2000, [2000] CJ, II, 209.

[85] On the parental duty of maintenance, see, for all, J.P.R. Marques, *Algumas notas sobre alimentos* (2000), 52–80.

fered economic loss. Entities such as hospitals and social services have a direct action *vis-à-vis* the tortfeasor, as prescribed in art. 495, 1 and 2 CC.

23. In case of wrongful life: Does the child have a damage claim against the physician or a health care institution?

133 There are many voices against allowing the claim of a child in a case of wrongful life.[86] The major argument against the claim is the absence of damage and causation. Also the *Schutzzwecktheorie* seems to be a bar to these claims. The duty to inform of the physician protects parents, not the child *a se.*

134 The Supreme Court (STJ 19 June 2001) denied such compensation,[87] in a very controversial decision, with the following reasoning. The violation of the duty to inform (of a possible malformation) only led to the deprivation of the parents' right to choose (to have or not have the child). Moreover, even if the Portuguese law recognized a right to non-existence, the minor as such could not sue the doctor.[88] Parents cannot intervene because parental care does not cover this personal decision on the right to non-existence[89] or the personal view of the minor concerning his own view of his limited existence.

135 For pecuniary damages, however, another set of arguments were presented. The court held that although the minor was making the claim (represented by his parents), the real victims were the parents.

136 The decision was severely criticised by some legal scholars whilst others applauded either the final solution or the legal reasoning.

137 As to the critics, it strips liability to its main aims: compensation and punishment. Furthermore, according to an equality principle,[90] physicians dealing with pre-natal life will be seldom liable. Costs of treatment and assistance should, therefore, be compensated, both to parents and the child.[91]

138 As far as non-pecuniary damages to the child are concerned, it is "doubtful"[92] that the courts should accept this head of damage.

[86] J.A. Dias (supra fn. 4), 501. Differently, G. de Oliveira, O direito do diagnóstico pré-natal in: *Temas de Direito da Medicina* I (1999), 175–176.

[87] STJ 19 June 2001, [2002] RLJ, 375; V.C. Correia, *Indemnização por wrongful life, a responsabilidade civil do médico no diagnóstico pré-natal, Centro de Direito Biomédico* (2003), 33.

[88] A.P. Monteiro, Portuguese case note, [2003] *European Review of Private Law*, 2, 220.

[89] V.C. Correia, Indemnização por wrongful life, a responsabilidade do médico no diagnóstico pré-natal, [2004] *Lex Medicinae*, 77, one can of course deny the right of non-existence, but is it really different from the right of a healthy, dignifying existence?

[90] A. Pereira (supra fn. 32), 387–390.

[91] F. Araújo, *A procriação assistida e problema da santidade da vida* (1999), 96–100 and A.M. Cordeiro (supra fn. 14), 281.

[92] A. Pereira (supra fn. 32), 390.

One of the most interesting features of Portuguese legal literature on wrongful life regards the link between the claims of the parents and the child. To some authors, wrongful birth actions play the role of pre-requisite to wrongful life actions.[93] If parents did not seek compensation from the practitioner, then the child cannot demand the latter[94]. Difficulties might arise since parents' interests and viewpoints might be radically different from the minors.[95] 139

24. Concerning liability for pre-natal injuries: Are third parties liable to the child? May the mother be liable to the child, for example for excessive consumption of alcohol or even for an omission to procure treatment?

Where there is malpractice during delivery, the child can sue the doctor, even under a contractual basis (*contratos com eficácia de protecção para terceiros*).[96] 140

The case law is rather reluctant to accept claims against parents. The reluctance is due to the fact that that liability amongst members of the family may aggravate bad relationships. If, for instance, a mother with H.I.V. decides to have a child, it is the fundamental right to have the child that must be protected.[97] 141

[93] V.C. Correia (supra fn. 89), 75.

[94] V.C. Correia (supra fn. 89), 75.

[95] A.P. Monteiro, Direito a não nascer?, [2002] RLJ, 382. Also stressing the possible contradiction between their interests, A.M. Cordeiro (supra fn. 14), 288.

[96] A.P. Monteiro, [2002] RLJ, 383. About this institute and its ruling, see J.S. Monteiro, Responsabilidade por informações, [1997] BFD, 45–60 and L.M. Leitão (supra fn. 40), 319–320. On the specific question of liability for pre-natal injuries and the child's legitimacy, C.M. Pinto, *Teoria geral do direito civil* (4th. edn. 2004), rev. by A.P. Monteiro and P.M. Pinto, 203.

[97] G. de Oliveira, H.I.V. e S.I.D.A. – 14 perguntas sobre relações de Família in: *Temas de Direito da Medicina* (1999) I, 175.

Children as Victims under Russian Law

Igor V. Kornev

I. Contributory Negligence

Are there any special provisions concerning contributory negligence if the tortfeasor is a child?

1 There are no special provisions concerning contributory negligence if the tortfeasor is a child. According to the general rule, contributory negligence on the part of the victim must be considered for the reduction of compensation.[1] However, if a victim has been injured, a court may not deprive him or her of compensation unless there was intent on his or her part to sustain the injuries.[2]

What are the rules governing contributory negligence of the child? Do such principles follow the same lines as those governing the negligence issue itself (mirror-image)? Does the fixed minimum age for children to be liable, if any exists, also apply to the contributory negligence of the child?

2 Generally, in the law of delicts the legal status of a person after fourteen is not different from the legal status of an adult. Thus, a child from fourteen to eighteen may be a tortfeasor and bear full personal liability and may be contributorily negligent when a victim. For children who are under the age of fourteen the same rules as those governing the negligence issue itself apply (mirror-image) – such children are presumed to be incapable of fault (intentional and negligent – both personal and contributory).

3 The Supreme Court has always supported the legal doctrine that a minor victim, who has not attained fourteen years of age cannot be contributorily negligent and even prohibited all courts from discussing this matter in their decisions.[3]

[1] See *Grazhdanskii Kodeks Rossiiskoi Federatsii* (Civil Code of the Russian Federation, GK RF), art. 1083, no. 2.

[2] See GK RF, art. 1083, no. 2.

[3] See O Sudebnoj Praktice po Delam o Vosmeshenii Vreda Prichinennogo Povreshdeniem Sdorovia 28 April 1994 (On Court Practice on Compensating of Injuries) Biull. Verkh. Suda RF, 1994, no. 7., 23(2).

Thus, if neither the minor tortfeasor nor his or her minor victim has attained fourteen years of age they cannot be in fault of any kind at all.

4 At the same time, the question of contributory negligence by the victim's parents or guardians arises. The plain implementation of the law dictates that only the minor tortfeasor's parents are to bear all the responsibility, which may be unfair when gross contributory negligence could have been found had the victim been an adult. There are a few decisions where the parents of a minor who had caused harm together with another minor proved that the harm had arisen mainly through the fault of the other minor's parents.[4] Thus, considering the mirror-image to negligence, this rule might theoretically be applied with respect to a victim minor who was contributorily negligent and to his parents. However, the author is not aware of such precedents.

What is the standard of care governing the behaviour of children in the context of contributory negligence? Is such standard determined by the same principles and criteria which are relevant to the duty of care incumbent upon the child in the context of him or her being held liable?

5 If a minor victim is older than fourteen, a usual adult approach towards contributory negligence is applied. The standard of care will be an adult standard without consideration of the minor's age. This standard is determined by the same principles and criteria which are relevant to the duty of care incumbent upon the child/adult in the context of being held liable.

II. Contribution in Equity

Is there a parallel (mirror-image) to liability in equity in the field of contributory negligence? If so, do the criteria determining liability in equity of the child also apply to the issue of holding him or her accountable for his or her contributory negligence?

6 Art. 1083 provides that the court may reduce or deny compensation having considered the property status of the tortfeasor with the exception of when harm was inflicted by the tortfeasor intentionally. This general rule may be applied to a child victim older than fourteen years of age. However, there is not any legally established mirror-image rule with respect to minor victims similar to the rule according to which an under-aged (under fourteen) minor tortfeasor may be compelled to compensate in equity. On the contrary, the prohibition on considering the contributory negligence of a child under fourteen stops courts from reaching such conclusions on the general grounds of art. 1083.

[4] See GK RF, art. 1083.

III. Miscellaneous

What are the rules for a situation in which the child is guilty of contributory negligence but the parents have also breached their duty to supervise? Is the child held accountable in any way for his or her parents' breach of the duty to supervise so that his or her claim for damages is reduced?

There is no direct rule that the failure of the parents to supervise adequately will be considered as a factor to reduce compensation for minors under or over fourteen years of age. However, a tortfeasor may try to prove that the harm was not inflicted through his/her fault, for example when infant children are injured having accessed dangerous areas (highways, construction sites, airports, railways, etc.). If compensation is awarded without fault (strict liability) for engaging in abnormally dangerous activities (e.g. machine operations) the child will still be entitled to full compensation but his/her parents will be considered as additional tortfeasors along with the tortfeasor who inflicted the actual injury. Thus, the parent will be responsible before the child for their own negligence and will have to compensate a part of the sum. 7

Do the rules of contributory negligence also apply in the area of strict liability? Do the rules of contributory negligence apply in the area of strict liability for traffic-accidents or other areas of tort liability?

The rules of contributory negligence do apply in the sphere of strict liability. According to para. 2 of art. 1083 of the Civil Code, in strict liability cases the compensation sum may be reduced or compensation may even be rejected if contributory negligence is established. However, if bodily injuries were inflicted compensation may only be reduced. This rule is applied both in traffic accident liability and other strict liability cases. Please see the example in para. 7. 8

Are adults held to a higher standard of care in their interactions with children or when children are or may be around?

There is no general provision that adults are held to a higher standard of care when children are around. There are a few exceptions to this rule. In special circumstances when children are likely to be around in particular places, special regulations impose such a higher standard of care on anyone who is engaged in particular activities – e.g. driving, construction works close to establishments for children, selling liquor, etc. Special regulations for personnel hired to work with children generally hold such personnel to a higher standard of care – childcare regulations, summer camp activity regulations, school outdoor and gym activity regulations. 9

IV. Insurance Matters

Are pupils covered by private or public accident (first-party) insurance?

10 Usually pupils are not covered by private or public accident (first-party) insurance. In the Soviet Union, when only one state-owned giant insurance company *Gosstrakh* (now *Rosgosstrakh*) existed, the insurance premiums were relatively small and state-fixed and it was common practice for parents to buy some sort of accident policy for children, though no obligation existed. Currently, there are no special regulations obliging parents, schools or other institutions to buy insurance policies for pupils and the cost of accident insurance premiums prevent a considerable number of families from buying such policies. However, many private schools, school districts or even individual public schools ask parents to buy accident insurance.

11 At the same time many summer camps, children's sport camps or other facilities where children engage in activities with high risk of injuries, normally insure participating children.

12 If a child is employed, studies at a professional college with scheduled production activities or is sentenced to a term in a juvenile facility, he/she may be covered by employment insurance introduced for jobs connected to harmful environments and prisoners pursuant to the Law "On obligatory accident professional and production workers social insurance".

Does this insurance cover any damage incurred on the way to school and back?

13 There may be different coverage provisions upon mutual agreement of the parties to the insurance contract regarding damage incurred on the way to school and back, etc. However, most common policies do not separate coverage for damage sustained on the way to school and back but just include different types of damages – traffic, transportation, weather disaster, etc.

Are there restrictions on damages recoverable by the child, e.g. with respect to loss of future earnings?

14 There are no such limitations. Any amount of compensation may be agreed upon by the parties to insurance contracts and any number of insurance contracts with respect to personal insurance may be concluded. Usually there is a lump sum payable upon the accident event.

V. Damage Issues

If damages for loss of earnings are available, what are the principles governing their assessment?

Damages for loss of earnings are available, on the principles established by the Civil Code. Art. 1085 of the Civil Code provides that the tortfeasor shall compensate the loss of earnings to the victim. This compensation does not depend on social security compensation, other possible pensions and earnings, which the victim receives or is entitled to receive because of the injury. The compensation for the loss of earnings is paid in addition to the compensation for the loss of health (calculated as medical services, treatment, etc.). For children who attain fourteen years of age compensation for loss of earnings may not be less than the minimum monthly living expenses (a figure established by the government, in 2005 – approx. € 80, in some provinces local governments do increase this sum, though insubstantially). After the start of employment the child has the right to receive from the tortfeasor the loss in earning constituted by the difference between his/her actual earning and the earnings of an employee having a similar job at the same place of employment. If a child was employed prior to the injury then the compensation may not be less than the sum equal to his/her earnings prior to the injury or than the minimum monthly living expenses. 15

Are there special rules for the assessment of damages sustained by a child, e.g. with respect to pain and suffering?

There is a general compensation for pain and suffering established according to artt. 1099–1101 of the Civil Code. This is an independent compensation established individually in each case. Amounts of such compensation are not established by rules of any kind and may depend on different circumstances but, according to the reported cases, it rarely exceeds 100.000 roubles (approx. € 3.000). 16

Does a small child have a claim for damages for pain and suffering if he or she is deprived of his or her parents by a tortious act? If so, may the claim be denied on the ground that the child does not feel the loss?

According to art. 151 of the Civil Code anyone who sustained pain and suffering has a claim for damages. A small child is not an exception. There are many cases when children of terrorist act victims claim for damages. However, irrespective of the initial claims, courts usually substantially reduce the sums claimed and such claims are normally directed against the state. There is no discussion as to whether a child of tender years may feel the loss but there are no examples where compensation was denied on this ground. 17

With respect to a damage claim for the costs of medical treatment: May the tortfeasor defend himself by pointing to the fact that the parents have a duty to maintain the child?

18 No. Costs of medical treatment, additional food, any additional expenditure of a victim, etc. are always recoverable; however, the tortfeasor may not be obliged to compensate in excess of what is spent by the parents as a result of the delict committed.

In case of wrongful life: Does the child have a damage claim against the physician or a health care institution? Concerning liability for pre-natal injuries: Are third parties liable to the child? May the mother be liable to the child, for example for excessive consumption of alcohol or even for an omission to procure treatment?

19 There are no examples of such suits but according to the general rules of art. 56 of the Family Code, which enables the child or state bodies to claim execution by parents of their parental obligations, such claims might be possible. General rules of the Civil Code also enable anyone to claim damages for harm and oblige the defendant to prove his or her innocence. However, monetary compensation in such cases might be comparable to the compensation for the moral harm (please see no. 16 above) and will not exceed € 1.000–3.000.

20 Moreover, there may be a conflict of laws. Pursuant to the Civil Code the child will not be able to claim compensation for loss of earnings or other types of damages as technically the harm was inflicted to a foetus and not to a person. According to art. 17 of the Civil Code, civil rights and obligations appear only after a person is born; similarly, according to art. 54 of the Family Code a minor is a person who has not yet attained eighteen years of age. Thus, a court may refuse a child's claim in cases of wrongful life both against his/her parents and any third parties.

Children as Victims under Spanish Law

Miquel Martín-Casals, Jordi Ribot and Josep Solé Feliu

I. Factual Introduction

1. What are the most common causes of injury to children in your jurisdiction? In what proportion of cases are actions brought for damages in tort? How many of these are successful? (Plus any other relevant factual data.)

Information available refers to the number of fatal incidents and of persons injured because of external causes (i.e. road traffic accidents, other types of accidents, intentional infliction of damage). Both sources provide a preliminary source of information regarding the most common causes of death and injuries to children in Spain. On the other hand, figures of incidents resulting in civil litigation are not available. Judicial statistics do not focus on the type of action brought to the courts or on the personal circumstances of the claimant or the amount. Both the number of successful claims and the amount of damages claimed for personal injury are thus very difficult to know. 1

Table 1. Number of deaths (unrelated to illness) (2002)[1]

	0–4	5–9	10–14	15–19
Road Traffic/Transport	58	48	63	417
Bad falls	7	6	5	17
Burnings/Drowning	46	13	8	26
Assault	7	4	2	14
Other Causes	11	11	9	47

Table 1 shows that the main cause of non illness-related death in children is road traffic accidents. 71.1% of fatal accidents involving youngsters aged 15 to 19 are due to that cause. The most likely explanation for such a high figure is that that children older than 14 years are allowed to drive mopeds and certain motorcycles. On the other hand, deaths of younger children in road traffic accidents are in proportion to the number of deaths in the case of adults. In striking contrast to that, death related to accidental burning or drowning amounts to ca. 5% of all deaths in children below 14 years. Accordingly, chil- 2

[1] Source: INEBASE Defunciones según causa de muerte 2002 <www.ine.es/inebase> © Instituto Nacional de Estadística, 2005.

dren appear to be substantially exposed to accidents that normally take place at home or while they are carrying out sports or leisure activities.

Table 2. Number of persons injured (last 12 months) (1999)[2]

	All Ages	**0–5**	**6–9**	**10–15**	**16–19**
Population	39,247,019	2,209,504	1,576,851	2,597,650	2,213,518
Road Traffic	669,029	4,877	13,977	19,920	98,228
Assault	322,598	3,654	15,982	32,803	36,475
Other Accidents	2,439,529	94,774	109,732	240,125	168,871

3 Table 2 upholds the conclusions drawn from Table 1 inasmuch as fewer children below 15 appear to be injured in road traffic accidents on average than adults: 1.7% of the population as a whole against only 0.2% (0–5), 0.8% (6–9) and 0.76% (10–15) in case of children. On the other hand, 4.43% of the children above 15 years suffered injuries in road traffic accidents, a figure rising dramatically to 14.5% in the case of children older than 16 and to 18.9% in the case of adults between 20 and 24. In addition, 9.24% of children aged 10 to 15 and 6.96% of children aged 6 to 9 were injured in other kinds of accidents. For children aged 10 to 15 these data show a figure substantially higher than the general average for all ages (6.21%). These data are consistent with the above-mentioned exposure of these age-groups to accidents consisting in accidental burning or drowning. Finally and surprisingly enough, Table 2 shows that more children aged 6 to 15 were injured by intentional physical violence (1.1%) than road traffic accidents (0.81%).

II. Damage Caused by Parents and Other Specific Third Parties

2. In what circumstances may a parent be held liable for an injury sustained by his or her child?

4 In Spanish law there is no specific exception or defence with regard to the tort liability of the parents for the damage that they cause to their children,[3] either on the occasion of their exercise of parental responsibility or resulting from the social contact that is usual between parents and children. Therefore, nothing prevents children from bringing an action for compensation for damage caused intentionally or unintentionally by their parents.

5 However, with regard to accidents involving children harmed by their parent/s, some writers have suggested that the lack of court decisions seems to indicate that, in practice, there is a *de facto* privilege.[4] This practice would adjust the

[2] Source: INEBASE Encuesta de discapacidades, deficiencias y estado de salud 1999 <www.ine.es/inebase> © Instituto Nacional de Estadística, 2005.

[3] By contrast to criminal law, where kinship can be the grounds for attenuation, aggravation or exclusion of criminal liability, according to the circumstances and the type of crime or misdemeanour (cf. artt. 23, 180.4 and 268.1 *Código Penal* (Spanish Penal Code, CP)). See infra section (a) of this question.

[4] J. Ferrer, Relaciones familiares y límites del derecho de daños, [2001] *InDret* 10, 13.

actual liability of the parents to the prevailing social rules and implies that the liability of the parents is restricted, in all likelihood, to cases where they have acted with intent or with gross negligence and, therefore, where the tortious act also qualifies as a crime or a misdemeanour.

In addition, it must be borne in mind that parents are included in the so-called *family privilege*, which excludes subrogation of the first party insurer in the action of the victim if the person causing the damage was any of his or her relatives in direct or collateral line within the third civil grade of consanguinity or his or her adoptive parent (art. 43 II *Ley del Contrato de Seguro* (Insurance Contract Act,[5] LCS)).[6] The legislature assumes thus that if the person causing the harm could be held liable, in practice the relationship of kinship existing between the parties would exclude this possibility and, therefore, it has also opted for excluding the possibility for the insurer to subrogate to the rights of the insured person.[7] As an exception, the insurance company could recoup from the parents if they acted with intent and their liability is covered by an insurance contract (art. 43 II *in fine* LCS). 6

In fact, only in a limited number of cases are civil actions brought by children against their parents. These cases are related to work or traffic accidents and there is some type of compulsory or voluntary liability insurance which provides for coverage of personal injuries.[8] 7

(a) In what circumstances may a parent be held liable for injury resulting from his or her intentional conduct? (Liability for intent.)

Usually this type of case triggers not only civil but also criminal liability. Therefore, the provisions encompassed in the *Código Penal* (Penal Code, CP) dealing with the so-called "tort liability resulting from crimes or misdemeanours punished by the law" shall apply (art. 109–122 CP). 8

Pursuant to art. 109.1 CP "the execution of an act described by the law as a crime or a misdemeanour entails the obligation to repair the harm thereby 9

[5] Ley 50/1980, 8 October, (BOE no. 250, 17.10.1980).

[6] On the other hand, art. 83 LCS lays down that "it is forbidden to contract insurance for cases of death of minors below the age of 14 and incapacitated persons" ("*No se podrá contratar un seguro para caso de muerte, sobre la cabeza de menores de catorce años de edad o de incapacitados*"). It is doubtful whether the legal prohibition applies to accident insurance (see J. Tirado Suárez, Comentario del art. 83 in: F. Sánchez Calero (ed.), *Comentario a la Ley del Contrato de Seguro* (2nd edn. 2001), 1649).

[7] F. Sánchez Calero, Comentario del art. 43 in: F. Sánchez Calero (supra fn. 6), 727. Some scholars also justify this rule with the fact that the collection of the credit against the person causing the harm could have negative repercussions, as a whole, on the household community to which the insured person belongs. Cf. A. Tato Plaza, *La subrogación del asegurador en la Ley del contrato de seguro* (2002), 188.

[8] See J. Ferrer, [2001] *InDret* 10, 13. For instance, in the context of traffic accidents as to the coverage of the occupants of the vehicle, see SAP Sevilla 5.10.2000 (JUR 2001\119306) (the mother brought a claim for compensation for the damage suffered by her child who was knocked down by his father while this latter was making a parking manoeuvre).

caused in the terms provided by the legislation" and according to art. 116.1 CP "every person who is criminally responsible for a crime or a misdemeanour is also civilly liable in the act which gives rise to damage".

10 However, a distinction must be drawn between parental conduct intended to cause death or personal injuries to the child and conduct directed only at harming his or her patrimony. Whereas the former usually qualifies as a crime or, at least as a misdemeanour,[9] intentional acts or omissions causing only financial detriment to the child (for instance, by harming intentionally his or her assets, damaging his or her belongings, stealing money from his or her bank accounts) do not necessarily give rise to criminal liability of the parents. According to art. 268.1 CP "spouses not legally or factually separated or who are in course of judicial proceedings of separation, divorce or nullity, and *natural or adoptive ascendants*, descendants and brothers, and relatives in law in the first grade who live together" are exempted from criminal liability for crimes to the patrimony committed against each other without violence or intimidation. On the other hand, art. 268.1 CP expressly states that in these cases the offenders shall nevertheless be subject to civil liability. Courts usually hold the relatives civilly liable in tort in the same decision in which the legal exemption of criminal liability is applied. As a matter of "procedural economy", these decisions usually also assess the amount of damages, except when there is not sufficient information in the proceedings to take this decision.[10]

In particular, in what circumstances may the parent be held liable for injury resulting from his or her physical chastisement of the child?

11 Spanish law lays down the foundations of the "right of correction" in art. 154 *Código Civil* (Civil Code, CC), a provision which establishes the legal contents of parental responsibility. According to the third paragraph of this provision, "in the exercise of parental responsibility the parents may request the assistance of the public authorities. *They may correct their children reasonably and moderately*".[11]

12 The "right of correction" is linked with the educational purpose of parental responsibility. Therefore, the only *reasonable* measures are those that may be justified as an instrument to provide the child with a proper education.[12] Moreover, the application of the measures of correction shall be mild and dependent upon their necessity and adequacy according to social customs.[13] The ne-

[9] In addition, Spanish Criminal Law recognises a special type of crime of domestic violence, which requires the abuse to be "habitual" and committed upon a member of the same family or household (see art. 153 CP).

[10] See for instance SAP Sevilla 24.7.2003, [2003] *Aranzadi Penal* (ARP), 580.

[11] "*Los padres podrán en el ejercicio de su potestad recabar el auxilio de la autoridad. Podrán también corregir razonable y moderadamente a los hijos*". See also art. 268 II CC as regards the legal guardian's right of correction.

[12] L. Díez-Picazo/A. Gullón, *Sistema de Derecho civil*, vol. IV (5th edn. 1992), 290.

[13] R. Bercovitz, Comentario del art. 154, *Comentarios a las reformas del derecho de familia,* vol. II (1984), 1057.

cessity will be ascertained on having taken into account the age and the behaviour of the child and the adequacy depends upon the proportion of the measure with respect to the child's conduct. Under no circumstances may the measures of correction be contrary to the dignity of the child as a human being.[14]

Is the application of physical violence upon the child in the exercise of the right of correction allowed? Traditionally it was accepted, although when it was deemed "excessive" it could call for the parent's criminal liability (cf. art. 420 CP 1973). Along the same lines, old decisions of the Criminal Chamber of the Supreme Court held that the right of correction exonerated the parents from criminal liability in cases of minor injuries or maltreatment (*obiter* STS 13.4.1982 (RJ 1982\2090) citing STS 13.2.1878). Currently, the prevailing view in legal writing is that *physical chastisement resulting in injuries* or *regular maltreatment* of the child is always unlawful and will never be justified as a legitimate exercise of the right of correction.[15] Consequently, the parents will be criminally prosecuted and may be held liable for the damage caused to their child.[16] 13

The only exception put forward by some scholars are the occasional physical chastisements that do not result in any kind of physical or psychical injury and which are applied within the educational aims of parental responsibility.[17] The impunity of such conducts, which certainly fit some provisions of the Penal Code (see art. 617.2 CP), will be based then upon the legitimate exercise of a right according to art. 20.7 CP. The main problem is that liability will depend too much upon the prevailing social opinion. Moreover, the trend of modern legislation seems to rule out any kind of violence as a means of achieving educa- 14

[14] For this reason, humiliating measures are forbidden. Cf. R. Bercovitz (supra fn. 13), 1057. Accordingly, art. 143.3 *Codi de Família de Catalunya* (Catalan Family Code 1998, CF) stipulates that "the father and the mother shall be entitled to correct the children over whom they have parental responsibility, in a proportionate, reasonable and mild manner. Such corrective and disciplinary measures shall be applied by the parents with full respect for their children's dignity and the parents shall refrain from imposing humiliating sanctions that attempt against their children's rights. For this purpose, the parents may exceptionally request the assistance and the intervention of public powers". (*"El pare i la mare poden corregir els fills en potestat d'una manera proporcionada, raonable i moderada, amb ple respecte per llur dignitat i sense imposar los mai sancions humiliants ni que atemptin contra llurs drets. A aquest objecte, poden solicitar excepcionalment l'assistència i la intervenció dels poders publics.*").

[15] See J.L. Lacruz/J. Rams, *Elementos de Derecho civil*, vol. IV (2002), 423; J. Castán Vázquez, Comentario del art. 154 in: M. Albaladejo (ed.), *Comentarios al código civil y compilaciones forales,* vol. III-2 (1982), 128; J.I. Rubio San Roman, Comentario del art. 154 in: J. Rams (ed.), *Comentarios al código civil,* vol. II-2 (2000), 1484. See also G. Quintero Olivares/F. Morales Prats/J.M. Prats Canut, *Manual de Derecho penal, Parte general* (2nd edn. 2000), 346; F. Muñoz Conde/M. García Arán, *Derecho penal, Parte general* (5th edn. 2002), 346; J. Cerezo Mir, *Curso de Derecho penal español*, vol. II (6th edn. 2001), 310.

[16] Moreover, the judge may take any other measure necessary in order to prevent the child from being harmed (art. 158.4 CC). The parental responsibility must be partially or completely terminated (see art. 170 CC).

[17] See, for instance, J. Cerezo Mir (supra fn. 15), 310 and J. Castán Vázquez in: M. Albaladejo (supra fn. 15), 128. See recently, in this sense, SAP Córdoba 9.3.2004 (La Ley 2004, 1365).

tional goals. Recent legislation has indeed enhanced the legal measures to prevent family violence and child abuse (for instance, by typifying regular "domestic violence" as a crime which is different from the injuries caused to the children and to other members of the family).[18]

(b) In what circumstances may a parent be held liable for injury resulting from his or her unintentional conduct? (Liability for fault.) Are there special rules for liability of the parents? E.g. are parents liable only in case of gross negligence? Are parents held to a lower or higher standard of care?

15 The only specific legal indication with regard to this topic can be found in the rules governing the parent's administration of the property of their minor children.

16 By contrast to the general approach which provides that the yardstick for due care is the conduct of a reasonable person or "buen padre de familia" (art. 1104 I CC), here the law provides that parents must administer the property of their children with the same standard of care that they use with regard to their own affairs (*diligentia quam in suis*, cf. art. 164 I CC).[19] Additionally, with regard to the loss or detriment of the assets administered by the parents, pursuant to art. 168 II CC, the parents will be liable only if they have acted with "intent or gross negligence".

To what circumstances may a parent be held liable for injury resulting from his or her failure to protect the child from harm? (Liability for omissions.)

17 To our knowledge this issue has arisen only in situations qualifying as conduct which is also punishable as a crime of child abuse, domestic violence or the like.[20]

18 One may single out two types of settings:

19 a) Cases in which the relevant omission had a direct causal connection with the harm suffered by the child. In these cases, the crime can be directly attributed to the defendant's *intent* or *negligence*. A case where there was an intentional omission of the defendant was STS 2ª 21.12.1993 (RJ 1993\9592), in which the father left his 11-month-old child alone in his flat for 50 hours. The child eventually died due to lack of food and to cold and the father was convicted for aggravated homicide.[21] A case where the defendant behaved with

[18] F. Muñoz Conde/M. García Arán (supra fn. 15), 346 and G. Quintero Olivares/F. Morales Prats/J. M. Prats Canut (supra fn. 15), 346.

[19] Art. 145.1 CF, by contrast, requires the parents to administer the property of their children "with the standard of care that is required by a good administrator".

[20] As to the identification of parent's fault with the victim's fault in contributory negligence, which *indirectly* amounts to the parents bearing the costs of their own fault as regards protection of their child against harm, see infra question no. 11.

[21] See also *Sentencia del Tribunal Supremo* (Supreme Court Decisions, STS) 2ª 27.10.1992 ([1992] *Repertorio de Jurisprudencia Aranzadi* (RJ), 8538) (parents who failed to take their daughter to medical services when her condition worsened dramatically).

negligence was SAP Barcelona 4.5.1995 (ARP 1995, 683), where the mother's neglect exposed her infant daughter to the risk – which eventually became fact – of being born at home without any kind of medical assistance.

b) Cases in which the relevant omission of the defendant has contributed to the damage to the extent that he or she had the duty to prevent the harm from occurring. In fact, a typical set of cases in which the courts attribute criminal (but also civil) liability to the offender because he or she is deemed to have committed a wrongful act by omission ("commission by omission", as laid down generally in art. 11 CP) are the cases in which one of the spouses (or partners) knows of and consents to the assault or abuse of his or her children by the other spouse or partner. In these sorts of cases, case law has proceeded unambiguously on the basis that parents have a special position which morally and legally requires them to take positive steps to protect their children from harm caused by third parties.[22] 20

Considering contribution to the criminal act performed by a third party, the parent may be convicted either as *author* or only as *accomplice*. In the first case, it can hypothetically be said that, had the defendant acted as required, the damaging event would have been avoided. In the case of complicity, in contrast, this hypothetical assessment of the facts only leads to the conclusion that displaying the required conduct would have made the crime more difficult to commit but would not in itself have prevented it from happening.[23] 21

Theoretically, the aforementioned classification has consequences not only as to the criminal liability but also with regard to the civil liability of the wrongdoers. Pursuant to art. 116.1 CP *in fine* "when two or more persons are convicted for a crime or a misdemeanour the courts shall stipulate the share for which each of them shall be held liable". Moreover, authors and accomplices are jointly and severally liable directly for their shares and subsidiarily for the shares of the rest of the responsible persons (art. 116.2 I CP).[24] 22

[22] See STS 2ª 22.6.1991 (RJ 1991\4793); 31.10.1991 (RJ 1991\7473); 6.10.1995 (RJ 1995\7400); 15.4.1997 (RJ 1997\2931); 26.6.2000 (RJ 2000\5801) and 22.1.2002 (RJ 2002\2631). Not only the parents: STS 2ª 9.10.2000 (RJ 2000\9958) declared guilty of sexual abuse the partner of a man who had raped his daughter while his custody because the former had the legal duty to take positive steps to avoid the criminal act since she was the "guardian in fact" of the child.

[23] See STS 2ª 9.10.2000 (RJ 2000\9958).

[24] Nevertheless, criminal courts seldom provide for apportionment of liability between the offenders on account of their being authors or accomplices. Concerning cases of omissions to prevent harmful acts against children, see for instance SAP Pontevedra 8.2.2001 (JUR 2001\135067) (conviction of the mother as accomplice to violation of two girls who were repeatedly raped by their father, because she did nothing to prevent the abuse from continuing after her daughters let her know about it). In that case, however, the court held the spouses' solidarily liable for compensation to their daughters of € 48,000 and € 12,000. See also SAP Pontevedra 3.4.2003 (JUR 2003\210174) and SAP Barcelona 11.4.2003 (ARP 2003, 649). On the other hand, SAP Madrid 11.7.2003 (ARP 2003, 803) declared the mother guilty of child abuse as accomplice but held her only *subsidiarily* liable for compensation.

3. In what circumstances may a third party (e.g. a school or local authority social services department) be held liable for failing to render a child positive assistance (e.g. by preventing parental abuse)?

23 We have not been able to find any decisions of Spanish courts which deal with the liability of a third party for failing to take positive steps to prevent a child from foreseeable harm caused by his or her parents or by a third party. In particular, decisions holding the social services liable for defective performance of their protection functions are lacking.

24 The only instances refer to accidents suffered by children while in custody a) or to damage caused by third parties for whom the defendant is held vicariously liable b).

25 a) As to the omission of safety measures that could have prevented a child placed under the custody of the social services from suffering harm see, for instance, STJ Madrid 26.11.2003 (JUR 2004\94416) (holding liable the relevant public body in an accident suffered by a 12-year-old pupil who had run away from the centre of custody). See also SAP Zaragoza 27.1.2003 (dealing with the death, on a camp site, of a child who was under the supervision of the organisers).

26 b) With regard to liability of the defendant for the acts of others, SAP Madrid 22.2.2002 (JUR 2002\116667) deemed a sports club subsidiarily liable for damage arising from sexual abuses committed by a paddle instructor on several minors placed under the custody of the club when taking part in a competition.

27 In disputes between social services and biological parents of children placed under the custody of the Public Administration, some recent decisions show that courts seem ready to admit that biological parents have a right to compensation when the restitution of the minor after unlawful termination of parental rights is impossible. The ground for the parents' claim would be the infringement of their parental rights in connection with their right to a fair trial. For instance STS 9.7.2001 (RJ 2001\4999) held that a woman who improperly waived her motherhood at the time of the birth of her daughter, and who was subsequently prevented by unlawful means from having the daughter with her, was entitled to obtain compensation from the Public Administration for the non-pecuniary losses related to the permanent deprivation of her parental rights. In fact, the Department of Social Services of the Government of Andalusia had agreed to pay her € 1.2 million in damages.[25] Along the same lines, SAP Sevilla 3.2.2000 (AC 2000, 56) admitted as a possibility that the social services were liable due to improper termination of parental rights and for the psychological harm caused to a child unlawfully abducted from her

[25] According to E. Corral García, El derecho a la integridad moral del menor como fundamento de la imposibilidad de la reinserción en su familia, [2003] *Aranzadi Civil* (ArC), 11.

mother and placed with a plurality of foster families. In that case, the mother had tried, unsuccessfully, to enforce several court decisions that held that she had not abused her daughter and that ordered the restitution of the child to her biological family. The court stressed that complying with the order issued by the court could reduce the final amount of the very likely award for damages. The Constitutional Court, however, eventually revoked this decision two years after on account of the right to the child's moral integrity and the fact that the restitution of the child to her family could produce new psychological harm to her.[26]

4. What limitations periods are applied to a child's claim?

28 With regard to a child's claim the general rule provided by art. 1932 I CC establishing that "rights and actions are extinguished by prescription, to the detriment of all kinds of persons, even juridical ones, in the terms provided by the law" applies. Therefore, the child's legal representatives must bring the tort claim for the damage suffered by the child within the period established by the law and, usually, within one year starting from the time in which the scope of the damage and the identity of the tortfeasor have become known (art. 1968.2 CC). Moreover, pursuant to art. 1932 II CC, minors shall always have the right of action against their legal representatives if the negligence of the latter was the cause of the prescription.

29 If the minor does not have a legal representative, the time period elapses all the same and the prescription of the action can be considered as damage caused by those persons who have the duty to request the constitution of guardianship in order to prevent the minor from being defenceless (cf. art. 229 CC and 183.1 CF).[27]

30 From 1 January, 2004 new provisions on prescription have entered into force in Catalonia. Among other changes, a new limitation period for extracontractual damage has been set up. According to art. 121–23 *Codi Civil de Catalunya* (Catalan Civil Code, CCC) the new limitation period is three years, starting from the time when the damage and the identity of the tortfeasor have become known (art. 121-23 CCC). In addition, contrary to the criteria laid down in the Spanish Civil Code, the new Catalan legislation provides that the limitation periods shall be suspended whilst the minors lack a legal representative (art. 121–6 § a). Moreover, the claims between the father or the mother and the children

[26] STC 221/2002, 25 November.

[27] But see SAN 31.1.2000 ([2000] *Repertorio Jurispridenica Contercioso* (RJCA), 128), dealing with a case in which the parents of a person infected with HIV as a result of treatment conducted by the public health system concealed this fact from him while he was a child. When he reached the age of majority and applied for the allowances set up by HIV-Infected Allowances Act 1993 (Real Decreto-ley 9/1993, 28 May) the public body contended that the limitation period had elapsed. The court turned down this decision stressing that the starting point of the limitation period was the moment at which the claimant had known about the disease and considered that the parents had acted reasonably in concealing the fact of the infection from him in order to spare him the worries related to AIDS.

subject to their parental responsibility (art. 121–6 § d) and between the minor and the tutor, the curator, the patrimonial administrator, the guardian *ad litem* and the foster parent (art. 121–6 § e) are also suspended. At any rate, however, under art. 121–24, thirty years after the damaging event any claim shall be deemed extinguished in spite of any kind of suspension thereof.

III. Contributory Negligence

5. Are there any special provisions concerning contributory negligence if the tortfeasor is a child?

31 No, there are no special provisions concerning contributory negligence when the tortfeasor is a child. Moreover, the Spanish Civil Code does not contain any provisions establishing general rules on contributory negligence.[28] Art. 114 CP, with regard to tort liability deriving from a crime or a misdemeanour, states that: "If the victim had contributed by his conduct to the occurrence of the damage sustained, the judges or the courts will be able to moderate the amount awarded for its reparation or compensation", but draws no distinction between adults and children. Other provisions referring to contributory negligence in cases of strict liability refer to contributory negligence (see infra questions nos. 12 and 13), but neither of them tackles the question of what happens when the tortfeasor is a child.

6. What are the rules governing contributory negligence of the child? Do such principles follow the same lines as those governing the negligence issue itself (mirror-image)?

32 a) When the victim is a child with tortious capacity, courts do not have any objection to establishing his or her contributory negligence and reducing compensation accordingly. In some cases, capacity is presumed and the conduct of the child is simply considered negligent.[29] By contrast, in some other cases decisions refer to the capacity of the child to realise and understand the possibility of suffering damage. So, for instance, in STS 15.3.1999[30] the victim was a 15-year-old boy who was run over by a train while walking close to the railway in an area where there were no fences. The Supreme Court reduced compensation by taking contributory negligence into account as "the victim was

[28] See on the subject F. Soto Nieto, La llamada «compensación de culpas», [1968] *Revista de Derecho Privado* (RDP), 409–427; R. de Ángel Yágüez, Com. art. 1902 in: I. Sierra Gil de la Cuesta (ed.), *Comentario del Código Civil, T. 8, Libro IV, De las obligaciones y contratos, art. 1790 al 1902* (2000), 438; R. M. Moreno Flórez, ¿Concurrencia de culpas o concurrencia de causas?, [1986] *Actualidad Civil* (AC), 2293; C. Rodríguez Marín, Culpa sin víctima y responsabilidad sin culpa, [1992] RDP, 113–132; J. Solé Feliu, La concurrencia de culpa de la víctima en la jurisprudencia reciente del Tribunal Supremo, [1997] *Anuario de Derecho Civil* (ADC), 867.

[29] So, for instance, in SSTS 27.6.1983 (RJ 1983\3691); 3.12.1990 (RJ 1990\9539); 7.2.1991 (RJ 1991\1151); 15.2.1995 (RJ 1995\851); 20.7.1995 (RJ 1995\5717); 11.12.1996 (RJ 1996\9015); 17.5.2002 (RJ 2002, 4974). See also C. López Sánchez, *La Responsabilidad civil del menor* (2001), 312.

[30] RJ 1999\2147.

15 years old when the accident occurred and, therefore, had enough reasoning and discernment to know the scope of his acts and the implications of what he was doing".[31]

b) With regard to children who have no tortious capacity, the prevailing opinion in legal writing is that in spite of this lack of capacity their contributory negligence must be taken into account in reducing compensation.[32] Some of the academics who share this opinion think that what has to be taken into account is not so much the presence or absence of tortious capacity but rather the "objective violation of norms of conduct or of general prudence through a behaviour that contributes to the creation of the damage".[33] 33

By following a similar opinion in several decisions, the Spanish Supreme Court has reduced compensation to victims who had no capacity to realise the existence of a danger adequately because of the objectively imprudent conduct of the victim.[34] In STS 1.2.1989[35] the defendant driver had run over an 8-year-old child who had unexpectedly stepped into the road. In its decision, the Court of Appeal had considered that one could not properly speak of contributory negligence due to the age of the child. However, the Supreme Court stated that "although the finding that there is no contributory negligence of the victim owing to age [...] must be upheld in cassation, it is however true that the decision takes the conduct of the minor when interfering with the causal link through his thoughtless but unexpected step into the trajectory of the vehicle very much into account". In the same sense, in STS 31.1.1992[36] (6-year-old child who stepped unexpectedly into the road), the Supreme Court held that it was proven that "the damage came from a negligent and silly conduct that was solely imputable to the victim".[37] 34

[31] In the same sense, see also, e.g. STS 25.9.1996 (RJ 1996\6655); 3.10.1996 (RJ 1996\7011); 12.3.1998 (RJ 1998\1286) and 29.5.1999 (RJ 1999\4382).

[32] For an overview on this point see M. Martín Casals, A través del espejo: Concurrencia de «culpa» de la víctima y culpa del causante del daño in: *Estudios Jurídicos en Homenaje al Profesor Luis Díez-Picazo,* vol. II (2003), 2471–2490.

[33] In this sense E. Gómez Calle in: *Tratado de Responsabilidad Civil* (2002), 1053 and 1091; J. Santos Briz, *La responsabilidad civil*, vol. I (1991), 112 and J. Solé Feliu, [1997] ADC, 874. See also STS 14.2.2000 (RJ 2000\675) and 7.3.2001 (RJ 2001\3974). Against this opinion F. Soto Nieto, [1968] RDP, 413.

[34] Corroborating this, F. Pantaleón, Comentario del artículo 1902 in: C. Paz-Ares/L. Díez-Picazo/R. Bercovitz/P. Salvador (eds.), *Comentarios del Código Civil*, vol. II (1991), 1998, who considers that it is a difficult problem to decide whether "objectively negligent" conduct of the victim who, due to his or her young age or insanity, cannot realise the danger to which he or she was exposed must reduce compensation and points out that "although some support can be found in decisions of the courts against reduction STS 1.2.1989 did declare itself flatly for reduction".

[35] RJ 1989\650, commented on by S. Díaz Alabart in [1989] *Cuadernos Cívitas de Jurisprudencia Civil* (CCJC) 19, 149–158.

[36] RJ 1992\540.

[37] For a similar decision, see also STS 28.5.1991 (RJ 1991\3940).

35 More recently, in STS 2.12.2002[38] the Spanish Supreme Court found in favour of the defendants, the Spanish railway company and the engine driver who had run over a 15-month-old child, because the accident occurred due to the exclusive fault of the victim.[39] STS 24.7.2002,[40] in a case where the victim was an 8-year-old girl who was run over by a train, adopted the same solution. The court exonerated the Spanish railway company by using two sorts of reasoning. According to the first, the railway company did not act with fault, as it adopted all the measures required by the applicable standard of care. Secondly, the court stated that even if the company could have been held strictly liable which is impossible under Spanish law, where railway accidents are regulated by general rules of tort based on fault its liability would have been excluded "when the damaging result would have occurred due to carelessness, mistake, omission or lack of sufficient diligence of the victim", which was considered to be the case.

36 In all these cases, the decisive element when establishing the percentage of reduction is the degree of participation in the causation of the damage.[41] In STS 13.2.2003,[42] a case where despite the victim being a minor without tortious capacity the Court of Appeal had evaluated her contributory conduct and reduced the award for damages, the Supreme Court stated that the decision was correct when it "considered that there were concurring causes, not *compensación* [...] *de culpas*, since it is not possible to think of culpability of a little girl, but only that her conduct concurs with the conduct of the defendant in the production of the damage". The truth is, however, that no matter what the Supreme Court calls it, "concurring causes" is not a legal institute different from contributory negligence and, for practical purposes, the practice cannot be distinguished from reducing compensation to victims who have no tortious capacity.

37 Given that the general provisions remain silent on this point, rule 1.2 of the Annex of the Road-Traffic Liability Act 1994 (hereafter LRCSCVM) offers a legislative argument in favour of a general rule concerning the relevance of contributory negligence of children when it states that "the case in which the victim has no tortious capacity and the accident occurs as a result of his conduct or his conduct contributes to it will be put on the same level as contributory negligence". However, this argument has been strongly criticised by some scholars, stating that this rule contradicts the idea of protecting minors, commonly accepted in Europe 20 years ago.[43] Besides, the provision does not state

[38] RJ 2002\10405.

[39] The parents had claimed an award of over € 480,000, without specifying whether it was for them or for the minor child.

[40] RJ 2002\6490.

[41] STS 1.2.1989 (RJ 1989\650). In legal writing, E. Gómez Calle, *La responsabilidad civil de los padres* (1992), 421 and J. Solé Feliu, [1997] ADC, 875. See also STS 9.3.1998 (RJ 1998\1269).

[42] RJ 2003\1045.

[43] L.F. Reglero Campos in: *Tratado de responsabilidad civil* (2nd edn. 2003), 816. See also M.Yzquierdo Tolsada, *Aspectos Civiles del Nuevo Código Penal* (1997) 152–153.

that the conduct of a victim without tortious capacity "is" contributory negligence, but only that "it will be put on the same level". Moreover, it must be borne in mind that this is a special Act.

Finally, some legal writers argue that art. 114 CP[44] furnishes the legal grounds for considering that a victim who has no tortious capacity can be considered, in spite of that, contributorily negligent. Against this opinion it must be pointed out, however, that while it is true that the provision does not expressly require the tortious capacity of the victim, it does not exclude it either.[45] 38

7. Does the fixed minimum age for children to be liable, if any exists, also applyl to the contributory negligence of the child?

There is no minimum age for children to be liable. Regarding contributory negligence of children who have no tortious capacity see supra question no. 6. 39

8. What is the standard of care governing the behaviour of children in the context of contributory negligence? Is such standard determined by the same principles and criteria which are relevant to the duty of care incumbent upon the child in the context of him or her being held liable?

The standard of care governing the conduct of children in the context of contributory negligence can hardly be specified in abstract terms. Courts usually resort to the circumstances mentioned in art. 1104 CC, which allows for it to be adapted to the circumstances of the case. Age is a relevant element, especially with children who have surpassed the first stage of childhood. In general terms, being a child usually justifies childish pranks, but not conduct that clearly shows a reckless disregard for danger.[46] While in their teens it can be regularly required that children comply with the general duties of care and in their late teens, before coming of age, the standard of care can hardly be distinguished from that which would govern the conduct of an adult. Although with regard to children with tortious capacity the standard for contributory negligence is, in principle the same as that which applies to determine their fault, the fact that children with no tortious capacity are also held contributorily negligent to some extent colours the standard for contributory negligence of children. According to some legal scholars, courts tend to focus their attention more on the wrongfulness of their conduct and, specifically, on the reckless disregard of risk or its voluntary assumption.[47] This may be true with regard to wrongfulness, which refers to an objective violation of norms of conduct by behaving in a way that contributes to causing the damage. However, it is diffi- 40

[44] See supra question no. 5.
[45] For these criticisms, see M. Martín Casals (supra fn. 32), 2478.
[46] J. Ferrer Riba/C. Ruisánchez Capelastegui, Niños y adolescentes, [1999] *InDret* 10, 8.
[47] See STS 3.10.1996 (RJ 1996\7011); 2.4.1998 (RJ 1998\1870); 31.12.1997 (RJ 1997\9195) and Administrative Chamber 29.10.1998 (RJ 1998\8421). Cf. J. Ferrer Riba/C. Ruisánchez Capelastegui, [1999] *InDret* 10, 8–9.

cult to talk here about "reckless disregard of risk" or even "assumption of risks", since children who cannot understand what damaging others means can hardly be said to "disregard risk" or assume it. What really occurs in practice is that courts either centre their attention on the objective violation of norms of conduct or pay attention to the strong interference of the conduct of the victim with the causal link (as has been stated supra in question no. 6).

IV. Contribution in Equity

9. Is there a parallel (mirror-image) to liability in equity in the field of contributory negligence? If so, do the criteria determining liability in equity of the child also apply to the issue of holding him or her accountable for his or her contributory negligence?

41 There is no liability of children in equity under Spanish Law.

10. If answered affirmatively: Is the fact that the child is privately or socially insured against the accident a factor to be considered? Is the existence of liability insurance of the tortfeasor to be taken into account? What factors have a bearing on the assessment of equitable contribution?

42 There is no liability of children in equity under Spanish Law.

V. Miscellaneous

11. What are the rules for a situation in which the child is guilty of contributory negligence but the parents have also breached their duty to supervise? Is the child held accountable in any way for his or her parents' breach of the duty to supervise so that his or her claim for damages is reduced?

43 Legal writing rejects the possibility of tortfeasors using the negligence of parents or guardians as a defence in order to reduce compensation when they, as legal representatives, file a claim of damages on behalf of their children. On the contrary, legal scholars contend that if it is proven that the contributory negligence of the child originated in lack of care on the part of his parents (*culpa in vigilando*), the parents will be liable together with the tortfeasor. If liability between parents and tortfeasor can be apportioned, everyone will be liable for their share. If it cannot be apportioned, the parents and the tortfeasor will be solidarily liable.[48] However, no decision has been found where the courts have considered the parents and the tortfeasor solidarily liable.[49]

44 By contrast, there are some decisions where parents make a claim in the name of their child and the court reduces compensation because of the contributory negligence (*culpa in vigilando*) of the parents. Thus, for instance, in STS

[48] Instead of many, see E. Gómez Calle (supra fn. 41), 430–431; F. Pantaleón in: C. Paz-Ares/L. Díez-Picazo/R. Bercovitz/P. Salvador (supra fn. 34), 1998 and J. Solé Feliu, [1997] ADC, 879.

[49] See also S. Díaz Alabart, [1989] CCJC 19, 157.

11.6.1991[50] a 4-year-old girl appearing from behind some parked cars stepped suddenly and unexpectedly into the road and a driver ran over her. The parents filed the claim acting as the legal representatives of their daughter. The Supreme Court held that the driver and the insurer were solidarily liable, but also took into account that the parents had been negligent in watching their daughter, and considered that this amounted to 50% in the creation of the damage. Accordingly, the Supreme Court ruled that the damages award had to be reduced in this proportion, and thus, that "the defendants had to compensate solidarily for only half of the damage sustained [...] taking into account that, owing to the negligence of the persons involved in the accident, apportionment of civil liability – which is considered to be 50% on each part – has to be made".[51]

STS 3ª 9.10.2001[52] reduced, by 50%, the amount of the compensation for the parents of a young girl for the damage suffered when her grandmother negligently took her to a breakwater, which was not properly signposted, and over which they both fell, with the result that the grandmother died and the granddaughter sustained serious injuries. STS 21.10.2002,[53] in its turn, found for the defendant, a company owner of a vending machine, in a claim brought by the mother of a 5-year-old child who was injured when the machine suddenly fell on him while he was playing with it where it was placed on a stand owned by his father. The court fully rejected the claim, pointing out that the father of the child was the only person to whom the injuries sustained were attributable, in his double condition of father of the child, therefore having a duty to supervise the minor, and owner of the stand who, therefore, had the duty to supervise the proper placement of the machine. 45

In other decisions, the parents sued both for themselves and, as legal representatives, for the minor as victim of the accident. When the parent's negligence in the care of their child has already been proven, the court makes two separate damages awards, one for the parents and the other for the child. In this case, however, children are also "identified" with the negligence of their parents and the Supreme Court declares, as in STS 27.9.1993,[54] that the parents' fault "must be reflected in the amount of the compensation award" that must be satisfied by the defendant to the child not only "by the operation of art. 1103 CC, which provides for a power of moderation by the courts, which is not special to obligations arising from contract, but also by obvious reasons of fairness and logic". 46

Generally, however, when the courts declare that they are reducing compensation for *culpa in vigilando* of the parents it is never clear whether the reduction 47

[50] RJ 1991\4439.

[51] Cf. S. Díaz Alabart, [1989] CCJC, 155, with more references to previous case-law. See also STS 30.6.1998 (RJ 1998\5288) and E. Gómez Calle (supra fn. 33), 1055.

[52] La Ley 2002, 995.

[53] RJ 2002\8438.

[54] RJ 1993\6746.

is limited to the award that parents receive for themselves or whether it refers also to the award to the child. So, for instance, STS 29.12.1998[55] referring to a case of an accident suffered by a 5-year-old girl during a school party. The party at which the parents were also present had been organised on the school premises by the association of parents. One of the activities involved filling balloons with hot air, and when lighting the alcohol burner the fluid caught fire and the daughter of the plaintiffs was seriously burned. The parents of the girl claimed damages acting both for themselves and for their daughter for an amount of 49,333,000 PTA (approx. € 300,000). The court of first instance, taking into account contributory negligence, reduced compensation to 34,436,992 PTA (approx. € 205,000). In cassation, the plaintiffs contended that contributory negligence did not apply to cases of children under 5 years of age but the Supreme Court rejected this argument because it understood that in the decision of the court of first instance contributory negligence did not refer to the child but to the parents and held that the school, the association of parents and the insurance company were jointly and severally liable and awarded 10,000,000 PTA (approx. € 60,000) to the parents and 20,000,000 PTA (approx. € 120,000) to compensate for the non-pecuniary loss of the victim.[56]

48 When the parents are acting for themselves as secondary victims of the damage that their child has sustained, legal scholars accept a reduction of compensation that derives from their lack of care in supervising the child. Normally, this situation arises when the child has died because of an accident.[57] Among many others, STS 23.2.1996[58] – a case in which the youngest daughter of the plaintiff died in a summer camp for schoolchildren – has followed this point of view. The child suffered from a chronic disease that caused her death after participating in some physical exercise that had been offered by the organisers of the camp. Her parents made a claim acting for themselves against the summer camp organisers. During the trial, it was proven that the parents had not reported the disease to the organisers of the camp. The Supreme Court held that the organisers were liable, but it reduced compensation on the grounds of contributory negligence of her parents. Their contributory negligence consisted in allowing their daughter to take part in a summer camp where children participate in exercises that were unsuitable to her physical condition, and in not providing the persons in charge of the camp with the necessary information about her health condition.[59]

[55] RJ 1998\9980.

[56] Cf. J. Ferrer Riba/C. Ruisánchez Capelastegui, [1999] *InDret* 10, 11. See also STS 17.9.1998 (RJ 1998\6544).

[57] E. Gómez Calle (supra fn. 41), 429 and F. Pantaleón in: C. Paz-Ares/L. Díez-Picazo/R. Bercovitz/P. Salvador (supra fn. 34), 1998.

[58] RJ 1996\1587.

[59] See also STS 16.5.2000 (RJ 2000\3930), dealing with the compensation claimed by the father of a 12-year-old child who sustained serious injuries in a hypermarket when riding on the shopping trolley with the approval of his father while going down on the conveyor belts of the centre.

12. Do the rules of contributory negligence also apply in the area of strict liability?

Yes. Contributory negligence appears frequently in Acts that establish strict liability as a device that can reduce and even exclude compensation. The relevant provisions are the following: 49

Art. 45 II Nuclear Energy Act 1964 (hereafter LEN),[60] which provides that if the operator of a nuclear plant proves that the damage was caused by or contributed to by the negligence of the victim, the Court may exonerate him wholly or partially from his liability. However, this possibility of exoneration is understood as a discretionary power of the court, not as a legal duty.[61] 50

Art. 9 Product Liability Act 1994 (hereafter LRPD),[62] which establishes that liability of the producer or of the importer may be reduced or disallowed when, on considering all the circumstances of the case, the damage is found to be caused both by a defect in the product and by fault of the injured person or any person for whom the injured person is responsible. 51

Probably, one of the clearest references to contributory negligence can be found in the LRCSCVM.[63] Art. 1.1 II LRCSCVM excludes liability of the driver for damage that can be attributed exclusively to the fault of the victim.[64] In the case of contributory negligence liability will be apportioned equitably and on awarding compensation the "importance of the corresponding concurring fault" will be taken into account (art. 1.1 IV LRCSCVM). In spite of the wording of the Act, what must be assessed in this case is to what extent the victim contributed to the causation of his own harm[65] and, in turn, to what extent the driver could have avoided the accident. For more details as regards traffic accidents, see infra question no. 13. 52

There also are other provisions which, although referring only to the exclusive fault of the victim, according to legal doctrine also include partial exoneration and thus a reduction of damages when the victim's negligence has also contributed to the harm. This is the case in art. 1905 CC, dealing with liability for 53

[60] Ley 25/1964, 29 April, *reguladora de la energía nuclear* (BOE no. 107, 4.5.1964).

[61] L. Díez-Picazo/A. Gullón, *Sistema de derecho civil,* vol. II (8th edn. 1999), 570.

[62] Ley 22/1994, 6 July, *de responsabilidad civil por daños causados por productos defectuosos* (BOE no. 161, 7.7.1994).

[63] *Ley de responsabilidad civil y seguro en la circulación de vehículos a motor* as established by the Additional Provision 8 of Ley 30/1995, 8 November, *de ordenación y supervisión de los seguros privados* (BOE no. 268, 9.11.1995) (Act about the Ordering and Supervision of Private Insurance, which modifies the Act of Use and Circulation of Motor Vehicles).

[64] So, for instance in STS 17.12.1992 (RJ 1992\10698) (pedestrian who steps onto the road) and in STS 31.1.1997 (RJ 1997\253) (motorcyclist who falls under the wheels of a lorry while driving on the hard shoulder of the motorway).

[65] This is confirmed by the fact that the Annex of LRCSCVM (I.2) puts "fault of the victim" on the same level as the case where the victim is not capable of fault and "the accident can be attributed to his conduct or the victim has contributed to the accident".

animals,[66] art. 33.5 Hunting Act (hereafter LC)[67] and art. 25 General Consumer Protection Act (hereafter LGDCU).[68]

54 Finally, although artt. 139 et seq. Legal Regime of Public Administrations and General Administrative Procedure Act (LRJAP)[69] do not mention contributory negligence in the area of liability of public bodies, legal doctrine and court decisions agree that in this area contributory negligence is also relevant.[70]

13. Do the rules of contributory negligence apply in the area of strict liability for traffic-accidents or other areas of tort liability?

55 In the area of strict liability for traffic-accidents art. 1.1 II LRCSCVM excludes liability of the driver for damage that can be attributed exclusively to the fault of the victim.[71] Indeed, this provision uses the expression "conduct or negligence of the victim", instead of the traditional "fault of the victim", and has been understood by legal scholarship as a legislative decision aimed to include, as a full defence, both acts of persons having tortious capacity ("negligence") and acts of those who do not have tortious capacity ("conduct").[72] In the case of contributory negligence, the amount of compensation will take into account the "importance of the corresponding concurring fault" (art. 1.1 IV LRCSCVM). In spite of the wording of the Act, what must be assessed in this case is to what extent the victim contributed to the causation of his own harm and, in turn, to what extent the driver could have avoided the accident.

[66] See I. Gallego Domínguez, *Responsabilidad civil extracontractual por daños causados por animales* (1997), 87.

[67] Ley 1/1970, 4 April, *de Caza* (BOE no. 82, 6.4.1970); L. Díez-Picazo/A. Gullón (supra fn. 61), 571.

[68] Ley 26/1984, 19 July, *general para la defensa de los consumidores y usuarios* (BOE no. 176, 24.7.1984). In this sense, L. Díez-Picazo/A. Gullón (supra fn. 61), 141.

[69] Ley 30/1992, 26 November, *de Régimen Jurídico de las Administraciones Públicas y del Procedimiento Administrativo Común* (BOE no. 285, 27.11.1992 [correction of mistakes by BOE no. 311, 28.12.1993 and no. 23, 27.1.1993]), amended by the Act 4/1999, of 23.1.1999 (Ley 4/1999, 13 January, *de modificación de la Ley 30/1992, de 26 November, de Régimen Jurídico de las Administraciones Públicas y del Procedimiento Administrativo Común* (BOE no. 12, 14.1.1999)).

[70] SSTS Cont Adm 10.4.2003 (RJ 2003\3504); 23.10.2003 (RJ 2003\7936); 29.3.1999 (RJ 1999\3241); 13.3.1999 (RJ 1999\3151); 21.4.1998 (RJ 1998\4045); 27.4.1996 (RJ 1996\3605); 7.10.1997 (RJ 1997\7393). See also E. García de Enterría/T. R. Fernández, *Curso de Derecho Administrativo,* vol. II (1999), 401 and L. Martín Rebollo, La responsabilidad patrimonial de las Administraciones Públicas en España: estado de la cuestión, balance general y reflexión crítica, [1994] *Documentación Administrativa* (Doc.adm.), 237–238, 62 et seq.

[71] So, for instance, in STS 17.12.1992 (RJ 1992\10698) (pedestrian who steps onto the road) and in STS 31.1.1997 (RJ 1997\253) (motorcyclist who falls under the wheels of a lorry while driving on the hard shoulder of the motorway).

[72] See supra question no. 6. Cf. L. F. Reglero Campos (supra fn. 43), 813–814.

14. Are adults held to a higher standard of care in their interactions with children, or when if children are or may be around?

There is no specific rule framed in these terms. However, in many cases where the victim is a minor and, especially, a very young child, courts tend to speak only of contributory negligence and not exclusive fault of the victim. In order to reach this outcome, courts usually assess the conduct of the defendant with very strict criteria. Thus, for instance, in STS 30.12.1999[73] the Supreme Court considers that the safety measures that had been adopted, which probably would have been sufficient in the case of adults, were insufficient with regard to children or young people. It held that the defendant had negligently omitted the security measures required according to the circumstances of the case, since it is foreseeable that these sorts of victims have a conduct "prone to facing danger in a thoughtless way".[74] 56

This approach can be confirmed by case law in a specific series of cases, usually involving children, which refer to accidents which occur in private premises where a device or machine which entails some sort of danger has been set up, or, more often, which is improperly used or operated. When analysing whether the safety measures adopted are suitable for preventing people from suffering harm, case law usually requires the taking into consideration of the conduct of persons who are foreseeably less thoughtful or careful.[75] 57

VI. Insurance Matters

15. Are pupils covered by private or public accident (first-party) insurance?

a) Public accident (first-party) insurance

Within the framework of Social Security there is a specific compulsory insurance scheme for students (art. 7.1 d) and 10.2 f) LGSS). This scheme is to be applied both to private and public schools and was introduced by the Act of 17 July, 1953[76] and regulatorily developed by the Order of 11 August, 1953[77], which passed the Rules of the Friendly Society of School Insurance (*Estatuto de la Mutualidad del seguro escolar* [hereafter, Estatuto]). After several amendments, it currently encompasses all students – with no further specification – who are Spanish or who reside in Spain and who are between 16 and 27 years old.[78] 58

[73] AC 2000\308.

[74] STS 14.2.2000 (La Ley 2000, 6367) considers that the centre had been contributorily negligent in the suicide attempt of a minor "because the same grade of maturity that can be required from an adult can not be required from a minor [...] and if the windows had been equipped with the appropriate protection devices the event could have been avoided".

[75] J. Ferrer Riba/C. Ruisánchez Capelastegui, [1999] *InDret* 10, 6.

[76] BOE no. 199, 18.7.1953.

[77] BOE no. 240, 28.8.1953.

[78] See J.L. Tortuero Plaza in: M.Alonso Olea/J.L. Tortuero Plaza (eds.), *Instituciones de Seguridad Social* (16th edn. 1999), 516–517; D. Lantarón Barquín, El régimen especial de la seguridad social de estudiantes: análisis de un régimen jurídico en vías de extinción, [1997] *Tribuna Social* (TS) 83, 53–60; R. Esteban Legarrete/A. Arqued Sanmartín, Pluriactividad y encuadramiento subsidiario en los regímenes especiales de la Seguridad Social de los trabajadores agrarios, del mar y de los estudiantes, [2001] *Aranzadi Social* (AS) 12, 1 et seq.

59 The specific characteristic of the risks covered by this compulsory school insurance is that they are related to studying. Art. 11 of the Rules define accident as "any bodily injury suffered by a student on the occasion of activities directly or indirectly related to his capacity as such, even those related to sports, meetings, study tours, training tours, or graduation tours, and the like, as long as these activities have been organised or approved by Teaching Institutions …".

60 The insurance does not cover accidents when these have been caused by *force majeure* unrelated to any school activity (art. 12 I and II Estatuto). By contrast, negligence of the student does not exclude coverage (art. 12 III Estatuto).

b) Private accident (first-party) insurance

61 Usually private schools and partially public funded private schools (the state assisted schools, so-called *escuelas concertadas*) offer to the parents of the pupils an accident insurance which includes health care and medication, as well as small amounts for cases of death and personal injury.

62 Public schools more frequently buy accident insurance which covers the pupils suffering accidents in the centre. Competences in mandatory education have been decentralised and some Autonomous Communities have underwritten collective insurance policies for the pupils with insurance companies. These policies usually distinguish different types of educational activities (workshops, work experience, kindergartens, etc.).

16. Does this insurance cover any damage incurred on the way to school and back?

63 The enumeration of art. 11 Estatuto is simply by way of example and, therefore, the insurance also covers the accident *in itinere* on the occasion of the student travelling from his home to school or back.[79]

64 Private insurance covers accidents suffered by the pupils while at school and while being transported to their domiciles, as well as the accidents that they may suffer on the occasion of excursions or complementary activities organised by the school.

17. Are there restrictions on damages recoverable by the child, e.g. with respect to loss of future earnings?

65 The compulsory (first-party) insurance covers health care and medication expenses until the injured victim is discharged, as well as a social security dis-

[79] See D. Lantarón Barquín, [1997] TS 83, 57 and STSJ Castilla La Mancha 25.10.1993 (AS 1993\4474).

ability benefit whose amount depends on the seriousness of the disability suffered:

a) *Absolute and permanent disability* results in entitlement to a benefit sum between 25,000 and 100,000 PTA (approx. € 150–600) per year [*sic*], which is calculated "in proportion to the studying time that has already elapsed without being wasted and to the reduction of further ability for the practice of a professional activity" (art. 20 Estatuto). 66

b) In the case of *serious disability*, the insurance entitles the victim to a life annuity of 24,000 PTA (approx. € 144.5) per year [*sic*]. 67

These amounts also cover the detriment resulting from the inability to continue studying and are fixed sums. However, they are compatible with the amounts that the victim might receive on the same facts from private insurance (art. 9 II Estatuto). By operation of the general rules on this subject, they are also compatible with the claim for tort liability against the tortfeasor and his insurer. 68

As can be seen from their amounts, these benefits have never been updated. In addition, the rule that provides that these benefits are not compatible with any other social benefits arising from the same risk if covered by the general Social Security Scheme is still in force (art. 9 Estatuto). Since benefits that can be obtained from the general Social Security Scheme are much higher in these cases, the practical importance of the benefits for school accidents is nil for those persons who, at the same time, are entitled to the benefits of the general Social Security Scheme or even any other scheme.[80] 69

VII. Damage Issues

18. If damages for loss of earnings are available, what are the principles governing their assessment?

The problem with compensation for loss of earnings in children has not been dealt with systematically. As a rule,[81] the assessment of damages in all cases has to be done "according to the circumstances of the case" which, as construed in the case law, does not mean the full discretion of the court, but a decision under the criteria of "prudence" and "reasonability".[82] Moreover, courts regularly award a lump sum which at most will reach the amount claimed for by the plaintiff and which will be assessed by the court at a rough guess that does not distinguish between the different heads of damages and sometimes, not even 70

[80] See R. Esteban Legarrete/A. Arqued Sanmartín, [2001] AS 12, 18.

[81] In general, see M. Martín/J. Ribot/J. Solé Feliu, Compensation for Personal Injury in Spain in: B.A. Koch/H. Koziol (eds.), *Compensation for Personal Injury in a Comparative Perspective* (2003), 274–285 (explaining also the system of compulsory tariffication provided for road-traffic accidents, which comprises pecuniary and non- pecuniary loss arising from temporary or permanent disability).

[82] Among many others, see STS 9.7.1998 (RJ 1998\5547).

between pecuniary and non-pecuniary losses.[83] Additionally, damage awards usually vary a lot from court to court.[84]

71 The same is true when the victim is a child. The courts follow the practice of awarding, according to their discretion, a lump sum that encompasses both pecuniary and non-pecuniary losses.[85] For their assessment, they take into account the seriousness of the injuries sustained by the victim and their impact on his or her life in the future.[86]

72 Regarding loss of earnings flowing from permanent disability, to this date no common method of assessing damages awards has been developed. The prevailing legal scholarship points out that compensation must cover living expenses for an ordinary life during an average lifespan,[87] but in practice courts usually assess a lump sum *ex bono et aequo* without taking into account actuarial methods of prediction and calculation that are widespread in areas such as life insurance or accident insurance. If the victim is a child, it is not usual to take into account either the activity that the victim might have carried out in the future or how the permanent disability may affect him in this respect or what compensation he should receive for the loss of the time for his studies while recovering from injuries.[88]

73 No model or scheme of compensation that takes into account how the injury sustained specifically affects the professional career of the victim has so far been developed or applied.[89] Neither is any commonly accepted yardstick available to assess the loss of earnings when the victim is a child or a student. However, it is feasible to venture that courts would unanimously reject the consideration of a particular career development with the corresponding calculus of loss of income as too speculative.[90]

[83] See for instance STS 15.11.2000 (La Ley 2000, 10874); 20.5.2002 (RJ 2002\5344) and 11.4.2002 (RJ 2002\3382).

[84] See for instance STS 8.11.1998 (AC 1998\21883); 19.4.1999 (La Ley 1999, 6184); 11.6.2002 (RJ 2002\4887) and 17.5.2002 (RJ 2002\6748).

[85] See SAP Burgos 10.2.1998, ARP 1998, 776, which awarded the same amount of compensation as for an adult on a day of sick leave.

[86] Thus, for instance, SAP Barcelona 21.7.2000 (AC 2001\30) awarded 100 MPTA (€ 601,000) to a 14-year-old child who suffered paraplegia as a result of the defendants' lack of care.

[87] See L. Díez-Picazo, *Derecho de daños* (1999), 324.

[88] See in this sense, E. Vicente Domingo, *Los daños corporales: tipología y valoración* (1994), 129. STS 11.3.2001 (RJ 2001\1520) awarded a child who had been injured by another child 3,000 PTA (€ 18) per day of sick leave, and leaves the assessment of the award "for long term bodily and mental effects and for compensation of loss of earnings in his job" to the moment of execution of the judgment.

[89] See for instance, STS 11.3.2000 (RJ 2000\1520) in a case of a child who suffered temporary disability and severe permanent consequences.

[90] As a general rule courts exclude compensation for "simple expectations or earnings that are doubtful or contingent". See, among others, STS 25.2.1998 (RJ 1998\1810); 21.10.1996 (RJ 1996\7235); 30.6.1993 (RJ 1993\5340) and 6.7.1983 (RJ 1983\4073).

19. Which of the child's non-material interests are protected in your jurisdiction? May the child, for example, sue for impairment of intellectual or social development, the onset of behavioural problems, or reduced employment prospects?

As a rule, children may claim for compensation for the same non-material interests as adults. However, neither Spanish courts nor legal scholarship, have so far considered the possibility of compensating for the impairment of intellectual or social development, the onset of behavioural problems, or the reduced employment prospects. 74

20. Are there special rules for the assessment of damages sustained by a child, e.g. with respect to pain and suffering?

No. The same rules regulating assessment of damages for an adult also apply to children. 75

21. Does a small child have a claim for damages for pain and suffering, if he or she is deprived of his or her parents by a tortious act? If so, may the claim be denied on the ground that the child does not feel the loss?

There are no specific rules providing for differences with regard to adults. Accordingly, the child has a claim for damages for pain and suffering and the claim cannot be rejected on the grounds that the child does not realise the loss. Even when the child is very little at the time of the accident which deprives him or her of the company of his or her parents and, therefore cannot realise what that loss means, he or she will realise it on growing up. As STS 2ª, 10.12.1997[91] stated "non-pecuniary loss, both current and future, that the death of a parent can cause to a child, even if parent and child had little contact with each other, must always be compensated for". 76

22. With respect to a damage claim for the costs of medical treatment: May the tortfeasor defend himself by pointing to the fact that the parents have a duty to maintain the child?

The fact that someone else covers the damage caused by the tortfeasor (insurer, social security, medical treatment costs paid by the parents) does not allow him to escape paying compensation for the damage caused. 77

23. In case of wrongful life: Does the child have a damage claim against the physician or a health care institution?

The Spanish Supreme Court has not decided on this question yet and legal scholarship has not devoted much attention to the topic so far. The opinion of legal writers who have dealt with the topic is twofold. On the one hand, there 78

[91] RJ 1997\8746.

are those scholars who are in favour of compensation for the child born with disabilities as long as it is proven that had the mother been duly informed she would have terminated the pregnancy. Additionally, sometimes this is even presumed from the mere fact that the mother decided to undergo the prenatal tests.[92] On the other hand, other scholars consider that, with regard to the *nasciturus*, the physician has no duty to prevent him from being born[93] or, conversely, that the legal system does not recognise that the child born with severe disabilities has any right not to be born.[94]

79 Along the lines of this second opinion, we think that, according to the values enshrined in the Spanish Constitution, the possible interest of the disabled child "in not being born" does not deserve protection and, therefore, its infringement does not give rise to liability in tort.

80 Although the right to life is a fundamental right enshrined in art. 15 CE (Spanish Constitution), the Spanish Constitutional Court in STC 53/1985, of 11 April refused to declare, that the foetus holds this fundamental right and preferred to treat unborn life as a "legal good protected by this provision of the Constitution [...] albeit not [...] a holder of the fundamental right". This gives rise to an obligation on the part of the State to make the protection effective through law, including, where necessary, criminal law. However, the court acknowledged that this protection must cease when it collides with the rights of the mother, such as the right to life, health or privacy and that the legislator does not need to impose criminal sanctions in these cases because the continuation of pregnancy would constitute an unbearable hardship for the woman concerned. Whereas in the therapeutic cause of abortion there is a conflict of interests between the foetus' life in the process of formation and the life of the mother, in the ethical and the eugenic causes the conflict occurs with regard to the mother's dignity and the free development of her personality. More specifically, in the case of the eugenic cause the exemption from punishment solves a conflict between life in the process of formation, which, despite malformations and disabilities, is protected by law, and the dignity and the free development of the personality of the mother. The issue is not that the law does not value the birth of disabled children positively, but simply that it is considered incompatible with dignity and with the free development of personality to impose upon a mother the continuation of pregnancy and to force her, this way,

[92] R. De Ángel Yágüez, Diagnósticos genéticos prenatales y responsabilidad (II), [1996] *Revista de Derecho y Genoma Humano/Law and the Human Genome Review*, 152.

[93] Cf. F. Pantaleón, Procreación artificial y responsabilidad civil in: II Congreso Mundial Vasco, *La filiación a finales del siglo XX* (1988), 271–276; and following him, M. Ureña Martínez, Comentario de la sentencia de 6 de junio de 1997, [1997] CCJC 45, 1113–1116 and G. Díez-Picazo, La imposibilidad de abortar: un supuesto más de responsabilidad civil, [1998] La Ley, 1706.

[94] See, in this sense, M. Martín Casals/J. Solé Feliu, Comentario a la sentencia de 7 de junio de 2002, [2002] CCJC 60, 1097–1121 and Cour de Cassation, 13 July 2001, arrêts 278, 279 and 280. Spanish case note, [2003] *European Review of Private Law* (Eur.Rev.Priv.L.) 2, 201–220.

to assume the grave duties of bringing up and taking care of a child who, as is already known, will be born with severe disabilities.[95]

This balancing of rights does not exist in the case of wrongful life. Art. 15 CE, as stated, protects life, but here there is not a conflict of interests between the right to life of the foetus and a hypothetical "right not to be born without serious disabilities". To recognise such a right would mean to admit that no-life must be preferable to life with disabilities and would entail that the life of disabled persons is valued negatively, as a harm for which compensation must be awarded. Moreover, it might lead further to an inquiry into whether the mother who has decided not to terminate pregnancy can be sued by her handicapped child for not having exercised an implausible sort of "right of prenatal euthanasia" in his or her name.[96] 81

24. Concerning liability for pre-natal injuries: Are third parties liable to the child? May the mother be liable to the child, for example for excessive consumption of alcohol or even for an omission to procure treatment?

a) Third parties are liable to the child, since the foetus enjoys constitutional protection as a "legal good protected by this provision [art. 15] of the Constitution".[97] The general rule of Spanish law set out in art. 29 CC considers the *nasciturus* as born with regard to all those effects that favour him or her under the condition, however, that he or she is finally born and meets all the conditions necessary to acquire civil personality pursuant to art. 30 CC (i.e. to have human figure and to live at least for 24 hours entirely detached from the womb of his or her mother). This rule has permitted Spanish courts to compensate for the non-pecuniary loss sustained by a child for the death of his father in a traffic accident, which occurred when he was still in the womb of his mother (*nasciturus*). Thus, for instance, SAP Barcelona 20.9.2000[98] declared that "although the «nasciturus» is not specifically referred to in the current tariffication scheme [the court refers to the scheme provided by the Act 30/1995 for compensation for death and personal injury in the cases of traffic accidents], this scheme may be applied as if he were just another child in accordance with art. 29 CC". It is true that in this case the foetus did not suffer any personal injury, but these cases illustrate that protection of *nascituri* is much broader and even encompasses non-pecuniary loss not resulting from personal injury. 82

There are also decisions which compensate children for the damage suffered as the result of negligent conduct on the part of the physician or the midwife 83

[95] See J.C. Carbonell Mateu/J.L. González Cussac, in Vives Antón et al., *Derecho Penal. Parte especial* (2nd edn. 1996), 112–113 and J.J. González Rus in: Manuel Cobo del Rosal (ed.), *Curso de Derecho Penal Español, Parte especial,* vol. I (1996), 130–131.

[96] See also, in this sense, R. Bercovitz, Comentario de la sentencia de 4 de febrero de 1999, [1999] CCJC 50, 859.

[97] Cf. *Sentencia del Tribunal Constitucional* (Constitutional Court Decisions, STC) 53/1985. See supra question no. 23.

[98] ARP 2000, 3289.

during labor and even before actual birth has occurred. Thus, for instance, they compensate the child for the consequences resulting from the lack of oxygenation of the foetus during birth which took place when the doctor on duty, in spite of the fact that he knew that the birth had started, preferred to keep on resting and left the delivery in the hands of the midwife.[99] A child has also been compensated for the consequences resulting from the conduct of a gynaecologist who arrived late for delivery, in spite of the fact that the midwife had called twice and informed him of the symptoms of foetal distress prior to birth.[100]

84 b) As far as we know, Spanish Courts have not had the opportunity to deal with cases referring to the damage caused by the mother by excessive consumption of alcohol or even by an omission to procure treatment, but we think that in these cases the self-determination of the mother is paramount and the child cannot bring a claim against her. In favour of this opinion it must be borne in mind that when art. 146 CP provides for the punishment of persons who on the grounds of "serious negligence bring about abortion" it excludes the criminal responsibility of the pregnant mother by declaring in section 3 that "pregnant women will not be punished pursuant to this provision". Along the same lines, art. 158 CP punishes those who, by serious negligence, commit a crime of injuries to the foetus, understood as conduct which, by any means or proceedings, causes the foetus an injury or an illness which seriously impairs his normal development or gives rise to a serious physical or psychical defect. However, art. 158 III CP also establishes that "pregnant women will not be punished pursuant to this provision". The consequence resulting from the regulation of these two crimes by the Criminal Code, although referring only to criminal responsibility, may well be the expression of a policy which aims at excluding, in general terms, any responsibility of the mother for the damage that she may negligently cause to her unborn child.

[99] See STS 27.5.2002 (RJ 2002\7159).

[100] SAP Barcelona 5.3.2003 (JUR 2003\198585).

The Child as Victim under Swedish Law

Bertil Bengtsson

1 In the case of contributory negligence on the part of the child, the general rules concerning such negligence are applied. Here, Swedish law is so different from most other European legal systems that a comparison is rather difficult as far as concerns the position of children.

2 The Swedish Tort Liability Act (TLA) makes a distinction between personal injuries on one hand, and damage to property and financial loss on the other. As for personal injuries, there is full liability notwithstanding contributory fault, except where there is intention or gross negligence on the part of the victim himself (or when the victim is a motorist who has driven negligently under the influence of drink). When wrongful death is concerned, compensation is reduced only if there was intent on the part of the deceased, in other words in suicide cases. Considerations of social policy and the arguments of loss distribution have also been important in cases of personal injury; in general, damages will be paid by liability insurance. Concerning damage to property and purely financial loss, the ordinary rules of contributory negligence apply; compensation is adjusted in accordance with considerations of reasonableness, above all the degree of fault on both sides. (Chapter 6 sec. 1 TLA.)

3 The result is that in case of injury, the child will get full compensation in almost all cases because the courts are very reluctant to describe negligence on the part of a child as gross. As for damage to property and financial loss, there is also a considerable tolerance towards children who behave in a thoughtless way, especially small children. When a child is a victim there is not the same tendency to apply an objective standard as when the child is tortfeasor (cf. B. Bengtsson, Children as Tortfeasors under Swedish Law in: M. Martín-Casals (ed.), *Children in Tort Law Part I: Children as Tortfeasors* (2006), no. 5). It is likely that the minimum age for a child victim to be considered negligent is higher, probably seven years or more.

4 Otherwise, considerations of equity do not play the same part as when the child is tortfeasor. The rules of the TLA are so very favourable to the victim in general that there is hardly any need to make it still easier for a child to claim damages. As for accident insurance, it might influence the compensation in case of inju-

ries; however, this problem will seldom arise because as mentioned above the law does not permit any reduction of compensation because of ordinary negligence. In case of damage to property, the existence of insurance can have some significance, though there are no cases dealing with this question.

5 If parents have neglected a duty of supervision, this will not have any influence on the possibilities for a child to claim compensation for personal injuries; only the fault of the victim himself can be a ground for reduction. On the other hand, when property belonging to the child is damaged, the child will be identified with the parent, and damages may be reduced as a consequence of the negligence of the parent.

6 The same rules of contributory negligence apply in the area of strict liability for traffic accidents or in other cases.

7 It is a natural consequence of the principle of fault liability that adults are held to a higher standard of care when dealing with children or in other cases when children are around, for instance in road traffic.

8 Pupils are very often protected by private insurance taken out by the municipality or the parents. The insurance may cover accidents on the way to school and back, though conditions vary.

9 Regarding damages recoverable in tort by the child, the same principles will prevail as for other victims, although it can be difficult to establish loss of future earnings for instance; here, courts must resort to a prognosis that can be very uncertain, or to a free estimation. Damages for personal injury will include costs of medical treatment necessitated by the injury. As for non-financial damage, the child is entitled to damages for pain and suffering in the same way as other victims. If the child is deprived of a parent, it is often entitled to damages under the head of pain and suffering for mental injury in the same way as other members of the family, although very small children will probably be denied such compensation.

10 The law concerning wrongful life and pre-natal injuries is not very clear, but probably the child would have no claim in the former case; as for pre-natal injuries, at least third parties can be liable to the child.

11 There are no special rules or special provisions for liability of the parents towards their children. Claims for damages seem to be very unusual in these situations, especially as such liability is usually excluded from liability insurance.

12 To sum up, the system of liabilities in the cases discussed above may seem complicated; however, in most cases claims will be directed only against the liability insurance of the parent or the liability insurance of the school, and in practice there is seldom any recourse against other parties.

Comparative Report

Comparative Report

Miquel Martín-Casals and Josep Solé Feliu

I. Introduction

1. What are the most common causes of injury to children in your jurisdiction? In what proportion of cases are actions brought for damages in tort? How many of these are successful? (Plus any other relevant factual data.)

Statistics and data concerning civil litigation related to accidents where children are involved are rather fragmentary in all countries under survey. Probably, one of the reasons for this is that judicial statistics do not usually focus either on the type of accident, the action brought to the courts or the personal circumstances of the claimant. Nevertheless, some reports provide some statistics concerning the sources of accidents involving children, irrespective of whether the accident is followed by judicial proceedings or not. 1

A conclusion that seems to be shared by all those reports including data in this respect is that, generally speaking, road traffic accidents are the main cause of death for children,[1] a result that agrees with the perceptions of parents regarding the most serious sources of danger to their children's lives.[2] Additionally, all statistics provided in this area show that the number of children of a certain age affected by traffic accidents increases the closer the age-group is to majority.[3] Thus, in England and Wales for instance, according to figures referring to the year 2000, the number of deaths of children in traffic accidents for the age-group between 0 and 4 years was 38, this figure increased up to 48 for the age-group between 5 and 9 years, and reached the number of 89 for children in the 2

[1] England and Wales no. 1; Germany no. 1; the Netherlands no. 2; Portugal no. 1; Spain no. 2.
[2] The Netherlands no. 2.
[3] Germany no. 1; Italy no. 2; the Netherlands no. 2; Spain no. 2.

age-group between 10 and 14 years.[4] In Germany, the figures for the year 2002 show that in the age-group between 0 and 10 years the number of deaths was 118, 115 in the age-group between 10 and 15 years and 852 in the age-group between 15 and 20.[5] Finally, in Spain, according to figures for the year 2002, the number of deaths for children within the age-group between 0 and 4 was 58, 48 in the age-group between 5 and 9, 63 in the age-group between 10 and 14 and then this number skyrocketed to 417 for the age-group between 15 and 19 years. In all likelihood, the significant increases for the higher age-group can be explained by the fact that in this age-group children start taking part in road traffic by driving mopeds, motorcycles and, finally, cars.[6]

3 After road-traffic accidents, burnings and drownings come second as the most common sources for accidents suffered by children in the countries under survey, in a proportion that tends to be more significant when children are of tender age.[7] Thus, for instance, it is pointed out that in the Netherlands whereas the rate of child mortality is 3.10 per 100,000 population in the case of road accidents, the rate of deaths is 1.17 in the case of drownings and 0.24 in the case of burns and scalds.[8] In England and Wales, according to figures for the year 2000, the total number of deceased children within the age-group from 0 to 14 years for drowning, choking, suffocation and burning was 132,[9] which by smaller age-groups, can be distributed as follows: from 0–4 years, 83; from 5–9 years, 22 and from 10–14, 27. In Spain, for the year 2002 the total number of deaths for burning and drowning for children between 0 and 19 years was 93, distributed as follows: for the age-group between 0 and 4, 46; for the age-group between 5 and 9 years, 13; for the age-group between 10–14 years, 8 and finally, for the age-group between 15 and 19, 26.[10]

II. Damage Caused by Parents and Other Specific Third Parties

2. In what circumstances may a parent be held liable for an injury sustained by his or her child?

(a) In what circumstances may a parent be held liable for injury resulting from his or her intentional conduct? (Liability for intent.) In particular, in what circumstances may the parent be held liable for injury resulting from his or her physical chastisement of the child?

4 This question refers to two different aspects: (1) whether there are specific rules dealing with the liability of parents for the harm they have intentionally

[4] England and Wales no. 1.
[5] Germany no. 1.
[6] Spain no. 2.
[7] England and Wales no. 1; the Netherlands no. 2; Portugal no. 1; Spain no. 1.
[8] The Netherlands no. 2.
[9] England and Wales no. 1.
[10] Spain nos. 1–2.

caused to their children and (2) whether these legal systems accept the so-called "right of chastisement" or not.

(1) With regard to the first aspect, there are no specific statutory rules or immunities for the benefit of the parents and all legal systems apply the general tort law rules to these cases.[11] When such cases reach the courts they tend to be dealt with by criminal courts, since they involve serious conduct such as sexual, physical or mental abuse, which qualify as crimes.[12] In most legal systems civil courts are reluctant to get involved in domestic affairs and therefore no decisions dealing with this topic are known.[13] However, in some countries, such as Italy, there is a recent tendency to deal in civil courts with cases involving infringements of the rights of personality of children perpetrated by their parents and to award compensation for the resulting non-pecuniary damage.[14] 5

(2) With regard to the so-called "right of chastisement", there are two groups of countries. In the first group, which includes Austria, Germany and Italy, physical chastisement of children is expressly prohibited by the law.[15] In this sense, for instance, § 146a Austrian Civil Code (*Allgemeines Bürgerliches Gesetzbuch*, ABGB) provides that "the use of violence and the infliction of physical or mental distress on the child are considered unlawful".[16] In its turn §1631 subs. 2 cl. 2 German Civil Code (*Bürgerliches Gesetzbuch*, BGB), since an amendment carried out in 2000, sets out that "Children have the right to an education free of violence. Physical punishment and mental distress and other humiliating measures are unlawful".[17] In Italy physical chastisement is also considered unlawful since the abrogation in 1975 of art. 319 Italian Civil Code (*Codice civile*, c.c.), which dealt with the necessary measures "to stop the bad behaviour of the child".[18] 6

In the second group, which includes Belgium, the Czech Republic, England and Wales, France, the Netherlands, Portugal and Spain,[19] physical chastisement, although not prohibited, is allowed under certain conditions only. *Inter alia,* these conditions are that physical chastisement must be necessary, ade- 7

[11] Austria no. 1; Belgium no. 1; Czech Republic no. 7; England and Wales no. 6; France no. 6; Germany no. 2; Italy no. 13; the Netherlands no. 6; Spain nos. 5–7.

[12] In this sense, for instance, Belgium no. 4; Italy no. 14; Portugal nos. 13–14; Spain no. 5.

[13] France no. 6; Italy no.14.

[14] Italy nos. 20–21.

[15] Austria no. 2; Germany no. 3; Italy no. 14.

[16] § 146a ABGB „Das minderjährige Kind hat die Anordnungen der Eltern zu befolgen. Die Eltern haben bei ihren Anordnungen und deren Durchsetzung auf Alter, Entwicklung und Persönlichkeit des Kindes Bedacht zu nehmen; die Anwendung von Gewalt und die Zufügung körperlichen oder seelischen Leides sind unzulässig". See Austria no. 2.

[17] § 1631 subs. 2 cl. 2 BGB „Kinder haben ein Recht auf gewaltfreie Erziehung. Körperliche Bestrafungen, seelische Verletzungen und andere entwürdigende Maßnahmen sind unzulässig." See Germany no. 3.

[18] See Italy no. 14.

[19] Belgium no. 5; Czech Republic no. 5; England and Wales no. 7; France nos. 6–7; the Netherlands no. 6; Portugal no. 15; Spain nos. 8–11.

quate or appropriate, reasonable or proportionate and not against the dignity of the child. The necessity may be ascertained according to the circumstances and taking into account the age and the behaviour of the child and the educational purpose of the measure.[20] Adequacy, appropriateness, proportionality or reasonableness seem to refer to the proportionality of the measure with respect to the child's conduct, to the extent of the measure itself or to its impact upon the child[21]. In this sense, for instance, art. 154 II of the Spanish Civil Code (*Codigo Civil*, CC) declares that parents "may correct their children reasonably and moderately".[22] It is clear, however, that the measures of correction may not in any case inflict personal injuries on the child or be contrary to his or her dignity as a human being.[23]

(b) In what circumstances may a parent be held liable for injury resulting from his or her unintentional conduct? (Liability for fault.) Are there special rules for liability of the parents? E.g. are parents liable only in case of gross negligence? Are parents held to a lower or higher standard of care? In what circumstances may a parent be held liable for injury resulting from his or her failure to protect the child from harm? (Liability for omissions.)

8 Most legal systems do not have specific rules and apply to these cases the general tort law rules.[24] This means, generally speaking, that parents who cause unintentional harm to their children are held liable according to the objective standard of the reasonable person. The exception can be found in Germany and, to a lesser extent, in Spain and Portugal.

9 In Germany § 1664 subs. 1 BGB, which provides a statutory basis for claims of the child against his parents for injuries inflicted by them, establishes a *privilege* and limits the parents' liability to cases of subjective fault (*diligentia quam in suis* (cf. § 277 BGB)). Thus, as long as parents do not act intentionally or recklessly, they merely have to observe the same level of care and diligence they follow in their own affairs. The justification for this privilege is the protection of the family against internal lawsuits which aim at little more than a redistribution of wealth from one family member to another.[25] A similar solution, even in the absence of a specific norm, is favoured in Austria by legal scholarship.[26]

10 In Spain there are specific rules which establish a privilege in favour of the parents with regard to the administration of the property of their minor chil-

[20] See, for instance Czech Republic no. 5; France nos. 6–7 and Spain no. 8.
[21] Czech Republic no. 5; England and Wales no. 7; France no. 7; Spain no. 8.
[22] Cf. art. 154 III CCS: "Los padres podrán en el ejercicio de su potestad recabar el auxilio de la autoridad. *Podrán también corregir razonable y moderadamente a los hijos*."
[23] So, for instance, Czech Republic no. 5; Portugal nos. 13–15; Spain nos. 9–10.
[24] Austria no. 3; Belgium no. 6; Czech Republic nos. 8–9; England and Wales nos. 8–9; France no. 8; Italy no. 12; the Netherlands nos. 8–9; Spain nos. 12–13; Sweden no. 11.
[25] Germany no. 2.
[26] Austria no. 4.

dren. By contrast to the general approach which provides that the yardstick for due care is the conduct of a reasonable person *(buen padre de familia)* (art. 1104 I CC), here the law provides that parents must administer the property of their children with the same standard of care that they use with regard to their own affairs (*diligentia quam in suis*) (art. 164 I CC). Additionally, pursuant to art. 168 II CC, with regard to the loss or detriment of the assets of children that their parents administer, they will be liable only if they acted with "intent or gross negligence".[27] Similar exceptional rules regarding the administration of the property of children also apply in Portugal, where according to art. 1897 Portuguese Civil Code (*Codigo Civil*, CC), parents must administer their children's patrimony as if they were administering their own patrimony, this is considered to be an exception deviating from the general yardstick of the *bonus pater familiae* (art. 487, 2 CC)[28].

3. In what circumstances may a third party (e.g. a school or local authority social services department) be held liable for failing to render a child positive assistance (e.g. by preventing parental abuse)?

11 Although there are no specific regulations imposing tort liability on schools or social services for the infringement of their specific duties to supervise "children in need", liability may arise under the general rules. Some countries establish statutory duties which impose some specific duties on social services to take care of children in need. Although the statutes providing for these duties do not establish compensation for the damage arising from their infringement, under certain circumstances compensation can be awarded if the neglect of these duties meets the general requirements for liability in tort.[29] Nevertheless, decisions holding social services liable for defective performance of their protective functions regarding minors against their parents are not found in the majority of countries.[30]

12 In England and Wales, by contrast, the liability of local authorities for the work of their social services departments has been a much-litigated issue in recent times. The duty of local authorities to safeguard and promote the welfare of "children in need" is established by the Children Act 1989 (cf. sec. 17). Accordingly, the authority must make inquiries about any child in its area who it has a reason to believe is suffering, or is likely to suffer, significant harm, and it must take such action as it considers necessary to safeguard or promote the child's welfare. These duties do not give rise directly to enforceable private rights, so their breach is not actionable in damages, but their negligent exercise may give rise to liability in common law negligence – provided a duty of care arises in the circumstances of the individual case.[31] After the Human Rights Act 1998 entered into force, and according to recent decisions such as

[27] Spain no. 13.
[28] Portugal no. 11.
[29] Austria nos. 8–13; Czech Republic nos. 12–17; France nos. 12–21; Germany nos. 4–5.
[30] Czech Republic no. 12; Germany nos. 4–5; Italy no. 22; Portugal nos. 21–24; Spain no. 20.
[31] England and Wales no. 11.

Z v. United Kingdom, local authorities have a positive obligation to protect children from inhuman or degrading treatment by their parents, and can be sued for compensation under the Act's own remedial mechanism.[32]

4. What limitations periods are applied to a child's claim?

13 As regards damage caused by parents to their children, most countries, such as Austria, Belgium, England and Wales, Germany, Italy, the Netherlands and, in Spain, Catalonia[33], establish that prescription is suspended and, therefore, that the time limitation does not start running until the child is no longer under parental responsibility, which regularly coincides with the child's majority.[34] This is also the case in France according to case-law.[35] In the Netherlands this suspension is even prolonged for another six months after the ending of parental responsibility (cf. art. 3:321 subs. 1 lit. b Dutch Civil Code (*Burgerlijk Wetboek*, BW)).[36]

14 Specific case examples are actions of the child against their parents for sexual abuse. This is the case, for instance, in Germany, where in the case of claims relating to violations of the so-called "right to sexual self-determination", the limitation period does not start running until the child has reached the age of twenty one (cf. § 208 cl. 1 BGB) and can be prolonged beyond this age when the victim continues to live together with the perpetrator in the same household until the victim moves out (cf. § 208 cl. 2 BGB).[37] A similar result is reached by Dutch case-law, according to which claims for abuse can be brought even after having reached majority under specific circumstances.[38]

15 In some other countries such as the Czech Republic, Russia, Spain and Sweden, there is no suspension and the general rules of prescription apply.[39]

III. Contributory Negligence

5. Are there any special provisions concerning contributory negligence if the tortfeasor is a child?

16 No country, except Austria, has specific rules on contributory negligence when the tortfeasor is a child.[40] In this country, the Austrian Civil Code, after

[32] England and Wales no. 12.
[33] Austria no. 14; Belgium no. 18; England and Wales no. 14; Germany no. 6; Italy no. 26; the Netherlands no. 11; Spain no. 27.
[34] Austria no. 14; Belgium no. 18; England and Wales no. 14; Germany nos. 6–7; Italy no. 26; the Netherlands no. 11.
[35] France no. 23.
[36] The Netherlands no. 11.
[37] Germany no. 7.
[38] The Netherlands no. 12.
[39] Czech Republic nos. 18–21; Russia no. 22; Spain no. 27; Sweden no. 11.
[40] See Czech Republic nos. 22–25; England and Wales no. 18; France no. 24; Germany no. 9; Italy nos. 32–35; the Netherlands no. 14; Portugal no. 34; Spain no. 28.

establishing the general rule on contributory negligence which calls for reduction when the victim has also contributed to causing the damage by his or her lack of self-protection (cf. § 1304 ABGB), regulates the specific case of contributory negligence when the tortfeasor is a minor whose damaging conduct has been induced by the injured party (cf. § 1308 ABGB). This provision establishes that in these cases the injured party cannot claim any compensation if he induced the damaging behaviour of the minor with fault.[41] Legal scholarship considers that this provision can also be applied, under the same circumstances, when the injured party is a child and the tortfeasor an adult, but not when both injured party and tortfeasor are minors, since in this case they are both equally worthy of protection and the application of different yardsticks would not be justified.[42]

6. What are the rules governing contributory negligence of the child? Do such principles follow the same lines as those governing the negligence issue itself (mirror-image)?

Most legal systems recognise, as a general rule, that damages are to be reduced when the victim's conduct has contributed to cause the harm. The only exception is probably Sweden where, although the same holds true concerning damage to property or pure financial losses, in the case of personal injuries there is full liability of the tortfeasor notwithstanding contributory negligence, except if the victim contributed to the harm intentionally or with gross negligence.[43] 17

In most legal systems, the so-called "mirror image" prevails, i.e. the idea that the principles applied to establishing liability also have to be applied correspondingly to contributory negligence, since contributory negligence is also related to the question of attribution or imputation of the damage. As a rule, this means not only that a line of causation between the conduct of the victim and the damage is required, but also that "fault" of the victim, understood as a lack of self-protection, must be established.[44] Therefore, children who have no tortious capacity cannot be held contributorily negligent. 18

The "mirror image" also applies in France, but it leads to a different result. To the same extent that children can be held liable in tort regardless of their age and capacity[45], according to the *Cour de Cassation*, they can also be held con- 19

[41] Austria nos. 15–19.
[42] Austria nos. 20–21.
[43] Sweden no. 2.
[44] Austria no. 22; Belgium no. 21; Czech Republic no. 28; England and Wales no. 19; France no. 25; Germany no. 10; Portugal no. 42; Russia nos. 2–4. In Italy and in the Netherlands this position has also been favoured by legal scholarship. See Italy nos. 33–34 and the Netherlands no. 17.
[45] See M. Martín-Casals, Comparative Report in: M. Martín-Casals (ed.), *Children in Tort Law, Part I: Children as Tortfeasors* (2005), no. 16.

tributorily negligent irrespective of "whether the child has been capable of discerning the consequences of his act" (cf. *Derguini* and *Lemaire* cases).[46]

20 Although in following the "mirror image" some legal systems introduce some nuances taking into account the specific characteristics of contributory negligence (such as the fact that, properly speaking, it is not fault which causes harm to others but lack of self-protection which does not minimise damage suffered by the victim). This is the case, for instance, in England and Wales, where legal scholarship points out that the test of negligence as applied to the conduct of claimants may be more "subjective" than the test of negligence applied to defendants.[47] Or in the Czech Republic, where it is emphasised that, whereas fault of tortfeasor is generally presumed by art. 420 of the Czech Civil Code (*obèanský zákoník*, OZ), this presumption is not extended to contributory negligence of the victim and, accordingly, "fault" of the victims may not be presumed.[48]

21 In other legal systems, such as those of Italy, Spain and the Netherlands, contributory negligence is not the "mirror image" of fault and children who have no tortious capacity and, therefore, cannot be held liable as tortfeasors, may, in spite of this fact, be held contributorily negligent if they have contributed to causing the harm.[49] In the Netherlands the harshness of the consequences of this rule is mitigated in the stage of so-called "equitable adjustment", which is regularly carried out when establishing contributory negligence. When establishing contributory negligence, the Dutch Civil Code takes an approach based on three stages: (1) imputable occurrence; (2) primary apportionment and (3) equitable adjustment (cf. art. 6:101 BW)[50] and with regard to children this approach means that: (1) first, it must be ascertained whether the victim has acted negligently that is, from an objective perspective and, therefore, without regard to his or her age. If this is the case, (2) then a causal apportionment should be applied. And, finally (3) this causal apportionment is fully equitably adjusted, having regard to the young age of the victim.[51]

[46] France nos. 31–32.
[47] England and Wales no. 19.
[48] Czech Republic nos. 28–29.
[49] France nos. 26–28; Italy nos. 33–34; Spain nos. 35–40; the Netherlands nos. 16–17.
[50] Art. 6:101 BW: "When the damage is partly caused by an occurrence that can be imputed to the injured party, the obligation to pay compensation is reduced by apportioning the damage between the injured party and the liable party in proportion to the degree in which the occurrences that can be imputed to the parties have contributed to the damage, provided that account is taken of the disparity in the seriousness of the respective faults, or other circumstances of the case to decide whether equity demands that an alternative apportionment or full recovery takes place or that the obligation to pay lapses" (translation by W. van Boom, the Netherlands nos. 15–16).
[51] The Netherlands nos. 18–22.

7. Does the fixed minimum age for children to be liable, if any exists, also apply to the contributory negligence of the child?

In most countries there is no minimum age,[52] but in Germany and Russia, where a minimum age for children to be liable exists, this minimum also applies to contributory negligence.[53] Thus, for instance in Germany, children under the age of seven cannot be held liable for contributory negligence, according to § 828 subs. 1 BGB (*mirror-image theory).* This minimum age is raised to ten years if the damage was sustained in an accident involving a motor vehicle, a railway, or a cable car (§ 828 subs. 2 BGB).[54] 22

In other countries, such as the Netherlands, where a minimum age exists but the mirror image theory is not applied, the minimum age is not reflected in contributory negligence and accordingly, children under the age of 14 can be held contributorily negligent. However, the age of the child can be taken into account at the stage of "equitable adjustment" which is carried out when establishing contributory negligence.[55] In Portugal, the minimum age existing for holding minors liable does not apply to contributory negligence and the prevailing legal scholarship requires imputability for considering a child contributorily negligent.[56] 23

Finally, in other countries such as Austria, the minimum age acts as a presumption only, i.e. children under 14 are rebuttably presumed not to have sufficient capacity of discernment and, therefore, they cannot be held liable unless it is proven that they have this capacity. According to the "mirror image" theory, the same rule applies to contributory negligence and for this reason, for children under 14 to be held contributorily negligent, the presumption of lack of discernment must be rebutted.[57] 24

8. What is the standard of care governing the behaviour of children in the context of contributory negligence? Is such standard determined by the same principles and criteria which are relevant to the duty of care incumbent upon the child in the context of him or her being held liable?

Since victims do not have the legal duty to protect themselves, it is generally acknowledged that in the case of contributory negligence the "fault" of the victim does not have the same meaning as the fault of the tortfeasor. However, following the mirror image idea, most legal systems apply the same standard.[58] In this sense, in Austria for instance, the same subjective standard ap- 25

[52] Czech Republic no. 30; England and Wales no. 20; France nos. 31–32; Italy no. 36; Spain no. 42.
[53] Germany no. 11; Russia no. 3.
[54] Germany no. 11.
[55] The Netherlands nos. 18–22.
[56] Portugal nos. 44–46.
[57] Austria nos. 24–25.
[58] Austria nos. 26–27; Czech Republic no. 32; England and Wales no. 21; France nos. 33–34; Germany nos. 12–13; Italy no. 37; the Netherlands no. 23; Spain no. 43.

plicable to fault applies to contributory negligence.[59] Other countries, such as Belgium, the Czech Republic, England and Wales, Germany, Italy, the Netherlands, Portugal, Russia and Spain,[60] which follow an objective standard for fault, apply this same standard to contributory negligence.

26 However, the foregoing assertion is clarified for some countries by adding that, in spite of the mirror image of fault, the legal system is more prone to taking subjective factors into account in the case of contributory negligence. In this sense it is affirmed in England and Wales that, although the test of a child's contributory negligence is formally the "mirror-image" of its negligence to others, there is a suspicion that in practice the test is made more "subjective" in the former case and is hence more lenient to the child".[61] A similar result can be reached in the Netherlands in the so-called "equitable adjustment" stage when establishing the contributory negligence of children,[62] or in Germany when considering the "circumstances of the case" according to § 254 subs. 1 BGB.[63] In Sweden, when contributory negligence is accepted – i.e. in all sorts of damage except personal injury – there is also a considerable tolerance towards children who behave in a thoughtless way, especially if they are small children.[64] In Portugal too some legal scholars consider that in the case of minors the abstract standard of care must be subjected to some flexibility.[65]

IV. Contribution in Equity

9. Is there a parallel (mirror-image) to liability in equity in the field of contributory negligence? If so, do the criteria determining liability in equity of the child also apply to the issue of holding him or her accountable for his or her contributory negligence?

27 According to the "mirror image principle", in Austria, Belgium, Germany and Russia, the rules concerning liability in equity are applied by analogy in the case of contributory negligence.[66] In Austria, when the child is the tortfeasor, the terms of liability in equity also apply when he or she is at fault in order to reduce the award for damages. Accordingly, when children are contributorily negligent the "mirror image" application might lead – if the other conditions for liability in equity are met – to a lesser reduction[67]. In Belgium, rules on liability in equity provided in art. 1386 *bis* Belgian Civil Code (*Code civil*, CC)

[59] Austria no. 27.

[60] Belgium no. 24; Czech Republic no. 32; England and Wales no. 21; Germany no. 12; Italy no. 37; the Netherlands no. 23; Portugal no. 48; Russia no. 5; Spain no. 43.

[61] England and Wales no. 21.

[62] The Netherlands no. 23.

[63] Germany no. 13.

[64] Sweden no. 3.

[65] Portugal no. 49.

[66] Austria no. 28; Belgium no. 25; Germany nos. 14–15; Russia no. 6.

[67] S. Hirsch, Austria in: M. Martín-Casals (supra fn. 45), no. 31.

regarding persons suffering mental disturbances are considered to be applicable in the case of victims who are insane and have been contributorily negligent.[68] In Germany the analogical application of liability in equity (cf. § 829 BGB) to cases of contributory negligence pursuant to § 254 subs. 1 BGB can take place not only when children do not have the intellectual maturity to understand their burden or onus of self-protection, but also when they do have this maturity. This is the case when a child has behaved as any ordinary child of the same age – and, therefore, has not failed to meet the burden of self-protection – but has failed to meet the adult standard. Accordingly, the mirror image application of liability in equity to cases of contributory negligence may lead to a reduction when, had the child been an adult, he or she would have been contributorily negligent.[69] In both Austria and Germany, however, this analogical application to cases of contributory negligence of children can only take place when the same strict requirements established by the law for liability in equity are met (cf. § 1310 ABGB and § 829 BGB).[70] In Russia the provision that establishes that, with the exception of cases of intentional infliction of harm, the court may diminish compensation under consideration of the wealth of the tortfeasor (cf. art. 1083 Russian Civil Code) may also be applied by analogy in cases of contributory negligence of the victim when the victim is a child older than fourteen years of age.[71]

In Italy, by contrast, there is no need for the rules of equity to be applied to contributory negligence since case-law does not follow the mirror image rule here and, regardless of their maturity, considers that children are contributorily negligent as long as there is a causal link between the child's negligence and the aggravation of the damage sustained by him or her.[72] In Portugal, although the issue is discussed by legal scholarship, the prevailing legal opinion seems to reject the application of equity in the field of contributory negligence[73]. 28

Finally, in Sweden it is considered that the rules of liability for fault are, in general, so favourable to the victim that there is no need for a mirror image application of these rules to contributory negligence of children.[74] 29

10. If answered affirmatively: Is the fact that the child is privately or socially insured against the accident a factor to be considered? Is the existence of liability insurance of the tortfeasor to be taken into account? What factors have a bearing on the assessment of equitable contribution?

The existence of accident insurance covering the damage suffered by the victim is considered as a relevant factor in most countries that recognise some 30

[68] Belgium no. 25.
[69] Germany nos. 14–15.
[70] Austria nos. 28–31; Germany no. 15.
[71] See Russia no. 6.
[72] Italy no. 34.
[73] Portugal nos. 52–53 and 55.
[74] Sweden no. 4.

sort of contribution of equity, such as Austria, Belgium, Germany and Sweden, because this is one of the factors that have to be taken into account when establishing the financial conditions of the victim.[75] In Sweden, however, the question may arise in cases of damage to property only, since in the case of personal injury the law does not permit any reduction in the compensation award, unless the victim has intentionally not met his or her burden of self-protection or has been grossly negligent in doing so.[76]

31 Most countries apply *mutatis mutandi* the other factors that are relevant for establishing liability in equity when children are in the position of tortfeasors (such as the financial conditions of the parties, the existence of liability insurance, the degree of fault of the child – or in Austria, in the absence of fault, even the degree of wrongfulness –, etc.) to cases of contributory negligence when children take the position of victims.[77] However, in none of the countries under survey do there appear to have been any judgments which can illustrate the application of the rules of liability in equity to these cases.

V. Miscellaneous

11. What are the rules for a situation in which the child is guilty of contributory negligence but the parents have also breached their duty to supervise? Is the child held accountable in any way for his or her parents' breach of the duty to supervise so that his or her claim for damages is reduced?

32 It seems clear that when the child has been contributorily negligent and, at the same time, his or her parents have also breached their duty to supervise, the defendant may seek both a reduction in his liability for the contributory negligence of the child and contribution from the negligent parents as co-tortfeasors.[78]

33 A different question is whether children are "identified" with the negligence of the persons who have the duty to supervise them in order to evaluate their contributory negligence, so that the breach of this duty leads to a reduction in the award of damages the child will receive. The vast majority of legal systems under survey stand for no identification and, accordingly, no reduction in the compensation award takes place in these cases.[79] In most cases, the parents breaching their duty to supervise will be considered solidarily liable together with the defendant[80] and the defendant will not be permitted to raise the breach of this duty as a defence of contributory negligence against the child.[81] This rule has, however, some exceptions. In Austria and Germany the rule of

[75] See M. Martín-Casals, *Comparative Report*, in: M. Martín-Casals (supra fn. 45), nos. 33–37.
[76] Sweden nos. 2 and 4.
[77] See Austria nos. 30–31; Belgium nos. 27–29.
[78] See in this sense, for instance, England and Wales no. 23.
[79] Austria no. 32; Belgium no. 30; Czech Republic no. 37; England and Wales no. 23; France nos. 40–43; Germany nos. 18–19; Italy no. 40; the Netherlands no. 26.
[80] See, for instance, Czech Republic no. 37 or the Netherlands no. 26.
[81] See, in this sense, for instance Italy no. 40.

no identification ceases when there is a contractual relationship between the child and the tortfeasor and the parents act as the child's auxiliaries.[82] A further exception may be found in Germany where the victim's conduct has merged with the parents' violation of their duty to supervise (for instance, when the parents' fault allowed for the self-damaging conduct of the child), so that both conducts can be considered as the same source of harm.[83]

In the countries under survey, identification as a general rule exists only in Portugal, Spain and Sweden. In Portugal, identification is expressly provided by art. 571 CC, according to which "the negligent act of the legal representatives of the victim and of persons the victim uses are put on the same level as the negligent conduct of the victim" (*"ao facto culposo do lesado é equiparado o facto culposo dos seus representantes legais e das pessoas de quem ele se tenha utilizado"),* but legal scholarship criticises its consequences.[84] In Spain, although the prevailing legal scholarship rejects identification, the fact is that when parents claim for damages on behalf of their children the courts regularly reduce the awards on account of their lack of care in supervising them.[85] Finally, in Sweden neglect of the parental duty of supervision has no influence in the case of personal injuries – since in this case contributory negligence does not apply – but in the case of damage to property the child is identified with his or her parents and damages may be reduced as a consequence of the negligence of the parents.[86] 34

12. Do the rules of contributory negligence also apply in the area of strict liability?

In all the countries under survey the rules of contributory negligence also apply in the area of strict liability. All reports point out that in cases of strict liability damages may also be reduced or excluded if contributory negligence of the victim is established.[87] 35

A different but related question is whether the rules of contributory negligence, irrespective of whether liability of the tortfeasor is for fault or strict, also apply when what contributes to the harm on the side of the victim is not his or her lack of self-protection but a source of danger (such as an animal or a thing) which is under his or her control ("operational risk"). That they also apply in this case is clear in Austria, where this application results either from provisions of specific strict liability statutes or by analogical application of the general provision on contributory negligence (§ 1304 ABGB). Although in 36

[82] Cf. Austria nos. 32–35 and Germany no. 18.
[83] Germany no.19.
[84] Portugal no. 57.
[85] Spain nos. 46–51.
[86] Sweden no. 5.
[87] Austria no. 36; Belgium no. 33; Czech Republic no. 38; England and Wales no. 24; France nos. 44–49; Germany no. 21; Italy no. 41; the Netherlands no. 27; Portugal nos. 60–62; Russia no. 8; Spain no. 52; Sweden no. 6.

these cases the apportionment of damages presents some difficulties because the factors that have to be compared (i.e. fault and risk) are not really commensurable, the prevailing legal opinion tends to equate operational risk with slight negligence.[88] In the Netherlands the victims also bear the operational risks in these cases and it is considered that the rules of contributory negligence may also apply when, for instance, the damage is not exclusively caused by the tortfeasor but also by an act of an animal or the defect of an object in the possession of an injured child who is 14 years of age or older. Since there children under 14 years of age cannot be held contributorily negligent, contribution might be shifted to his or her parents in the form of strict liability.[89] Thus, it is pointed out that in the case, for instance, of a ten-year-old child who while walking his dog is injured in a fight between his dog and someone else's, the child cannot be held contributorily negligent and can claim damages in full from the owner of the other dog; in turn, this owner may claim against the parents of the child for contribution.[90]

13. Do the rules of contributory negligence apply in the area of strict liability for traffic-accidents or other areas of tort liability?

37 In all countries, contributory negligence rules apply in the area of strict liability for traffic accidents or other areas of tort liability. In England liability for traffic accidents is based on fault, but contributory negligence may be a defence in the other areas where strict liability exists. The application of the rules of contributory negligence to cases where children are victims of traffic accidents is aggravated in Spain by the fact that the Spanish Road Traffic Act provides for reduction for contributory negligence both when children have tortious capacity and when they do not have it.[91] In practice, this can lead to a reduction in damages even when victims of a very tender age suffer serious personal injuries.

38 In some countries, however, statutes or case-law provide specific rules for the protection of children. Thus, in Belgium for instance, art. 29*bis* cl. 6 of the Act of 21 November 1989 (W.A.M. Act) aiming to protect vulnerable victims of traffic accidents, provides that compensation can only be refused if the victim wanted both the accident and its consequences to happen. However, regarding children, this only applies to minors older than 14, whereas in the case of victims younger than 14 contributory negligence is always excluded and they will obtain full compensation.[92] Also with the aim of protecting children, the case-law developed by the Dutch Supreme Court since the 90's completely excludes contributory negligence when children up to 14 years of age are involved in traffic accidents as bicyclists or pedestrians, even if they have heavily contributed, in a casual sense, to the occurrence of the accident. This rule,

[88] Austria nos. 36–37.
[89] The Netherlands no. 27.
[90] The Netherlands no. 28.
[91] Spain no. 54.
[92] Belgium nos. 22 and 34.

however, does not apply if they have contributed to the harm intentionally or recklessly.[93]

In Germany the minimum age for a child to be held liable and – according to the mirror application of these rules to contributory negligence – to be held contributorily negligent is 7 years. However, this minimum age is raised to 10 years if the damage was sustained in an accident involving a motor vehicle, a track railway, or a cable railway (§ 828 subs. 2 cl. 1 BGB). Accordingly, the reduction in damages for contributory negligence is ruled out, as a matter of law, if the child has not reached the age of 10, unless the child intentionally contributed to his damage (cf. § 828 subs. 2 cl. 2 BGB). This general rule, however, may have exceptions as, for instance, when the child harmed himself by having an accident with a car parked in a lawful manner, since in these cases the car cannot be considered a source of danger. When the child is over the age of 10, no reduction will take place if his conduct merely reflects his inability to behave as a prudent adult. Contributory negligence will only apply if his conduct fails to meet the standard of conduct of children of the same age.[94] 39

France probably enjoys the most famous regulation for the protection of certain classes of victims, including children.[95] The Act of 5 July 1985, commonly known as *"Loi Badinter"*, provides that if a non-driving victim is a child under 16 years of age (or a person over 70 years or, whatever his or her age, with at least 80% permanent disability), the rules of contributory negligence do not apply and, consequently, the victim may obtain full compensation for personal injuries regardless of the weight of his or her contribution to the accident.[96] When the age of the victim is between 16 and 70 years (or when his or her permanent disability is less than 80%), contributory negligence of the victim will be taken into account only if his or her "fault" is "inexcusable" (i.e. according to case-law "voluntary fault of exceptional seriousness, exposing, without valid reason, the person causing it to a danger of which he should be aware") and "the exclusive cause of the accident".[97] Since both requirements are hardly ever met, courts tend to award full compensation in most cases.[98] However, these favourable rules for the victims do not apply either to damage to property suffered by the victim or when the victim was driving the vehicle involved in the accident.[99] 40

[93] The Netherlands nos. 20 and 29.
[94] Germany nos. 22–24.
[95] France nos. 50 et seq.
[96] France no. 55.
[97] France no. 54.
[98] France no. 53.
[99] France nos. 58–60.

14. Are adults held to a higher standard of care in their interactions with children, or when children are or may be around?

41 In all countries, adults may be held to a higher standard of care – or, more accurately, more care may be demanded of them, though the standard remains that of the reasonable person – when children are or may be around.[100]

42 In some countries such as Austria, Germany, England and Wales and Russia, there are even specific provisions that refer to this circumstance. Thus, in Austria § 3 Austrian Road Traffic Act (*Straßenverkehrsordnung*, StVO) considers that every user of the road may rely on other persons observing the provisions regarding the use of the road, unless he has to presume that the person is a child.[101] Similarly, in Germany this principle of confidence in the conduct of the others (*Vertrauensgrundsatz*) finds its exception when children are around; thus, pursuant to § 3 subs. 2 German Road Traffic Act (*Straßenverkehrsordnung*, StVO), drivers have to be particularly careful in the vicinity of children since minors are less able to control their conduct and to behave prudently.[102] In England and Wales sec. 2 subs. 3 lit. a Occupiers' Liability Act 1957 provides that an occupier, in discharging his duty under the Act, must be prepared for the fact that children are likely to be less careful than adults.[103] In Russia similar provisions can be found in the area of transport regulations, childcare regulations and other regulations.[104]

43 In other countries, such as Belgium, France, Italy, Portugal and Spain, the need to be more careful when children are around seems to be derived from the "circumstances of the case", which is one of the factors used to adapt the objective standard of care to the characteristics of the particular situation. Thus, in Belgium, the behaviour of an adult must be tested against the abstract standard of a *bonus pater familias* in the same circumstances. According to this, the interaction of children in the neighbourhood is to be considered as one of the circumstances that the judge can take into account in order to assess whether an adult has or has not behaved according to the required standard of care.[105] In France, the conduct of the tortfeasor is assessed *in abstracto,* i.e. with reference generally to the conduct expected from a *bon père de famille*. When establishing his liability, however, the circumstances external to the tortfeasor must also be taken into account, and the conduct that could be expected from a "reasonable man" in similar circumstances is considered. Although one of these circumstances may be the fact that there are children around, courts rarely state expressly that adults are subject to a special duty of

[100] Austria no. 40; Belgium no. 35; Czech Republic no. 46; England and Wales no. 26; France no. 61; Germany no. 25; Italy no. 43; the Netherlands no. 30; Portugal no. 69; Russia no. 9; Spain no. 55; Sweden no. 7.

[101] Austria no. 39.

[102] Germany no. 25.

[103] England and Wales no. 26.

[104] Russia no. 9.

[105] Belgium no. 36.

care in their interactions with children.[106] In Italian law, a general principle imposes a higher degree of care on adults in relation to children when children are involved in their activities. Indeed, the degree of care must be established in the light of the prevailing circumstances, as for instance, when an adult drives a car near school premises where there are children playing, in which case the courts mention that such circumstances require particular care.[107] Finally, in Portugal the "circumstances of the case" pursuant to art. 487, 2 CC,[108] or in Spain "the circumstances of the persons, time and place" (cf. art. 1104 I CC)[109] are also the factors usually referred to by courts when requiring a higher degree of care from adults interacting with children.

VI. Insurance Matters

15. Are pupils covered by private or public accident (first-party) insurance?

In some countries such as Austria, the Czech Republic, Germany, Portugal and Spain, schools have the duty to take accident or first party insurance to cover the accidents their pupils may suffer.[110] In Austria, however, insurance is compulsory in public schools only; although there are no specific legal provisions as regards private schools, private school principals, teachers or parents' associations tend take out voluntary group accident insurance for the pupils.[111] In the Czech Republic, Germany, Portugal and Spain both public and private school pupils are covered by a special Social Security scheme which is compulsory.[112] Moreover, the pupils may also be covered by optional private insurance, which may be bought independently, included in the family accident insurance (as is the case in the Czech Republic)[113] or contracted as voluntary group insurance (which happens in Spain).[114] 44

In other countries such as Belgium, England and Wales, France, Italy, the Netherlands, Russia and Sweden, schools have no legal duty to provide accident insurance for their pupils.[115] However, in all these countries, in some way or other, children may be protected by voluntary accident insurance. In England, for instance, although accident insurance is normally regarded as a matter for the parents, not for the schools, there have been various initiatives to encourage schools to take out accident insurance for their pupils.[116] In Russia many schools, either public or private, also ask parents to take out insur- 45

[106] France no. 61.
[107] Italy nos. 43–51.
[108] Portugal no. 69.
[109] Spain nos. 55–56.
[110] Austria nos. 41–44; Czech Republic nos. 47–48; Germany no. 26; Portugal nos. 79–80; Spain nos. 57–63.
[111] Austria nos. 41–43.
[112] Czech Republic nos. 47–48; Germany no. 26; Portugal nos. 76–80; Spain nos. 57–60.
[113] Czech Republic nos. 49–50.
[114] Spain nos. 62–63.
[115] Belgium no. 37; England and Wales no. 26; France nos. 64–65; Italy no. 52; the Netherlands no. 31; Russia no. 10; Sweden no. 8.
[116] England and Wales no. 27.

ance.[117] Voluntary insurance, either individual or collective, is also taken out by parents, schools or municipalities in Belgium, France, Italy, the Netherlands and Sweden.[118]

16. Does this insurance cover any damage incurred on the way to school and back?

46 With the exception of the Czech Republic, in all countries where accident insurance is compulsory the insurance also covers accidents that occur on the way to school and back.[119] In Germany the provisions establishing public accident insurance coverage expressly include the harm suffered on the way from school to an official event and are also interpreted broadly in order to include harm suffered during detours if they are motivated by infantile curiosity or playfulness.[120] In Austria and in Spain the corresponding provisions are also subject to a broad interpretation by the courts in order to cover all the activities that children carry out in their condition as pupils.[121] In Portugal, there is a provision establishing coverage of "*seguro escolar*" for accidents occurring on the normal way from home to school and back, and in a period immediately before or after classes. Nevertheless, it only covers *minors* that are not being accompanied by an adult who, by law, is obliged to supervise the child.[122] In the Czech Republic, by contrast, accidents occurring during the journey from the place of residence to the entrance of the school and back are not covered by the compulsory accident scheme.[123]

47 In the countries where no legal duty to insure exists, such as Belgium, France, Italy and Sweden, coverage will obviously depend on the conditions established in the voluntary insurance policy, but usually policies will cover these accidents.[124]

17. Are there restrictions on damages recoverable by the child, e.g. with respect to loss of future earnings?

48 In most countries, recovery of damages does not undergo general restrictions when the victims are children. Loss of future earnings is compensated for in most countries, but here the situation is rather disparate.

49 Among those countries where accident insurance is compulsory, future earnings are compensated for in Austria and Germany according to the general

[117] Russia no. 10.
[118] Belgium no. 37; France no. 64–65; Italy no. 55; the Netherlands no. 31; Sweden no. 8.
[119] Austria no. 41; Czech Republic nos. 51–53; Germany no. 27; Portugal nos. 90–92; Spain nos. 68–69.
[120] Germany no. 27.
[121] Austria no. 41; Spain nos. 68–69.
[122] Portugal no. 91.
[123] Czech Republic nos. 51–53.
[124] Belgium no. 38; France no. 67; Italy nos. 56–58; Sweden no. 8.

rules and without any specific limitations. In Austria case-law compensates for future earnings according to the circumstances of each case.[125] In Germany the Civil Code provides specifically for compensation for the loss of professional advancement and occupational prospects (cf. § 842 BGB), a head of damages which is different from the impairment of the ability to work and which must be claimed for expressly and separately.[126] In Spain by contrast, whereas the law compensates for loss of future earnings according to the circumstances of the case, the compulsory insurance scheme provides ridiculously low awards.[127]

In those countries where accident insurance is not compulsory, future earnings are also compensated for in one form or other (as, for instance, in Belgium and France, according to the loss of chance doctrine).[128] However, whether compensation for loss of future earnings will be included in insurance policies will obviously depend on the terms of the particular policies.[129] 50

VII. Damage Issues

18. If damages for loss of earnings are available, what are the principles governing their assessment?

In most countries the assessment of damages for loss of earnings is governed by the general principles and by the idea that the harm has to be compensated for according to probability of the usual course of events.[130] The main differences are to be found in the method the various legal systems use to assess this course of events and in the depth of detail that they go into. 51

Thus in Germany, for instance, if the child's professional development is foreseeable, the loss of earnings has to be estimated on the basis of an ordinary advancement in the career that the child would have chosen; if he had to abandon his education due to the accident, the court will examine his prospects of success, according to his talents and, if these are not apparent, according to his family background. The amounts thus established, however, are usually discounted according to the existing grade of uncertainty.[131] In England and Wales the loss of earnings is normally assessed by reference to average national earnings, though evidence that the child could have been expected to have higher or lower earnings than average may be taken into account. The calcula- 52

[125] Austria no. 45.
[126] Germany no. 28.
[127] Spain nos. 70–75.
[128] Belgium no. 39; France nos. 70–71; Italy no. 59; Sweden no. 9.
[129] So, in England and Wales no. 28, it is unlikely that insurance policies cover children for earnings that they have never made, while policies taken out by adults may cover loss of future earnings.
[130] Austria nos. 46–49; Belgium no. 40; England and Wales no. 30; Germany nos. 30–31; Italy nos. 60–61; the Netherlands nos. 34–35; Portugal nos. 99 et seq.; Russia no. 15; Spain nos. 76–77.
[131] Germany nos. 30–31.

tion is carried out by reference to the expected annual loss, multiplied by a figure which takes as its starting point the number of years for which the loss is expected to continue. This sum is discounted for the vicissitudes of life and the fact that there is accelerated payment and, since these factors have great weight when the claimant is a child, the discount is much greater than would be expected in the case of an adult.[132] In Portugal, legal scholarship and case-law have pointed out some objective factors in order to assess loss of earnings of children. Thus, for instance, when students have lost some sort of financial support, as in the case of scholarship, this would be taken into account. If there is a proved professional option, the courts can take into consideration how difficult it is to get a job in that profession and what is the corresponding average income. The intelligence of the victim and his or her persistence in studies, as well as success at school, are factors from which one can infer a predictable successful career. Finally, it is considered that the average national income, combined with the previous factors when they exist or considered on its own, seems to be the fairest solution.[133] In Spain, by contrast, it is not usual to take into account either the activity that the child might have carried out in the future or how the permanent disability may affect him in this respect or what compensation he should receive for the loss of the time devoted to his studies while recovering from injuries. All these items seem to be too speculative and in practice the courts assess a lump sum *ex bono et aequo* without using clear methods of prediction or calculation.[134]

53 In Belgium and France the question of loss of earnings is treated according to the doctrine of loss of a chance. The opportunity lost, however, cannot be too speculative, since courts require that the losses caused to the victim by the lost opportunity are "direct", "real" and "certain".[135] Accordingly, these requirements can be easily met when the person who suffers the accident is a student who is already advanced in his career but not when the victim is a child of tender age.

54 Whereas in some countries such as Austria, Germany and the Czech Republic the payment of loss of earnings is in the form of an annuity[136] in other countries, such as Spain, it is usually a lump sum.[137] In the Netherlands the courts may award damages either as a lump sum or as a periodic allowance; in practice, however, the parties generally prefer the payment of a lump sum, partially on taxation grounds.[138]

[132] England and Wales no. 30.
[133] Portugal nos. 105–111.
[134] Spain nos. 78–79.
[135] See Belgium no. 40; France no. 72.
[136] Austria no. 49; Czech Republic no. 60; Germany no. 31.
[137] Spain no. 76.
[138] The Netherlands no. 35.

19. Which of the child's non-material interests are protected in your jurisdiction? May the child, for example, sue for impairment of intellectual or social development, the onset of behavioural problems, or reduced employment prospects?

In general terms, all legal systems protect the same non-material interests of victims regardless of whether they are adults or children. In some countries such as Austria, Germany, England and Wales, Italy, the Netherlands and Russia[139] non-pecuniary losses are compensated for if they are consequential upon personal injury or the result of the infringement of certain protected interests (such as freedom, honour, one's name, one's image or sexual self-determination). German law admits compensation under § 253 BGB for non-pecuniary losses such as pain and suffering and loss of amenities of life where a child has sustained personal injury and suffered a permanent disability. As far as loss of amenities is concerned, it is even thought, in Germany, that the amount awarded should be increased for the simple reason that a person injured at a minor age will have a long time to live with the handicap.[140] However, in Austria it is required that compensation be either statutorily provided for or that the tort was committed with intent or gross negligence.[141] In Italy, beyond the cases of impairment to health, non-pecuniary losses are recoverable only if they are statutorily established, i.e., generally speaking, if a crime has been committed.[142] By contrast, other countries such as Belgium, France, Portugal and Spain, have general principles allowing recovery of non-pecuniary losses.[143] 55

However, this division between countries that are more reluctant to compensate for non-pecuniary losses and those which are more prone to do so is not reflected in their positions with regard to compensation for certain harms such as the impairment of intellectual or social development, the onset of behavioural problems, or reduced employment prospects. Thus, for instance in France and in Spain, although other non-pecuniary harms can be compensated, neither legal scholarship nor courts consider the possibility of compensating for these abovementioned types of damage as such.[144] In Belgium, although decisions compensating this type of damage do not exist, legal scholarship does not exclude the possibility of bringing claims for educational negligence.[145] Decisions compensating for these sorts of damage are not found in Austria, the Czech Republic, Germany or the Netherlands either.[146] In the Netherlands, at least in theory, the impairment of development may result in a claim for material damages, e.g. the loss of future earning capacities or the loss of future job opportunities, as well as 56

[139] Austria nos. 50–51; Germany no. 32; England and Wales no. 31; Italy no. 66; the Netherlands no. 36; Russia no. 16.
[140] Germany, question 19.
[141] Austria no. 51.
[142] Italy nos. 13–21.
[143] Belgium nos. 41–42; France nos. 74–76; Portugal nos. 114 et seq.; Spain no. 80.
[144] France nos. 74–76; Spain no. 80.
[145] Belgium no. 42.
[146] Austria no. 52; Germany, question 19; Czech Republic no. 64; the Netherlands no. 36.

for the non-pecuniary consequences (for example loss of enjoyment and prospects). In most cases, however, the damage will be too hypothetical to be valued, and this is probably true for other countries also.[147] By contrast, in Portugal the impairment of intellectual or social development and the onset of behavioural problems are taken into account in the head of damage *"prejudizio de afirmaçao pessoal"*. This head of damage encompasses the negative effect of damage in social life and also the disturbance in one's self-confidence, in particular the feeling of inferiority usually associated with handicaps.[148]

57 Among all countries under survey, England and Wales seems to be the only legal system where, in several cases, claimants have actually alleged that their school negligently failed to address their special educational needs (e.g. relating to dyslexia), or over-zealously addressed their special educational needs, with the consequent impairment of their intellectual and social development. However, it is considered now that such loss is best regarded as purely economic, and not as a personal injury, with damages to be awarded for the diminution of the claimant's employment prospects, and liability premised upon the school's assumption of responsibility for the child's development.[149]

20. Are there special rules for the assessment of damages sustained by a child, e.g. with respect to pain and suffering?

58 In all countries under survey there are no special rules for the assessment of damages when the victims are children and the same rules applicable to adults apply to children.[150]

21. Does a small child have a claim for damages for pain and suffering, if he or she is deprived of his or her parents by a tortious act? If so, may the claim be denied on the ground that the child does not feel the loss?

59 Some legal systems recognise as a general rule that close relatives of a victim are entitled to damages for pain and suffering arising from his or her death.

60 This is the case in France, Portugal, Russia, Spain and Sweden.[151] In Portugal, the Civil Code expressly provides that descendents can claim compensation for pain and suffering when deprived of their parents, or even grandparents if parents are no longer alive (art. 496.2 CC)[152].

[147] The Netherlands no. 36. In Austria however – and this is probably also true for most countries – compensation for reduced employment prospects may be awarded if it results from disfigurement.

[148] Portugal no. 114.

[149] England and Wales no. 31.

[150] Austria nos. 56–58; Belgium no. 43; Czech Republic nos. 70–71; England and Wales no. 32; France no. 77; Germany nos. 32–33; Italy no. 72; the Netherlands no. 37; Portugal no. 119; Russia no. 16; Spain no. 81; Sweden no. 9.

[151] France no. 80; Portugal no. 122; Russia no. 17; Spain no. 82; Sweden no. 9; in Italy the situation is under debate (Italy no. 75).

[152] Portugal no. 122.

The same is true for the Czech Republic, but in this case the award is limited to the sum of approx. € 8,000 when the fatal injury was caused to the parent of the child.[153] This fixed sum is similar to bereavement damages existing in England and Wales, but here it must be stressed that the Fatal Accidents Act 1976 does not provide for the award of bereavement damages where a child loses his parents, though it does, under certain conditions, if the positions are reversed and the parents lose their child.[154] In Belgium, in case of fatal injury caused to the parent of the child, the award is fixed – according to the so-called "*Indicatieve tabellen*" – at the amount of € 7,500 when the child was living together with his or her parent or € 3,750 when the child was not living with him or her any longer. However, this kind of damage is not always awarded. Furthermore, the amounts of € 7,500 and € 3,750 can be increased or decreased on the basis of concrete circumstances.[155] 61

In other countries such as Austria, and as already referred to, in England and Wales, Germany and the Netherlands, as a rule children cannot claim for damages for pain and suffering in these cases, although in Austria a recent decision does not appear to follow this trend and awards damages in cases where the harm has been caused with intent or gross negligence.[156] In Austria, Germany and England and Wales, however, an exception is made when the harm suffered by the relative is a bodily injury consisting in damage to his or her own health caused by the shock of watching the death of a parent or upon learning of it (the so-called "nervous shock" or "*Schockschaden*"). Compensation for nervous shock must meet the strict requirements established by case-law and is not granted lightly.[157] Damages for nervous shock can be also awarded in the Czech Republic.[158] 62

Regarding the possibility of denying compensation to a child when he or she is too young to feel the loss, it is obvious that in those countries where compensation for pain and suffering resulting from the fatal accident of a parent is not generally admitted, the question may arise in the above-mentioned exceptional cases only. In Austria, although there are no decisions on these cases, legal scholarship favours compensation.[159] In Germany, what seems to be relevant in order to obtain compensation is that the minor has suffered an injury to his or her health, not the fact of whether the loss is felt.[160] 63

Among those countries where compensation is generally admitted, the positions vary. Thus, whereas in Belgium, Portugal, Russia and Spain there is no discussion on whether compensation must be treated differently when chil- 64

[153] Czech Republic no. 75.
[154] England and Wales no. 33.
[155] Belgium nos. 44–45.
[156] Austria nos. 59–60; England and Wales no. 33; Germany nos. 34–35; the Netherlands no. 38.
[157] Austria no. 59; Germany no. 35; England and Wales no. 33.
[158] Czech Republic no. 73.
[159] Austria no. 60.
[160] Germany nos. 35–36.

dren do not feel the loss,[161] in Sweden it is considered very probable that compensation will be denied when children are of tender age.[162]

65 Finally, in Italy the claim for damages by small children against persons causing the death of their parents has provoked wide debate. However case-law is very disparate on this and thus, while some courts award compensation on the grounds that the right of the child to receive a balanced upbringing by both parents is violated when one parent has been killed, others refuse compensation in these cases.[163]

22. With respect to a damage claim for the costs of medical treatment: May the tortfeasor defend himself by pointing to the fact that the parents have a duty to maintain the child?

66 In none of the countries under survey may the tortfeasor raise the defence that the costs of medical treatment are not recoverable because parents have a duty to maintain the child.[164] In Austria and Germany it is considered that the purpose of the parent's obligation is to benefit the child, not to release the tortfeasor from liability.[165] In Germany the general principle establishing that the tortfeasor is not to be released from his obligation to compensate the victim at the expense of those who have to pay maintenance is expressly stated in the Civil Code (cf. § 843 subs. 4 BGB)[166] and in the Netherlands this principle has been expressly stated by case-law[167].

23. In case of wrongful life: Does the child have a damage claim against the physician or a health care institution?

67 As is well known, the term "wrongful life" refers to cases where a child brings a claim for damages for being born with a serious mental or physical impairment which existed prior to birth and which, in contrast to prenatal injuries, was not caused by medical malpractice. One of the particular features of this case is that this impairment could not have been cured even if it had been detected and the only way to prevent the child from suffering it would have been a termination of pregnancy. The negligence of the physician consists in not informing the mother in due time about the existence of this impairment in order to allow her to decide whether to carry out a legal termination of pregnancy or not. The difference between cases of wrongful life and those of so-called "wrongful birth" is that, although in both cases the child is born with a serious

[161] Belgium no. 45; Portugal no. 124; Russia no. 17; Spain no. 82.
[162] Sweden no. 9.
[163] Italy nos. 75–76.
[164] Austria nos. 61–62; Belgium no. 46; Czech Republic nos. 78–80; England and Wales no. 34; France nos. 81–82; Germany nos. 36–37; Italy nos. 77–83; the Netherlands no. 40; Portugal no. 131; Russia no. 18; Spain no. 83; Sweden no. 9.
[165] Austria no. 61; Germany no. 36.
[166] Germany no. 36.
[167] The Netherlands no. 40.

impairment, in the case of wrongful life the person who brings the action for damages is the impaired child (or the parents on his or her behalf) and in the case of wrongful birth the person who brings the action is the mother in her own name or both parents also in their own name. In the cases of wrongful birth, the parents bring the claim for the damage they have suffered as a result of not being able to decide about having a child with such serious impairments. In the case of wrongful life, the claim can only be based on the fact that the child was born at all and now has to put up with a life of severe restrictions due to his or her impairment and with the enormous expense usually associated with his or her health condition.

Whereas in the case of wrongful birth the mainstream tendency is to compensate parents for the damage resulting from having a child with such serious impairments, in the cases of wrongful life most legal systems under survey do not deal with the case or, when they do, they reject compensation. So, for instance in the Czech Republic, Russia, Spain and Sweden there are no cases decided by the courts and legal scholarship does not seem to have devoted much attention to the topic so far.[168] 68

By contrast, higher courts in Germany, Austria, Italy and Portugal, and lower courts in England have decided cases of wrongful life and have not awarded damages to the claimant. This is the case, for instance, in Germany where the Federal Supreme Court denied the child any claim for damages, both in tort and in contract, i.e. on the grounds of the contractual relationship between the mother and the doctor. The child was held not to have a claim for damages in tort pursuant to § 823 subs. 1 BGB, since the doctor was not under a duty to prevent the life of a disabled child. In the eyes of the court, such a duty would be against the core idea of tort law which is to protect the integrity of personal rights, with the right to life being the most solemn of all. Moreover, the child could not derive a claim for damages from the contractual relationship between the mother and the doctor either. Since the law vests the right of abortion in the mother alone and for her own interest, the court held that the contract cannot be construed to confer an implied right to be aborted on the child. Finally, it was also argued that every human being had to accept his life as it has been given to him and had no claim against others to prevent or destroy it.[169] Along the lines of the German Federal Supreme Court, the Austrian Supreme Court did not compensate for such a claim either, considering that one had to accept one's life as it was created by nature and therefore had no right to being killed or being prevented from being born. In Italy, a decision of the *Corte di Cassazione* in 2004 confirmed the non-existence of a right not to be born, arguing in the light of the principle of solidarity (art. 2 Italian Constitution) and the general principle of art. 5 c.c., which prohibits acts causing a permanent reduction or loss of psycho-physical integrity[170]. 69

[168] Czech Republic no. 81; Russia no. 19; Spain no. 84; Sweden no. 10.
[169] Germany no. 39.
[170] Italy no. 86.

70 In Portugal, a decision of the Supreme Court in 2001 denied compensation to a child based on the reasoning that the violation of the duty to inform (of a possible malformation) on the side of the physician only led to the parents being deprived of the right to choose whether to have the child or not, but did not violate any right of the child.[171] In England the subject was already dealt with many years ago by a decision of the Court of Appeal[172] where compensation was rejected taking into account that the claim was contrary to public policy and disclosed no reasonable cause of action. Imposing a duty on the doctor to advise an abortion on grounds of the child's likely disability would "make a further inroad on the sanctity of human life … [and] would mean regarding the life of a handicapped child as not only less valuable than the life of a normal child, but so much less valuable that it was not worth preserving." In addition, it was utterly impossible to put a value upon the child's loss in such a case, which required a comparison between life in the child's present condition and not being born at all, and to determine the degree of disability that would entitle the child to bring such an action.[173] As can be observed, this reasoning has many points in common with those used much later by the German and Austrian Supreme Courts.

71 In some of these countries, however, a sector of legal scholarship has not agreed with these decisions. Some German legal scholars have criticised this case-law, arguing that only a claim for damages vested in the child would guarantee him sufficient financial means after the death of the parents and have considered it to be contradictory to deny the child a claim for damages under a reference to respect for human life, on the one hand, and on the other to put the dignity of the child's life in peril by disallowing him the necessary funds, obliging him to rely on social aid in a situation where need is greatest. Other scholars add that the doctor should be responsible for his professional failure, and that there are no reasons to release him from his burden at the expense of the tax-payer. It has also been argued that acknowledgement of liability in tort would not only provide for compensation but would also allow the determination of professional standards of care.[174] In Italy some isolated opinions have also drawn attention to the need to re-examine rejection of such claims on the basis of technological and scientific development.[175] Also, in England and Wales, case-law rejecting wrongful life claims has attracted considerable academic criticism, with some commentators going so far as to call for the recognition of a cause of action for wrongful life in English law. It is said that the facts in *McKay v Essex AHA* arose before the implementation of the Congenital Disabilities (Civil Liability) Act 1976, which supersedes all previously effective legal provisions governing liability to children in respect of their congenital disability, and the Court noted that the Act's passage effec-

[171] Portugal nos. 134–135.
[172] England and Wales no. 35 and *McKay v. Essex AHA* [1982] QB 1166.
[173] England and Wales no. 35.
[174] Germany no. 40.
[175] Italy no. 87.

tively precluded wrongful life claims relating to births from its in-force date in 1976 on. It has been suggested, however, that the subsequent extension of the Act to make specific provision for infertility treatments has opened the door for wrongful life claims in a limited set of circumstances, namely, where the disability results from negligence in the selection of a damaged embryo to place in the mother, or damaged gametes to create the embryo, but this has yet to be tested in court.[176] However, when closely analysed from a comparative perspective, one could consider that these cases resemble more the problems related to prenatal injuries than those posed by wrongful-life.

In a minority of countries, such as France – albeit for a certain time, only –, Belgium and in the Netherlands – quite recently – compensation for wrongful life has been admitted. In France in the famous *Arrêt Perruche*-decision the *Cour de Cassation* granted compensation both to parents and to the impaired child in a case where, due to the negligence of a laboratory and of a doctor, it was not possible to find out that a pregnant mother had contracted rubella and, therefore, the parents had been prevented from exercising their right to terminate the pregnancy and the child deprived of the chance not to be born.[177] The legislature did not take long to act following the often visceral response of many in the legal community to the *Perruche* decision, and passed Act no. 2002-303 of 4 March 2002, relating to the rights of the sick or injured and the quality of the healthcare system. The Act stipulates that "no one may seek redress for losses resulting merely from the fact of his birth", which brings to an end to the ongoing debate around the issue of wrongful life. As regards the question of fault on the part of the healthcare professional, the Act adds that "the person born with a disability due to medical negligence (*faute médicale*) may obtain compensation for his losses provided that the negligent act directly caused the disability or aggravated it or prevented measures from being taken that might have attenuated it". This means that for the case of wrongful life, although the child cannot bring a claim in tort against the physician, he is not left without redress, since the Act states that "any disabled person, whatever the cause of his disability, is entitled to full support of the state"[178]. In this case, compensation is shifted from the tort law system to the so-called "national solidarity", or in other terms, specific social security instruments, but the *Office national d'indemnisation des accidents médicaux* (ONIAM) is only authorised to compensate for losses resulting from medical accidents where the level of disability exceeds a specified threshold, something which means that victims suffering from less serious impairments are to be excluded from its provisions.[179] It must be emphasised, however, that while a child may not be granted compensation on the basis of wrongful life, his parents may still be entitled to compensation for their own losses resulting from the child's wrongful birth.[180] 72

[176] See England and Wales no. 35.
[177] France no. 84.
[178] France nos. 86–88.
[179] France no. 88.
[180] France no. 89.

73 In Belgium two recent decisions, issued in 2002 and 2004 by the Civil Tribunal of Brussels, declared that a wrongful life claim of a child was admissible. The Court expressly admits to having been influenced by the French *Perruche*-case, and in the last decision of 2004 declared that the claim introduced by the legal representative of the child tended "to the reparation of a wrongful life", but that "the postulated damages were limited to the consequences of the impairment" and "the question was not the compensation for the damage of being born or not".[181]

74 In the Netherlands the Supreme Court recently decided in the *Baby Kelly*-case to allow claims concerning wrongful life. In this case, the obstetrician had negligently refused to apply prenatal diagnostics. As a result Kelly was born with severe congenital defects. Kelly and her parents sued for material and non-pecuniary losses, including the non-pecuniary loss suffered by the severely disabled Kelly herself. Specifically, the Dutch Supreme Court awarded compensation (1) for maintenance of the child, including the extra costs deriving from her handicap; (2) for non-pecuniary losses arising from the infringement of the parent's self-determination; (3) for the non-pecuniary losses suffered by the child herself; and (4) the costs of the psychiatric treatment of the mother[182]. In the decision, the Supreme Court anticipated some of the criticisms that could have been opposed to the adopted solution. Thus, it stated that the claim was allowed not because non-existence was better than living with severe disability, but because Kelly (and other severely disabled children) had a right to compensation if a third party had acted negligently with respect to her well-being. Consequently, according to the Court, the decision should not be understood in the sense of holding the disabled child to be inferior, but rather as making her life more bearable. At the same time, the Supreme Court explicitly declared that as the right of non-existence was not at stake, the child cannot sue his parents for not having aborted.[183]

24. Concerning the liability for pre-natal injuries: Are third parties liable to the child? May the mother be liable to the child, for example, for excessive consumption of alcohol or even for an omission to procure treatment?

75 All legal systems admit the right of the child to be compensated for pre-natal injuries caused by a third party, even when at the time of being injured the child was not yet born.[184] Most legal systems follow the fiction of the *nasciturus,* i.e. that although the foetus is not a living human being yet, he is considered to have full legal capacity before birth if later born alive and, accordingly, if the child is born alive, third parties will be liable to him or her.[185]

[181] Belgium no. 47.
[182] The Netherlands no. 44.
[183] The Netherlands no. 47.
[184] Austria no. 66; Belgium no. 48; Czech Republic no. 82; England and Wales no. 36; France nos. 92–93; Germany no. 46; Italy nos. 89–90; the Netherlands nos. 48–51; Portugal no. 140; Spain no. 88; Sweden no. 10. A different result seems to be reached in Russia (Russia no. 20).
[185] Austria no. 66; Belgium no. 48; Czech Republic no. 82; England and Wales no. 36; Germany no. 46; Italy no. 91; Spain nos. 88–89.

With regard to the liability of mothers for damage caused to their children due to excessive consumption of alcohol or an omission to procure treatment during pregnancy the positions are split. In some countries such as England, Germany, Portugal and Spain, as a rule mothers cannot be held liable. In Germany, whereas a sector of legal writing rejects liability completely, arguing that pregnancy is part of the mother's sphere of privacy protected by the German Constitution (cf. artt. 2 para 1, 1 para 1 *Grundgesetz*, GG), other legal scholars hold that, since the right to abortion as enshrined in § 218 of the German Criminal Code (*Strafgesetzbuch*, StGB) shows that the mother's right to dispose of the child's life is not without limits, mothers may be held liable in the terms of § 1664 subs. 1 BGB, i.e. if they have acted intentionally or recklessly (taking into account the standard of care that the mother meets in her own affairs). The underlying idea is that the interests of mother and child have to be balanced in order to protect the child and, by the same token, allow the mother a lifestyle that is not subjected to exaggerated exigencies.[186] Along the same lines, it is considered in Spain that the self-determination of the mother is paramount and that the child cannot bring a claim against her, except when the harm has been caused with intent (cf. art. 145.2 Spanish Penal Code (CP) and probably, also when it has been caused with gross negligence.[187] In Portugal, case-law is reluctant to accept claims against parents in order to avoid bad relationships between family members.[188] In England, by way of exception, liability of the mother for damage caused to the child may arise if the claim relates to the mother's negligent driving of a motor vehicle when she knew (or ought reasonably to have known) that she was pregnant: she is deemed to owe the same duty to take care for the safety of the unborn child as the law imposes on her for the safety of other people, and may be held liable to the child if it is born with disabilities as a result of her breach of that duty. This exception is clearly motivated by the independent legal requirement that users of motor vehicles be insured against third-party risks.[189] In Sweden, liability does not seem to exist either, since such liability is usually excluded from liability insurance.[190] However, it seems that there are no cases deciding this issue in any of these countries. 76

No cases can be found either in Austria, Belgium, the Czech Republic, France or the Netherlands,[191] but the national reporters, at least in theory, do not exclude the possibility of compensation. However, it is also considered that the basic requirements for establishing liability may be very difficult to prove in practice.[192] In Italy compensation has been awarded at least in one case.[193] 77

186 Germany no. 47.
187 Spain no. 90.
188 Portugal no. 141.
189 England and Wales no. 36.
190 Sweden no. 11.
191 Austria no. 67; Belgium no. 49; Czech Republic nos. 83–84; France nos. 96–100; the Netherlands no. 51.
192 Belgium no. 49; Czech Republic no. 84; France no. 96.
193 Italy no. 96.

Final Conclusions

Final Conclusions: Policy Issues and Tentative Answers

Gerhard Wagner

I. Introduction

As our common research project drew to a close, the question was raised what the upshot of our comparative endeavours was. Is it possible to identify a legal system in Europe which provides the "optimal" solution to the problem, i.e. that deals with children in tort law in the most satisfactory way? What would be the answer if national lawmakers willing to reform their own system of tort law asked for advice? Is there a particular model on which to build the relevant sections of a prospective European Civil Code? 1

These questions are far-reaching indeed. In a final meeting in Tossa de Mar, held in September 2005, the participants discussed these questions without being able to agree on every single detail. As was to be expected, there are differing views with regard to the many policy issues which have to be tackled in devising a special system of tort law for children, both in their role as tortfeasors and as victims. As the comparative studies revealed, there are major differences between the several national legal systems in Europe, and 2 it would be astonishing indeed if these differences were a result of mere happenstance rather than an expression of divergent normative principles and viewpoints.

II. Tort Law Principles

3 Another preliminary point that had to be considered was that the challenges that children pose for any system of tort law had already been the subject of deliberation within the European Group on Tort Law. Not surprisingly, the Principles of European Tort Law cover most of the issues that solicit attention when defining the liability of children, parents and other institutions as well as the protection of children as victims[1].

1. The Principles of European Tort Law

4 As far as the liability of parents is concerned, Art. 6:101 PETL opts in favour of fault-based liability but reverses the burden of proof such that the parents have to establish that they have conformed to the required standard of conduct in supervising the child properly. Since Art. 6:101 PETL is not limited to parents but applies to any "person in charge of another who is a minor", the same principle of liability for fault with reversal of the burden of proof also governs the liability of schools, kindergardens and other institutions.

5 The PETL do not contain specific provisions on the personal liability of children such as age limits. However, Art. 4:102 para 2 PETL provides for an adjustment of the objective standard of care enshrined in Art. 4:102 para 1 PETL where the relevant person cannot be expected to conform to it "due to age". Thus, the behaviour of children is not measured against the same demanding standard as the behaviour of an adult. In the eyes of the European Group on Tort Law, adjustment of the standard of care was preferable to the definition of age limits below which a minor was protected from liability because it allowed for more flexible solutions[2]. The same principles carry over to the area of contributory fault which is dealt with in Art. 8:101 PETL. Although the text of the Principles is silent on this issue, the commentaries make it clear that a finding of contributory fault on the part of the victim requires application of Art. 4:102 para 2 PETL as well[3]. Thus, the behaviour of the child is measured by the same yardstick, regardless of whether it stands in the shoes of a tortfeasor or in those of a victim.

2. The Study Group on a European Civil Code

6 The rival to the Principles of European Tort Law are the "Principles of European Law: Non-Contractual Liablity Arising out of Damage Caused to Another – PEL Liab.Dam.", drafted by the Study Group on a European Civil Code[4]. The liability of parents and other supervisors is addressed in Art. 3:104 PEL

[1] European Group on Tort Law (ed.), *Principles of European Tort Law* (2005).
[2] P. Widmer (supra fn. 1), Art. 4:102 no. 9.
[3] M. Martín-Casals (supra fn. 1), Art. 8:101 no. 11.
[4] Available on the internet under <http://www.sgecc.net>.

Liab.Dam. Under Art. 3:104 PEL Liab.Dam. parents are liable for the torts committed by their children provided that the child was under fourteen years of age, that the tortious conduct of the child would have been deemed careless if it had been the conduct of an adult, and provided that the parents are unable to prove that they supervised the child with the required diligence (Art. 3:104 para 3 PEL Liab.Dam). Thus, the Study Group on a European Civil Code applies the same system of fault-based liability with a reversal of the burden of proof as the European Group on Tort Law, the major difference being that the PEL Liab.Dam. limit the responsibility of parents to torts committed by children younger than fourteen years.

As to the personal liability of the child, again, the two sets of Principles converge. Under Art. 3:103 PEL Liab.Dam. a person under eighteen years of age is liable only in so far as "that person does not exercise such care as could be expected from a reasonably careful person of the same age in the circumstances of the case". In other words, the PEL Liab.Dam. also adjust the objective standard of care enshrined in Art. 3:102 PEL Liab.Dam. in taking the limited capabilities of children into account. However, the Study Group goes one step further in adding a fixed minimum age that shields children falling below the threshold from liability completely. Under Art. 3:103 para 2 PEL Liab.Dam a person under seven years of age is not accountable for causing damage intentionally or negligently. In any case where a child may not be held liable in circumstances where the same conduct shown by an adult would have triggered the obligation to pay damages, liability in equity may still be established under Art. 3:103 para 3 PEL Liab.Dam. 7

3. *The Scope of Discussion*

Of course, it is impossible to discuss the general issues underlying the status of children in tort law without touching upon the basic choices which were made by the tort law groups in setting up their competing sets of principles. Still, there was consent that it was neither possible nor desirable to subject the provisions drafted by the European Group on Tort Law and the Study Group on a European Civil Code to review. As the participants were either members or friends of the European Group on Tort Law it was thought pointless to restage the deliberation process of the Group and to take a second round of votes on the several choices made. It appeared equally unattractive to focus on the – few – points of divergence between the Principles of European Tort Law and the Study Group Principles in order either to denounce the latter or to celebrate the former. 8

The general belief was that the research that had been conducted was special in its solitary focus on children on the one hand and its comprehensive scope that also concerned the liability of parents, supervisors, schools etc. as well as insurance issues on the other. Therefore, a major part of the final discussion dealt with the general question of the interrelationship between the liability of the child and those of parents, third parties as well as insurance carriers. It was 9 in this area that the project produced truly original insights and in this sense created valuable guidelines for policymakers confronting the status of children in tort law. Everything that follows after the general choice in favour of one "system" or the other seems to be at once of minor importance and subject to rather little disagreement. The fact that there are so few points of divergence between the two sets of Principles is evidence of this fact.

III. The Overarching Choice: A One-Tier or a Two-Tier System of Liability

1. The Two-Tier Model

10 The Principles of European Tort Law adopt a two-tier system of liability for damage caused by children. One tier is the personal liability of the child. Although the child does enjoy a privilege by not having to conform to the objective standard of care it still runs the risk of incurring liability for the damage caused intentionally or negligently. In other words, the child does not enjoy immunity.

11 The second tier is the liability of parents. Their responsibility may be established next to the one of the child, with the victim having the choice between the two sets of defendants. However, the circle of potential defendants may even be larger than this. If the child committed the tortious act while away from home, e.g. while in a children's yard or school, the institution or the school board may be liable as well. In this sense, one may even speak of a three-tier liability system. However, in most cases, the scope of the responsibilities incumbent upon schools and other educational institutions will be coordinated with the remaining responsibilities of the parents.

12 In sum, the victim of a tort committed by a child has the choice of either seeking recourse against the minor tortfeasor itself or against an adult supervisor of the child – be it a parent or an institution. The liability of each class of potential defendant – children, parents, third parties – must be established on its own ground and is dealt with separately. This is true both for legal doctrine and for litigation practice. In the courtroom, establishment of the personal responsibility of the child does not automatically trigger the liability of the parents or of a school board and vice versa. As far as legal doctrine and lawmaking is concerned, the principles governing the responsibility of the child are discussed and established in separation from those underlying the liability of parents and of third parties.

2. The Unitary, One-Tier Model

13 The counterimage of the model just described is something that might be called the "one-tier-system" of liability for the torts of minors. Under this approach, the liability of children and of third-party supervisors remains intact on paper. In practice, the costs of accidents caused by minors are channelled towards the parents and their liability insurer. As a matter of fact, the child

usually lacks the funds to pay up damage claims raised by third party victims anyway. The victim has a strong interest to access the family funds held in the name of the parents. The easiest and most direct way to accommodate this interest is the introduction of strict liability of the parents for the torts of their children.

The parents may of course buy liability insurance, and if they do so, the liability of themselves as supervisors of the child is covered along with the liability of the child in person. Once this sort of family liability insurance is blended into the picture even the liability of third parties like schools and children's yards loses much of its attractiveness. The victim has little incentive to establish the responsibility of third parties, which is usually based on fault where it may easily turn to the liability insurance of the family of the child. The liability of the third party is relevant only for potential rights of recourse of the insurance carrier. 14

In the typical scenario, then, only a single head of liability, i.e. parental liability, in conjunction with the pertinent insurance cover are relevant. The central question is whether the law should take this state of affairs into account, and if so, how. A legal system may remain passive and just recognize the fact that the victim looks for the defendant who is easiest to pursue and who enjoys the protection of insurance coverage. The alternative strategy is to exploit the workings of litigation practice and deliberately to channel the costs of damages caused by children to one single entity, an insurance carrier. All that is needed to accomplish this is widespread liability insurance and a trigger, i.e. the definition of a single head of liability that allows the victim to access the funds collected by the insurance carrier. In this sense, such a system is a "one-tier" solution to the problem of accidents caused by children. 15

IV. The French System of Channelling Liabilities

1. *Exposition*

a) Strict Parental Liability

Like in many other areas, it is again French law which stands out in following its own path. In the present context, it represents the legal system that goes furthest in deliberately channelling damage claims towards the parents and the insurance carriers standing behind them. 16

The crucial elements of the French law of delict that do the trick are threefold. The first step is strict liability of the parents for the torts of their children[5]. In making the parents strictly liable, the liability of the child becomes moot. In the ordinary case, it is the parents who are in command of the financial means necessary to cover the damages of the victim. If the parents are liable in each 17

[5] France, Part I, nos. 94 et seq.

and every case in which the personal liability of the child may be established, then the victim will ordinarily turn to the parents only.

b) Quasi-Mandatory Liability Insurance

18 The second element of French law that reinforces the focus on the parents is widespread liability insurance. The above reasoning that the parents will be the ones in a financial position to cover the damage claim holds true in cases involving minor damage only. In a very small number of cases, the child will be richer than its parents, but in quite a large number of situations, the parents will lack the funds to pay up the damage claim too. Be that as it may, family liability insurance eliminates the judgment proof problem and provides the parents with the necessary financial means to meet the claim of the victim. In addition, because the liability of the child is insured against as well, the insurance carrier has no right of recourse as against the child[6]. In this sense, it is a true family insurance policy.

19 To be sure, family liability insurance is not compulsory in France. Although there is no legal obligation to seek out insurance, the fact is that close to 100% of French families in fact do enjoy the protection of an insurance cover[7]. The almost complete penetration of French society is accomplished by a number of factors, with the most important being a deeply rooted social habit to buy such insurance along with strong pressures to do so. The central actors in the effort to supply every family with such a policy are the elementary schools[8]. Their officers are obliged to advise parents who register their children for school attendance to take out insurance. In case the parents are not covered yet and seem unwilling or unable to do something about this, they even assist the parents in obtaining an insurance contract. The French insurance industry, in turn, seems ready to accept each and every risk the schools refer to them in doing the underwriting work of the insurance carriers.

20 It is important to note that family liability works differently in systems that impose strict liability on the parents for the torts of their children. In these systems, the parents are automatically liable if their child is liable. The case that only the child is liable but not its parents cannot occur. Therefore, it makes no sense to pursue claims against the child. The child effectively "drops out of the picture". Without intending any moral stigmatization, it may be said that the child is reduced to the status of an animal or a car, i.e. it is a mere conduit to establish the liability of the parents.

21 The effect that the liability of the child becomes moot is reinforced by insurance law. Ordinarily, liability insurance coverage does not extend to intentional torts or, more precisely, the intentional infliction of harm[9]. This exclusion

[6] France, Part I, nos. 75 et seq.
[7] France, Part I, nos. 64, 66, 72 et seq.
[8] France, Part I, no. 74.
[9] See, e.g., Germany, Part I, no. 34.

becomes problematic once two different actors may be held liable for the same damage. In this situation, the exclusion only applies to the insurance contract of the tortfeasor who in fact acted intentionally, not to the other tortfeasor who is liable on other grounds, be it vicarious liability, be it strict liability. In the case of family liability insurance, the exclusion of intentional torts only works against the liability of the child who acted intentionally but not against the liability of the parents who are strictly liable for the torts of their child[10]. Again, the effect is that the victim is well advised to rely on the liability of the parents only and to ignore the child altogether.

Up to this point, a number of reasons have been mentioned which together create a channelling effect towards parental liability. The triangle comprised of the victim, the child and the parents thereby is reduced to a bilateral relationship between the victim and the parents, with the insurance carrier standing behind the parents in order to pick up their liability. 22

c) Disregarding the Liabilities of Third Parties

At first blush, one might suppose that the situation just described changes once third parties enter the picture. The standard scenario is that the child causes damage while at school. Here, the channelling effect towards the parents and their insurance carrier seems to break down as the victim might have a viable claim towards the school or another third party. 23

This supposition is not supported by reality as it exists in France. One reason of course is that the liability of the parents is easy to establish if it is strict. Systems operating on the basis of fault, be it with or without a reversal of proof, necessarily run into problems if the child causes damage while away from home. In cases where the whereabouts of the child do not in itself amount to carelessness on the part of parents, e.g. if the child attends a public or otherwise well-reputed school, it is very difficult to establish the breach of a duty of supervision on the part of the parents. Naturally, the victim looks to the school or other institution in search of liability. 24

Under a system of strict parental liability like the French one, there is no need to turn to the third party[11]. Rather, the school or other institution may be left out of the picture as well. Strict liability does not require a finding that the parents had a chance to avoid the accident, i.e. that they did anything wrong in bringing up or supervising the child. The mere fact that it is their child who caused the damage is sufficient[12]. Given that families are insured against liability, the victim will not bother with a potential liability of the third party but will ignore the latter and stick with the parents and their insurer. This effect, that third parties who may be liable themselves, drop out of the picture, may 25

[10] France, Part I, no. 68.

[11] This is only a rough description of the rather complex set of rules and cases; see France, Part I, nos. 134 et seq.

[12] France, Part I, nos. 121, 149 at fn. 190.

be the true explanation for the vigilance with which French schools seek to guarantee that each and every of its pupils enjoys the benefit of family liability insurance.

d) Dispensing with Fault on the Part of the Child

26 A final cornerstone of the French system is that strict liability of the parents has been stretched beyond limits in that the courts have dispensed with the requirement of tortious behaviour on the part of the child[13]. The parents are answerable not only for the torts committed by their child but in fact for any damage that was caused by their offspring, regardless of whether or not the child was at fault. Their liability is not even contingent on a finding that the behaviour of the child, judged against the objective standard of care incumbent upon an adult, was careless. Even where the child showed the same diligence that would have been sufficient to free an adult person from liability, the parents are liable anyway.

27 Whatever one may think of this rule in terms of principle, there is no doubt that it reinforces the channelling effect towards parental liability and its insurance coverage. To put it bluntly, the victim would be silly to try to establish the personal liability of the child itself, i.e. to grapple with issues like capacity and carelessness, instead of turning to the parents whose liability may be established without proving anything like capacity and fault on the part of the child, let alone fault on the part of the parents themselves.

e) Conclusion

28 To sum up, the French system is one which places parental liability and their liability insurance in the centre and pushes everything else to the sides, i.e. the personal liability of the child as well as potentially responsible third parties. The upshot is a channelling of damages claims towards the parents and their liability insurers. The key features of the system are:

- Strict liability of parents for damage caused by their children, regardless of whether the child itself was at fault.
- Close to complete protection of families by liability insurance policies covering both the liability of the child and of the parents. Coverage of damage claims arising out of intentional torts committed by the child. No right of recourse of insurance companies against the child.

2. *Evaluation I: Advantages of the French System*

29 The French system may appear strange to many outside observers but that must not foreclose a fair evaluation of its strengths and weaknesses. Let us begin with the strengths.

[13] France, Part I, no. 114.

a) Full Compensation of Victims

It is generally agreed that the compensation of victims is a principal goal of tort law. The French system is very good in accomplishing this aim. Close to every family enjoys the protection of liability insurance, and the law of extra-contractual liability makes sure that the funds of the family insurance carriers may be accessed with ease. The introduction of strict liability on the part of the parents in combination with the elimination of the requirement of delictual – intentionally harmful or careless – behaviour on the part of the child work to the effect that indemnification is guaranteed for every victim that can show it has sustained damage caused by a child. In terms of compensation of victims, this is the utmost private law can do. 30

b) Comprehensive Risk Spreading

The lowering of the threshold of liability of the parents to such an extreme extent as done in France could not be supported if the families were left alone with the associated burden of damage costs. A system of strict liability is in need of liability insurance which must be readily available and widely used in order to allow the families to pool their risks. The French system achieves this result with informal means, i.e. with the help of school officers who pressure families to contract for insurance as a precondition for school attendance. 31

In a world where close to every family enjoys the protection of liability insurance, the costs of accidents caused by children as well as the harm inflicted through their intentional acts is shifted on to insurance pools and ultimately to society at large. In this sense, both the risk of suffering injury at the hands of a child and the corresponding risk of the family to be burdened with the resulting damage costs is spread among the general public. Precisely because the general public is the best risk bearer available, this outcome is optimal under the risk spreading goal of tort law. 32

c) Low Transaction Costs

The French law with respect to tortious behaviour of children may be summed up in the rule that parents are automatically liable for harm done by their children. Because the threshold for liability is so low, it takes very little to plead a claim for damages and to prove the relevant facts. Fault on the part of the child is not an issue, and a failure on the part of the parents to educate and supervise the child is irrelevant too. Therefore, the outcomes to be obtained under the rule of parental liability are clear and readily foreseeable. 33

Claims for damages are handled by insurance companies who treat such claims on a rational basis, defending them only where this seems worthwhile. Because the requirements for liability of the parents are so weak, there is little scope for defence work. Thus, the claims may easily be settled without judicial intervention. 34

d) Conclusion

35 The above evaluation employed the three criteria developed by *Calabresi* to provide guidance in the choice between different compensation systems[14]. As it turned out, the French system looks good on all three prongs of the test.

3. Evaluation II: Disadvantages of the French System

36 As the surveys of national legal systems conducted within the course of this project have made clear, the French system stands out against the ones of other European nations. Therefore, one must raise the question as to whether there is a downside to the French solution.

a) Incentives to Take Care

37 The traditional view is that tort law is not only concerned with a redistribution of damage costs after the fact but also aims at preventing accidents from occurring in the future. This position has gained fresh support from the law-and-economics movement which regards deterrence as the primary goal of tort law[15].

38 In contrast to a belief held by parts of the legal profession, the preventive effect of tort law is not restricted to fault-based liability but extends to strict liability[16]. Therefore, it is to be expected that the imposition of strict liability on parents for the damages caused by their children provides incentives to educate their children towards prudent behaviour and supervise them accordingly. This incentive will be as strong as in a system making parental liability contingent on a failure of supervision.

39 Pure systems of strict liability are thought to produce adverse effects on the part of the potential victims as their incentives to take care are weakened. However, this problem may be easily dealt with by reducing the damage claim in cases of contributory negligence which French law of course does.

40 In terms of incentives to take care, the main problem of the French solution is not strict liability but liability insurance[17]. A person who knows that any damage caused will be picked up by a third party – i.e. an insurance carrier – has little incentive to take costly precautions in order to avoid harm. Why should parents invest in educating their children in the name of safety if their failure to do so merely results in increased payments of an insurance carrier but has no influence whatsoever on their personal balance sheet? Why stand up to the

[14] G. Calabresi, *The Costs of Accidents* (1970), 26 et seq.

[15] S. Shavell, *Foundations of Economic Analysis of Law* (2004), 177 et seq.; H. Kötz/G. Wagner, *Deliktsrecht* (10th edn. 2006), nos. 59 et seq.

[16] S. Shavell (supra fn. 15), 179 et seq.; H. Kötz/G. Wagner (supra fn. 15), no. 500.

[17] Cf., generally S. Shavell (supra fn. 15), 262 et seq.; H. Kötz/G. Wagner (supra fn. 15), nos. 78 et seq.; G. Wagner, Comparative Report in: idem (ed.) *Tort Law and Liability Insurance* (2005), no. 77.

unnerving conflicts with one's children if the insurance carrier takes care of their failures anyway?

The insurance industry of course has means to fend off the destruction of incentives to take care just described. Pertinent instruments to cope with moral hazard include the risk-rating of premiums, bonus/malus-schemes, deductibles and exclusions[18]. However, very little from this menu of tools seems to be used by French insurers[19]. They charge flat premiums which are the same for all households, bonus/malus-schemes do not exist and deductibles are not negotiated. The attempt of French insurers to exclude coverage for intentional infliction of harm on the part of the child has been thwarted by the *Cour de Cassation*[20]. Thus, an adolescent of seventeen years who sets a row of cars on fire in the street of a *banlieu* has virtually nothing to fear in terms of civil liability. Of course, he is personally liable for the damage caused intentionally, and this liability is not covered by family liability insurance. However, his parents are liable as well, in their relationship with the insurer, the exemption for intentional acts does not apply, and therefore, the damage claims of the car owners will be covered by the insurance carrier. Where a child in the true sense of the term, i.e. less than ten or fourteen years of age, commits an intentional tort, one may still classify this as imprudent, playful behaviour and grant insurance coverage. In contrast, tortfeasors close to the age of majority might wilfully use the insurance coverage as an invitation for wrongdoing. In terms of prevention, this outcome is a nightmare. 41

Compelling as these concerns may be on a theoretical level, their impact in practice might be comparatively modest. After all, premiums charged under family liability insurance policies seem to remain well within the range that is to be observed in other countries as well. In absolute terms, the policy is still cheap, with prices well below 100 Euros. The explanation for this astonishing result is likely to be multifold. First of all, one has to bear in mind that the quasi-compulsory system of family insurance prevalent in France effectively forces the good risks – the diligent families – in one pool together with the bad risks – families where the parents do not care about education and supervision of children. As long as the majority of families remain diligent, the total effect on premiums might be negligible. Whether this outcome will obtain depends, of course, on the ratio of diligent families to negligent families. If the former outnumber the latter by far, then the effects of cross-subsidization will not be strong enough to result in a palpable rise in insurance premiums. 42

But why should the large majority of parents continue to educate and supervise their children properly? Part of the answer may be that careless behaviour of children poses risks not only to third parties but also to themselves. A child that is careless on the street may cause an accident in which the victim with 43

[18] G. Wagner (supra fn. 17), no. 78.
[19] France, Part I, no. 65.
[20] Cass. civ., 12 March 1991 in [1991] JCP, II, no. 21732 note Bigot; France, Part I, no. 68.

the most severe injuries will be the child itself. The incentive to teach a child the rules of the road and other precautionary habits is strong even if the child and the parents are shielded from liability completely – as in fact they are in France.

44 The above reasoning does not carry over to intentional torts. The smashing of cars in a *banlieu* does not put the health of the minor tortfeasor itself on the line. Rather, the sole risk of loss is on third parties. In such cases, the criminal law is likely to fill up much of the loss in incentives that the suspension of the deterrent effects generated by tort law causes. The wilful destruction or damaging of things belonging to someone else is a crime in every country, and everywhere, minors above a certain age are subject to criminal liability. Therefore, the criminal sanction stands ready to deter wrongful behaviour. Of course, the criminal law only works if it is enforced in practice which it is not in cases of widespread riots as well as in most instances of casual, every-day vandalism. However, these gaps in law-enforcement are likely to haunt tort law as well – if the police fails to catch the offenders, then the private victim will have no chance to collect its damages either.

45 Taken together, the effects just described may provide an explanation for the otherwise puzzling fact that the French system of parental liability and family insurance destroys whatever incentives to take care and abstain from intentional wrongdoing that the private law of tort creates.

b) Burdening Families

46 It has already been indicated – somewhat hesitantly – that the French doctrine of strict parental liability treats children like animals or cars, that is like a source of danger which the "owner" keeps at his peril. Quite obviously, though, children are human beings and they deserve to be treated as such. In addition, the demographic problems haunting Europe counsel against a legal rule that "penalizes" parents for having and educating children.

47 It is a well received teaching of the economic analysis of law that strict liability works to reduce the amount of the activity to which it attaches[21]. Strict liability for animals works to internalize all the costs of keeping an animal to its owner, thereby adds to the total cost of keeping an animal and as a consequence reduces the number of animals kept. If this reasoning is transferred to the area of interest here, it means that strict liability of parents for the damage caused by their children adds to the cost of raising a child and in the end will cause the "marginal" parents, i.e. those who were close to refraining from having a child, to opt in favour of abandoning the plan of rearing a child.

48 Even if one is prepared to apply the economic rationale which was developed for activities with measurable costs and benefits to the case of children, doubts

[21] S. Shavell (supra fn. 15), 193 et seq.; H. Kötz/G. Wagner (supra fn. 15), nos. 72 et seq., 503 et seq.

remain. To begin with, the simple fact is that France has one of the highest birth rates in Europe whereas Germany, which entertains a system of fault-based liability of the parents for the torts of their children[22], has one of the lowest. Whatever the effect of the French law of delict is, it is obviously not strong enough to deter French couples from having children. – In truth, any other outcome would be surprising. It has to be kept in mind that, in France, the costs of accidents caused by children are not borne by the families but shifted on to a professional risk carrier. For the reasons expounded above, the premium charged by insurance companies for family liability insurance policies are modest[23]. In addition, they are flat, i.e. the same for every family, without regard to the number of children and their accident-proneness. Thus, the adverse effect that families with children in general, and those with many children in particular are burdened with the costs of damage caused by their offspring does not materialize. To the contrary, the costs of injuries caused by minors are borne by all the families carrying liability insurance, i.e. the public at large. Because the costs of damages are "socialized" instead of attributed to the individual family, the French system cannot have the effect of reducing the number of children.

4. Conclusion

What is the learning of the French experience? The views entertained within 49
the group of participants remained divided. Most observers were ready to admit that the French system "worked" well but still insisted that it was wrong in principle.

It was thought wrong to treat a child like a "source of danger", particularly so 50
because it remained unclear whether minors, on average, really cause higher social losses than adults. Unfortunately, there seem to be no reliable data which allow an estimate of the losses caused by an average adult throughout a particular period of time and their comparison to the respective number for children. It might be the case that children are even less accident-prone, at least as far as third parties are concerned. After all, most of the accidents caused by children merely hurt themselves rather than third parties. The most dangerous things of everyday life – tools, cutlery, weapons, cars, matches and the like – are usually operated by adults and beyond the reach of children.

But be this as it may, it seemed obvious that children are by no means compa- 51
rable to sources of abnormal danger for which their keeper is strictly liable – like animals, cars or nuclear power plants[24]. Strict liability of the parents for the wrongs committed by their child would therefore run into the face of the rationale of strict liability. For these reasons it might be wrong in principle to impose strict liability on parents. The interest of the victim in obtaining com-

[22] Germany, Part I, nos. 48 et seq.

[23] Cf. supra, IV. 3. a.

[24] Cf. Art. 5:101 Principles of European Tort Law (supra fn. 1); Art. 3:202 seq. PEL Liab.Dam. (supra fn. 4).

pensation is not strong enough to overcome the principle of fault-based liability. There are many classes of victims who sustain injuries and have to put up with them unless they are able to identify someone who caused the injury and establish negligence on the part of the injurer. Why should it be any different where the injury has been caused by a minor? Why should the law create a privilege in favour of victims who were injured by a child rather than by an adult? What happens if the total amount of damages exceeds the limit of the insurance cover and thus eats away at the financial livestock of the family? These questions are impossible to answer satisfactorily unless one grants the goal of victim compensation absolute priority. The majority within the group was not prepared to do so.

52 For these reasons, the "grand solution" offered by French law does not carry the day. Comparative analysis is pushed back to a two-tier-model of liability for damage caused by children, treating parental responsibility separate from personal liability of the child.

V. Specifying Principles of Liability

1. Parental Liability

53 After all that has been said above, it follows easily that the foundation of parents' liability should be fault. The legal systems working on the basis of fault tend to focus the duties of care incumbent upon the parents on the supervision of the child[25]. This is an outdated concept. A child that is supervised around the clock and until the age of majority will never be a responsible person but rather a candidate for a psychiatrist. What parents really have to do is to educate their children, i.e. to inform them about the danger of everyday life and to train them in dealing with those dangers. In this context, it is inevitable to expose children to some risks in order to make them accustomed to deal with dangerous situation on their own. With regard to small children, the most important thing parents have to do is not supervision either but to engage in every effort to keep them away from sources of danger – from matches, from ponds, from the street etc. It is only in exceptional cases that supervision is the kind of precaution which the parents should adopt. For these reasons, the fault requirement is to be understood in a broad sense: it is not only about supervising the children but also about educating, teaching and training them, as well as placing them into situations where they are able to learn how to manage themselves.

54 Along with the debate on the basis of liability of the parents for the damage caused by their children, the question was raised as to which system was more adequate: the *"single rule"* model adopted in Austria and in Germany or the *"graduation of liability"* model followed in the Netherlands. The former adopts a single rule, e.g. fault-based liability with a reversal of the burden of

[25] See, e.g., Germany, Part I, nos. 48 et seq., 69 et seq.

proof[26], for the liability of parents with regard to minors of all ages. In contrast, Dutch law distinguishes between three stages depending upon the age of the child and provides different liability rules for parents with respect to every single stage. In the Netherlands, these rules range from strict liability for children under fourteen years of age, over fault-based liability with a reversal of the burden of proof for children aged fifteen or sixteen years, and ordinary liability for fault without a reversal of the burden of proof for children older than sixteen until they reach the age of majority[27].

The Dutch model certainly has its virtues. Its main advantage is that it balances the capabilities of the parents to control the child – which decrease with increasing age – against the capacity of the child to control its own behaviour – which increases with increasing age. Still participants tended to favour a single rule model of fault-based liability to be applied with flexibility, instead of a graduation of liability model. It was thought that the standard of care is flexible enough to take such differences into account, imposing more intensive duties on parents of small or problematic children and relaxing their duties if a well-educated child approaches the age of majority. 55

2. Liability of Third Parties

Once the group opted for fault as a basis of parents' liability, this led to the conclusion that in the case of third parties being held liable for damage caused by children, the fault principle should apply as well. 56

Within a system that bases both the liability of parents and the one of third parties on fault, the relationship between the two sets of duties to take care must be defined. In contrast, where the liability of the parents is strict, it takes priority over the responsibility of third parties, as far as litigation practice is concerned. However, for the reasons set out above, strict liability of parents was rejected. 57

As to the relationship between parental duties and those of schools, it was thought, again, that the fault principle itself provided the necessary structure. A clear cut solution allocating liability exclusively to the school for damage caused in the course of school attendance was rejected. Parental liability for torts committed by their children during school hours will be exceptional but cannot be ruled out altogether. Where the parents violated a duty of care, e.g. did not prevent their child from carrying a weapon to school, their personal responsibility is out of the question. Likewise, the liability of the school depends on whether it failed to supervise its pupils properly. 58

The same principles should apply where the liability of an employer of the child for damage caused in the course of employment is in issue. 59

[26] Austria, Part I, nos. 164 et seq.; Germany, Part I, nos. 48 et seq.
[27] Netherlands, Part I, nos. 10 et seq.

3. *Personal Liability of the Child*

a) Keeping Personal Liability Alive

60 For the reasons expounded above, the group was not prepared to follow the French model and to let the minor "disappear from the scene". First of all, it would be wrong in principle to deny personal responsibility where it may be established under general principles and notions of fault. As a practical matter, there may well be cases, albeit rare, where the parents lack the financial means to cover the victim's claim whereas the child is in command of such assets.

61 Especially in cases involving severe personal injuries, the liability of the child may result in an obligation to pay damages for the rest of the child's life, i.e. a life that has just begun. The adverse effects of liabilities of crushing magnitude must be acknowledged. However, it would amount to an overreaction to rule out the personal liability of the child altogether. Rather, the problem should be taken care of either by way of a reduction clause or by insolvency law[28].

b) Capacity

62 There is no doubt that capacity is a prerequisite for personal liability in tort, at least if it is fault-based. The controversial issue here is whether it is advisable to fix a certain minimum age below which the child enjoys immunity. The national legal systems give divergent answers, and even the efforts at European harmonization of tort law differ, with the Principles of European Tort Law eschewing such a solution (Art. 4:102 para 2 PETL) while the Principles of the Study Group embrace it (Art. 3:103 para 2 PEL Liab.Dam.)[29].

63 Given the diversity of opinions, participants refrained from providing any specific recommendation as that would require putting the Principles of European Tort Law on the stand or even re-drafting them. In any case, the issue should be approached with a pragmatic attitude. The two alternative solutions merely employ different means to achieve a common end, i.e. to isolate minors from liability who are unable to discern dangers and to manage themselves. The definition of a fixed minimum age (Art. 3:103 para 2 PEL Liab.Dam.) has legal certainty on its side whereas abstention from such definition and sole reliance on the moderation of the standard of care (Art. 4:102 para 2 PETL) has the virtue of flexibility. A compromise between the two "extremes" would be to define a minimum age for capacity but to relegate it to the status of a presumption that is rebuttable where justice so requires. This suggestion gained a lot of support but did not reach unanimous agreement.

[28] See infra, V. 5.
[29] See supra, II.

c) Standard of Care

Closely related to the concept of capacity is the moderation of the objective standard of care where the behaviour of children is in issue. In fact, the two concepts are interchangeable as Art. 4:102 para 2 PETL shows. 64

In substance, there is some disagreement among the legal systems surveyed in that most countries apply an objective standard of care whereas others opt in favour of a subjective standard. However, with regard to children, all legal systems – with the sole exception of the French one[30] – agree that the reduced capacity of children to behave carefully must be taken into account. 65

d) Liability in Equity

Liability in equity is used in some countries to supplement fault-based liability of the child[31]. Where it is impossible to establish liability for fault, either because the child lacked capacity or because it conformed to the standard of care incumbent upon a child of its age but still violated the objective standard of care designed for adults, liability in equity may fill the void. It is predicated on the case that the harmful act of the child would have amounted to negligence if it had been performed by an adult but must be exonerated under the special standard of care applicable to children. Under this concept, the child may still be answerable for the damage caused if the circumstances of the case so require, i.e. if the minor tortfeasor is strikingly more wealthy than the victim. 66

Participants discussed the issue of liability in equity at length without reaching an unanimous conclusion. In favour of a rule holding the child liable in equity it was argued that such a category is a valuable stone within the mosaic of a flexible system of liability. In cases where the child was not at fault in the true sense of the term, it has to internalize the costs of the damage it caused only if it can easily handle the burden associated with such liability. It would also be a mistake to think that liability in equity is an outdated concept without much bearing on legal practice. The widespread use of liability insurance makes many children wealthy at least vis-à-vis the victim of a tort. If the existence of liability insurance were taken into account in determining the wealth of the child – which is a matter of dispute in some legal systems[32] – then liability in equity could play an important role even in the modern law of torts. 67

In spite of these potential virtues, liability in equity remained suspect to some participants. It was argued that it is inconsistent first to celebrate the fault-principle and then abandon it where the result achieved looks unattractive on equitable grounds. Moreover, one may question whether the distribution of wealth should really be a concern of the law of torts. *Richesse oblige* is a prov- 68

[30] France, Part I, nos. 27 et seq.

[31] M. Martín-Casals, *Comparative Report*, Part I, nos. 24 et seq.

[32] See Germany, Part I, nos. 22 et seq.; M. Martín-Casals, *Comparative Report*, Part I, nos. 35 et seq.

erb but hardly a sound principle on which to ground responsibility in tort. The historical background of liability in equity in Germany was the relationships between rich rural aristocrats and their dependent workers, a background that has completely vanished after World War II. Today, liability in equity would only gain steam if it were directed against the deep pockets of liability insurance carriers. It may be doubted whether it is sound policy to allow the insurance tail to wag the liability dog.

4. *Insurance*

69 The group concluded that once strict liability of parents for damage caused by their children had been rejected, a mandatory insurance scheme was out of the question as well. Of course it is always possible to argue that it is in the best interests of potential tortfeasors to take out liability insurance but this paternalistic view alone is not strong enough to justify public intervention into private affairs. The argument that it is impossible for the child to buy insurance itself does nothing to reverse this result. In most cases, parental liability is in issue along with personal liability of the child such that the wealth of the parents is at stake as well. As a consequence, the parents have a strong incentive to buy liability insurance. Once they do so, the cover automatically extends to the personal liability of the child as well. Therefore, it is not clear why the state should intervene and force insurance contracts upon parents against their will.

70 In addition, mandatory insurance schemes always involve an element of redistribution of wealth, away from good risks and into the pockets of bad risks. As insurance companies are unable, or rather: not allowed, to weed out the bad risks, i.e. families with a high propensity to cause recoverable damage, the disproportionately large amount of damage costs for which they are responsible will in part be shifted to the good risks who will see their premium payments misapplied to cover costs which were caused by others who relax in their efforts to behave carefully and prudently.

71 Finally, it must be borne in mind that the costs of administering a scheme of compulsory insurance are likely to be considerable. The government would have to regulate a whole range of issues, like the scope of the insurance cover and of exclusions, if any were allowed, minimum sums of coverage would have to be defined and so on. In addition, the duty to monitor compliance with the scheme would have to be vested in a public authority, be it a school, a social security agency or the like. Of course, all this is manageable – but it is not costless.

5. *Reduction Clause*

72 It has already been mentioned that personal liability of the child may result in obligations of crushing magnitude which the tortfeasor will have to service for the rest of his or her life. The problems associated with this risk could be solved by making liability insurance mandatory; an idea that was rejected by

the reasons set out above[33]. It is also true that a system of strict parental liability also lends itself to eliminating or at least alleviating the risk to the child, depending on the allocation of the financial burden within the intra-family relationship between the minor tortfeasor and its parents. But again, strict liability of the parents did not win the support of the group either[34].

A system of personal liability of the child on the basis of fault and voluntary liability insurance creates the risk that the child may be burdened with crushing and life-long liabilities is serious. As Germany runs a system of the kind just described, pertinent cases have come before the courts in this country, and they evidenced that the problem is not confined to negligence but also haunts intentional torts[35]. The boundary between mere inadvertence (negligence) and intention is slim anyway, and the playfulness and recklessness typical of children may also drive them to commit an intentional tort. 73

There are two different tools available which can fix the problem of crushing liabilities, i.e. a reduction clause[36] and insolvency law[37]. The former is the intra-tort-law solution which does not have to rely on another branch of the law. A reduction clause would allow the judge to reduce the damages due below the compensatory level in order to avoid overburdening the child-defendant. The solution within the context of insolvency would be to provide the debtor in bankruptcy with a fresh start by discharging personal debts to the extent they remain unpaid after distribution of all available assets of the debtor. 74

The central argument in favour of the insolvency solution is that crushing liabilities are no speciality of tort law but haunt other areas of private law as well. Loan agreements are a case in point but also failed business plans of all sorts. A consistent policy of debtor protection would require lawmakers to insert reduction clauses into a large number of subject-matter areas, such as the law of consumer credit, business credit, guarantees, torts etc. Instead of following this course it seems preferable to provide a uniform solution to the problem and to place it into the context of insolvency law. In fact, many European jurisdictions now have pertinent provisions on personal bankruptcy on their insolvency codes which allow consumers a fresh start by discharging debts incurred[38]. 75

In spite of this reasoning, the majority of participants remained inclined to embrace the tort-law-solution, i.e. a reduction clause. It was thought that a reduction clause was a necessary corollary of applying an objective standard of care to the child – even if the minor age is taken into account. Placing a specific privilege in tort law reflects the acknowledgment that persons are not to be 76

33 See supra, 4.
34 Supra, III.
35 Germany, Part I, nos. 42 et seq.
36 Cf. M. Martín-Casals, *Comparative Report*, Part I, no. 32.
37 Cf. M. Martín-Casals, *Comparative Report*, Part I, no. 65.
38 See Germany, Part I, no. 46; Netherlands, Part I, no. 34; England and Wales, Part I, no. 29.

held fully responsible until they reach the age of majority. In addition, the potential for disproportionate liabilities inherent in tort law was seen as a major justification for a reduction clause. Tort liabilities were thought to differ from contractual obligations as only the latter were incurred voluntarily. Only in the area of tort, a minor slip or blunder could cause major damage which in turn might result in a crushing liability. The mechanisms of insolvency law, on the other hand, were not seen equally suited to protect tortfeasors from disproportionate liabilities. Provisions on personal bankruptcy do not exist in every country and even where they exist bankruptcy still carries a moral stigmatisation of the debtor. Furthermore, insolvency law makes it rather difficult and cumbersome for the individual to obtain a fresh start. In consumer bankruptcy, the insolvent debtor must earn the fresh start by the handing over all his assets to his creditors. In most countries, additional requirements must be satisfied, like a multi-year waiting period during which the debtor is confined to the state of subsistence. For these reasons, the majority was in favour of an intra-tort solution, i.e. a reduction clause.

VI. The Child as Victim

77 The major issue discussed with respect to children as victims was whether they should be accorded a privilege on and above the moderation of the objective standard of care (e.g. Art. 4:102 para 2 PETL)[39]. Under the traditional so-called "mirror-image" rule, the victim must accept a reduction of its damage claim if the tortfeasor can establish that the victim failed to comply with the general duty of care. Thus, the objective standard of care cuts both ways and obliges the would-be tortfeasor as well as the potential victim. Under this principle it is understood that moderations of the objective standard in favour of children also apply in the context of contributory negligence. In this context also, the child is to be held at fault only if it failed to live up to the standard of a reasonable child of the same age. The French law of the so-called loi Badinter famously goes one step further than that and privileges children even more in excluding the defence of contributory negligence with regard to claims growing out of traffic accidents if the victim is a child below sixteen years of age[40]. A similar provision, albeit limited to children less than ten years of age, has been introduced into German law[41].

78 Against this background, the issue arises as to whether children should enjoy a broader exemption from the defence of contributory negligence where they are involved in accidents caused by adults. It is obvious that many adult activities pose very substantial risks to the well-being of children. Motor traffic is of course the most striking example. Every year thousands of children in Europe lose their lives on the street, and many more are seriously injured. The activity of driving a motor car in itself poses a serious threat to the life and physical integrity of children. Psychological studies have shown that children

[39] Supra, II.
[40] France, Part II, no. 55.
[41] Germany, Part I, no. 71; Germany, Part II, no. 24.

below a certain age are unable to adequately assess the speed and distance of approaching cars and interrelate this data with its own path of movement. As a result, they are typically much more vulnerable to the risks created by motor traffic than an average adult. The driver of a car, in turn, is usually in a position to discern the particular vulnerability of minors in their vicinity, and to adjust his level of care accordingly. Therefore, it may well be argued that the claims of children injured in motor traffic should not be reduced upon a showing that the minor victim did not behave properly.

In spite of these considerations, opinions on what the proper reaction of the 79
law should be remained divided. Some participants defended the mirror-image-rule and thought it wrong in principle to depart from it in certain classes of case. To accord children a special status in their role of victims of tortious acts would open up Pandora's Box. Other social groups could follow and also claim privileges in the area of contributory negligence. If the fault principle got it right in general, it should also be followed in particular cases. Mere pity for the fate of injured children, understandable as it is, was no sufficiently compelling ground for abandoning the general framework of tort law.

Others were more willing to compromise principle with the exigencies of par- 80
ticular factual situations. It was thought that a privilege should more easily be granted where the tortfeasor enjoyed the protection of compulsory liability insurance. Under this assumption, the additional damages awarded to the child would not fall on the adult tortfeasor but on the pool of premium payers, i.e. the public at large. The limitation to areas where liability insurance is mandatory reflected the resolve of not making liability contingent on the fact whether the defendant carries insurance or not.

Index

The letters refer to the country reports, the numbers refer to the marginal notes. The country reports are marked by the international letter symbols: A stands for Austria, B for Belgium, CZ for the Czech Republic, D for Germany, E for Spain, EW for England and Wales, F for France, I for Italy, NL for the Netherlands, P for Portugal, RUS for Russia and S for Sweden. The Comparative Report is marked by C, the Final Conclusions by FC.

Publications

Principles of European Tort Law

Volume 1: *The Limits of Liability: Keeping the Floodgates Shut.*
Edited by Jaap Spier.
Kluwer Law International,
The Hague. Hardbound.
ISBN 90-411-0169-1. 1996, 162 pp.

Volume 2: *The Limits of Expanding Liability. Eight Fundamental Cases in a Comparative Perspective.*
Edited by Jaap Spier.
Kluwer Law International,
The Hague. Hardbound.
ISBN 90-411-0581-6. 1998, 244 pp.

Volume 3: *Unification of Tort Law: Wrongfulness.*
Edited by Helmut Koziol.
Kluwer Law International,
The Hague. Hardbound.
ISBN 90-411-1019-4. 1998, 144 pp.

Volume 4: *Unification of Tort Law: Causation.*
Edited by Jaap Spier.
Kluwer Law International,
The Hague. Hardbound.
ISBN 90-411-1325-8. 2000, 161 pp.

Volume 5: *Unification of Tort Law: Damages.*
Edited by Ulrich Magnus.
Kluwer Law International,
The Hague. Hardbound.
ISBN 90-411-1481-5. 2001, 255 pp.

Volume 6: *Unification of Tort Law: Strict Liability.*
Edited by Bernhard A. Koch and Helmut Koziol.
Kluwer Law International,
The Hague. Hardbound.
ISBN 90-411-1705-9. 2002, 444 pp.

Volume 7: *Unification of Tort Law: Liability for Damage Caused by Others*
Edited by Jaap Spier.
Kluwer Law International,
The Hague. Hardbound.
ISBN 90-411-2185-4. 2003, 335 pp.

Volume 8: *Unification of Tort Law: Contributory Negligence.*
Edited by Ulrich Magnus and Miquel Martín-Casals.
Kluwer Law International,
The Hague. Hardbound.
ISBN 90-411-2220-6. 2004, 300 pp.

Volume 9: *Unification of Tort Law:* Multiple Tortfeasors.
Edited by W.V. Horton Rogers
Kluwer Law International,
The Hague. Hardbound.
ISBN 90-411-2319-9. 2004, 313 pp.

Volume 10: *Unification of Tort Law: Fault.*
Edited by Pierre Widmer.
Kluwer Law International, The Hague. Hardbound.
ISBN 90-411-2098-X. 2005, 391 pp.

Tort and Insurance Law

Volume 1: *Cases on Medical Malpractice in a Comparative Perspective.*
Edited by Michael Faure and Helmut Koziol.
Springer, Vienna/New York.
Softcover. ISBN 3-211-83595-4.
2001, 331 pp.

Volume 2: *Damages for Non-Pecuniary Loss in a Comparative Perspective.*
Edited by W.V. Horton Rogers.
Springer, Vienna/New York.
Softcover. ISBN 3-211-83602-0.
2001, 318 pp.

Volume 3: *The Impact of Social Security on Tort Law.*
Edited by Ulrich Magnus.
Springer, Vienna/New York.
Softcover. ISBN 3-211-83795-7.
2003, 314 pp.

Volume 4: *Compensation for Personal Injury in a Comparative perspective.*
Edited by Bernhard A. Koch and Helmut Koziol.
Springer, Vienna/New York.
Softcover. ISBN 3-211-83791-4.
2003, 501 pp.

Volume 5: *Deterrence, Insurability and Compensation in Environmental Liability. Future Developments in the European Union.*
Edited by Michael Faure.
Springer, Vienna/New York.
Softcover. ISBN 3-211-83863-5.
2003, 408 pp.

Volume 6: *Der Ersatz frustrierter Aufwendungen. Vermögens- und Nichtvermögensschaden im österreichischen und deutschen Recht.*
By Thomas Schobel.
Springer, Vienna/New York.
Softcover. ISBN 3-211-83877-5.
2003, 342 pp.

Volume 7: *Liability for and Insurability of Biomedical Research with Human Subjects in a Comparative Perspective.*
Edited by Jos Dute, Michael G. Faure and Helmut Koziol.
Springer, Vienna/New York.
Softcover. ISBN 3-211-20098-3.
2004, 445 pp.

Volume 8: *No Fault Compensation System in the Health Care Sector.*
Edited by Jos Dute, Michael G. Faure, Helmut Koziol.
Springer, Vienna/New York.
Softcover. ISBN 3-211-20799-6.
2004, 492 pp.

Volume 9: *Pure Economic Loss.*
Edited by Willem H. van Boom, Helmut Koziol and Christian A. Witting.
Springer, Vienna/New York.
Softcover. ISBN 3-211-00514-5.
2004, 214 pp.

Volume 10: *Liber Amicorum Pierre Widmer.*
Edited by Helmut Koziol and Jaap Spier.
Springer, Vienna/New York.
Softcover. ISBN 3-211-00522-6.
2003, 376 pp.

Volume 11: *Terrorism, Tort Law and Insurance. A Comparative Survey.*
Edited by Bernhard A. Koch.
Springer, Vienna/New York.
Softcover. ISBN 3-211-01867-0.
2004, 313 pp.

Volume 12: *Abschlussprüfer. Haftung und Versicherung.*
Edited by Helmut Koziol and Walter Doralt.
Springer, Vienna/New York.
Softcover. ISBN 3-211-20800-3.
2004, 180 pp.

Volume 13: *Persönlichkeitsschutz gegenüber Massenmedien/The Protection of Personality Rights against Invasions by Mass Media.*
Edited by Helmut Koziol and Alexander Warzilek.
Springer, Vienna/New York.
Softcover. ISBN 3-211-23835-2.
2005, 713 pp.

Volume 14: *Financial Compensation for Victims of Catastrophes.*
Edited by Michael Faure and Ton Hartlief.
Springer, Vienna/New York.
Softcover. ISBN 3-211-24481-6.
2006, 466 pp.

Volume 15: *Entwurf eines neuen österreichischen Schadenersatzrechts.*
Edited by Irmgard Griss, Georg Kathrein and Helmut Koziol.
Springer, Vienna/New York.
Softcover. ISBN 3-211-30827-X.
2006, 146 pp.

Volume 16: *Tort Law and Liability Insurance.*
Edited by Gerhard Wagner.
Springer, Vienna/New York.
Softcover. ISBN 3-211-24482-4.
2005, 361 pp.

Volume 17: *Children in Tort Law, Part I: Children as Tortfeasors.*
Edited by Miquel Martín-Casals.
Springer, Vienna/New York.
Softcover. ISBN 3-211-24480-8.
2006, 476 pp.

Volume 19: *Tort and Regulatory Law.*
Edited by Willem H. van Boom, Meinhard Lukas and Christa Kissling.
Springer, Vienna/New York.
Softcover. ISBN 3-211-31133-5 (forthcoming).

European Tort Law Yearbook

European Tort Law 2001.
Edited by Helmut Koziol and Barbara C. Steininger.
Springer, Vienna/New York.
Softcover. ISBN 3-211-83824-4.
2002, 571 pp.

European Tort Law 2002.
Edited by Helmut Koziol and Barbara C. Steininger.
Springer, Vienna/New York.
Softcover. ISBN 3-211-00486-6.
2003, 596 pp.

European Tort Law 2003.
Edited by Helmut Koziol and Barbara C. Steininger.
Springer, Vienna/New York.
Softcover. ISBN 3-211-21033-4.
2004, 493 pp.

European Tort Law 2004.
Edited by Helmut Koziol and Barbara C. Steininger.
Springer, Vienna/New York.
Softcover. ISBN 3-211-24479-4.
2005, 674 pp.

European Tort Law 2005.
Edited by Helmut Koziol and Barbara C. Steininger.
Springer, Vienna/New York.
Softcover. ISBN 3-211-31135-1.
200, 715 pp.

Principles of European Tort Law

Text and Commentary.
By European Group on Tort Law.
Published by Springer, Vienna/New York.
Softcover. ISBN 3-211-23084-X.
2005, 282 pp.

Springer and the Environment

We at Springer firmly believe that an international science publisher has a special obligation to the environment, and our corporate policies consistently reflect this conviction.

We also expect our business partners – printers, paper mills, packaging manufacturers, etc. – to commit themselves to using environmentally friendly materials and production processes.

The paper in this book is made from no-chlorine pulp and is acid free, in conformance with international standards for paper permanency.